HUMAN
ASSOCIATIVE
MEMORY:
A Brief Edition

THE EXPERIMENTAL PSYCHOLOGY SERIES

Arthur W. Melton • *Consulting Editor*

1972   MELTON and MARTIN • *Coding Processes in Human Memory*
1973   ANDERSON and BOWER • *Human Associative Memory*
        McGUIGAN and LUMSDEN • *Contemporary Approaches to
                                Conditioning and Learning*
1974   GARNER • *The Processing of Information and Structure*
        KANTOWITZ • *Human Information Processing:
                      Tutorials in Performance and Cognition*
        KINTSCH • *The Representation of Meaning in Memory*
        MURDOCK • *Human Memory: Theory and Data*
1975   LEVINE • *A Cognitive Theory of Learning:
                    Research on Hypothesis Testing*
1976   ANDERSON • *Language, Memory, and Thought*
        CROWDER • *Principles of Learning and Memory*
1977   STERNBERG • *Intelligence, Information Processing, and
                       Analogical Reasoning:
                       The Componential Analysis of Human Abilities*
1978   POSNER • *Chronometric Explorations of Mind*
        SPEAR • *The Processing of Memories: Forgetting and Retention*
1979   KIHLSTROM and EVANS • *Functional Disorders of Memory*

HUMAN
ASSOCIATIVE
MEMORY:
A Brief Edition

JOHN R. ANDERSON
Carnegie-Mellon University

GORDON H. BOWER
Stanford University

LAWRENCE ERLBAUM ASSOCIATES, PUBLISHERS
1980   Hillsdale, New Jersey

This book is dedicated to our wives

Sharon Anthony Bower

and

Lynne Marie Reder

Lawrence Erlbaum Associates, Inc., Publishers
365 Broadway
Hillsdale, New Jersey 07642

Library of Congress Cataloging in Publication Data

Anderson, John Robert, 1947–
  Human associative memory.

  Bibliography: p.
  Includes indexes.
  1. Memory. 2. Association of ideas. I. Bower, Gordon H., joint author. II. Title.
BF371.A53   1980   153.1'2   79-28349
ISBN 0-89859-020-5

Printed in the United States of America

CONTENTS

PREFACE TO BRIEF EDITION   vii

PREFACE TO FIRST EDITION   ix

1. **INTRODUCTION**   *1*
   1.1. Concern for Sufficiency Conditions   *2*
   1.2. Neo-Associationism   *3*
   1.3. The Fundamental Questions   *6*

2. **ASSOCIATIONISM:**
   A HISTORICAL REVIEW   *9*
   2.1. Associationism: An Overview   *9*
   2.2. Aristotle's Associationsim   *16*
   2.3. British Associationsim   *18*
   2.4. Associationsim in America   *26*

3. **RATIONALIST COUNTERTRADITIONS**   *39*
   3.1. The Rationalist Approach   *39*
   3.2. Gestalt Theory   *44*
   3.3. The Reconstruction Hypothesis   *56*

4. **AN OVERVIEW OF HAM**   *63*
   4.1. The Information-Processing Approach   *63*
   4.2. HAM'S Structures and Processes   *65*
   4.3. The Simulation of HAM by Computer   *70*

5. **THE STRUCTURE OF KNOWLEDGE**   *79*
   5.1. The Representation Problem   *79*
   5.2. The Propositional Representation   *83*

6. **THE RECOGNITION PROCESS**   *101*
   6.1. The MATCH and IDENTIFY Processes   *101*
   6.2. Experimental Tests of the
        MATCH Process   *112*
   6.3. Stimulus Recognition   *125*

7. **MODEL FOR SENTENCE LEARNING**   *129*
   7.1. The Mathematical Formulation   *129*
   7.2. Location-Agent-Verb-Object   *141*

8. **FACT RETRIEVAL**   *153*
   8.1. Fact Retrieval   *153*
   8.2. Evidence for HAM's Search Strategies   *159*
   8.3. Semantic Memory   *171*

9. **VERBAL LEARNING**   *181*
   9.1. A Propositional Analysis of
        Verbal Learning   *181*
   9.2. Paired-Associate Learning   *185*
   9.3. Imagery   *194*

10. **INTERFERENCE AND FORGETTING**   *207*
    10.1. Forgetting in HAM   *207*
    10.2. Comparison to Other
          Interference Theories   *217*

11. **PROBLEMS AND NEW ISSUES**   *231*
    11.1. Representation   *231*
    11.2. Learning   *235*
    11.3. Retrieval   *238*
    11.4. Final Remarks   *241*

REFERENCES   *243*

AUTHOR INDEX   *253*

SUBJECT INDEX   *257*

PREFACE TO BRIEF EDITION

We wrote the HAM book six years ago. Six years provides some perspective on one's work. This perspective has led us to construct this new edition of the book. As the reader should be able to tell by comparing the thickness of the two books, the principle transformation between the original and the revision has been deletion. We have dropped some sections that are simply out of date. Others were dropped that seem, in retrospect, not very essential to our message in the original book. Other deletions involve analyses that either proved to be far off target or have been replaced by substantially better analyses. What remains (approximately 50% of the original text) is either what we feel still committed to or, if not that, what we feel is important as background for understanding current important issues in the literature. A major goal of this edition is to make the more important points of the original HAM book available at a more economical price. If someone needs the deleted analyses and experiments, the full version of the book remains available.

This edition contains two major parts. First is the historical analysis of associationism and its countertraditions. This still provides the framework that we use to relate our current research to an important intellectual tradition. This is reproduced without comment from the original book; historical analyses do not need as rapid revision as theoretical analyses.

The second part of the book reproduces the major components of the HAM theory. As we see it today, the major contribution of that theory was the propositional network analyses of memory and the placement of those representational assumptions into an information-processing framework. We have reproduced our specification of the HAM representational assumptions. Although there are problems with certain specifics of this representation, we feel content with most of it.

Also, several assumptions about the processes that operate on this memory representation still seem like good ideas. One is our idea about how pattern recognition operated in such a system. The conception we developed in HAM conceived of recognition as pattern matching. This conception has become even more important in subsequent theoretical developments (e.g., JA's ACT theory). Closely related is the idea that retrieval from long-term memory takes place through this graph matching process. Although certain essential details have proven wrong, many aspects of this retrieval model are with us still, and even our inadequate assumptions serve as important starting points for organizing current research.

Another major contribution of HAM concerned its analyses of how sentential and other factual knowledge is learned. Although it has attracted a fair number of alternative proposals, our stochastic model of sentence learning is still a real contender. Further, we provided an analysis of many of the traditional analyses of imagery and forgetting. We have changed our minds on some specific claims, but these analyses are still the basic way we conceive of verbal learning phenomena.

Certain aspects of the HAM theory presented here have proven to be incorrect or, if not incorrect, are in considerable dispute. We have appended a new chapter to review briefly these aspects and the issues they raise.

So, in summary, we have tried to use the passage of time to give a more focused rendition of the HAM book. What remains in this book represents, in our mind, what is still important and significant.

Preparation of this revision was supported by grant BNS-78-17463 from the National Science Foundation to John Anderson and by grant MH-13905 from the National Institute of Mental Health to Gordon H. Bower.

John R. Anderson and Gordon H. Bower

PREFACE TO THE FIRST EDITION

This book proposes and tests a theory about human memory, about how a person encodes, retains, and retrieves information from memory. The book is especially concerned with memory for sentential materials. We propose a theoretical framework which is adequate for describing comprehension of linguistic materials, for exhibiting the internal representation of propositional materials, for characterizing the "interpretative processes" which encode this information into memory and make use of it for remembering, for answering questions, recognizing instances of known categories, drawing inferences, and making deductions. This is all a very tall order, and we shall be gratified if a fraction of our specific hypotheses prove adequate for long. However, what is more significant is the overall framework and theoretical methodology within which specific hypotheses are cast: we sincerely hope that this framework would have a singular value that would outlive its specific details.

How have we arrived at the theoretical framework to be proposed? We will answer this question at two levels—first, in terms of a brief autobiography; second, in terms of a broader historical context. When the first author (JA) arrived at Stanford University as a graduate assistant to the second author (GB), there was an ongoing research program concerned with organizational and imaginal factors in various memory tasks. As we tried to become precise, even quantitative, in fitting organizational theory to free recall data, its difference from associationistic models of free recall seemed to evaporate, frankly because neither theory had been formulated with any real precision up to that time. Eventually, JA developed a semi-successful computer simulation model of free recall, FRAN; however, the data base of FRAN (or its memory representation) was fundamentally associationistic in character.

The problem with FRAN, as with other free recall models, is that it could not understand language: it treated a sentence as though it were a string of unrelated words. Consequently, it was decided to put FRAN aside and to search for a theory and model that would be able to represent the information in sentences and describe how they are learned and remembered. This required that both of us learn a fair amount of linguistics, psycholinguistics, and computational linguistics, a task in which we were aided by Herbert Clark and Roger Schank of the Stanford faculty. We had also begun some empirical investigations of sentence memory, expecting to find support for a Gestalt-like theory but instead finding associationist-like phenomena (these are reviewed here in Chapter 11).

The outcome of rather intensive ruminations and discussions was the theory, HAM (for Human Associative Memory) proposed herein. This was first worked out in detail in a long "dissertation proposal" by JA which had several goals: to present an associative theory of sentence memory, to report evidence relevant to it, to relate the theory to the historical tradition of associationism, and to indicate how a few standard "verbal learning" phenomena might be interpreted in terms of this approach. That document formed the basic outline for this book. The language parser and question-answerer of HAM were written as a LISP program by JA, and its operation is illustrated in Chapter 6 here. That proposal led us into a productive set of discussions and experiments, many of which are scattered throughout this book. Given the volume of results and the number of things we wanted to say about them, it became clear that a book rather than piecemeal publications was the appropriate way to communicate the theoretical framework and its supporting evidence.

In the Spring of 1972, we began collaborative writing of this volume; each day was filled with hours of fruitful discussions followed by our individual writing efforts. In these discussions we came to adopt characteristic roles—JA as the proposer, interpreter, and defender of HAM, and GB as the critic, provider of more problems, the demander of greater generality. However, like most fruitful interchanges, ours were free-wheeling, and we adopted various roles as the occasion demanded. Only a fraction of the analyses and problems solved appear in these pages. The discussions and writing turned out to be both personally and intellectually the most gratifying moments of our collaboration.

Now, let us briefly indicate the historical context of this work. First, our work falls within the tradition of philosophical associationism, which stretches from Aristotle through the British empirical philosophers to current psychology. We found so much of value in that rich intellectual tradition that we felt honor-bound to cite chapter and verse from it to show its contemporary relevance. This we do in Chapter 2, along with criticizing that tradition and anticipating how our theory of memory differs from it.

Second, this work owes a special debt to those scientists doing research on human memory, both researchers from the "verbal-learning" tradition and those using the "organizational" approach. Chapters 14 and 15 here explicitly deal with the verbal learning literature, whereas the influence of the organizational approach to memory should be apparent in chapters 3, 8, 11, 13, and 14.

The third intellectual tradition impinging on our research is the theoretical work in modern linguistics, especially that on transformational generative grammar of Noam Chomsky, his associates, and the whole movement he has promulgated. Although we deal with models of linguistic *performance* for only limited domains, we are nonetheless indebted to the formal analyses of the linguists for suggesting these models. Linguistic theories are reviewed in Chapter 5 and issues concerning the representation of propositional information occur repeatedly throughout our work (e.g., Chapters 7, 8, 9, 11, 13).

Our final intellectual debt is to the research workers in artificial intelligence, to those like Minsky, McCarthy, Newell, and Simon who have shaped the conceptual development of that entire area, but more specifically to those who have dealt with computer models for natural language understanding and for question-answering. A review of language understanding programs (those of Woods, Winograd, and Schank) is contained in Chapter 5, and a review of models for "long-term semantic memory" (specifically, Quillian's and that of Rumelhart, Lindsay, and Norman) is contained in Chapter 4. Our theoretical framework has a special likeness to that being developed by Rumelhart, Lindsay, and Norman at the University of California at San Diego, and that developed by Walter Kintsch at the University of Colorado. It is indicative of the *Zeitgeist* that our work was begun independently and in relative ignorance of theirs, and only later did we become acquainted with the details of their approach. Special visits to La Jolla and Boulder provided us with detailed information about their theoretical projects, and we are pleased to have this opportunity to thank these scientists and their research students for their intellectual help, encouragement, and hospitality.

These four distinct areas, then, provide the intellectual and historical backgrounds for our theory of human memory. As does every lengthy research project or book, ours has accumulated a number of specific debts to individuals who have helped bring this enterprise to fruition. First, we acknowledge the general support of the faculty and graduate students in cognitive psychology at Stanford University; the general climate of intellectual stimulation there clearly provided the reinforcing and educational contingencies needed to initiate, encourage, and maintain our theoretical enterprise. We appreciate those colleagues—Arnie Glass, Steve Kosslyn, Perry Thorndyke, and Keith Wescourt—who allowed us to report their previously unpublished experiments. Ed Feigenbaum was very helpful in our development of the simulation program and provided us with help when the simulation began to exceed the capabilities of the campus facility.

We solicited and received constructive comments from many colleagues, and the final version of the book is clearly better because of them. Bob Crowder, Jim Greeno, Reid Hastie, Marcel Just, Steve Kosslyn, Alan Lesgold, Elizabeth Loftus, Gary Olson, Lance Rips, Ed Smith, Dave Tieman, and Wayne Wickelgren all have commented on portions of the book. To them we give our thanks. A special note of thanks goes to Lynne Reder who read the book in its entirety and pointed out passages in need of better exposition.

The research reported here and preparation of the manuscript was supported through a research grant to GB, number MH-13950, from the National Institutes of Mental Health. We are pleased to acknowledge Drs. George Renaud and John Hammack of the NIMH staff for their helpful encouragement and support of this research and of its writing. Yale University also helped JA's writing by easing the burden on its new assistant professor and by making resources available for him to supervise the book through its final draft. During the final revisions, GB was supported by the Center for Advanced Study in the Behavioral Sciences and by research funds from NIMH.

We owe a special thanks to the several individuals who have been closely involved with the physical preparation of the manuscript. First among these is Joyce Lockwood, GB's secretary, who typed the first one and a half versions of the book, making sense out of our scrawls while exhibiting patient forebearance in the face of a frustrating barrage of corrections to corrections. The final one and a half versions of the manuscript were typed by JA's secretaries at Yale, Barbara Psotka and Glenna Ames. We appreciate the swift and reliable clerical help they have provided to us. A special thanks also goes to Larry Erlbaum, our publisher, for providing moral support as well as expediting those technical matters associated with shepherding a manuscript through to publication. Finally we are obliged to several authors and publishers who gave permission to quote or to reproduce figures from their publications, and we have acknowledged their contributions in the appropriate places of the text.

John R. Anderson and Gordon H. Bower

March, 1973

1
INTRODUCTION

And I gave my heart to seek and search out by wisdom concerning all things that are done under heaven; this sore travail hath God given to the sons of men to be exercised therewith.

—Solomon

Two years ago, we set out to develop a theory of human memory, a theory which was to span a wide range of mnemonic phenomena. We are now humbled by the immensity of this task; human memory is a complex mental capacity, and our ability to comprehend man's mind appears at times quite limited. But Solomon calls us to the task of understanding, to be "exercised" by its sore travail. And so we tried. In countless hours of conversations, we discussed, proposed, role-played, argued, laughed, cajoled, reasoned, debunked, and just plain talked to one another about the problems of human memory. The time has come for us to commit to print a fraction of the things we have thought about human memory in the hope of helping others to think about this problem—which we consider to be the supreme intellectual puzzle of the century.

The theory of human memory which we will articulate will seem overly ambitious but still terribly programmatic; no one can realize this better than we ourselves. So why bother? What does Psychology need with another fragmentary theory of memory? After all, a long parade of memory theories since Plato's have been offered with great fanfare, hopeful enthusiasm, and persuasive arguments. Most of these were soon consigned to the loneliness of library tombs, accumulating dust to hide their insignificance. A very few of these writings become classics. But no one really believes the classics; they are read only to provide jousting partners for later opponents and voyagers on the seas of the unknown.

It is commonplace that the Zeitgeist in current psychology opposes global theories such as the one to be presented. It is said, instead, that one ought to work

1

on limited hypotheses for small, manageable problems—categorization effects in free recall, verification latencies for negative sentences, search of items in short-term memory, and so on ad infinitum. Indeed, we have been told by many respected colleagues in psychology that we will surely fail because we "are trying to explain everything." Of course, we are not. Human memory is but a very small part of the psychological domain. To make a salient contrast, a criticism we are apt to receive from colleagues outside of psychology (e.g., artificial intelligence) is that we are far too narrow in our perspective and aims.

The reason for writing a theoretical book on human memory is the belief that we have something important to offer. In rejecting the earlier global theories, modern research on human memory has overreacted to the opposite extreme; it has become far too narrow, particulate, constricted, and limited. There is no overall conception of what the field is about or even what it should be about. There is no set of overarching theoretical beliefs generally agreed upon which provide a framework within which to fit new data and by which to measure progress. Were we describing an unhappy personality, we would say that the contemporary study of memory has lost its sense of direction, its sense of purpose, and it is drifting aimlessly with much talent but little focus. This point was stated forcibly by a recent, informed but highly critical review of the field (Tulving & Madigan, 1970).

1.1.   CONCERN FOR SUFFICIENCY CONDITIONS

Laboratory studies of memory appear under the inexorable control of a distinct set of "experimental paradigms," a standard set of "tasks," which seem by their nature to spew out an unending string of methodological variations and empirical studies. But the phenomena studied are becoming further and further removed from the manifestations of memory in everyday life. There would be nothing necessarily wrong with this esoterica provided psychologists had some clear conception of how their research and theories would eventually fit together into a system adequate to explain the complexities of everyday human memory. But, on the contrary, it appears that we psychologists are totally unconcerned about having our psychological theories meet certain *sufficiency conditions*. It is not enough that a theory make adequate ordinal predictions for a particular situation and experiment; in addition, it should be shown that its principles are sufficient to play a part in the explanation of the total complexity of human behavior. For instance, one could require of a model of memory that it be sufficiently powerful to succeed in simulating question-answering behavior.

When we began to concern ourselves with sufficiency conditions, we were forced to fundamental reconceptualizations regarding the nature of memory. We found that memory could no longer be conceived as a haphazard jumble of associations that blindly record contiguities between elements of experience. Rather, memory now had to be viewed as a highly structured system designed to record facts about the world and to utilize that knowledge in guiding a variety of performances. We were forced to postulate entities existing in memory which have no one-to-one correspondence with external stimuli or responses. As discussed in Chapter 2, such structures violate the Terminal Meta-Postulate of classical associationism and stimulus-response psychology. It also became necessary to postulate the existence in the mind of highly complex parsing and inferential systems which function to interface the memory component with the external world. Furthermore, we were forced to postulate the existence of innately specified ideas in the form of semantic primitives and relations. We will therefore be proposing and arguing for a radical shift from the associationist conceptions that have heretofore dominated theorizing on human memory.

This shift is most apparent in the unit of analysis which we adopt. Unlike past associative theories, we will not focus on associations among single items such as letters, nonsense syllables, or words. Rather, we will introduce *propositions* about the world as the fundamental units. A proposition is a configuration of elements which (*a*) is structured according to *rules of formation*, and (*b*) has a *truth value*. Intuitively, a proposition conveys an assertion about the world. The exact structural properties of our propositional representation will be set forth in Chapter 5. We will suppose that all information enters memory in propositional packets. On this view, it is not even possible to have simple word-to-word associations. Words can become interassociated only as their corresponding concepts participate in propositions that are encoded into memory. However, propositions will not be treated here as unitary objects or Gestalt wholes in memory having novel, emergent properties. Rather, propositions will be conceived as structured bundles of associations between elementary ideas or concepts. However, our insistence that all input to memory be propositional imposes certain *well-formedness* conditions on the structure of the interidea associations. This notion of structural well-formedness is one that was completely lacking in past associative theories and was at the heart of many rationalist attacks on associationism.

1.2. NEO-ASSOCIATIONISM

We shall use the term "neo-associationism" to denote this new conception of human memory. While it introduces substantial deviations from past associationist doctrines, it still maintains a strong empiricist bias. We feel that the full significance of these theoretical assumptions can only be appreciated when one understands the associationist tradition out of which they came. Therefore, we have devoted Chapter 2 to an analysis of the associative tradition that extends from Aristotle through current American psychology. We will argue that a defining feature of associationism has been its *methodological empiricism*. That is, all associationists have accepted as their task the job of taking the immediate sense-data available to them and constructing their theory directly from these, always letting the data dictate the nature of the theory. This is contrasted in Chapter 3 with the *methodological rationalism* which attempts to first arrive at abstract, sufficient conditions, or constraints for the phenomena at hand, and then tries to relate these abstractions and conceptual constraints to the empirical world.

The contrast we are making between methodological empiricism and methodological rationalism corresponds (not surprisingly) to the more frequently made distinction between empiricism and rationalism. In the strong version of empiricism, the mind begins as tabula rasa, and all knowledge is a consequence of the passive encoding of experience. The strong version of rationalism claims that the mind begins highly structured and all significant knowledge derives from the mind's initial structure. According to the rationalists, the role of experience is simply to stimulate the mind to derive that knowledge. Methodological empiricism and rationalism are not concerned with the origins of human knowledge, but rather with procedures for developing a scientific theory. However, we can almost derive a definition of each by substituting "scientific theory" for "mind" in the above statements of empiricism and rationalism. That is, methodological empiricism claims a scientific theory can be built up from immediate data by the blind procedure of generalization; whereas, methodological rationalism insists the theory builder must bring the essential structure of the theory to the phenomena to be explained.

Neo-associationism represents a profane union of these two methodologies. There is no attempt at a "creative synthesis" of these two positions; we simply pursue both methods in parallel in constructing a theory. The result is a theory that irreverently intermixes connectionism with nativism, reductionism with wholism, sensationalism with intuitionism, and mechanism with vitalism. Depending on the theoretician's propensities, the mixture can be claimed to be either more rationalist than empiricist or vice versa. The mixture we will offer is still strongly empiricist, much more so than the other neo-associationist theories that we will examine.

The various neo-associationist theories of memory (e.g., Simon & Feigenbaum, 1964; Collins & Quillian, 1972b; Rumelhart, Lindsay, & Norman, 1972), including our own, have been cast in the form of computer simulation models of memory. This is no accident. The task of computer simulation simultaneously forces one to consider both whether his theory is sufficient for the task domain to be simulated and also whether it can deal with the particular trends found in particular experiments.

Our therorizing and experimentation are specifically oriented towards memory for linguistically structured material. With such interests, one cannot help but make constant contact with the recent ideas in linguistics. The linguistic work, particularly of Chomsky, Fillmore, Lakoff, Katz, Ross, and their associates, is important for a second reason. These linguists have argued effectively for the importance of sufficiency conditions in linguistics. As a consequence, over the past decade rationalism and mentalism have become strongly entrenched in linguistics. The rationalist "revolution" has been imported from linguistics into psychology. Thus, the developments in linguistics are an important source behind the neo-associationist developments.

Two substantial chapters are being devoted to an extensive historical and theoretical review of efforts related to our own. This is clearly out of character for a typical "research volume." The usual practice for American psychology is to restrict its focus to the last 5 or 10 years of experimentation centered around a narrowly circumscribed topic. This practice is lamentable since true scholarly endeavor would seem to require an appreciation of the historical and intellectual context within which that scholarship occurs. Without knowledge of that context, it is not possible to discriminate between significant theoretical advance as opposed to elaboration of an established paradigm. Chomsky (1968) has argued persuasively for a similar historical perspective in linguistics.

Our work began in the typical intellectual isolation of experimental psychology, but we constantly found ourselves being led into discussions of issues about which we know very little. Therefore, we have tried to trace the connections between our work and that which had occurred in past centuries or which was occurring in related fields. Our perception of what questions were important changed; similarly, the character of the theory and research to be presented is very different from what we had originally projected and from the typical fare that one finds in psychology. It can only be appreciated in the perspective of the historical context that we set in the first two chapters. One of the incidental advantages of a theory so constructed is that it provides the reader with an integrated viewpoint from which to perceive his own experimental research, related research in psychology and other fields, and the relationship between this research and what has happened in past centuries.

Following these two review chapters, the remainder of the book serves as a forum for presenting our theory and research. We have many experiments to report that have not appeared before in print. We will also review and comment upon a large number of recent experiments that seem particularly interesting with respect to the issues that we are raising. Although there is no attempt to review extensively the literature in human memory, we do hope to establish theoretical connections among many different areas of experimentation in psychology.

To preview the contents of the later chapters, Chapter 4 provides a general overview of our model of long-term memory. We have christened the model HAM, an acronym for Human Associative Memory. The subsequent three chapters set forth most of the substantive theoretical assumptions of that model. The character of presentation varies considerably from one chapter to the next. In Chapter 5, entitled "The Structure of Knowledge," we propose a structure in which information will be encoded and stored in long-term memory. In Chapter 6 we will ask how the memory system recognizes that it has experienced something before. This issue, of how current stimuli contact old traces, is a point of notorious difficulty for other accounts of memory. Finally, in Chapter 7 we will present a stochastic model of how incoming information is encoded into long-term memory.

The remaining chapters will be concerned with relating our theory to various areas of research and experimentation. In Chapter 8 we will examine the question of how long-term memory is searched for information, to decide whether or not some fact is known or some statement is true. This is the problem of *fact retrieval*. In Chapter 9, we will discuss how our model would perform in the typical verbal learning paradigms such as paired-associate learning and free recall. Finally, in Chapter 10 we will discuss how different information inputs interfere with one another to produce forgetting. We will compare our model of this process with past theories of interference and forgetting.

1.3. THE FUNDAMENTAL QUESTIONS

There are well-known advantages to vagueness in constructing a theory; it protects the theory from disconfirmation. The typical strategy is to articulate the theory at those points where it makes contact with confirming evidence, but otherwise to shroud it in sufficient vagueness so that any other present or future data cannot unambiguously disconfirm the model. We have tried to avoid this tactic. Not only is our theory vulnerable to future disconfirmation; it also clearly fails to handle a number of the existing facts. The points of misfit will be openly acknowledged at the appropriate places. It is difficult to determine how serious these failures are. In a complex model like HAM it is always possible to introduce some special assumption that will handle any particular discrepancy. Also, the misfits may indicate a mistake in one particular assumption rather than a flaw in the grand theoretical design.

The fundamental issue at stake with respect to our theory is its neo-associationist character. This is not to be found in any particular assumption, but rather pervades diffusely throughout the whole enterprise. Our strong computer-simulation orientation has led to a class of controversial assumptions. Information processing in HAM tends to be in terms of discrete units called ideas and associations, and it proceeds in sequential steps, whereas parallel, interactive processes are assumed to be minimal. Can one really claim that a human processes information in this discrete, serial manner? But the physiology of the brain is very different from that of a serial, digital computer, and analogue, parallel processes would not seem out of character for that mysterious organ (cf. Von Neuman, 1958). Perhaps, then, our theory has been too strongly determined by what is easy to simulate on a computer rather than by considerations of psychological plausibility. That is one fundamental question.

Another source of difficulty with our theory may arise from our strong empiricist leanings. We have insisted that all knowledge in memory should be built up from input to the memory. We have denied that memory has any capacity to spontaneously restructure itself into more useful forms. Perhaps we have made memory too passive, too much of a tabula rasa. That is a second fundamental question.

On the other hand, we have granted the mind a great deal of self-structuring power in our assumptions regarding the perceptual parsers that transform external stimuli into memory input, or the various inferential and problem-solving abilities that enable the system to make intelligent use of the information recorded in memory. One is forced to postulate such powerful mechanisms in order to interface a memory with the world. The postulated mechanisms are enormously more complicated than any of the theoretical devices that have been previously postulated in associative theories. Perhaps, if we had complicated the proposed memory system, we could have simplified the interfacing apparatus. That is a third fundamental question.

Another possible flaw in the grand design has to do with our insistence on making the propositional representation fundamental. We will want to encode perceptual as well as linguistic input into this uniform propositional base. Perhaps we are choosing a representation that is too logical and abstract. Perhaps the primary representation of knowledge is of some diffuse, sensory sort; and our ability to encode information propositionally in this original base comes about only after much conceptual development and training in abstraction. This is a fourth fundamental question.

These are the sorts of questions that will hound us throughout this enterprise. We cannot claim that there is any great initial plausibility to our particular formulation. But we feel it is important that we develop that formulation as explicitly as possible and raise the questions we have about it. Our formulation provides a concrete realization of a certain theoretical position. It provides something definite for research workers to discuss, examine, criticize, and experiment upon. It is hoped that some resolution will be eventually achieved with respect to the fundamental theoretical questions. We hope that others will be encouraged to provide and motivate other explicit models of fundamentally different theoretical positions. If this happens, our goal will have been achieved, whatever is the final judgment with respect to HAM. We will have shifted the focus of experimental psychology from the articulation of narrow paradigms to an analysis of the significant questions concerning human memory. To attempt this may be a pretentious ambition, but it is a primary purpose and justification of this book.

2
ASSOCIATIONISM: A HISTORICAL REVIEW

> *In our inquiry into the soul it is necessary for us, as we proceed, to raise such questions as demand answers; we must collect the opinions of those predecessors who have had anything to say touching the soul's nature, in order that we may accept their true statements and be on our guard against their errors.*
>
> *—Aristotle*

2.1. ASSOCIATIONISM: AN OVERVIEW

Associationism has a tradition that extends over 2,000 years, from the writings of Aristotle to the experiments of modern psychologists. Despite the existence of this clearly identifiable *theoretical tradition*, there is not a well-defined monolithic *theoretical position* which can be called associationism. Past associative theories differ one from another both in details and in basic assumptions. While all major associative theorists have agreed on a few fundamental points, there are more fundamentals on which there exist no such consensus. So, we are faced with an apparent paradox: How can we identify a coherent associative tradition but no coherent associative theory?

The unifying feature of associationism lies in its empiricist methodology, not in any substantive assumptions that it makes. That is, all associationists have taken as their task the job of using the immediate data available to them (e.g., introspections, stimulus-response contingencies, etc.) and constructing the human mind from these with minimal additional assumptions. Depending upon the data they considered important and upon personal idiosyncracies, different theorists achieved somewhat different mental reconstructions. However, because of the common methodology, their psychological systems tend to share certain metafeatures. Four such features seem to universally typify associationism:

9

1. Ideas, sense data, memory nodes, or similar mental elements are associated together in the mind through experience. Thus, associationism is *connectionistic.*

2. The ideas can ultimately be decomposed into a basic stock of "simple ideas." Thus, associationism is *reductionistic.*

3. The simple ideas are to be identified with elementary, unstructured sensations. (The meaning we want to assign to "sensation" is rather generous in that we intend to include internal experiences, such as involved in emotion.) Because it identifies the basic components of the mind with sensory experience, associationism is *sensationalistic.*

4. Simple, additive rules serve to predict the properties of complex associative configurations from the properties of the underlying simple ideas. Thus, associationism is *mechanistic.*

We claim that these four features of associative theories are defining features of associationism because they are the highly probable consequences of the empiricist methodology that constructs such theories.

It might seem that the empirical validity of these four metafeatures might then be crucial to evaluating associationism. If one of these assumptions were to be proven false, that would prove that associative theories are wrong. However, it is doubtful whether any of these assumptions is of the sort that it could be subject to empirical falsification. After all, they are metafeatures of the theory rather than definite predictions about observable behavior. These metafeatures become manifest in particular theories in the form of particular predictions that may be falsified or verified, but it seems that the metafeatures are not subject to empirical disconfirmation. But before pursuing this point further, we should examine the four meta-assumptions in more detail.

Connectionism. Regarding connectionism, one must distinguish whether the discussion concerns associationism as a theory of human memory or as a theory of all mental phenomena. Connectionism, with its implicit empiricism, is a controversial assumption within the general associative plan of trying to explain all mental processes with one basic principle. It is not at all obvious that all our mental processes have been connected together through experience. Indeed, in our own model we do not subscribe to the notion that the mind has been totally "wired up" by experience. Some of the important mental processes described in our model are much more naturally viewed as innate rather than acquired mechanisms.

In contrast to the doubtful character of connectionism as the universal principle of mental phenomena, it would seem entirely innocuous as a principle of memory. To say that memory consists of ideas connected by experience would seem to be almost tautological. In this respect, it is interesting to note the uncritical tendency among psychologists to apply the "associationistic" label to any theory of memory that refers to connections or associations. This practice is reducing associationism to an empty descriptive notion. Associationism as a theory of memory gets its cutting edge from the remaining three distinguishing features. They serve to impose some restrictions on the character of the "connections."

Reductionism. This is sometimes called "elementarism," and the doctrine is fairly clear: It is assumed that there are certain elements (the simple ideas) that are distinguished by the fact that all other ideas are built up from them. The phrase "built up from" is somewhat vague, but a formalization of that notion will be offered in Chapter 5, where the memory structure of HAM is discussed. Some readers might question whether reductionism has any empirical significance; wouldn't every theory of human memory subscribe to such a metaprinciple? The answer is "Definitely not." The classic counterexample (although there are others) is Gestalt theory, which argued many phenomena defied reductionistic analysis (see Chapter 3).

Sensationalism. Certainly no one would quarrel with the claim that representations of sensory data constitute part of the contents of the mind. However, from Plato to Chomsky, there have been radical rationalists who have denied the sensationalist's claim that all knowledge has a sensory base. Indeed, it will turn out that a few non-sensory elements are required in our model.

Mechanism. The mechanistic feature of associative theories is at once the most imprecise and the most controversial. Stated crudely, the claim is that man is a machine and his nature and behavior are to be understood in mechanical terms. Ever since Democritus gave his original mechanistic account of the human soul, the issue has been a controversy of some stature. Since La Mettrie attempted to refute Descartes' claim that man is not machine, the matter has been a violent debate (witness the recent book by Dreyfus, 1972). The problem, however, is that our concept of what it is to be a machine is exceedingly imprecise and is continually being revised as we construct more intelligent automata. However, we do have reliable intuitions about what it means to be mechanistic. Many principles in our model will be unanimously judged as mechanistic and, no doubt, distasteful for that reason to some readers. Mechanistic assumptions such as those in our model tend to display an affinity for simple, linear, and discrete processes and an aversion for mass, interactive, and continuously varying processes.

We have argued that these four features have significance with respect to theories of the mind, although connectionism without the other three is an empty claim with respect to human memory. Nonetheless, it seems unlikely that any single feature can be subject to direct empirical falsification. There is a certain vagueness inherent in each of these metafeatures. One can empirically falsify the manifestation of these features in a particular model (for instance, our own), but it seems that it will always be possible to come up with another set of similar assumptions to explain the offending data. Indeed, much of the history of experimental psychology is the continuing saga of antiassociationists demonstrating the weakness of a particular associative theory, only to find the theory quickly changed and no longer subject to the old attack. This elusiveness of the four metaprinciples should not be surprising since they reflect methodological biases that are not really subject to empirical disconfirmation.

To summarize our conclusions, we claim that associationism is a historical tradition distinguished by its attempts to reconstruct the human mind from sensory experience with minimal theoretical assumptions. This approach contrasts with rationalistic theories which have attempted to work from basic a priori principles. As a consequence of its empiricist methodology, all associative theories have been distinguished by the four metafeatures enumerated above. While these metafeatures can be manifested in empirical predictions that are subject to disconfirmation, the metafeatures themselves would seem fairly immune.

The Terminal Meta-Postulate

However, there is one feature which tends to haunt associative theories, which can be given precise statement, and which can be proven in error. This is the Terminal Meta-Postulate (TMP) which was so dubbed by Bever, Fodor, and Garrett (1968). This postulate should be viewed as a particularly likely manifestation of associationism's metafeatures. The postulate may be divided into three statements, one statement corresponding to each of three associative metafeatures.

1. *Sensationalist Statement.* The only elements required in a psychological explanation can be put into a one-to-one correspondence with potentially observable elements. These elements may themselves be observable stimuli or responses, or they may be derived from such observables. These derivatives have been variously known as intervening variables, mediating responses, sensations, perceptions, images, or ideas.

2. *Connectionistic Statement.* The elements in Statement 1 become connected or associated if and only if they occur contiguously.

3. *Mechanistic Statement.* All observable behavior can be explained by concatenating the associative links in Statement 2.

While many past associative theories have assented to the TMP, there are theories which are commonly agreed to be associative and which violate this principle. Many of the classical British associationists (see Section 2.3) admitted an irreducible principle of similarity and so would reject Statement 2, although all of the British associationists do seem to have accepted Statements 1 and 3. Aristotle (Section 2.2) rejected all three claims. We have followed his lead and have done likewise in our model. Therefore, to claim that the TMP is a defining feature of associationism, as some of our colleagues have, is just false.

Here we will illustrate a fundamental flaw in the TMP. In our demonstration we will be using the same example as employed by Bever et al. (1968). This is the mirror-image language which is typically employed as a structure that cannot be generated by *finite-state automata* or *regular grammars* (see Hopcroft & Ullman, 1969, for a formal exposition of such technical terms). Any mechanism satisfying the TMP cannot produce behaviors more complicated than can these formal automata or grammars. For instance, Suppes (1969) has established the equivalence between finite-state automata and S-R theory. Rather than becoming enmeshed in the formal theory of automata, however, we will try to make our points at a more conversational level.

In a mirror-image language, the sequence of elements in the first half of a string (or sequence) must be mirrored in the second half. For instance, if a and b were the only elements of the language, Table 2.1 gives examples of strings which are acceptable and strings which are not. Consider how a TMP system might try to deal with such a mirror-image language. Note that in grammatical strings, a can be followed by either a or b, and b can be followed by either a or b. Then, in accordance with Statements 1 and 2, we would have to postulate that the following

TABLE 2.1

A Mirror-Image Language

Grammatical	Ungrammatical
aa	ba
abba	aaab
bbbb	bbabaa
abaaba	bbabb

four associations are formed: $a \rightarrow a$, $a \rightarrow b$, $b \rightarrow a$, $b \rightarrow b$. These four associations do suffice to generate all the grammatical strings of our language. The first grammatical string in Table 2.1 could be generated simply with the association $a \rightarrow a$; the second could be generated by concatenating $a \rightarrow b$, $b \rightarrow b$, and $b \rightarrow a$, and so on for other strings. But the reader has probably already noted the difficulty. This TMP system generates too much. For instance, from the association $b \rightarrow a$ we can generate the ungrammatical string ba.

The basic problem with the TMP system is that it has no means of recording what it did early in the string so it can unwind the mirror image of that sequence in completing that string. To use a term popular in some psychological circles, a TMP system can have no "plan of action." It is easy enough to construct a system capable of generating all and just the strings of our mirror-image language. A context-free grammar to do this is given in Table 2.2. Also in Table 2.2 is a tree structure generated by the grammar. Bever et al. (1968) argue that it is the element X in the rewrite rule of the grammar which violates the TMP. However, this is to confuse a description of the formal grammar with the mechanism that implements the grammar. Nonetheless, when we examine such a mechanism we will find ample violations of the TMP.

However, before we turn to that mechanism, the reader should be clear about what is the problematical aspect of the mirror-image language in Table 2.1. The

TABLE 2.2

A Grammar for the Mirror-Image Language

Rewrite Rules

$X \rightarrow a\,X\,a$

$X \rightarrow b\,X\,b$

$X \rightarrow \phi$

difficulty is that this language permits an indefinite number of embeddings of strings within strings. This embedding introduces dependencies between elements at arbitrary distances in the final string. For instance, the first and last element of a mirror-image string must match. Such dependencies cannot be captured in a finite-state automaton.

In Table 2.3 is the flow chart of a minimal system that is adequate to generate mirror-image languages. This system requires a push-down stack (PDS), a device

TABLE 2.3

Flow Chart of Push-Down Stack Machine for
Mirror-Image Language

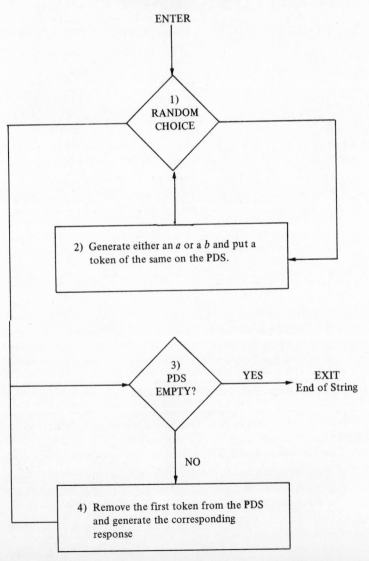

that stores objects and returns them according to the principle of last-in, first-out. This PDS clearly violates Statement 1 of the TMP. When we examine the flow chart, prescribing use of the PDS, we find further violations of the TMP. Consider how the string *abba* would be generated: The mechanism enters the random-choice box 1, and decides to move to box 2. Here it generates an *a* and puts an *a* token on the PDS. It cycles through the choice-box 1 and returns to box 2, this time to generate a *b*. Correspondingly, a *b* token is stored on the PDS. The contents of the PDS are now the tokens *b* and *a* in that order. The mechanism returns to choice-box 1 and then proceeds this time to decision-box 3. As the PDS is not empty, our mechanism proceeds to box 4, where it takes the first element from the PDS. This is a *b* token, and the system correspondingly generates a *b* response. It cycles through the choice-box 3 and back to box 4. Here it removes the last token from the PDS and generates an *a*. Upon returning to box 3, it finds the PDS empty and exits having successfully generated the string *abba*. The various operations we have been describing are clearly not encoded according to Statement 2 of the TMP or performed according to Statement 3. So we have violated all three conditions. Further violations of Statement 1 are the *a* and *b* tokens which were stored in the TMP. These *a* and *b* tokens are not responses nor response derivatives. Responses are not elements that reside for indefinite periods on push-down stacks. They rather occupy a brief moment in time and space.

Therefore, to generate the mirror-image language, we were forced to postulate a number of structures and processes only *abstractly* related to external observables. This is just what the TMP cannot abide. To end our discussion of the TMP on a technical note: In our "conversational" exposition we have been basically using the fact that a push-down automaton can and a finite-state automaton cannot accommodate the mirror-image languages. However, it is well known that any push-down automaton can be replaced by an equivalent finite-state automaton if we set a finite limit to the length of the push-down stack. A push-down automaton like that in Table 2.3 with a stack of length n can only generate (or recognize) mirror-image strings of length $2n$. But this is not objectionable, since there are certainly short-term memory limitations on the length of strings that we realistically can generate or recognize. Hence, it might be questioned whether we have shown the TMP to be in error, since there is a finite-state automaton that will handle mirror-image strings bounded by some upper length. However, this argument overlooks two important facts. First, the translation of a finite-stack push-down automaton into a finite-state automaton involves an enormous complication in terms of number of states. Essentially, each possible mirror-image string up to length $2n$ must be individually recorded by a distinct set of states. Secondly, by Statement 2 of the TMP, each transition in the state diagram must encode a contiguity in experience. But this is nonsense. We do not learn the mirror-image language by being exposed to all possible sequences of length up to $2n$; rather, a minute's study of the rules in Table 2.2 is sufficient. So this is one example of the importance of distinguishing questions of logical equivalence of two models from questions of their relative empirical plausibility. It is on the latter basis that we would reject any model based on the TMP.

To return to the main line of our historical exposition, in the following three sections of this chapter we will examine three types of associationism. The first is the associative analysis of human memory that Aristotle gave 2,300 years ago. His conception of memory was dominant until the time of the British associationists, beginning with Thomas Hobbes. The British empiricists extended the domain of associationism from Aristotle's original concern with human memory to encompass all mental phenomena; they also tried to make the associative doctrine a basis for their epistemology. The third type of associationism is the brand of associationism developed in America under the influence of functionalism and behaviorism.

Throughout this historical survey, we will try to distinguish the claims of associationism that are relevant to memory from those claims relevant to the more ambitious enterprise of reconstructing all of the human mind on a single principle. This distinction will be forced at times because, as we will see, some of the associationists denied that memory existed as a phenomena distinct from other aspects of consciousness.

2.2. ARISTOTLE'S ASSOCIATIONISM

Aristotle's associationism is found almost exclusively in his brief essay "On Memory and Reminiscence." However, it is best understood in the context of his general philosophy. In contrast to the extreme sensationalism of the sophists or the extreme rationalism of Plato, Aristotle provided a satisfying combination of empiricism and rationalism. In contrast to Plato, Aristotle supposed that all knowledge is derived through perception; there are no innate ideas. However, he supposed that the human mind does not contain a raw record of past sensory experience. Rather, Perception involves a creative action by Reason which imposes form on the incoming sensory data. The Reason makes use of various *analytical a priori propositions* in performing this task. Without the Reason to constantly structure and interpret incoming data, the mind would supposedly be a confusing mass of particulars. A role similar to the Reason in Aristotle's theory is exemplified in our model by such items as the perceptual and linguistic parsers and the inference-making processes. As with Aristotle's Reason, components of HAM's mechanisms are assumed to be innate rather than acquired from experience.

Aristotle's theory of memory is clearly sensationalistic. In fact, he believed that memory was part of the primary faculty of sense perception in that memory was the mechanism by which past sensory experience could be examined. A memory had the same relation to an original sense perception as a picture has to that of which it is a representation—i.e., memory provides a likeness of the original sensory experience. Even memory for "intellectual objects" such as numbers was alleged to involve the faculty of sense perception in that the intellect required its object to be presented to the mind by that faculty. Thus, as in all associationist theories, the structure of the input to and output from the memory component is identified with the structure of the percept. However, in contrast with many later theorists, Aristotle assumed that the mind imposed a great deal of structure upon the percept.

Aristotle's theory of perception, and hence his theory of memory, is also reductionistic in that he considered the perception of an object to be composed of the perception of its various sensible properties—color, smell, size, form, etc. Aristotle proposed the existence of a "common sense" which plays a central role in the construction of the object from its basic properties. It serves to unite the diverse sensations that come in by the various modalities and to cognize properties of the object which are not modality-specific (e.g., motion, number, shape, and magnitude). Aristotle took his theory about the encoding of the input with little modification from Plato's analogy of the wax-seal impression: "The process of movement involved in the act of perception stamps in, as it were, a sort of impression of the percept, just as persons do who make an impression with a seal [Beare, 1931, 450a30–450b1]." The important feature to note about this approach is that it identifies perception of an object as a necessary and sufficient condition for formation of a memory trace. This contrasts sharply with the emphasis commonly found in American associationism on the role of reinforcement in the formation of associations.

Aristotle's discussion of the retrieval process is commonly used to justify identifying him as the first associationist. He noticed something systematic in the chain of thoughts which resulted in the recollection of particular facts. He isolated three sorts of relationships that governed the succession of these thoughts: similarity, contrast, and contiguity of exemplars in past experience, which were to become the favored three principles of the British associationists. Aristotle also noted the importance of frequency, intensity, and good order in the construction of the associations. He thought that recollection involved a voluntary act of probing memory with some thought that was likely to bring about the desired memory by an associative train of thought: "Accordingly, therefore, when one wishes to recollect, this is what he will do: He will try to obtain a beginning of a movement whose sequel shall be the movement he desires to reawaken [Beare, 1931, 451b30]." Aristotle is making a distinction here between the selection of a probe, which is subject to strategic considerations, and the response of memory to this probe, which proceeds automatically. Aristotle called the automatic response of memory to a stimulus an "act of remembering," but if there was also strategic selection of the probe, he called the total act *recollection*. The former, the act of remembering, was allegedly a power possessed by all animals; but the latter, recollection, was possessed only by man, who alone had the faculty of deliberation and the capacity to make inferences. A similar distinction will appear in our model, separating the strategic selection of a probe from the automatic operation of a memory component in response to a probe.

At points in this examination of Aristotle's theory of memory, we have noted how closely it resembles our own in contrast to more recent formulations. Indeed, the British associationists, to be examined next, seem to have only introduced error into the Aristotelean conception. There are several reasons for this apparent advanced character of Aristotle's theory of memory. First, it is very sketchy. Many of the later errors occurred when the associationists took on the necessary task of filling in the details. Second, not content with Aristotle's original concern with human memory, later associationists extended the domain of associationism to all mental phenomena. Therefore, they could not provide the tailor-made analysis for human memory that Aristotle did. Finally, Aristotle's theory of memory was built upon the background of his careful and sophisticated epistemology. In contrast, the British associationists did not have such guidance to overview the construction of their associative theory. Rather, they tried to base their epistemology upon their analysis of the human mind.

2.3. BRITISH ASSOCIATIONISM

In the 200-year period from Thomas Hobbes ("Human Nature," 1650) to Alexander Bain (*The Senses and the Intellect*, 1859), associationism took on a very definite and ambitious form. Initially, with Hobbes and John Locke, associationism was just a minor part of free-wheeling empiricist expositions that boldly jumped from philosophy to psychology to sociology to political science. With Bishop Berkeley and David Hume, association psychology was called in to help buttress their epistemological views. With David Hartley, the connection between the psychological theory and the philosophical systems was cut. Hartley took the incomplete analyses of his predecessors and built a detailed psychological doctrine around them. Later associationists such as John and James Mill and Alexander Bain suggested variants on Hartley's system, but all basically conformed to the pattern Hartley had set forth.

One way to survey British associationism would be to provide a chronology of the 200-year period, noting what the principle figures said and how they differed one from another. However, excellent surveys of this kind already exist (e.g., Boring, 1950; Warren, 1921) and there is no need to reduplicate past efforts. Instead we shall try to extract and examine the global characteristics of British associationism. This is the way to isolate the weaknesses in their system that we must be careful to avoid in ours. In this analysis of British associationism it is necessary to focus on three aspects of their theory: first, their concept of an "idea," the unit out of which the mind was constructed; second, their concept of the association which connected the ideas together; and third, their concept of the associative process by which past experience determined current thought. There are serious weaknesses in each concept.

The Simple Idea—The Building Block of the Mind

As noted above, Aristotle identified the input and output of memory very closely with perception. This sensationalism is also present in the British associationism. Locke emphasized that all knowledge could be analyzed into discrete simple ideas like "roundness" and "redness," and that such simple ideas were all derived from experience—either directly through the senses or through reflection and self-observation. This conception of the simple idea was repeated by most of the later British writers.

Locke also outlined how complex ideas arose from associations of simple ideas. For instance, the complex idea of an apple would be composed, in part, from the simple ideas of roundness and redness. One of the immediate embarrassments to the associationists was that all the convincing introspective evidence for the association of ideas indicated that complex rather than simple ideas were linked by associations. It was never made entirely clear how complex ideas (which are interassociated bunches of simple ideas) could become directly connected by a single association in a way that could preserve the original mechanistic conception of an association as a link between two elements of the mind. It seems that a bunch of interconnected ideas could come to behave as a single idea.

In any case, according to the British associationists, the "terminal vocabulary" of the human mind is provided completely by elementary sensations and reflections. More complex ideas are just compounds of simple ideas. In more recent times, a similar notion dominated experimental psychology, namely, that behavior should be analyzable in a theoretical language that uses as its terms only stimuli and responses that are observable (at least in principle). This is the "Terminal Meta-Postulate" (TMP), which we discussed and criticized earlier. As shown there, a descriptive system satisfying the TMP cannot perform recursive mental operations, which are necessary to account for the creative aspects of language behavior and are probably necessary for other human behaviors as well. However, our concern with associationism is not with its adequacy as a model for human thought or language, but rather as a model for human memory, a subcomponent of our total mental hardware. Does the TMP lead to similar difficulties in the restricted domain of memory? There are some convincing demonstrations that it does.

The Need for a Type-Token Distinction

One of the problems with the TMP is that it would strain the storage capacity of any physical system. Consider James Mill's (1869) famous reconstruction of what is involved in the concept of a house:

> Brick is one complex idea, mortar is another complex idea; these ideas, with ideas of position and quantity, compose my idea of a wall. My idea of a plank is a complex idea, my idea of a rafter is a complex idea, my idea of a nail is a complex idea. These, united with the same ideas of position and quantity, compose my duplex idea of a floor. In the same manner my complex idea of glass, and wood, and others, compose my duplex idea of a window; and these duplex ideas, united together, compose my idea of a house, which is made up of various duplex ideas [pp. 115-116].

To paraphrase, a vast number of complex ideas and duplex ideas (associations of complex ideas) must be associated together to represent a house. Each of the complex and duplex ideas requires many associations between simple ideas. Thus, an enormous number (i.e., at least in the thousands) of simple ideas and associations would go into constructing the relatively simple concept of a house. The storage requirements to represent all our concepts and knowledge in such a format would be enormous. On this basis alone such a representation is untenable. However, such considerations of storage requirements did not weigh heavily on the British associationists. While some like Hartley occasionally lapsed into physiological speculations, the spirit of the age was such that pragmatic questions, like that of storage requirements in a physical system, were ignored. However, in this age of the computer, the problem immediately comes to mind.

In this age of the computer, the problem also has a well-known solution, the so-called type-token distinction (e.g., see Simon & Feigenbaum, 1964). However, the type-token distinction brings with it abandonment of the Terminal Meta-Postulate; i.e., elements are permitted which do not correspond to sensations or other externally observable referents like responses. The type-token distinction permits one to define each concept just once in memory. For instance, instead of embedding into the house concept the duplex idea of a window with all its complex ideas and associations, a single element is used to stand for the concept of a window in the definition of a house. This element is a "token" which "points" to the "type" for window. It is only the type node that collects together all the associations defining what a window is. This allows efficient structuring of information, since knowledge about windows needs to be stored just once in memory, even though the concept of a window can be used in constructing many other concepts. A significant feature of this analysis is that it introduces, as elementary unanalyzable units, some theoretical objects (namely, the tokens) which are not derived from elementary sensations. These tokens are not "copies" of sensations. If they were they would have to contain all the associative complexity of the type. Hence, the Terminal Meta-Postulate of British associationism is violated by the type-token distinction.

A similar difficulty stems from the fact that the same idea can enter into more than one association. For instance, suppose two sequences of colors were flashed at a subject—the first, red, blue, green, and the second, yellow, blue, orange. By the principle of contiguity, he could remember the first sequence by forming associations from the idea of red to the idea of blue and thence to the idea of green; by similar means he could represent and remember the second sequence. Letting arrows represent associations, these representations are illustrated in Figure 2.1a. Upon inspection, the difficulty with this representation should be immediately apparent. There is an association from red to blue and one from blue to orange. Given this structure, it is likely that the subject may recollect the sequence red-blue-orange, but this sequence in fact never occurred. This hypothetical example illustrates a very general point; if we have many associations leading to an idea and many associations leading from the idea, then the representation must have some way to determine which predecessors go with which successors.

One solution to this problem would be to have multiple copies of a particular idea and to use a new copy for each association. This would result in a representation like that shown in Figure 2.1b. One difficulty with this proposal is that it would require a great deal of storage to represent multiple copies of very complex ideas. A second problem arises when we ask how one would ever retrieve the old associations that an idea had entered into if every time we thought of the idea we found ourselves with a new, virgin copy of that idea. A better solution is again to introduce "tokens" of these ideas as in Figure 2.1c. These tokens are connected by further associations to the types which contain the prototypical representation of the ideas. Hence, it is possible to retrieve the old associations that an idea has entered into by following the associations from the prototypical type to its various tokens.

A further difficulty created by acceptance of the Terminal Meta-Postulate is that it committed the British associationists to a strong nominalist position. That is, all simple ideas were ideas of particular sensations, and all complex ideas were formed

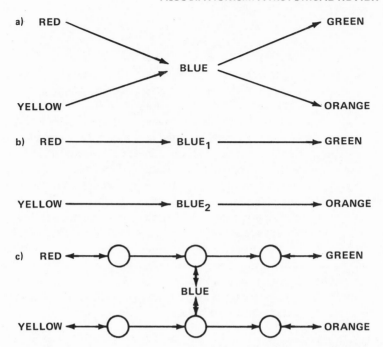

FIG. 2.1. Alternative associative structures: (*a*) the British conception; (*b*) with multiple copies of ideas; and (*c*) with the type-token distinction. See text for discussion.

from these particular ideas. Such an approach cannot tolerate any truly universal ideas—that is, elements that are completely abstracted away from particular elements of reality. How, then, were they to accommodate the fact that we appear to have ideas of universals, such as the generic idea of man? They argued that we have a word (e.g., "man") to denote the general idea, and that the word becomes associated to a complex idea composed of the collection of individuals to whom the generic title has been applied:

> The word, man, we shall say, is first applied to an individual; it is first associated with the idea of that individual, and acquires the power of calling up the idea of him; it is next applied to another individual, and acquires the power of calling up the idea of him; so of another, and another, till it has become associated with an indefinite number, and has acquired the power of calling up an indefinite number of those ideas indifferently. What happens? It does call up an indefinite number of the ideas of individuals, as often as it occurs; and calling them up in close connexion, it forms them into a species of complex idea [J. Mill, 1869, p. 264].

This analysis is unsatisfactory on multiple grounds. It is an enormous complication in the mental representation to insist that the general idea is an aggregate of all its individual instances. It is more economical to grant the mind the power to introduce a new element, the idea of the universal concept which is an abstraction from the instances. Moreover, without the distinction between particular and general ideas, it seems impossible to explain how we can identify the defining properties of a general concept as contrasted with accidental properties of particular instances. For example, all the knives one has seen may have had wooden handles, but having wooden handles is still not a defining property of knives. In contrast, serving the function of cutting is one of the defining properties of a knife.

The Terminal Meta-Postulate also denies the possibility of any innate knowledge and insists that all knowledge be a record of past experience—which, of course, is the extreme empiricist position. But, on this account, certain elements of our knowledge become inexplicable. For instance, as Hume demonstrated, there can be nothing in our experience to lead us to the notion of causality. So why do we perceive causality in the relation of events, and not just spatiotemporal contiguity? As Kant concluded, our understanding of causality (or at least our predisposition to perceive causality) must be a priori, or built in as part of our mental hardware.

So, the Terminal Meta-Postualte appears to have been the source of a host of related difficulties in the British associationist account of the mind. This questionable assumption was not part of Aristotle's original formulation. While it has been generally accepted in American associationism, particularly as a result of the behaviorist epistemology, we were soon forced to abandon it in our attempts to develop an explicit simulation model of human memory.

The Association—The Mind's Glue

In the previous section we examined and criticized the British conception of the idea. In this section we examine the associations which were alleged to hold the ideas together. We will begin by reviewing some of the agreed-upon properties of associations and will conclude by noting some difficulties with the British conception of an association. The problem with the British conception of the association is basically that it provides no useful way to represent the different relations that are expressed by different associations, nor for expressing the structural properties inherent in an associative configuration.

Contiguity and Similarity

Generally, the associationists distinguished between the *successive associations* which control the sequencing of thoughts in the stream of consciousness, and the *synchronous associations* which combine simultaneous ideas into more complex ideas. Contiguity in time was particularly important in the formation of a successive association, whereas contiguity in space was important for the formation of a synchronous association. Hartley attempted to reduce contiguity in space to a special case of contiguity in time, claiming that contiguity in space was effective only in that spatially contiguous objects or properties are likely to be perceived in temporal contiguity. However, all other major British associationists preserved the distinction between successive and synchronous associations. Much of what the British associationists included under the title of successive association is of little interest to our present concern with human memory, although such associations were supposed to play an important role in the British explanation of language and thought.

Similarity has frequently been mentioned as a principle governing the association of ideas. Both Hartley and James Mill, however, insisted that contiguity was the sole relation governing association and that similarity could be derived from it:

> Resemblance only remains, as an alleged principle of association, and it is necessary to inquire whether it is included in the laws which have been above expounded. I believe it will be found that we are accustomed to see like things together. When we see a tree, we generally see more trees than one; when we see an ox, we generally see more oxen than one; a sheep, more sheep than one; a man, more men than one [J. Mill, 1869, p. 111].

This sort of associationistic argumentation has been attacked by numerous critics seeking an easy prey (e.g., Koffka, 1935; Köhler, 1947; Deese, 1965). These attacks are somewhat unjustified, since Locke, Berkeley, Hume, and Bain all accepted similarity as an irreducible law of associationism. Indeed, even John Stuart Mill rebelled against his father on this issue. On the same page as we find the preceding quote of the elder Mill, we can find this footnote added by J. S. Mill:

> The reason assigned by the author for considering association by resemblance as a case of association by contiguity, is perhaps the least successful attempt at a generalisation and simplification of the laws of mental phenomena, to be found in the work. It ought to be remembered that the author, as the text shews, attached little importance to it. And perhaps, not thinking it important, he passed it over with a less amount of patient thought than he usually bestowed on his analyses [J. Mill, 1869, p. 111].

In the domain of human memory, contiguity does deserve a special status, since memories are generally of what has been spatially or temporally contiguous in our past experience. It is an interesting question, however, whether similarity among contiguous ideas or events facilitates our memory for them. One issue in the debate between Gestalt theory and modern associationism has been whether a concept of similarity is also needed for memory.

While most of the British philosophers admitted the possibility of association through similarity, they focused on the factor of contiguity. This is witnessed by the number of subprinciples enunciated within British associationism whose only purpose was to augment the principle of contiguity. Specifically, vividness of experience, frequency of experience, duration of experience, and recency of experience were all suggested as determining the strength of a particular association. This set of principles should sound very familiar to experimental psychologists, since they have generated a great many experiments on memory and verbal learning.

A point worth mentioning here is that the British associationists explicitly assumed that the mind could acquire new associations by "deliberate reflection," by thinking over a set of prior associations and noting new relations or inferences. For example, having learned how children keep dogs and cats for pleasure, a person may later be taught a new concept of a *pet*, as a domesticated animal kept for pleasure rather than utility; a later moment of critical reflection could then bring together the two associations relating "dog," "animal kept for pleasure," and "pet," thus setting up the internal contiguity necessary for the new association "dog-pet" to be formed. It is rather like the modern accounts of "mediated generalization," or how the associations A-B and B-C can strengthen the association A-C. What is wrong with the doctrine is not the unobservable character of its constructs (to which radical behaviorists would object), but rather that the mechanisms governing "reflection" are not given any satisfactory explanation and the theory becomes either totally descriptive or irredeemably vitalistic. To this day there is no well worked out theory of how the mind spontaneously interrogates its own knowledge to construct new knowledge.

The Mechanistic versus the Chemical Conception

One of the problems in interpreting British associationism is to determine what exactly an association was intended to be. Hume referred to it as "a gentle force which commonly prevails." In more recent times, psychologists have talked about the probability that one idea will elicit another. This notion is frequently referred to as "mental mechanics"; each association is simply a semideterministic link between independent ideas. Mental mechanics is to be contrasted with the "mental chemistry" view most clearly espoused by J. S. Mill (1889):

> When impressions have been so often experienced in conjunction that each of them calls up readily and instantaneously the ideas of the whole group, these ideas sometimes meld and coalesce into one another, and appear not several ideas but one. These, therefore, are cases of mental chemistry, in which it is proper to say that the simple ideas generate, rather than that they compose the complex ones [p. 558].

Warren (1921) argued that the chemical analogy is just as representative of British associationism as is the mechanical one. He quoted passages from Hobbes, Locke, Berkeley, Hume, and Hartley to show that they all admitted the possibility of the chemical analogy. It seems only James Mill rejected it. However, Warren failed to recognize that the writings of each of these authors was dominated by the mechanistic conception. None of the associationists, including J. S. Mill, developed the chemical analogy to any systematic conclusions.

Associations Express Relations

There is one problem with the conception of the association developed by the British school which cannot be rectified by either increasing the role of similarity or by introducing the possibility of the chemical analogy. The problem is that items that we know to be related in different ways are assumed to be connected in the mind by one and the same sort of association. For instance, in our mind a dining room is associated with eating, a glutton with eating, a fork with eating, and a steak with eating. How is it that we know that the relation expressed by the first association is one of location to act, the second is that of actor to act, the third of act to instrument, and the fourth of act to object? All are connected by the same one sort of associative link. No doubt James Mill would argue that these differences could be captured by considering each of the above examples as part of a larger network of associations, so that the relation in each case could somehow be "computed" from the position of the association in the network. However, no one has ever described exactly how this computation proceeds. All recent attempts to simulate human memory with an associative model have had to resort to labeling the associative links with the various relations they express (i.e., Anderson, 1972; Quillian, 1968; Schwarcz, Burger, & Simmons, 1970).

While most of the British associationists insisted that there was no need for relations, several notable exceptions are to be found at the periphery of the associationist's camp. Thomas Brown (1820) of the Scottish school had quite clearly seen the need to introduce the relation as distinct from the two interconnected ideas, and he made the relation an important part of his philosophy of the mind. Also in the last days of British associationism, Herbert Spencer (1890) proposed that associations expressed rudimentary relations which were distinct from the elements associated.

In addition to not admitting relations, the British theory also failed to have any conception of well-formedness in an associative structure. That is, they claimed that any idea could be associated with any other idea with which it is spatiotemporally contiguous. But on the contrary, as will be seen in the Gestalt analysis of perception, the elements tend to become organized into certain groupings which in turn tend to become organized into hierarchical structures. A similar need for hierarchical structures will arise when we deal with linguistic material. The point is, as Aristotle apparently understood, that the mind imposes a particular form on the incoming elements of experience. A system such as that proposed by the British associationists which denies such an organizing force would appear likely to produce a chaotic mass of uninterpretable associations.

The Associative Process

We have so far focused on what might be called the *structural* assumptions in British associationism. The two principle constructs considered were those of the idea and the association. We will now examine the *process* assumptions of British associationism.

As a general rule, the British associationists failed to discriminate among the process of encoding information, the memory structure that encoded that information, and the process of retrieving information from that memory structure. Let us consider in this light Hartley's classic statement of the law of association:

If any sensation A, idea B, or muscular motion C, be associated for a sufficient number of times with any other sensation D, idea E, or muscular motion F, it will at last excite d, the simple idea belonging to the sensation D or, the very idea E, or the muscular motion F [Hartley, 1749, p. 102].

Note that there is no mention at all of a memory structure; rather, Hartley is stating a functional principle that relates a history of past experiences to a current psychological event. Hartley argued that remembering was a mental activity basically no different from thinking or imagining. Remembering just like these other activities was determined by the sequencing of associations in the mind. The only difference was "the readiness and strength of the associations by which they (the memories) are cemented together." If we do not assume that each step (association) in the thinking through of a problem had to be embodied in a memory trace, why assume this about memory. In our opinion, the fatal flaw in Hartley's argument is the assumption that a pure associative analysis is applicable to thinking or imagining. Aristotle was correct in restricting the associative analysis to memory.

This refusal of the British associationists to recognize the existence of memory traces is another instance of the extremities to which one can be led by an untempered empiricist approach. We will shortly return to this question of whether it is necessary to postulate memories. This was a point of debate between John Watson and Bertrand Russell. Watson, taking a similar position to Hartley's, argued that memory was just a matter of "verbal habits." It is to American associationism, in which Watson played such an important role, that we now turn.

2.4. ASSOCIATIONISM IN AMERICA

The bridge between British associationism and American associationism is the experimental psychology that developed in Europe under the influence of such figures as Wundt, Müller, and Külpe. The focus of the German research was on the introspective analysis of consciousness. The Germans introduced some novel theoretical ideas into the British conception—for instance, apperception, imageless thought, and the determining tendencies. However, the main effect of the German work was to articulate and develop the structural assumptions of the associative doctrine developed in Britain. There are excellent analyses of this early period in German psychology (e.g., Boring, 1950; Mandler & Mandler, 1964) that clearly describe the important issues and concepts. We have nothing to add to these sources. However, if the significance of our theory of memory is to be appreciated, it is important that we provide a separate analysis of certain developments that occurred in America.

Since most of the first generation of American psychologists received their training in the German laboratories, one might have expected to find in America a similar concern for articulating the structural assumptions of associationism. However, this was not the case. Over the first half of this century, associationism in America has almost completely disintegrated as a coherent theoretical position. In America associationism very nearly died due to its wide acceptance in academic psychology. Just as a scientific theory can be killed by scientists' widely ignoring it, so can a theory almost die from neglect because everyone accepts its basic premises and proceeds to work on technical details within the framework of those premises, details which may not be critically relevant to the truth of that framework. Remember that associationism began as a set of "structural" ideas regarding how our mind is constructed—regarding the content of our memories, how our memories are acquired, and especially how our memories are organized. What happened to associationism in America was that it was accepted and adopted by functionalism and then behaviorism, but it lay fallow while these schools and their exponents pursued other aims.

Functionalism

The psychology practiced by the Germans is known as structuralism—that is, the concern is with the observation, analysis, and description of the elements and contents of the mind—our sensations, feelings, thoughts, decision-making considerations, emotional conflicts. A deliberate attempt was made to reconstruct the patch quilt that is our conscious experience from these mental elements. The favored technique for gathering data was introspection, direct "observation" of one's own mental states and mental acts.

In America the cards were heavily stacked against this Teutonic brand of structuralism, despite Titchner's valiant efforts to make it palatable to his American colleagues. At the turn of the century, pragmatism and functionalism were the philosophical doctrines capturing the imaginations of American psychologists, and William James and John Dewey were the dominant intellectual figures. Pragmatism and functionalism were both very "action-oriented" programs, on the one hand analyzing philosophical ideas in terms of their consequences for practical actions, and on the other hand using the effective actions carried out by a particular "function of the mind" to characterize and elucidate that part of the mind (e.g., volition, imagination, memory). One appeal of such approaches is their potential for action research in real-life settings, with consequences for policy changes in educational or social practices. It was this seductive appeal to "relevance" that attracted American psychologists; it was also the forerunner of the present-day concern of behaviorists with the "control of behavior." Many of the early American psychologists were educational psychologists, employed in settings demanding effective, practical educational proposals. How very different all this was from the world of the withdrawn German introspectionist sitting in a quiet dark laboratory muttering to himself, straining to describe the essence of an afterimage!

Associationism was adopted by Functionalism because it was the most serviceable "learning theory" at hand to meet the needs of the educators. But associationism would have to change its previous emphasis and goals to make it more useful and relevant. A leading figure in American psychology, Edgar Robinson (1932), tells us why:

> Now it would be foolish to deny that the theory of associationism under British care put an unwarranted emphasis upon the intellectual functions, and the contentions of the theory became strongly colored by philosophical doctrines of mind to which we, today, feel superior [p. 5].
>
> British thought, until well into the nineteenth century, was strongly associational, but the associationism of our times is not to be understood as simply a continuation of the British tradition. The emphasis that our writers have put upon association requires for its explanation reasons why the conception has had a peculiar fitness for the American environment. Perhaps because the American public has had an eager faith in the practical advantages of learning, the American scholar has felt a great call to be useful. Our philosophy has tried several doctrines, but pragmatism has been its one wholehearted theory. Our physics has been a little mathematical, but very experimental. Our psychology has had its doctrines of sensation and of

instinct, but these have been minor matters as compared with association, which opens up the school room. We can see why, then, among the numerous conceptions that might have dominated psychological thought, association should have a genuine appeal. The texture of experience is something about which nothing can be done. Innate capacities are merely the limits within which an energetic improver of humanity can work. But association strikes at the heart of education. It holds a promise that changes can be worked in human nature, because it is, in fact, a theory of such changes [pp. 4-5].

In such hands, association becomes the instrument of behavior change, of "behavior modification," a means for altering human nature. Because of this emphasis on behavior change, "memory" became the study of behavior modifications resulting from experience; the theory of memory was transmuted into "learning theory." Association was virtually ignored as a principle for reconstructing the structural organization of a person's world knowledge; association simply became the name for the hypothetical substrate of the brain acted upon by a set of procedural rules for controlling and modifying behavior. The theory of dynamics crowded out the deeper view of static organization. The quotation from Robinson summarizes the spirit of the times and helps us understand why associationism took the turn it did. That is, American pragmatism favored a strongly functional analysis of mental life and behavior change, which orientation was simply incompatible with the theoretical elaboration of associationism, which is primarily a structural theory.

Behaviorism

The radical behaviorism of John Watson was an ideological explosion on the American scene that immediately preempted the schools of functionalism and pragmatism. It was a philosophical as well as a psychological theory regarding mind and behavior; even today, some 60 years later, the ideas of John Watson are very much with experimental psychologists; some of his preachings are our very staff of life.

We will not attempt here a careful exposition of the views of behaviorism. To briefly mention but a few main tenets: Watson emphasized that psychology should be an objective science, with its subject matter describable in physicalistic terms (i.e., stimulus histories and observable behaviors of an organism), that introspections were unreliable observation bases, and that substantive psychological theories must predict objective behaviors. Watson argued in particular against the postulation of any psychological event, action, or state which did not have immediately observable indicants or consequents. These indicants were invariably alleged to take the form of muscular or glandular responses at some bodily location. Thus, specific emotional feelings might be identified with particular patterns of response by the viscera, glands, and smooth muscle system; thinking was identified with subvocally talking to oneself; the imagining of lifting a weight was nothing but slight tensions in appropriate muscles of the forearm, and so on. Watson emphasized observable, peripheral activities (responses, behaviors) as the only objective meaning assignable to statements regarding mental states or processes. He also adopted wholesale two further ideas current at the time: first, from Pavlov and Bechterev, the notion of the conditioned reflex was adopted as the basic unit of skilled performance, and as a paradigm (and vocabulary) for describing all learning; second, from early associationism, Watson adopted the idea that complex movements, performances, or skills are analyzable into a number of separate, simple units (reflexes), put together in novel patterns or sequences to form new complex behaviors. This is very like Locke's idea of how new concepts are formed by new combinations of elementary sensory ideas.

Behaviorism became wedded to functionalism in the years 1920 to 1960 in American "learning theories," in the systematic positions of Thorndike, Guthrie, Hull, Miller, Spence, and Skinner. Association was adopted as a primitive notion by all; but the operation of various secondary laws became of issue to many of the systematists. The development and enrichment of the associative organization of memory held no importance at all for these theorists. A list of the "hot controversial" issues of the 1930–1970 period serves in part to illustrate how far from center stage were developments in associationism:

1. What is the effective stimulus for transposition (relational) responding (e.g., Spence versus Köhler)?

2. Do animals learn by selecting entire hypotheses to solve a problematic situation or by gradually strengthening correct responses? Does the animal learn about all the components of a complex stimulus to which he responds or only about a selected cue on each trial (e.g., Lashley versus Spence)?

3. Can learning occur without reward or punishment (e.g., by contiguous experience alone)?

4. What is the common property of all reinforcing events? Of all punishing events (e.g., drive or need reduction hypothesis)?

5. Does reward influence what is learned or only what is performed (e.g., latent learning, latent extinction)?

6. Can stimulus-stimulus associations be learned without responses or reinforcements (sensory-sensory preconditioning experiments)?

7. Can learning occur without the overt response actually occurring (curare studies)?

8. Is the learned response best characterized as a muscular movement or as an approach by any means to a significant external stimulus ("place versus response" issue)?

9. Do responses of the autonomic nervous system ("involuntary") and skeletal ("voluntary") musculature differ in their fundamental laws of learning? Can involuntary responses be conditioned in the operant manner through the actions of rewards and punishments?

10. Do rewards act automatically to strengthen preceding responses or is the effect mediated by awareness of the S-R reinforcement contingencies? Do rewards act by their satisfying effects or by providing directive information?

This sample is representative of the class of controversial issues occupying the energies of American learning theorists during the past 50 years. They are questions posed largely within the stimulus-response framework, and they concern interpretations of the controlling effect on behavior of reinforcing and discriminative stimuli. Few of these controversies center around the structure of knowledge, the correct representation of the myriad bits of learnings that a person (or animal) acquires over its lifetime. If stimulus-response (or S-R) psychologists were pressed on this question of the structure of knowledge, they would probably reply that "knowledge" is coordinate with a set of S-R pairs: in situation S_i, make response R_j. The S's and the R's might be rather complex situations and performances (e.g., swerving a car to avoid a pedestrian; answering "Washington" when asked to name the capital of the U.S.A.), but these are themselves analyzable in terms of sequences of stimuli, responses, and response-produced (proprioceptive) stimuli. (This latter notion, used in many S-R discussions of thinking, is that a response has stimulus consequences which feed back as possible cues for later responses. For example, coordinated walking depends upon stretch-receptors in the leg and hip muscles feeding back signals to the spinal cord regarding the relative locations of the limbs in the stepping cycle.)

The S-R listing above could be augmented in theory by permitting "implicit mediating responses" and their implicit stimuli. A good example of an implicit response is "silently saying" a word to oneself; the implicit proprioceptive stimulus from such silent speech is a bit difficult to imagine, but might possibly be identified with particular time-varying patterns of tension in the articulatory muscles of the larynx, tongue, and lips. The presumed distinction between such implicit S-R events and the nebulous "ideas" of earlier associationism was based on the following restrictions:

1. The postulated implicit R's were restricted to those which are fractional copies of large-scale responses; essentially, if the experimenter could just "turn up the gain on the amplifier," these implicit responses would look and sound just like overt responses, and have all of their properties (e.g., be learned according to the same laws).

2. The only implicit stimuli are those corresponding to feedback from implicit responses.

With these sorts of restrictions on the implicit S's and R's, the addition of such pairs to the S-R listing of knowledge does not, in our opinion, appreciably expand the power of S-R theory to deal with the structure of memory (Fodor, 1965, has argued for a similar opinion). The criticisms associated with the Terminal Meta-Postulate apply full force to this variety of S-R theorizing. There are, furthermore, in our opinion rampant confusions and misconceptions regarding what can and what cannot be represented and reasonably explained in terms of mediating S-R chains (e.g., Osgood, 1968; Staats, 1969). The apparent power of mediating events comes about because S-R theorists literally abandon Strictures 1 and 2 above, and allow their "mediating" S-R events to take on precisely the surplus meanings of such notions as *idea, concept, meaning, image,* and *referent* which had been current in the mentalist vocabulary of British associationism.

Behaviorism and Neo-Associationism

In later chapters we will be proposing a neo-associationist theory which goes counter to many of the philosophical commitments of behaviorism since it uses notions like *idea, concept, feature,* and *image* as basic elements and uses relational associations as the "glue" for connecting these terms together into significant patterns. In this section, we critically analyze the memory representations implied by behaviorism; we also bring up and answer some standard criticisms we can anticipate from some S-R quarters against our neo-associationism.

There will be essentially two main criticisms that the strict S-R theorists could level against the general viewpoint of HAM. Like most present-day cognitive theories, HAM requires the postulation of a complex memory structure (data base plus interpretive procedures) which cannot be directly observed (or "operationally defined") but which we presume to intervene between a person's initial contact with some information and his later use of his memory of that information to guide a variety of performances. B. F. Skinner, an eloquent behaviorist, has criticized the postulation of *any* intervening variables, states, or structures that are not directly observable. He states his objection to any sort of postulated inner states as follows (also, see Figure 2.2):

> In each case we have a causal chain consisting of three links: (1) an operation performed on the organism from without—for example, water deprivation; (2) an inner condition—for example, physiological or psychic thirst; and (3) a kind of behavior—for example, drinking. . . . The objection to inner states is not that they do not exist, but that they are not relevant to a functional analysis. We cannot account for the behavior of any system while staying wholly inside it; eventually we must turn to forces operating on the organism from without. Unless there is a weak spot in our causal chain so that the second link is not lawfully determined by the first, or the third by the second, then the first and third links must be lawfully related. If we must always go back beyond the second link for prediction and control, we may avoid many tiresome and exhausting digressions by examining the third link as a function of the first. Valid information about the second link may throw light upon this relationship but can in no way alter it [Skinner, 1953, pp. 34–35].

The situation to which Skinner refers may be seen in Figure 2.2, where arrows depict functional relationships between variables. With one independent variable and one dependent variable, it is clearly uneconomical to introduce the intervening variable ("thirst"), since it is eliminable by functional arrow 3 relating just the observable variables. On this point there is no argument. The counterargument—stated effectively by Bergman (1953) and N. E. Miller (1959)—is that intervening

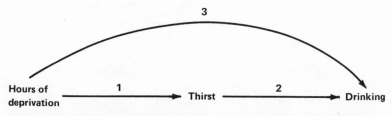

FIG. 2.2. An illustration of Skinner's argument for the elimination of intervening variables.

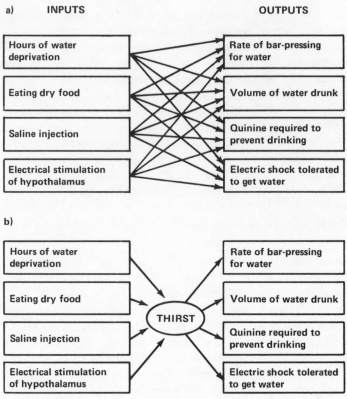

FIG. 2.3. An illustration of Miller's argument for the utility of intervening variables.

variables become economical in situations where there are multiple input and multiple output variables. The situation is properly depicted in the top and bottom panels of Figure 2.3 (adapted from N. E. Miller, 1959). In the top panel, with 4 independent determinants of "thirst" and 4 dependent indicators, there are 16 different functions to be discovered ($m \times n$ in general). The bottom panel, which introduces an intervening variable, also illustrates the economy of the postulation; here, only 8 ($m + n$ in general) relations must be determined, 4 relating the input variable to degree of thirst, and 4 relating thirst to the output variables. If this were a "unitary" intervening variable, then the former 16 S-R functions would be decomposable into 4 S-T and 4 T-R functions as shown in the bottom panel of Figure 2.3.

Most "neo-behaviorists" accepted the logic of this argument, saw the value of intervening variables, and so proceeded to postulate them with abandon. Clark Hull's theory, for example, was based on the postulation of one after another intervening variable (see Koch, 1954, for a critical review). Most of these concerned performance variables like stimulus intensity, drive intensity, incentive motivation, response fatigue, and the like. The basic associative intervening variable was simply "habit strength," conceptualized as an S-R bond. Thus, regarding the structure of knowledge, the main intervening variable in Hull's system was still just an S-R connection. This basic assumption exemplifies the so-called Terminal Meta-Postulate mentioned earlier which supposes that the only admissible elements (terms) in a description of behavior are those that map one-to-one onto observable stimuli or responses. Just as the failure of the TMP was a fundamental weakness of the empiricism of British associationism, so does it also point to a similar weakness in stimulus-response psychologies. Our theory, in rejecting the TMP, therefore is rejecting not only Skinner's radical behaviorism but all S-R associative conceptions. They are just not powerful enough to capture the complexity of human memory or language.

Behaviorism and the Reconstruction of Memories

Lest these criticisms of behaviorism appear too arid and abstracted away from the context of human memory, which is the focus of this book, let us examine the early behavioristic account of memory due to Watson, since it puts the issues in bold relief.

Watson did not think that "memory" was a useful term; he thought it had no place in an objective psychology. Insofar as the term has meaning, it refers, says Watson, to retention of a habit. He especially emphasized our memories of psychomotor skills such as golfing, swimming, and, for animals, running mazes and escaping from puzzle boxes. Here, memory considered as activation of a sequence of habitual reflexes does not seem too terribly implausible (except to ethologists, cyberneticists, and other connoisseurs of animal behavior or human skilled performance). But for describing man's ability to recollect past events, Watson relied heavily on the formation, retention, and reactivation of verbal and visceral habits to carry the burden of explanation. He explains as follows:

> What the man on the street ordinarily means by an exhibition of memory is what occurs in some such situation as this: An old friend comes to see him, after many years' absence. The moment he sees this friend, he says: "Upon my life! Addison Sims of Seattle! I haven't seen you since the World's Fair in Chicago. Do you remember the gay parties we used to have in the old Windmere Hotel? Do you remember the Midway? Do you remember _____," ad infinitum. The psychology of this process is so simple that it seems almost an insult to your intelligence to discuss it, and yet a good many of the behaviorists' kindly critics have said that behaviorism cannot adequately explain memory. Let us see if this is a fact.
>
> When the man on the street originally made the acquaintance of Mr. Sims, he saw him and was told his name at the same time. Possibly he did not see him again until a week or two later. He had to be re-introduced. Again, when he saw Mr. Sims he heard his name. Then, shortly afterwards, the two men became friends and saw one another every day and became really acquainted—that is, formed verbal and manual habits towards one another and towards the same or similar situations. In other words, the man on the street became completely organized to react in many habit ways to Mr. Addison Sims. Finally, just the sight of the man, even after months of

absence, would call out not only the old verbal habits, but many other types of bodily and visceral responses [Watson, 1930, pp. 235-236].

He sums up by saying:

By "memory," then, we mean nothing except the fact that when we meet a stimulus again after an absence, we do the old habitual thing (say the old words and show the old visceral–emotional–behavior) that we learned to do when we were in the presence of that stimulus in the first place [p. 237].

The basic difficulties of this viewpoint are easily brought out. Most of them hinge upon an inadequate conception of linguistic competence. Indeed these criticisms of Watson's views appeared clearly in writings by Bertrand Russell in 1927, in reply to Watson's 1924 book. It is with some embarrassment that we note that Russell's critique was not noted and appreciated by psychologists until about 30 to 40 years after it was written. The criticisms can be listed quickly. First, people need not respond overtly and verbally to an event at the time of witnessing that event in order later to show retention of knowledge about that event. Common examples are remembering scenes, episodes, or pictures in mental imagery that has no linguistic counterpart. An artificial laboratory example is to have a subject later report verbally the names of pictures of famous people shown to him while his vocal apparatus is occupied, say, with rapidly subtracting threes successively from a starting two-digit number.

A second, and more critical, point is that recollection of Mr. Addison Sims can be stimulated and retrieved by a multitude of different stimuli (queries or "probes"). One whole class of retrieval cues refers to visual appearances of Mr. Sims himself, although seen perhaps in radically changed settings. Another whole class of cues is linguistic queries, such as: "Do you know a Mr. Sims?" "Do you know anyone from Seattle?" "Who did you meet at the World's Fair?" etc. Finally is a whole class of ill-defined "retrievals" wherein our knowledge of some earlier event is used for later effective actions, such as reserving a room at the Windmere Hotel when next in Chicago because of its past association with happy times. In short, knowledge about the events surrounding meetings with Mr. Sims is a complex set of conceptual relations, and a very diverse variety of inputs (perceptual and linguistic) can tap into that knowledge structure. It is senseless to argue for retrieval here on any basis of "similarity" between the retrieval cue and a knowledge structure; one's answer to "Who did you meet in Chicago?" might possibly be explained in terms of the similarity of that probe to an earlier implicit statement like "Here I am in Chicago meeting Mr. Sims"; but it would not explain why a trivial surface variation on the probe such as "*Why* did you meet in Chicago?" elicits an entirely different answer.

A third difficulty with Watson's "verbal habit" account of memory is that it ignores our ability to paraphrase and recast linguistically the basic conceptual facts about events. One can say "I met Mr. Sims on the commuter train to Chicago" just as well as "While riding into the Windy City on the 8:35, I bumped into Joe"; for an appropriate audience and context, these two sentences assert the same propositions or conceptual relations despite their having almost no content words in common. Also, one may use either sentence indiscriminately to recall the same fact. Moreover, one may translate a learned set of conceptual relations into entirely different domains to make the recollections palpable; for example, if one were bilingual, his experiences with Mr. Sims might be described in a foreign language; if an artist, he might draw sketches of Mr. Sims, and so on. In such cases there is no possibility that one is reproducing overt responses which occurred upon the earlier occasion of meeting Mr. Sims. Russell (1927) expresses the case regarding Watson's view of memory as follows:

> It is not our actual language that can be regarded as habitual, but only what our words express. In repeating a poem we have learned by heart, the language is habitual, but not so when we recount a past incident in words we never used before. In this case, it is not the actual words that we repeat, but only their meaning. The habitual element, therefore, if it really accounts for the recollection, must not be sought in words. This is something of a difficulty for the Watsonian theory of language. . . . [Two different sentences may] have nothing verbally in common, yet they may relate the same fact, and I may use either indifferently when I recall the fact. Thus my recollection is certainly not a definite verbal habit. Yet words are the only bodily movements by which I make known my recollections to other people. If the behaviorist tells me that my recollection is bodily habit, and begins by telling me that it is a *verbal* habit, he can be driven by such instances to the admission that it must be some other kind of habit. If he says this, he is abandoning the region of observable fact, and taking refuge in hypothetical bodily movements invoked to save a theory. But these are hardly any better than "thoughts."
>
> This question is more general than the problem of memory. Many different forms of words may be used to express the same "meaning," and there seems no reason in mere habit to account for the fact that we sometimes use one form of words and sometimes another when we "think" of that which all the various forms of words express. The association seems to go, not direct from stimulus to words, but from stimulus to "meaning" and thence to words expressing the "meaning.". . . It is such facts, among others, that make it difficult to explain the mechanism of association, whether in memory or in "thought" in general, if we assume that words, or even sentences, are the terms associated [Russell, 1927, pp. 73-75].

The words of Russell have surprising cogency in our post-Chomskian world of linguistic deep-structure. In current-day terms, Russell was arguing that habits defined over surface strings of verbal units (words) will not suffice to account for paraphrastic descriptions of witnessed events.

Although the criticisms above have centered upon how our linguistic competence confounds a simplistic S-R view of event memory, we hasten to point out that the logical point is the same as that made earlier regarding the theoretical economy made possible by introducing thirst as an intervening variable. Just as we should not identify "thirst" with hours of deprivation nor with drinking, so should we avoid identifying our memory of the Sims episodes with a particular verbal descriptive sequence. Multiple "responses" sensitive in varying ways to multiple "stimuli" are made possible by the memory structure representing those episodes. The memory structure in HAM is here conceived to be a network of associative relations among abstract semantic concepts—an interrelated set of "meaningful propositions"—and for sufficiently rich structures there are almost limitless stimulus probes by which we can tap a limitless supply of answers ("responses") from such an abstract structure. In this sense, the prior "$(m + n)$ versus $(m \times n)$" argument for theoretical economy applies as well to this postulation of a meaningful conceptual structure as our encoding of and memory of the Sims episodes.

Although our point (or Russell's, really) regarding multiple inputs and outputs of a memory structure has been argued with respect to verbal memories, we strongly suspect that a similar argument could be made for the memories established by simple Pavlovian or operant conditioning procedures with either man or animal. A man can easily detect and frame for himself propositions expressing such contingencies as "When this blue light comes on, if I press this lever, I will get a nickel; otherwise, I get nothing for pressing." That simple knowledge structure will "mediate" effective responding in a variety of altered circumstances. For example, the experimenter may alter details of the response (e.g., "use your left hand instead of your right"), or pay off in convertible tokens rather than nickels, or verbally alter the contingencies (i.e., "there will be no more nickels"), and the subject will quickly adjust his response appropriately. Also, the person exposed to these contingencies can use what he has learned to describe the contingency verbally, either to himself or to a friend in need of nickels.

These examples are still using the verbal subject. What of animals in such simple learning tasks? What complex "abstract structure" is, say, a dog learning when a tone is consistently followed by a painful, noxious stimulus? There is no reason to deny a priori that dogs and other nonverbal organisms can form the equivalents of elementary propositions encoding the temporal sequence of significant events. To be absurdly concrete, suppose the dog acquires an associative structure expressible as the proposition: "In experimental situation S, a high-pitched tone is followed within a few seconds by a painful stimulus to my left front paw." If this proposition is combined with other general propositions, such as "If a limb is about to be injured, move it away to avoid injury," the dog could "derive" the command to flex its left paw when the tone sounds.

The claim is that such conceptual propositions capture the flavor of the dog's behavior, especially in new situations. (This was Edward Tolman's main position.) Thus, it is known that the overt paw-flexion response need not occur during learning. Blockage of the neuromuscular junctures with a curare-like drug prevents all overt responses, yet the tone-shock association may be established under curare, and then later tested with positive results (i.e., conditioned paw withdrawals to the tone) after the drug has worn off. Also the tone-pain association institutes a totally different "repertoire of responses" in the dog from the tone in other situations. Thus, in a later appetitive instrumental conditioning situation, the tone will serve as a "conditioned emotional stimulus" suppressing appetitive behavior. The tone can also be used as a "punishing" event, supporting passive avoidance learning; also, its onset can initiate various kinds of previously learned escape behavior, and its termination can "reinforce" escape behavior. There is, thus, a diverse class of different behaviors affected by the tone-shock experience. Beyond this, there are probably other means to induce a similar memory structure in the dog. For example, the tone could be paired with other painful stimuli like burns, loud noises, nausea, or pinpricks delivered to the left paw.

The tenor of these comments is that for even a nonverbal organism and for a singularly simple connection such as "tone-shock," we still require for its representation an intervening propositional structure which can account for multiple determinants, multiple contexts of retrieval of that information, and multiple varied "behavioral indices" related to that learning. Thus, our arguments against the behavioristic conception of memory can also be advanced with some plausibility for elementary conditioning with animals, although admittedly the arguments lack the force of those available on the issue when dealing with language-rich human adults. Part of the battle fought by E. C. Tolman, arguing for a "cognitive theory" to explain animal behavior, was concerned with just such points.

Interference Theory

We have argued in the foregoing that the successes and excesses of functionalism and behaviorism led to the intellectual stagnation of associationism as a theory of memory. The primary exception to this stagnation has been the appearance of the associative interference theory of forgetting. Although suggested by a number of earlier researchers (e.g., Müller & Pilzecker, 1900), modern interference theory dates its beginnings from McGeoch's (1932) formulation, and it has been developed and researched by several generations of intellectual offspring of McGeoch. The British associationists had concentrated almost exclusively on the conditions favorable for acquisition of new information; the interference theorists turned the tables and concentrated instead on the conditions that promoted forgetting of already-learned materials. This yielded some new perspectives on the problems of memory.

A rich set of concepts and interlocking facts has been developed under the auspices of modern interference theory. The learning of laboratory materials tends to interfere with memory for other laboratory material that was learned before and after it. The basic variables in these experiments and multiple variations thereof have by now been quite systematically explored and catalogued. The facts of interference are very important to associationism because they appear to be so easily explained within an associationist framework. We consider these facts sufficiently important that we will devote a later chapter (Chapter 10) to reviewing the well-established facts about interference and illustrating how our model, HAM, can accommodate these facts.

The work of the interference theorists is, in our opinion, the major substantive accomplishment of associationism in America. Postman's assessment of the scene over a decade ago is still right on target:

> Interference theory occupies an unchallenged position as the major significant analysis of the process of forgetting. The only serious opposition has come

from the trace theory of the Gestalt psychologists, but that point of view has thus far proved experimentally sterile and resistant to rigorous test. As a result, the recent years have seen little debate about the basic assumptions of interference theory. Developments in the study of forgetting have consisted largely of extensions and refinements of interference theory and of methodological advances in the measurement of retention [Postman, 1961, p. 152].

Of the criticisms that might be leveled against interference theory, one of the most serious from our point of view is that interference theorists have not devoted much effort to systematically developing the associative theory of memory in which their theory of forgetting is embedded (see Melton, 1961, for a similar opinion). There has been little concern for demonstrating that their conception of memory meets the necessary "sufficiency conditions" for a theory adequate to the full range of mnemonic phenomena. They have adopted the restrictions of behaviorism, so that the "S-R habit" is the only conceptual tool interference theorists have for explicating or representing the knowledge that a person possesses. They have a weak view of the retrieval process and provide no account of interference, deduction, and reconstruction in acts of remembering. Interference theory is also conspicuously remiss in characterizing the associative organization of long-term memory in a realistic way, and it fails to clarify exactly how that associative organization is brought into play when we add new facts, new strategies, and new procedures to our knowledge. Interference theory, like other branches of psychology, has not provided a realistic model of language use, nor of learning and forgetting of propositional materials. Its exponents have said relatively little about interference with thematically meaningful materials, and some researchers have even doubted that interference has any bearing on memory for meaningful materials. What interference theory lacks is approximately what our theory, HAM, supplies; namely, a systematic theory about how the person brings his cognitive equipment to bear upon comprehending, storing, retrieving, and using propositional information for inference, question answering, and action.

3
RATIONALIST COUNTERTRADITIONS

Reminiscence is the faculty of the soul by which it receives the forms it had known before being associated with the body.

—Plato

3.1. THE RATIONALIST APPROACH

Experimental psychology in America is pervaded by the firm conviction that any theory of memory will have to be basically associative in character. This claim, we are convinced, is fundamentally wrong. This chapter reviews two counterexamples to this mistaken generalization, namely, Gestalt theory and the reconstruction hypothesis, both exemplifying the rationalist methodology. Unfortunately, both of these approaches will turn out to be rather sketchy when considered as memory theories. This is not surprising because, in the rationalist conception of matters, memory is a very complicated but essentially uninteresting topic for study.

As a consequence of their sketchiness and vagueness, neither theory provides a strong alternative to our model, HAM, which is an unfortunate state of affairs. We will report as sympathetically as we can what these theorists have said in their writings about human memory. We leave to those with rationalist leanings the task of developing or extrapolating either of these theories to the point where they could become strong competitors to associative theories.

In contrast with the associationist's commitment to methodological empiricism, the rationalist approach attempts to begin with certain "truths" or "first principles" about the human mind. The primary methodology is use of intuition, insight, and reason. By these means the basic structure of a mental phenomenon is supposed to emerge, and one should eventually be able to formulate the abstract principles that are really at the heart of the phenomenon. Once these first principles have been formulated, the remaining task is to relate them to observations of particular real world phenomena. Lest anyone think that this is an absurd manner in which to proceed, he should realize that a similar rationalist methodology has been one of the principal means by which many of the major theoretical advances have occurred in the physical sciences.

We argued in Chapter 2 that the methodological empricism of associationism tended to leave it branded with certain higher-order properties or metafeatures. We think we can make a plausible case for the position that the methodological rationalism also tends to generate certain metafeatures in the theories it generates. Furthermore, in rough correspondence to each of the four features of associationism, it is heuristic to consider an opposing four features typically allied with rationalist theories. Corresponding to connectionism in associationism one typically finds *nativism* (innatism) in the rationalist theory; corresponding to reductionism one finds *holism*; corresponding to sensationalism one usually finds *intuitionism*; and corresponding to mechanism there may be *vitalism* (or antimechanism). We will give a brief discussion of each of these theses.

Nativism

The most extreme form of nativism was that stated by Plato: All knowledge of any importance was alleged to be innately recorded in the human mind. The point of experience was merely to bring out that knowledge in explicit form. Plato did not deny that sensory experience could be recorded in a more or less direct form in the human mind; but he argued that such knowledge was inconsequential and a source of error. The particular facts of the world were ephemeral, changing, and untrustworthy compared to the enduring truths of pure reason. Plato's nativism is very nearly the antithesis of connectionism, which asserts that all knowledge arises from linking together the elements of experience.

Subsequent rationalist theorists, however, have not taken nearly so extreme a position as that of Plato. Instead they have argued a more moderate position that a certain *class* of *principles* is innately given in the "apparatus of the mind" which constrains it to impose particular structures or to project hypotheses of a special type upon the multifarious flux of sensory experience. Some typical examples in the literature of rationalism are such distinctions as that between self versus others, or material versus spirit, and the alleged universality of such beliefs as the principle of causality, or the principle of inductive inference, or the belief that "laws of logic" dictate our "laws of thought." Other examples of pertinence to psychologists include the rationalists' belief that man's perceptual system is so preset that it "naturally" interprets a two-dimensional retinal mosaic as a projection of a three-dimensional visual space; or that it is so preset that it construes the physical world in accordance with the axioms of Euclidean geometry.

A recent and vigorous rationalist argument has been given by Chomsky (1968) and Katz (1966) for language acquisition. Chomsky assumes that the facts of language force us to conclude that the child, considered as a language-acquisition device, must begin life innately endowed with a small set of *linguistic universals* both as in regards to some basic concepts (e.g., syntactic or semantic distinctions) and in regards to grammatical principles (e.g., a bias for transformational grammars, a potential for distinguishing surface versus deep-structure propositions, a potential for cyclic recursion, etc.). According to this view, these various innate settings bias the child to construct a rather sophisticated "theory" of the grammar underlying his native language, and to do so despite the fact that the speech he hears around him is ungrammatical, chaotic, and prone to errors. It should be remarked in passing that our model HAM begins, as does Chomsky's language-acquisition device, with a rather rich set of syntactic primitives for analyzing sentences.

The rationalism-empiricism controversy has revolved around the issue of innatism, not so much differing with regard to the existence of innate principles, but rather differing with regard to the nature of the types of mental *capabilities* which were assumed to be innate. For even John Locke, a strong critic of innate ideas in his *Essay Concerning Human Understanding*, assumed that the mind has an *innate* capacity to associate contiguous experiences, and to reflect upon experiences. The critical nature of these assumed innate mechanisms has been pointed out by Katz (1966) in regard to the rationalist-empiricist debate:

> The basis for the controversy is not, as it is often conceived in popular discussions, that empiricists fail to credit the mind with any innate principles, but rather that the principles which are accorded innate status by empiricists do not place any substantive restrictions on the ideas that can qualify as components of complex ideas or any formal restrictions on the structure of associations which bond component ideas together to form a complex idea. On the empiricist's hypothesis, the innate principles are purely combinatorial devices for putting together items from experience. So these principles provide only the machinery for instituting associative bonds. Experience plays the selective role in determining which ideas may be connected by association, and principles of association are, accordingly, unable to exclude any ideas as, in principle, beyond the range of possible intellectual acquisition [pp. 240–241].

Katz is arguing that associations that record contiguous experiences are not sufficient to constrain the nature of the mind nor of the child's interpretation of what his language is like. We hold a similar view, and so have endowed our model from the outset with a highly structured linguistic-perceptual "parser." Associations enter in HAM only in encoding ("learning") the structured output of a rather rich interpretative parser. Whereas associations represent and hold memories, the input to the memory component is structured logically in a manner resembling a Chomskian context-free phrase structure grammar. Therefore, HAM's memory for certain information is structured only insofar as its perceptual interfacing mechanisms impose a particular logical description onto its inputs; HAM's memory simply records rather passively the structural trees output by its parser. We have no detailed model for language acquisition; we know it is absurd to say that a baby should begin life with all the sophisticated interfacing and parsers with which we endow the "adult HAM." Exactly which parts and perceptual mechanisms of HAM should be degraded to get a viable model of the child is not obvious and is clearly not a simple scientific problem.

Nativism is not per se a theory of memory; in fact, the two notions are literally at opposite poles. Nativism becomes a meaningful position when it is used to characterize the properties of mental processes involved in perception (of space, of linguistic utterances) or in reasoning (inductive generalization, deductions). Of course, it is with respect to just these processes (perception, reasoning) that the rationalist attacks on associationism-empiricism have been most vigorous and successful.

Holism

Just as reductionism leads to theories that are cast in terms of the microproperties of experience, so holism leads to theories that are cast in terms of the global properties. This holist bias manifests itself at two levels in rationalist approaches to memory. First, there is the claim that the total memory structure has properties that cannot be predicted (or are very difficult to predict) from a knowledge of the underlying parts and their configuration. The whole is alleged to have novel properties that are quite unlike the properties of the parts comprising the whole. This is the doctrine of emergent properties to be examined in greater detail when we review Gestalt theory.

A second level revealing the holistic character of rationalist theories is in the insistence that it is in principle impossible to study the memory system by itself, that the functioning of the memory system is inextricably intertwined with the functioning of the total organism. Therefore, to understand memory, it is necessary to come to an understanding of the whole mind. For example, this attitude appears frequently in assertions that memory is not reproductive but rather reconstructive, or that remembering bears strong resemblances to "problem solving," or that all sorts of rules and inferential procedures are called in by "higher mental processes" in order for the person to reconstruct an event from memory. This viewpoint, that memory necessarily implicates diverse inference and problem-solving routines both at the time of input (e.g., comprehending a sentence) and at output (e.g., reconstructing an event), is at direct odds with our proposal that there exists a *strategy-free component* of memory (viz., that is modeled in HAM) that functions independently of the rest of the mental system; the strategies (e.g., use of mnemonic imagery in encoding, use of reconstructive searches in decoding, etc.) are assumed to operate in interfacing the memory system to the external world, but do not determine the operation of the memory once the input tree or probe (query) tree has been specified.

Intuitionism

In opposition to the empiricist tradition, the rationalist believes that intuitions about mental phenomena are much more important than any empirical data that he might obtain. His intuitions provide immediate access to the data central to the problem that he is studying, while empirical observations are always subject to contamination from unknown sources, to problems of replicability, multiple interpretations, questions of generalizability, and the whims of nature. So it is not surprising that the rationalist, when faced with an experiment that disconfirms his theory, will doubt the data and not the theory; the defense is frequently couched in terms of the alleged "artificiality" of the experimental situation in contrast to "real life" situations.

In most sciences, this is all that intuitionism amounts to, namely, a particular methodological bias about how to proceed in experimentation. However, in psychology intuitionism is something more because psychology is the study of the very animal that possesses these valuable intuitions. Hence, to the rationalist an important piece of data is the subject's introspections about the psychological processes under study. In contrast, the radical empiricist rejects intuitions as an acceptable form of data; and while milder mannered empiricists accept such data as indicators of internal processes, they refuse to regard intuitions as any more important than other data that can be brought to bear upon the matter. Clearly, the most successful form of this rationalist reliance on intuitive judgments is to be found in the modern linguistic tradition initiated by Chomsky which relies almost exclusively on intuitions of native speakers regarding the grammaticality of particular sentences. However, we shall also presently see that Gestalt theory and the reconstruction hypothesis place great emphasis on having their theories correspond to introspections about the memory processes.

Concerning human memory, intuitionism also manifests itself in judgments about what are the important matters that are worth explaining. While associationism focuses on the sensory contents of memory (i.e., the events that the subject reports remembering), the intuitionist is likely to focus on the subjective experiences of the "remembering act" itself. A good example would be the subjective experiences of a person caught mid-flight in a "tip of the tongue" state, in which a word or name hovers tantalizingly just outside the grasp of complete retrieval (see Brown & McNeill, 1966). As a second example, the rationalist is likely to emphasize how the mind abstracts an underlying schema or principle from a range of experiences with particular instances of a concept or rule, whereas the empiricist would emphasize storage of particular exemplars and only gradual and fragmentary abstraction of the schema or prototype (see Reitman & Bower, 1973). These points of divergence serve to contrast intuitionism with the "sensationalism" of the associative tradition. The intuitionist does not deny that sensory information is stored in some form in memory; rather he denies that this is the interesting feature of memory. He emphasizes instead processes such as abstraction, schematization, inference, and reconstruction.

Vitalism

Like mechanism, vitalism is a feature that is vague and hard to pin down, although we have reliable intuitions about what it implies. Originally, it was invoked by biologists who believed that the complexities of living organisms or the consciousness of human beings could not be explained in terms of reduction of these phenomena to the natural laws of physics and chemistry. Instead, it was proposed that new laws would have to be introduced to describe the vital forces behind such phenomena. Beyond this is the connotation of vitalism that relates it to the antithesis of mechanistic explanations. In psychology, for example, antimechanistic positions would include such things as the idea that "determining tendencies," "intentions," or "purposes" guide chains of associations (or responses) so as to achieve particular goals, and that they do so in a manner not reducible to mechanistic principles. With regard to vitalism, such examples now seem less antimechanical in the light of the developments in cybernetics, servomechanisms, equilibrium-seeking machines, executive programs, and algorithmic searches of problem graphs directed at achieving a hierarchy of goals (see Ernst & Newell, 1969). A plausible form of the antimechanistic position in psychology asserts that some psychological phenomena can never be captured or explained in any significant way by theories modeled on serial, digital computers. For instance, it might be asserted that one's immediate awareness and subjective experience of the world cannot be modeled in such a machine (see Hook, 1961). Or it might be argued that the mind is not remotely like a serial computer (but rather like a parallel, analog computer), that it exhibits holistic "field influences" in its actions in complex ways suggesting that present-day mechanistic accounts are misguided (see Dreyfus, 1972, for a recent critique from this viewpoint of research in artificial intelligence).

As was the case with the four metafeatures of associationism listed in Chapter 2, these opposing metafeatures of rationalism are not directly subject to empirical falsification. Rather, they insinuate themselves into particular predictions of particular models, and only the latter are subject to empirical falsification. Also, while these features are common properties of a rationalist model, they may also be accidental features of an associative model. For instance, our model HAM will be nativistic regarding the perceptual parsers, and perhaps vitalistic in that it assumes the existence of an executive program that directs the information processing. But other components of HAM are connectionistic and mechanistic in character.

3.2. GESTALT THEORY

Gestalt theorists were frequently criticized (see Buhler, 1926; Selz, 1926) for using other researchers' results as discoveries for Gestalt theory. The earlier researchers had already noted the significance of the results. So the Gestalters were asked what was so revolutionary about the theory they were proposing. To understand why Gestalters were able to shake the psychological world with shopworn demonstrations, let us consider just one example of how one class of demonstrations was incorporated into Gestalt theory. The illustration comes from research on *form qualities* or, as Christian von Ehrenfels (1937) called them, Gestaltqualitat.

The basic problem concerned the perception of form. In viewing a square, we experience more than four separate lines; we also perceive immediately the relationship of "squareness" that inheres in their particular configuration. Similarly, in hearing a musical tune, we perceive more than the individual notes; we perceive the melody, which is provided by the relationships among the notes. Before the time of the Gestalt theorists, the standard analysis of these phenomena, exemplified by Ehrenfels, was to assert that there were "non-sensory" elements in perception; in addition to perceiving the sensory elements (the Fundamente), it was said that we perceived their relationship (the Grundlage) as an additional element.

The important feature of this classical analysis is that it preserved the reductionism of associationism. It did not deny that all experience could be decomposed into a finite set of specifiable elements; it rather asserted only that higher-order, relational elements had also to be recognized in the analysis. The Grundlage was no more important than the Fundamente; indeed, according to Ehrenfels, the Grundlage was definitely subordinate, depending as it did on the Fundamente. Ehrenfels (1937) described his own results as follows:

> The decisive step in the founding of a theory of Gestalt-quality was my own assertion: When the memory-images of successive notes are present as a simultaneous complex in consciousness, then an idea (Vorstellung), belonging to a new category, can arise in consciousness, a unitary idea, which is connected in a manner peculiar to itself with the ideas (Vorstellungen) of the complex of notes involved [p. 521].

It was just this elementalism or atomism that the Gestalters objected to. They had made the same observations on form quality but they concluded something very different from them. They claimed that the elements in the perception of the whole were not preserved; rather, the perception of the relation transcended the elements and formed a new Gestalt. The new, emergent properties of the Gestalt could not be predicted by considering the elements themselves. In fact, perception of the elementary parts was transformed because of the whole. As Wertheimer (1944) described the matter:

> The whole cannot be deduced from the characteristics of the separate pieces, but conversely; what happens to a part of the whole is, in clear-cut cases, determined by the laws of the inner structure of its whole [p. 84].

This is a typical example of how the rationalist proceeds in a scientific endeavor. Nothing in the data about perception of squares or melodies directly indicated the need to overthrow elementalism. Within the established paradigm Ehrenfels had provided a fairly satisfactory elementalist analysis of the phenomena. Only a rationalist coming upon the phenomena with his preconceived model would have interpreted the phenomena in the way that the Gestalters did. With that theory the Gestalters were to reinterpret most of the mental world that the associationists had been so confident that they understood thoroughly. In this way, the elementary phenomena of Gestaltqualitat which were the source of satisfactory but not very inspiring analyses in the hands of associationists became ammunition for a revolution in the hands of the Gestalters.

After these brief historical remarks, we now examine the Gestalters' approach to human memory and how that view differs from associationism. However, first we will have to sketch in some of the details in the Gestalt theory of perception because, as had Aristotle and the British associationists before them, the Gestalters identified the input to the memory system with the perceptual data that the organism was registering. Indeed, as much as Aristotle, and more than the British associationists, the Gestalters refused to admit a truly separate faculty for memory. They supposed that mnemonic phenomena would be explained by the same principles that govern perception. "Association" was just a label for the coherence of elements resulting from the organization or assimilation of elements into a unitary perception or conception. Of course, people can remember their own thoughts and other data not immediately derived from perception, but the Gestalters claimed that the structure of this data was ultimately derived from perception. For this reason, Gestalt theory is sensationalistic; that is, it identifies the contents of memory with encodings of perceptual experience.

The Gestalt Theory of Perception

Since both Gestalt and associationist theories are sensationalistic, it is not surprising that the basic disagreements between them concern the nature of perception rather than the nature of memory. Gestalt theory and associationism confront each other on the topic of memory because both wanted to apply their analysis of perception to memory. The basic Gestalt objection was that the associative analysis was reductionistic and mechanistic, attempting to analyze experience into atomic sensations and then mechanistically build up all of human knowledge from these elements. Appropriately, Gestalt theory is usually dated as originating with the discovery of the phi phenomenon, the experience of apparent movement (e.g., the motion of flashed still pictures seen at the cinema) that could not be decomposed into a sequence of atomic sensations. It still stands today as a clear demonstration that the mind imposes organization on incoming sensory data, that the perception of the whole series takes on emergent properties above and beyond the properties of its parts (although modern neurophysiology [e.g., Barlow & Levick, 1965] suggests the Gestalters may have been wrong about the neural mechanisms). However, the reductionist postulate of associationism is too elastic to be emphatically disconfirmed by such a demonstration. Only that specific brand of reductionism advocated by Titchner and his associates was upset by the phi phenomenon. They had conjectured (incorrectly) that the perception of motion would be made up from a continuous sequence of "still" perceptions of the object as it traveled through its course. Other associationists simply changed the specific brand of reductionism so as to permit the perception of motion as one of the atomic elements in their analysis.

The Gestalt-associationist controversy was not over what the atomic elements might be in a psychological analysis, but over whether such elements existed at any level. The Gestalters insisted that psychology would only succeed if it considered the whole phenomenon "from the top down." The "whole" was alleged to have emergent properties that could not have easily been predicted by examining the parts. These wholistic properties determined how the parts would be perceived, and not vice versa. According to the Gestalt account, there was nothing mysterious or magical about the emergence of new properties in a whole. Emergent properties are found in many *dynamic* processes that have turned out to be quite amenable to scientific analysis. Köhler, the physicist among the Gestalt group, frequently invoked the concept of "dynamic self-distribution," as in the following quotation:

Dynamic distributions are functional wholes. Take, for example, a simple electric circuit. The differences of potential and the densities of the current distribute themselves among the conductors in such a way that a steady or stationary state is established and maintained. No part of this distribution is self-sufficient; the characteristics of local flow depend throughout upon the fact that the process as a whole has assumed the steady distribution [Köhler, 1947, p. 136].

The Gestalt literature is replete with such references to physical processes, all done to demonstrate that the postulation of "dynamic principles of organization" was respectable and scientific. However, one can concede the respectability of such concepts but still criticize the Gestalters for failing to provide an explicit or systematic process interpretation of relevant psychological phenomena. Instead, their work was largely a matter of argument and demonstration that the prevailing mechanistic interpretation of psychological phenomena was not adequate.

Koffka and Wertheimer used the phrase "law of Prägnanz" to reference essentially the same concept as Köhler's "principle of dynamic self-distribution." As Koffka (1935) described the law of Prägnanz"

It can briefly be formulated like this: psychological organization will always be as "good" as the prevailing conditions allow. In this definition the term "good" is undefined. It embraces such properties as regularity, symmetry, simplicity and others which we shall meet in the course of our discussion [p. 110].

The well-known Gestalt laws of similarity, proximity, closure, and good continuation in determination of perceptual groupings and perceptual organization can be seen as special instances of the law of Prägnanz"

The dynamic organization of experience not only creates wholes, but also segregates whole units from one another. These are not independent processes; the fusion of parts into unit-wholes necessarily implies that those parts not members of the same unit-whole will be segregated, separated, and assigned to other units. Köhler conceived of a hierarchy of successive segregation of parts followed by unification. An illustration is provided in Figure 3.1. At one level of analysis, each dot is segregated from every other. However, at another level they merge into a black "figure 8" against its background of white dots. At a still higher level, the "8" and its background merge into a single unit which is segregated as a picture from the surrounding frame. As Köhler (1947) described the matter:

Groups which consist of separate members have a special interest for theory inasmuch as they prove that a given unit may be segregated and yet at the same time belong to a larger unit. In our last example one dot represents a continuous detached entity. None the less it is a member of a larger whole, the number, which is detached from a wider area. There is nothing peculiar about such a subordination of units. In physics, a molecule constitutes a larger functional whole which contains several atoms as subordinate wholes. Functionally, the atoms belong to the molecule-unit; but in this unit they do not altogether lose their individuality [p. 144].

This description corresponds in part to the associationist conception of how ever more complex ideas are compounded out of simple ones. However, it is important

FIG. 3.1. An example that demonstrates a hierarchy of perceptual unification and segregation.

to emphasize the difference in the two conceptions. In the Gestalt account, at each level with the formation of a whole-unit there would be new emergent properties arising which would not be derivable by any simple summation of the properties of its parts. Furthermore, the Gestalters would reject the possibility of a fixed set of ultimately simple ideas, which belief was fundamental to the associationist's viewpoint.

The Gestalt Theory of Memory

As noted earlier, the Gestalt theorists identified the input to memory with perception. Gestalters would propose that the outputs from memory would also have a structure isomorphic to the original perception. To bridge the temporal gap between the input and the output, the Gestalters postulated the existence of an enduring *memory trace*, which conception is central to their theory of memory. They assume that the current input creates an active process which will remain in a "subdued" form as a trace. This information is stored in substantially the same form as the original perception. As Köhler (1938) described the matter:

> Neural events tend to modify slightly the state of the tissue in which they occur. Such changes will resemble those processes by which they have been produced both in their pattern and with respect to other properties [p. 236].

Recall simply involves a reactivation of the trace; effectively, it is a renewal of the same perceptual process as that corresponding to the original input. So, one idea was that the trace is an active process continuing in the nervous system.

A second, unrelated Gestalt principle was that of *isomorphism*, which supposed that the structure of phenomenal experience would be isomorphic to the structure of the underlying neural processes (whatever that means). The combination of these two ideas led to an apparent paradox; why is it that we are not simultaneously conscious of all past experiences that have been recorded as memory traces? To solve this problem, Koffka proposed that a trace would be represented in consciousness only if the dynamic processes underlying it were of sufficient intensity. Most memory traces, of course, would be too weak to reach consciousness. Recall, then, involves amplifying the intensity of a particular trace. This notion, coincidentally, is approximately the same as that of Freud (1933), who assumed that certain ideas and memories lay dormant in the unconscious until activated ("cathected") with an appropriate charge of libidinal energy to raise them over the threshold of consciousness.

Just as the associationists, the Gestalters proposed that the individual elements were connected together in memory and that recall involved going from one element (the cue) to another (the response). However, they rejected the associationist's claim that the memory trace consisted simply of the two independent elements plus a connecting bond. The elements were thought to be *fused* together or organized into a unitary trace. Köhler (1947) stated the alternatives thusly:

> We do not know what happens in recall. The only thing which we seem compelled to assume is some connection between the traces of two processes, A and B, so that reactivation of A leads to recall of B rather than of any facts with which A has not been associated. Now, in this respect two hypotheses are possible. If we believe that, in becoming associated, A and B remain two mutually neutral facts which merely happen to occur together, then some special bond, such as a particularly well conducting group of fibers, may be regarded as an adequate basis of the association. In full contrast to this view, we may, however, reason as follows: When an A and a B become associated, they are experienced not as two independent things but as members of an organized group-unit. This may perhaps now be taken for granted. But with this premise the neural situation cannot consist of two separate parts of which one corresponds to A and the other to B. Rather, the unitary experience indicates that a functional unit is formed in the nervous system, in which the processes A and B have only relative independence. If this is the case, we cannot expect two separate traces to be left when A and B are no longer experienced. Traces, we said, tend to preserve the organization of the original process. Thus only one trace will be established, which represents the functional unit by which it was formed. And in this trace, A and B will exist only as relatively segregated sub-units. Consequently, by virtue of their inclusion within one trace, A and B will be just as well "connected" as they could ever be by means of a special bond [pp. 269-270].

Since the traces formed in memory were permanent recordings of the units formed in perception, the Gestalters could easily explain the classical laws of association. The factors of contiguity, similarity, cause and effect, and so on, underly the "laws of association" because these factors corresponded to Gestalt laws governing the formation of organized units—namely, the laws of proximity, similarity, and good-continuation. Moreover, unlike the associationists, the Gestalters could handle the mnemonic advantage of meaningful material, since meaningful material was alleged to be easily organized into conceptual units.

The Asch Demonstrations

Particularly compelling illustrations of this Gestalt viewpoint in memory have been provided in demonstrations by Asch and his co-workers (see Asch, 1969; Asch, Ceraso, & Heimer, 1960; Prentice & Asch, 1958). Asch investigated the perceptual arrangements which lead to what he calls "coherence" or "unitary" patterns of two otherwise distinguishable visual forms. These are more easily illustrated (see Figure 3.2) than described; Asch's papers should be consulted for other examples. Asch is typically asking one question with these examples: "If I want to have two forms or properties naturally cohere in memory, how should I best arrange for them to be related perceptually at the time I present them for memorization?" In the top two lines of Figure 3.2, a constitutive relation is illustrated; for example, the shape of a rhombus is exemplified in outline by small pluses (the mode, or second form). Presentation of a list of such unitary figure-mode combinations results in far better "associative recall" (of the two forms appropriately paired) than does presentation of outlined figures paired with a row of mode forms alongside (the nonunitary displays on the right of Figure 3.2). Asch would say that the figure on the left is seen as a single unit, as "a rhombus composed of pluses," so that the two forms are inextricably bonded (organized) together. In contrast, the nonunitary display on the right is seen as two isolated units (an outline rhombus and a row of pluses), related only by their spatial contiguity (as are all other pairs in Asch's nonunitary list); consequently, the isolated figures are difficult to organize into a single unit. Therefore, after studying a list of such nonunitary pairs, the subject will be poorer at recalling "plus" when cued with an outlined rhombus than will

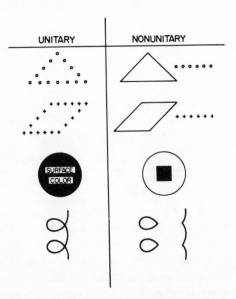

FIG. 3.2. Examples of unitary relations among components of a figure. (Reproduced from Bower, 1970a.)

be the subject exposed to the unitary figure. The third line of Figure 3.2 illustrates a similar coherence between a form and its surface color; one can more easily associate a "circular shape" with a "red color" if it is seen as a "red circle" rather than a "red patch" inside a "circular-shaped form" (see Asch, 1969; Arnold & Bower, 1972).

A similar mnemonic benefit arises from unitary pronunciation of the two elements of a verbal paired-associate item. Asch (1969) used pairs of nonsense syllables (like DAT–NIC) with subjects instructed to pronounce them cyclically either as a fused unit ("DATNIC") or as separate syllables ("DAT"–"NIC"). Arnold and Bower (1972) extended the finding with (consonant vowel)– (consonant) pairs, with some subjects instructed to pronounce each unit of the pair separately (e.g., LO-M as "low-emm"), whereas others were instructed to fuse the elements into a single syllable (e.g., "LOM"). Subjects learned under either incidental or intentional learning instructions, and retention was tested by cued recall of each pair with the left-hand member (e.g., present LO as a cue for recall of M; or DAT as a cue for recall of NIC). In all cases, recall was about twice as good for subjects given "unitary pronunciation" instructions as for subjects told to use "separate-unit pronunciation" rather than fused pronunciation. It may be noted that in all these cases the recall test cue is the separate unit itself (e.g., LO or DAT), which, being more similar to its code during acquisition of the pair, would seem to involve less generalization decrement than when input required fused elements. Nonetheless, the powerful effect of perceptual unitization in memory was sufficient to offset this differential generalization decrement for the two cases.

Such demonstrations illustrate the importance of perceptual relationships in determining how easily two properties or forms become associated in memory. They are not the sort of result that classical associationism was prepared to deal with, since the basic relations of "contiguity" of the two forms are more or less equated in the unitary versus the nonunitary pairs. In terms of our theory, HAM, such results as Asch's are obviously relevant to the type and complexity of the description issuing from the "perceptual parser," which serves in turn as the input to memory. It is plausible to assume that Gestalt laws of grouping would be built into the perceptual parser, and· that it would contain as part of its descriptive vocabulary such primitive relations as "form x is composed of y's," or "x is the surface of y," or "x fits into y as part to whole," etc. Given these relational primitives, then the description delivered to HAM's memory by the perceptual parser will be very much simpler and compact (and require fewer "associations" to be learned) for unitary displays than for nonunitary displays. To illustrate, "a rhombus composed of small pluses" is a shorter perceptual description than is "an outline rhombus to the left of a row of small pluses." Recall differences would accordingly be expected to follow these differences in complexity of the perceptual descriptions input to HAM's memory.

To summarize: Asch's demonstrations illustrate nicely the sort of criticisms Gestalt psychologists have been making with regard to classical associationist theory, but it is unclear how seriously they upset more modern associative notions like our own.

The Gestalt Theory of Forgetting

The Gestalters also tried to use a few of their insights regarding perception to explain forgetting. If the trick could be done successfully, they would have interference theory (modern associationism) at a distinct disadvantage in regard to parsimony. By invoking their dynamic laws of perception, the Gestalters would not need to introduce any new postulates for memory. The same "dynamic laws of organization" that are alleged to impose structure upon a perceptual field would also tend to transform incoherent and poorly organized memory traces over time into traces that displayed better organization. If the transformation were too drastic, the trace would lose its original identity and would thus effectively disappear. But if the transformation were not too extreme, recall of the trace would display some systematic distortion in the direction of a better organization. A long history of research has been aimed at testing this prediction of systematic distortion of memories, particularly regarding a person's memory for geometric forms. The literature was reviewed by Riley (1962). His conclusion was that the mass of empirical evidence on the issue is largely negative with respect to the Gestalt position. There are assuredly distortions in memory for forms, but they seem to be predictable not so much by Gestalt "good figure" biases as by (a) assimilation of the memory of the input figure to a common cultural stereotype (proactive interference ?), and/or by (b) assimilation of the input form to a common verbal code or label used at the time of input, which coding distorts the reproduction of the form in a relatively constant manner over varying retention intervals.

In addition to the alleged autonomous effects of organizing principles within the trace, Gestalt theorists also assumed that a trace could be transformed through interactions with other traces and processes. We have already noted that Gestalters held that unification and segregation of a perception took place at several levels. Correspondingly, memory traces were alleged to form a hierarchical structure of groupings. This idea has recurred in a slightly changed form in the writings of the modern "organizational" theorists (see Miller, 1956; Mandler, 1967; Bower, 1970b). According to the Gestalters, because of this hierarchical structure, what might be considered an individual trace at one level participated in a larger trace system at a higher level and was thus connected to other traces. So, via the dynamic laws of organization, traces would mutually affect one another within hierarchies. It was by this means that the Gestalters tried to explain the facts of interference uncovered by modern associationism (see Chapter 10). For example, to handle effects of similarity on retroactive interference, it was supposed that similar traces would tend to disappear into larger trace systems by virtue of the law of similarity.

The Gestalt Theory of Retrieval

Koffka (1935) stated that a current stimulus would serve to recall a fact with which it had been associated by setting up an active neural process that would communicate with the original trace. He introduced a particularly opaque concept to try to illustrate how the current process would make contact with the memory trace. The underlying principle is that a dynamic system such as memory would tend to move in the direction of equilibrium. With this in mind, the reader may evaluate for himself the following quote from Koffka (1935) which gives the Gestalt notion of retrieval:

It is therefore no new hypothesis if we apply this general principle to the problem of the selection of a trace by a process: This selection must have something to do with the nature of the process, it must further one kind of development of this process rather than others. Let us call the kind of development which is thus being furthered the stability of the process, just to have a convenient name. The actual choice will then depend upon this stability. Those traces will communicate with the process which will give it the particular stability it needs. When we say that in this way our problem has become a problem of organization we say nothing new, but with this formulation we connect our problem with others, the solution of which has been previously indicated. Again, in this aspect also, memory appears not as an entirely new function with completely new laws, but as a special case of a very general function [p. 598].

This conception of retrieval allegedly permits the Gestalters to explain why the active process corresponding to a probe tends to evoke traces of similar mnemonic processes, because one principle of good organization in perception is the law of similarity. By this means, they believed they could give a decent account of how the famous *Höffding step* was accomplished. The Höffding step refers to the problem of how the perception of a particular object (e.g., a particular cameo of Abe Lincoln) can selectively retrieve past memories of the generic representation of the object in memory. Höffding (1891) had used this required contact between the "percept" and "idea" to demonstrate the need for a law of similarity in any psychological reconstruction of recall. (Indeed, we use something like it in HAM.) The Gestalt theorists argued that it was their version of the law of similarity that was needed to explain the communication between the probe and the trace. For example, Köhler (1947) noted that the single vertical line in Figure 3.3*B* was a much better probe for recall of Figure 3.3*A* than were the series of bars in Figure 3.3*C*. This was the case despite the fact that the series of bars represented a much larger part of the original pattern than did the single bar. However, the series of bars was presumed to set up a perceptual process very dissimilar to that of Figure 3.3*A*, and so could not communicate with the trace of this original pattern.

A basic problem of this "similarity" approach to retrieval is that it is vague and unrevealing. Between any three multidimensional objects or events *A, B, C,* there are a multitude of possible comparisons; on some dimensions, event *A* may be closer to *B*; on other dimensions, *A* may be closer to event *C*. The question is how to weight the various components of "similarity" so as to come out with unambiguous predictions; different weightings of this or that similarity lead to different predicted outcomes. Without independent assessment of "psychological distances," explanations of phenomena in terms of the "similarity" of the probe and the retrieved trace will tend always to have high post hoc credibility but low predictive validity.

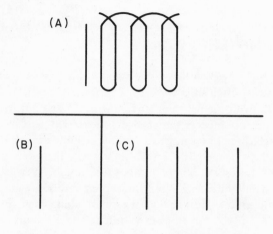

FIG. 3.3. Gestalt demonstration: The probe in (B) is a much better cue for recall of (A) than the probe in (C).

A Difficulty with Gestalt Theory

The most serious difficulty with the Gestalt theory of memory is that it has not been given an extended, explicit formulation by any of its proponents. The Gestalters, particularly Köhler, always wrote as if the only explicit or satisfactory formulation of their principles would be a neurophysiological one. Given our incomplete knowledge of the nervous system, they excused themselves from the task of concretizing their theory. In sympathy, one must consider that they may have been correct in their claim that an adequate expression of Gestalt theory awaited a more detailed neurophysiological theory. The great stumbling block to a formalization of their theory is the claim that the whole has emergent properties. One needs a basis for lawfully predicting what the emergent properties will be when a set of elements are united. A neurophysiological theory appears to provide the only possible basis. (The particular neurological speculations of Köhler have not fared at all well in the empiricist's marketplace; see Lashley, Chow, & Semmes, 1951; Sperry & Milner, 1955.)

It should be clear that the Gestalt theorists were not saying that there can be no adequate theory of the interactions arising when elements are merged into a whole. An analogy to chemistry should make the Gestalt position clearer. When oxygen and hydrogen are combined, the resultant is water. For a long while in chemistry, there were no means by which to explain what the properties of water would be (e.g., its wetness) from the properties of the elements oxygen and hydrogen (which are gases). In a very real sense, water was a "whole" whose emergent properties could not be explained from the properties of its parts. About all that the chemists could do was to give a descriptive statement, describing the properties of the emergent substance produced when oxygen and hydrogen were combined. Psychology, the Gestalters claimed, is at this stage of explanation. The Gestalt "law of Pragnanz" corresponds to the chemist's descriptive statements about the results of putting elements together in certain ways. Today chemistry has satisfactory theories regarding the emergent properties of chemical compounds. In the case of water, the emergent properties came to be understood in terms of the angle at which the two hydrogen atoms attach themselves to the oxygen atom. This level of analysis and its attendant properties were not available to the earlier chemists. Similarly, the Gestalters would argue, we do not yet have a satisfactory neurophysiological level of analysis, but the time will come when such an analysis will verify the Gestalter's claims.

We will close our discussion of Gestalt theory by emphasizing its importance to the topic of human memory. Because it is imprecise, its value is not so much that it provides another way of understanding memory, but rather that it makes us constantly think critically about and defend the reductionistic and mechanistic assumptions in a theory like HAM. Corresponding to the Gestalt demonstrations of the dangers in reductionism and mechanism in perception, there are demonstrations in memory, such as those of Asch mentioned earlier, which show that good, unitary figures are better remembered than nonunitary patterns.

There is a second class of memory phenomena that makes the same point regarding the benefit of "good organization" of the material to be learned, and this is the matter of "mnemonic devices." It has been known since ancient times that the best way to remember arbitrary sets of material is to introduce meaningful relations between the to-be-remembered items. The essential character of all such mnemonic devices (see Bower, 1970a; Norman, 1969) is that, in Gestalt terms, they attempt to merge the disjoint elements to-be-associated into a unitary perceptual or conceptual whole. For instance, if a subject is asked to remember the paired-associate pair *cow-boot*, a most effective device would be for him to image a cow wearing large rubber boots. Or, if he finds imaging difficult, he might produce a linguistic proposition of the form "The cow is wearing boots." An important characteristic of such mnemonic devices is that they make the information to be remembered more memorable by adding further information. But this addition of further information should mean more elements to associate together, so, on most associationist accounts, such mnemonics should make the task harder rather than easier. It was evidence of just this sort that forced the staunch associationist Müeller, as quoted by Katona (1940), to concede that we can learn "by uniting members of a series into solid groups through collective apperception [p. 23]."

It should be understood that we are not claiming that such demonstrations constitute incontrovertible evidence against associationist theories. Such claims would make this book rather pointless. Besides, we have argued in Chapter 2 that associationism is a metatheoretical position that is not directly subject to empirical falsification. The fact that the best remembered material appears to go against the spirit of associationism is an embarrassment to every existing associationist theory. However, being embarrassed is not the same as being proven false. In fact, it will turn out that we can handle many such phenomena in our theory HAM when we fully develop its assumptions in later chapters—about how information is encoded, about how processing time is distributed in the creation of associations, about the interaction between associative structure and new associations, and so on.

3.3. THE RECONSTRUCTION HYPOTHESIS

A standing debate in psychology concerns whether the mind should be analyzed into just static *elements* or qualities of consciousness, into just mental *processes*, or into both such aspects (see Boring's [1950] discussion of the schools of act and content in Germany). The Gestalters' analysis of memory tended to be a static one. That is, they spoke of each experience being recorded in memory as a separate trace, although they assumed that these traces could change spontaneously over time or through interaction with other traces. Recall was to be construed as a reactivation of that trace, as the reappearance of the original perception before "the footlights of consciousness" (to use William James' expression). It is just this sort of "reappearing trace" theory that Bartlett (1932) and Neisser (1967) have objected to most vehemently. Their alternative is what we have called the *reconstruction hypothesis*. They have argued that in perception or thought we *construct* mental objects out of the elementary sensory or cognitive data at hand rather than passively register and classify the events. This is the "analysis by synthesis" model of perception. Neisser, following Bartlett, has also argued that the same sort of approach can be applied to memory, that in remembering we bring to bear our total conceptual repertoire in reconstructing the original experience that we are trying to remember. In one of the more cogent descriptions of this position, Neisser (1967) writes as follows:

This is not to say that the stimuli themselves are copied and stored; far from it. The analogy being offered asserts only that the role which stored information plays in recall is like the role which stimulus information plays in perception. In neither case does it enter awareness directly, and in neither case can it be literally reproduced in behavior except after rather special training. The model of the paleontologist, which was applied to perception and focal attention in Chapter 4, applies also to memory: out of a few stored bone chips, we remember a dinosaur. To assert otherwise, to defend the Reappearance Hypothesis, would be to adopt an attitude reminiscent of naive realism in perception. It represents a fallacy in both contexts. One does not see objects simply "because they are there," but after an elaborate process of construction (which usually is designed to make use of relevant stimulus information). Similarly, one does not recall objects or responses simply because traces of them exist in the mind, but after an elaborate process of reconstruction (which usually makes use of relevant stored information) [p. 285].

The fundamental difficulty with this approach is its vagueness and incompleteness of statement. By analogy, memory is likened to "constructive processes in perception"; but these are themselves in dispute, not explicitly formulated, and not very well understood. For instance, there is no commonly agreed upon formulation of analysis-by-synthesis models of pattern recognition nor any consensus concerning what stored information they require. Nor is there any clear demarcation between such models as contrasted with "passive classifiers" which (by using stored information) feed forward expectations or hypotheses regarding what is the most plausible next stimulus (see Morton, 1969). Also, no matter how much construction and "fleshing out" of a memory may go on, it surely must begin with and be guided by some coherent bits of information, some "bone chips." And what are these but memory traces? How does the system decide which groups of "bone chips" go together? How does a cue retrieve one rather than another set of "bone chips" to begin the task of reconstruction? What are the reconstructive activities? Are they just "problem-solving" or "story-telling" routines that make use of formerly learned material to fill in, in a thematically plausible manner, a fragmentary, degraded memory trace? The paleontologist's "construction" of a dinosaur from a few bone chips is a striking metaphor, but why should we believe that it is not misleading?

Bartlett's Schema

These and numerous other such queries can be raised regarding the reconstruction hypothesis. We may look into Bartlett's (1932) book, *Remembering*, to try to find answers. For Bartlett, the important organizing factor behind such reconstructive recall was what he called the "*schema*." As he defined it, the schema was "an active organization of past reactions, or of past experiences, which must always be supposed to be operating in any well-adapted organic response [p. 201]." Bartlett is borrowing this notion of a schema from Head (1920), who had used it to refer to something like a person's moment-by-moment "knowledge" of where his various limbs (arms, legs) are located in space around his trunk. This "model" or schema is updated moment by moment by information that comes in as the person moves a limb or adjusts his posture; the "model" is also responsible for sending out commands to other bodily parts to make compensatory adjustments so as to maintain the body in upright balance. However, Bartlett wanted to use this notion to explain the vastly more varied and complicated behavior that we call remembering. The schema concept had been designed to handle the moment-to-moment adjustment of limbs in postural movements, and it is not obvious how it applies to the behavioral flexibility characteristic of human memory.

Bartlett (1932) clearly realized this difficulty with Head's notion of a schema. For example, he stated the problem of retrieval from memory in the following terms:

A new incoming impulse must become not merely a cue setting up a series of reactions all carried out in a fixed temporal order, but a stimulus which enables us to go direct to that portion of the organized setting of past responses which is most relevant to the needs of the moment [p. 206].

To solve the retrieval problem, Bartlett proposed a particularly opaque process:

An organism has somehow to acquire the capacity to turn around upon its own "schemata" and to construct them afresh. This is a crucial step in organic development. It is where and why consciousness comes in; it is what gives consciousness its most prominent function [p. 206].

Of great importance in this constructive activity is the subject's general attitude about the material he is trying to recall. It is this which determines the reconstruction of a schema in recall:

It may be that what then emerges is an *attitude* towards the massive effects of a series of past reactions. Remembering is a constructive justification of this attitude; and, because all that goes to the building of a "schema" has a chronological, as well as a quantitative significance, what is remembered has its temporal mark; while the fact that it is operating with a diverse organized mass, and not with single undiversified events or units, gives to remembering its inevitable associative character [p. 208].

We find such crucial passages a little hard to follow.

Neisser (1967) interprets Bartlett's schema concept as a cognitive structure, which he defines as a "nonspecific but organized representation of prior experience [p. 287]." The schemata, according to Neisser, are produced by the constructive act of recall. We do not store the schemata in memory, however; rather what is stored in memory are traces of the processes by which the original experience was constructed. So, for instance, the mnemonic representation underlying a perceptual memory would be traces of the perceptual processes that occurred during the original perception. Thus, we do not remember what happened but rather how we cognized what happened.

Neisser's Executive

Bartlett's idea of the person "turning around" upon his schemata and reconstructing them has been interpreted by Neisser (1967) in terms of problem-solving routines carried out by an *executive*, a concept borrowed from computer science. The executive component of a computer program is characterized as follows:

Most computer programs consist of largely independent parts, or "subroutines." In complex sequential programs, the order in which the subroutines are applied will vary from one occasion to the next. In simple cases, a conditional decision can lead from one subroutine to the next appropriate one: "transfer control to register A if the computed number in register X is positive, but to register B if it is negative or zero." In other situations, however, the choice between register A and register B may depend on a more complicated set of conditions, which must be evaluated by a separate subroutine called "the executive." Common practice is to make all subroutines end by transferring control to the executive, which then decides what to do next in each case [pp. 295-296].

Readers with philosophical acuity will see the executive as a vitalistic vestige within the mechanical model, a vestige to which all varieties of irreducible "faculties" are assigned. The decisions it makes, the goals it sets, the priority-rankings of subgoals it will work on, its cutoff time for stopping work on fruitless subproblems, etc., are not explained by the program itself; rather they are an assumed set of capabilities and "values" assigned to the program by its designer.

The designer, in some respects, is mimicking the effects of an evolutionary history in installing these components in the "innate wiring" of the machine. In the informal discussions of cognitive psychologists, the executive is assigned diverse and wondrous abilities; it has free will, purposes, intentions, goal priorities, etc. For example, the executive "decides," in the light of motivational and situational constraints, whether or not to begin reconstructing a memory to satisfy a given retrieval cue, or whether to switch attention from one train of thought to a newly arriving stimulus of some significance. In these respects, the executive plays somewhat the same explanatory role as the old "inner homunculus" of prescientific theories.

This concept of an executive is certainly alien to the spirit of stimulus-response associationism, which would want to inquire into why the executive behaves as it does. The counterargument is that something like an executive is almost a logical necessity for running complex, hierarchically organized programs, and the informal abuses of the concept in loose discussions should not be counted against the basically mechanical nature of the concept. At any level of behavioristic (or mentalistic) analysis, certain capabilities and operations have been accepted temporarily as primitives (e.g., the ability to "decide" whether two symbols match). The fundamental difference between the executive and the homunculus is that the executive is a mechanistically specified computational algorithm: its designer knows exactly the "rules" by which it operates. On the other hand, the homunculus is just another unanalyzed man, whose behavior can be predicted no better than that of the person within which the homunculus resides.

Winograd's Program

In searching for a concrete realization of what Bartlett and Neisser must be saying, we have found a recent dissertation by Terry Winograd (1971) to be a useful theoretical paradigm. Winograd's aims were in the direction of artificial intelligence, not psychology, and he certainly is not consciously in the tradition of Bartlett and Neisser. Nonetheless, his dissertation offers an interesting illustration of what it might mean to store procedures for reconstructing a memory rather than to store the memory itself. In Winograd's system, knowledge is expressed in terms of programs that will operate on the world or on other programs. For instance, linguistic assertions are stored in the data base as procedures that may be evoked when the system is faced with some task to perform such as answering a question or constructing a particular block scene in its small toy environment. By representing knowledge as procedures, Winograd (1971) claims to have gained "greater flexibility than a program with a fixed control structure, in which the specific knowledge can only indirectly control the process of understanding [p. 13] ." It is not clear how to evaluate Winograd's claim that representing knowledge as procedures is superior to systems that represent knowledge as data separate from program. There is no denying that Winograd's system is one of the most impressive natural language understanding systems in computer science. However, it appears to us that the credit for the success of the system really goes to its abstract, logical structure and not to its use of procedures for representing knowledge. It would seem possible to translate from Winograd's program representation of knowledge into a network representation which is logically equivalent. In fact, at points in his dissertation Winograd seems to concede this point or similar ones. For instance he writes: "Is there anything in common between grammars which are networks and grammars which are programs? The reader may have already seen the 'joke' in this question. In fact, these are just two different ways of talking about doing exactly the same thing! [p. 201]"

Evidence for the Reconstruction Hypothesis

Bearing in mind the Winograd type of explication, it would seem that the Bartlett-Neisser reconstructive hypothesis is a workable idea. But why should anyone favor it over the reappearing-trace hypothesis? Several lines of evidence are traditionally marshaled for this viewpoint. They mostly concern the fact that some memories are strongly biased by the particular mood, motives, interests, beliefs, and personality of the person who is remembering. One of Bartlett's famous demonstrations illustrated how recall of an Indian folktale ("The War of the Ghosts") became progressively transformed over time to fit into the cultural assumptions of his English subjects. Further, Neisser notes how adaptive memory is, that our memories are seldom repeated exactly but rather appear in new combinations appropriately suited to the tasks at hand. If the trace hypothesis were correct, Neisser (1967) argues, then we would expect that "repetition of earlier acts or thoughts should be the natural thing, and variation the exception [p. 280]." He also notes the importance of motivation or interest to memory, that we tend to remember what we want to.

Important to the reconstructive hypothesis is the analysis that Bartlett and Neisser give to perception. Both argue against the simple imprinting of impressions on a relatively passive wax tablet, which has been the underlying metaphor in associationist conceptions of perception, and to a lesser extent in the Gestalt conception. They argue rather that perception must involve an active process of using the elements of experience to construct a meaningful perception out of them. Gregory (1970) has offered a similar view of perception. If this analysis of perception is correct, then Bartlett and Neisser would have parsimony on their side in their analysis of memory. If the original perception is constructed, why not just assume that the memory of the perception also results from the same sort of constructive procedures.

As mentioned earlier, we find these remarks or arguments rather unconvincing. We readily admit that a trace theory which has only the potential to revive old experiences verbatim is inadequate for the complexities of human memory. Indeed, we have argued this same point at several places in the last chapter. But that is no reason to dispense entirely with a trace system; rather we feel that the trace system should be properly viewed as only one component of a total mental system that has the capacity for such things as deduction, strategic probing, inference, strategic guessing, selective attention, and so forth.

There is no doubt, however, that both Bartlett and Neisser would insist that a theoretical separation of memory from the rest of the mental system is inherently misguided. Indeed, in a sense, they would deny that "uncontaminated" experimentation on human memory could be a realistic or desirable goal. Neisser (1967) states his position as follows:

> The simplifications introduced by confining the subject to a single motive and a forced set of alternative responses can be justified only if motivation and cognition are genuinely distinct. If—as I suppose—they are inseparable where remembering and thinking are concerned, the common experimental paradigms may pay too high a price for simplicity [p. 305].

Concluding Observations

In conclusion, it is interesting to note that the Gestalt memory theory and the reconstruction hypothesis agree on the four metafeatures of a rationalist approach, but yet they are really quite different. As theories of memory, the issue of *nativism* is not really applicable to them. But both theories are clearly *holistic* in the two senses outlined in Section 3.1. Firstly, they emphasize the interactions among the contents of the total memory system; and secondly, the memory system is seen in unity with the rest of the faculties of the mind. But the principles which govern the interactions within whole memories and which unify the memory system with other systems are the dynamic laws of organization in Gestalt theory, whereas in reconstruction theory they are the procedures for generating plausible constructions, given certain traces as clues. A similar sharp contrast of the two theories is seen in the kind of *intuitions* which have guided the development of the theories and which the theories try to explain. The Gestalters concentrated on intuitions about how innate organizing forces structure whole units, whereas Bartlett and Neisser emphasize intuitions about how a person's attitudes and interests actively determine the character of his memories. The fourth rationalist feature, *vitalism*, was manifest in the dynamic laws of Gestalt theory but in the form of a purposeful "executive" within the reconstruction hypothesis.

In these two chapters we have examined two contrasting methodologies for constructing a theory of human memory. Methodological empiricism attempts to work from raw data to more and more general statements about memory. In contrast, methodological rationalism begins with lofty first principles and then attempts to relate these to empirical phenomena. In terms of a spatial metaphor we may say methodological empiricism works from the bottom (raw data) up but that methodological rationalism works from the top (lofty principles) down. Having now completed our review of both the rationalist and empiricist attempts at theories of memory, we must conclude that both methodologies appear subject to serious difficulties. The regrettable feature that seems characteristic of rationalist enterprises is that of stagnation. After the initial insights and intuitions have given shape to the theory, there is an absence of any further development or articulation of the hypotheses regarding memory. It is rarely made explicit with detail and rigor how a memory system so conceived will explain the empirical phenomena at hand. Subsequent experimentation seems to be little more than repeated demonstrations that there *really* are processes like the theory postulates. In terms of the top-down metaphor we used to describe rationalist theory construction, it seems that the theory never obtains a broad, elaborated, and firm empirical foundation. The theory remains suspended in mid-air, as it were.

Of course, it is just as easy for the rationalist to retaliate with criticisms of the empiricist enterprise. By focusing on the need to build a theory around particular data, the empiricist may frequently miss the fundamental characteristics of the phenomena at hand. We see evidence for this in the preceding chapter—for instance, with respect to associationism's blindness of the flaws in the Terminal Meta-Postulate. The empiricist methodology has a myoptic view of the world. In terms of our bottom-up metaphor, the empiricist methodology seldom gets beyond unconnected low-level theories, a complaint which runs rampant among surveyors of the contemporary scene of confusion (e.g., Tulving & Madigan, 1970). The connecting theoretical superstructure is never successfully imposed on these low-level theories. Moreover, the rationalist would argue that by the very nature of the enterprise, it is unlikely that the low-level theories could ever produce an adequate foundation for the necessary superstructure.

As indicated before, the neo-associationist methodology tries to proceed simultaneously from an abstract characterization of the problem downwards and from the empirical data upwards. It is too early to tell whether this methodology avoids the problems of the pure rationalist and the pure empiricist. Perhaps we will just be compounding the difficulties of both approaches. It is unclear whether it is any easier to get a meeting in the middle than it was for the rationalists to touch empirical ground or for the empiricist to reach the lofty goal of a sufficient and unified theory.

4

AN OVERVIEW OF HAM

I see no reason to believe that intelligence can exist apart from a highly organized body of knowledge, models, and processes. The habit of our culture has always been to suppose that intelligence resides in some separated crystalline element, call it consciousness, apprehension, insight, gestalt, or what you will, but this is merely to confound naming the problem with solving it.

—Marvin Minsky

4.1. THE INFORMATION-PROCESSING APPROACH

A disappointing outcome of our review of memory theories is that there appears to have been relatively little progress, at least until fairly recently. Indeed, one could argue that Aristotle's sketchy outline was the most advanced conception. Although it is too early to decide whether neo-associational models will constitute a significant theoretical advance, they certainly provide that prospect.

The progress now being made in theories of memory has to do, we think, with the advent of the information-processing approach in psychology. Until the last two decades there were only three principal ways to study the mind. First, there was introspection where one observed the operation of his own mental processes insofar as they were accessible to observation and description. The unreliability of introspection, as a source of data, has been greatly exaggerated. In the imageless thought controversy, for instance, the real issue did not seem to be what the basic introspections were, but rather how to interpret them. The original assumption of the introspectionists was that the data of introspection would simply and unambiguously determine a satisfactory psychological explanation. But this simply asks more of introspection than it can provide. Introspections are valid psychological data, but they cannot be expected to ever constitute or easily generate a theory. There is just too much "low-level processing" going on below the level of consciousness, not open to introspection which must be inferred from behavior. Skinner's (1953) analysis of how we learn to introspect about private mental events—to discriminate them, label them, describe them, and generally to be aware of them—suggests very severe limitations on the sorts of revelations that can be expected to come from "self-observation."

The behaviorist-functionalist approach was another attempt to arrive at a psychological theory via a particular experimental methodology. In this approach, man is viewed as a "black box" into which various stimuli go and out of which various responses come. For the radical behaviorist, the task of psychology is, *experimentally*, to record what responses are elicited by what stimulus conditions and, *theoretically*, to make generalizations about these stimulus-response contingencies. The nature of the processes going on inside the black box is of little interest to this account because the behaviorist does not believe that knowledge will advance one's ability to predict and control the behavior of the black box; as Skinner says, "The Outside Story has to be told first." On this account, the task of psychology is that of specifying the input-output functions that will serve to predict specified behaviors under specified conditions. The layman has always thought that this approach is unduly restrictive, and he is right. As we argued in Chapter 2, the task of specifying that grand input-output function is conceptually intractable unless one is permitted to speculate about the mental structures and processes underlying the behavior.

The problem remains of how to specify these structures and processes. In this age of scientific materialism, the layman has a ready solution: Let's talk about brain structures, neurons, electrical potentials, biochemical transmitters, and the concrete, physical happenings that we all know ultimately underlie man's behavior. The physiological psychologist pursues this solution in earnest. It is another attempt to arrive at a theory by an experimental methodology and it has similar fatal flaws. The neural activity involved in the typical question answering of a human is undoubtedly a matter of enormous complexity. We could never grasp it in terms of which neuron is exciting which others in what ordered patterns; at that level, the matter is simply too complex. The problem is analogous to trying to understand question answering in a computer program at the level of the electrical circuitry of the computer. And, almost certainly, the computer is much simpler physically than the human brain. The level of analysis is just too microscopic to be of any psychological utility. In the computer, we must talk of and characterize abstract objects called programs and data structures. So, also in understanding man, we must resort to postulation of abstract mental structures and processes.

The information-processing approach, then, is not a methodology for experimenting; it is rather a methodology for theorizing. An attempt is made to characterize abstractly the commodity, information, which is to be handled by the mental processes. One of the early characterizations of "information" measured its uncertainty in terms of *bits* (see Shannon, 1948). The uncertainty approach led to some interesting research (see Garner, 1962), but it was relatively useless as a theoretical tool. The problem was that the bit gave a very poorly articulated characterization of the information. More recent information-processing theories have attempted to characterize the information in terms of such things as chunks, features, associations, semantic markers, phrase structures, lists, discrimination nets, and propositions. As the descriptions of the information have become more articulated, the theories composed out of them have become more successful. The basic units in our theory will be semantic primitives (simple ideas), complex ideas constructed from these, and associations that connect the ideas. From these, propositional structures will be composed to provide a higher-order level of analysis.

4.2. HAM'S STRUCTURES AND PROCESSES

Having a viable characterization of the information, it then becomes possible to characterize the processes that transform or make use of the information as it proceeds through the system. Such characterizations are frequently given in terms of flow charts, and we follow this convention in introducing HAM. Figure 4.1 is an outline of the information flow occurring between the reception of stimuli and the emission of various responses. We will have very little to say about many of the system components in Figure 4.1. Our major theoretical contributions will all concern the component labeled "memory." Nonetheless, we have added the many arrows and components to illustrate how the memory component fits into the total mental picture.

First, we assume that the external information is registered by sensory receptors, transformed and recoded into higher-order features, and then held in

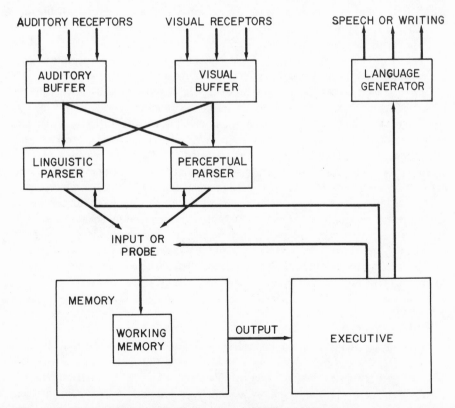

FIG. 4.1. The architecture of HAM's mental system.

limited-capacity auditory and visual buffers. We have absolutely nothing to say about these sensory processes except that they happen. In the next stage, the task of the parsers is to analyze what is in these buffers and to produce a meaningful description of it, suitable for transmission to and storage in long-term memory. The linguistic parser is designed to operate on symbolic information. It does not produce a description of the signals residing in the buffers, but rather a description of the conceptualization referenced by the symbols in the buffer. Its primary function is obviously to translate natural language statements into conceptual descriptions, but it presumably can be evoked to handle other symbolic systems such as formal logic. We will later examine how the linguistic parser functions and how it is to be interfaced with long-term memory.

In contrast to the linguistic parser, the perceptual parser simply tries to build up a description of the sensory contents contained in the buffers. Given current evidence about lateralization of function (e.g., Gazzaniga, 1967; Gazzaniga & Sperry, 1967; Kimura, 1963; Milner, 1968), it is intriguing to speculate that in most adults the linguistic parser may be localized in the left cerebral hemisphere and the perceptual parser may be in the right hemisphere. Obviously, the same stimulus can be analyzed and given very different descriptions by the two parsers. The linguistic parser would take a visual stimulus like the words "Nixon cried" and send off to memory a conceptualization equivalent to "The president of the U.S.A. shed tears," whereas the perceptual parser would build up a conceptualization equivalent to "The pattern, *Nixon*, occurred to the left of the pattern *cried*." We will develop in the next chapter the representation in which these conceptualizations are expressed. It will be argued there that the output of either parser is expressed in the same representational format.

The outputs of these parsers are sent as inputs or probes to be matched to the contents of long-term memory. This is the process generally known in psychology as stimulus recognition. It will be discussed in detail in Chapter 6. These probes and their matching structures in long-term memory are sent from the long-term memory component to the executive (the arrow labeled "Output" in Figure 4.1). The executive has very general control over all information processing in the system. It has at its disposal powerful problem-solving and inferential capacities which can be used in deciding how to direct the information processing. These capabilities will be called upon periodically to explain the intelligence displayed by HAM in allocating its mnemonic resources. The final component in Figure 4.1 is the language generator. This component is evoked to output answers to questions, to request further information to disambiguate a piece of discourse, and so forth. Again, we will have almost nothing to say about the language-generation process.

An Example

With this outline of the system architecture, it will be informative to trace a particular piece of information through encoding, storage, and retrieval. When a novel sentence is received like "In a park a hippie touched a debutante," it is analyzed into a binary graph structure like Figure 4.2. This graph structure is initially held in working memory. A separate tree structure is composed for each proposition in the sentence. Because our example sentence involves only one

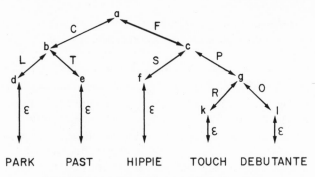

PARK   PAST   HIPPIE   TOUCH   DEBUTANTE

FIG. 4.2. A prototypical output from the parser.

proposition, the graph structure in Figure 4.2 is a simple tree. The graph in Figure 4.2 is composed of nodes interconnected by labeled arrows. The nodes are represented by lower case letters and the labels on the arrows by upper case letters. The letters representing nodes are arbitrarily chosen and simply facilitate reference to a particular node. In contrast, the labels indicate specific semantic relations holding among the nodes. There is just a finite set of possible semantic relations or labels. Note also that function words like *a* are not maintained in HAM's representation. Any semantic information conveyed by choice of function words is expressed in graph-structure configuration and by the choice of labels.

Each propositional tree is divided into two subtrees—a *context* subtree and a *fact* subtree. The arrow labeled with a *C* points to the context subtree and the arrow with an *F* to the fact subtree. Intuitively, the nodes in the tree represent *ideas* and the links *relations* or *associations* between the ideas. Therefore, in Figure 4.2, node *a* represents the idea of the total proposition, node *b* the idea of the context, and node *c* the idea of the fact. Effectively, the proposition is asserting that fact *c* is true in context *b*. The context node *b* is further subdivided into a *location* node *d* and a time node *e*. The arrows leading to these nodes are labeled *L* and *T*, respectively. Similarly, the fact node *c* leads by an *S* arrow to a subject node *f* and by a *P* arrow to a *predicate* node *g*. That is, the fact is composed of a predication *g* being asserted about a subject *f*. Finally in this example, the predicate node *g* leads by a *R* arrow to a *relation* node *k* and by an *O* arrow to an *object* node *l*. So, what is being predicated of *f* is that it has relation *k* to *l*.

This completes the binary divisions in the proposition. The node *d* represents a particular park, *e* a particular past time, *f* a particular hippie, *k* a particular touching, and *l* a particular debutante. These are connected by the *membership* relation, ε, to the general concepts of *park, past, hippie, touch,* and *debutante*. These general nodes already exist in memory and represent our ideas of each concept. Connected to each is an associative structure giving the meaning of the general idea. A much more complete analysis of HAM's representation is provided in Chapter 5. There we also attempt to motivate the structural assumptions that underlie these representations.

The concept nodes, in which the tree structure is anchored, are assumed to be preexisting in memory before receipt of the sentence. However, all the structure above the concept nodes is new and records the novel information in the sentence. To encode this sentence, each of the 13 working-memory links above the concept nodes must be transformed into long-term memory associations. A stochastic model describing this encoding process is developed and tested in Chapter 7.

When the parser receives a question (e.g., "Who touched the debutante?"), it constructs a probe tree to represent the query. This probe tree is held in working memory while HAM attempts to match it to a corresponding structure in long-term memory. The best-matching long-term memory structure is generated as the output. The executive uses the information in the output in its attempt to generate an answer to the question. If the information is insufficient, the executive may construct a new probe and send it to memory requesting further output. Three of our later chapters will be devoted to examining various aspects of this retrieval process.

The executive can also be a source of information input to memory. That is, the executive can reflect upon its own opinions and form spontaneous propositions of its own—e.g., "I guess I don't really agree with Nixon's policy" or "I've just discovered that the fourth power of 3 is 81." These also can be sent to long-term memory as inputs and encoded.

From this description it should be clear that the executive has very general powers and plays a central role in the information processing schematized in Figure 4.1. It directly receives outputs from memory, can send probes and inputs to memory, and determines the generation of speech. Finally, it can communicate with the parsers and send useful information to them (e.g., that a particular parse does not make sense).

The Strategy-Free Component of Memory

A particular mnemonic performance in the laboratory is behavior whose characteristics are determined by all the components mentioned in Figure 4.1. However, our concern is really only with the long-term memory component. We have to consider the other components only out of the need to make contact with experimental data. The executive is a particularly annoying source of complication in the analysis of the memory experiments, for it determines the mnemonic strategies, heuristics, and tricks that a subject may evoke to make his learning task easier. Research aimed at delimiting the information-processing characteristics of human memory often finds itself bogged down in a tangle of idiosyncratic tricks employed by subjects (see Anderson, 1972; Prytulak, 1971; Reitman, 1970; Tieman, 1971).

We shall assume that long-term memory, itself, is strategy-invariant, that probes are always matched to memory in the same way, that identical outputs will be generated to identical probes, and that a given input always is represented and encoded in the same manner. Mnemonic strategies enter the picture in terms of the strategic selection of probes and inputs which are to be sent to memory and in terms of interpretations given to the output. That is, we claim that all these troubles are to be localized in the "executive component" of Figure 4.1. We will argue that verbal learning paradigms such as paired associates or free recall are particularly likely to elicit such strategic complications. That is, subjects restructure and edit what they encode in memory in order to make it more meaningful. Most of our research is concerned with sentences or larger linguistic units. It was our hope that, with such material, subject-imposed structure would be less frequent, and the transformations between stimuli and memory representations would be more direct and predictable. However, we are sometimes forced to consider the complications of unexpected mnemonic strategies even with such sentential materials.

It is a claim of considerable empirical import to state that there is a core strategy-free memory component common to all memory performances. The claim is equivalent to asserting that memory performance can be analyzed into a large set of mnemonic strategies plus this common strategy-free component. If so, the task of analyzing a particular memory performance can be divided into two smaller and hence more tractable subproblems—that of specifying the memory component and that of specifying the prevailing strategy of the subject. Moreover, if we succeed in characterizing the core memory component common to all behaviors, we have only one of these subproblems left in analyzing any further memory performances, viz., specifying the strategy adopted in the particular situation. The reader should appreciate that this decomposition may in fact be impossible for human memory. As noted in Chapter 3, both the Gestalters and the reconstruction theorists asserted that it was impossible to extricate memory from such matters as problem solving and inference. If they are right, this whole theoretical enterprise will come crashing down on our heads.

A Formalization of the Strategy-free Component

Formalization is an appropriate goal for any scientific theory. However, there are dangers in forcing a theory prematurely into a formal cast. This tends to stunt the theory, fix it in its misconceptions, and prevent needed insight and revision. For whatever reason, certain types of reconceptualizations are easier if the theory is in a "rough and ready" form. This rough and ready form need not lack in clarity or precision, but it often lacks succinctness and elegance. Many of the ideas we will present are still in this state of informal development.

However, there does come a point when formalization becomes a stimulus rather than a hindrance to further theoretical development. It serves to separate the central assumptions from the tangential and to identify the points where further thought is required. Some of our theoretical ideas are achieving this needed formalization—particularly our ideas about the strategy-free component of memory. We will now provide a formal definition of this strategy-free component. This definition provides the superstructure for the formal developments in the next chapter. We will characterize the strategy-free component $\mathfrak{M}$ as an ordered six-tuple:

$$\mathfrak{M} = \langle \mathfrak{I}, \mathcal{P}, \mathcal{O}, \mathcal{S}, \mathcal{E}, \mathcal{D} \rangle$$

where $\mathfrak{I}$ is the set of possible inputs
$\mathcal{P}$ is the set of possible probes
$\mathcal{O}$ is the set of possible outputs

$\mathcal{S}$ is the set of possible memory structures

$\mathcal{E}$ is an encoding (or "learning") function such that $\mathcal{E}: \mathfrak{I} \times \mathcal{S} \times t \to P(\mathcal{S})$, where t is the time for which the input is studied, and $P(\mathcal{S})$ is the power set of $\mathcal{S}$ (i.e., the set of all possible subsets of $\mathcal{S}$). The encoding process $\mathcal{E}$, is the mechanism by which the structure of memory is modified to record new information. $\mathcal{E}$ maps into more than one possible memory structure because the encoding process is probabilistic rather than deterministic.

$\mathcal{D}$ is a decoding function such that $\mathcal{D}: \mathcal{P} \times \mathcal{S} \to P(\mathcal{O})$. This is the mechanism by which memory, $\mathcal{S}$, is probed, $\mathcal{P}$, to determine what is recorded there. The function maps onto the powerset of the outputs, $P(\mathcal{O})$, to accommodate the probabilistic character of the decoding process.

The elements $\mathcal{P}, \mathfrak{I}, \mathcal{O}$, and $\mathcal{S}$ will be discussed in Chapter 5. They constitute the *structural components* of the theory. The decoding function $\mathcal{D}$ is discussed in Chapter 6 on stimulus recognition, and the encoding function $\mathcal{E}$ in Chapter 7 on learning. They constitute the *process assumptions* of our theory.

A word of warning is appropriate here about our use of the word *encoding*. In the psychological literature it is most often used to refer to the transformation of a stimulus into an internal representation. We will use the term in this way sometimes—for instance, in our discussion of parsing. However, "encoding" has acquired a second meaning in our research—that exemplified in the above definition of the strategy-free component of memory. Here it refers to the transformation of the temporary representation of information in the input tree into a permanent representation in long-term memory.

4.3. THE SIMULATION OF HAM BY COMPUTER

One advantage of the abstract character of an information-processing theory is that one need not be concerned with the details of the physical realization of the theory in the brain. However, the characterization is sufficiently explicit that it should be capable of implementation in a number of physical systems. In particular, we should be able to implement HAM as a simulation program in a serial, digital computer. We have accomplished a partial simulation of the system outlined in Figure 4.1. The core strategy-free memory component is fully specified as a series of programs and data structures in the programming language, LISP.

It is important to be clear about the relationship between the theory and this simulation program. We make no claim that there is any careful correspondence between the step-by-step information processing in the simulation program and in the psychological theory. Rather, there is a *functional* correspondence to be made between various *mental processes* we postulate and various *programs* (LISP functions) that we have implemented. A particular program is equivalent to a mental process in terms of its *effect* on the abstract informational structures, but not necessarily in other respects. So, for instance, there will be no necessary correspondence between the time for a program to run and the time for the process to occur in the head.

Thus, the computer simulation of our theory is to be construed in the same sense that one construes computer simulations of theories in physics or in other sciences. We are simulating at a gross level some effects the theory predicts, but no ontological significance should be attributed to the operations (LISP functions or electrical componentry) that are evoked to produce the simulation. The computer is only a *computational tool* for explicitly checking the predictions of the theory, for determining whether all the specified mental processes are in fact fully specified, and whether they can work together as claimed.

This stance is not always taken with regard to computer simulations advanced as psychological theories. The claim is sometimes made (e.g., Newell & Simon, 1961) that the program is the theory. That is not the case for HAM, and we wish to make this denial explicit. HAM represents a very complicated set of speculations about human memory. Only some of these are represented in the simulation program. Moreover, the simulation program does not serve as an embodiment of this subset of the theory; rather, it is but one test of the adequacy of that subset.

Despite these disavowals, the reader is sure to suspect that the task of computer simulation has been a strong influence on the character of our theory. It has, and we worry about it. That is, one factor that has determined our theory is that it should be easy to simulate on a digital computer. Algorithmic computability is likely to be confused with psychological simplicity or plausibility of a process. Furthermore, programming a computer is a great stimulus for theoretical creativity. A solution to a programming problem often suggests a corresponding psychological mechanism. We would hardly want to criticize the machine for stimulating our creativity, but we do realize it stimulates us in the direction of computer-like mechanisms, and the brain is not a serial, digital computer. However, the tactic of developing a theory so that it is simulatable does not differ in principle from developing a theory so that it is mathematically tractable. The practice of simplifying theories to make them tractable is quite acceptable in science because of the necessity of testing scientific claims. However, it is a practice that is dangerous because computational tractability is not always compatible with scientific accuracy. Whether our theory is seriously flawed by this influence remains to be determined.

Our simulation program functions in a question-answering task domain. That is to say, we have programmed an interactive system to which we may assert facts and of which we may ask questions. The program accepts English sentences from a teletype, the sentences representing either assertions or questions. If it receives an assertion, it will type back a description of the memory structure it has formed in the course of encoding that assertion. If it receives a question, it will search its memory for an appropriate answer. This simulation program may be regarded as a test of the sufficiency of our theory. That is, it demonstrates that the theory is sufficient to generate behavior approaching the complexity of that found in the world outside the laboratory.

The Interface Problem

However, much more than HAM's strategy-free memory component must be simulated in order to have an operative system. This strategy-free component by itself comprises what is called a *fact-retrieval system* in the literature of artificial intelligence. That is, it is a memory system which, given a description of the desired information (a probe), will search memory for some piece of information that is similar to it, and then return this information as output. However, much more program must be written if one is to interface such a fact-retrieval system with the outer world, in order to produce a well-behaving *natural language question-answering system*. A linguistic parser must be written to transform natural language sentences into appropriate input for the memory. A number of executive routines must be written to guide the parser, to selectively search the vast memory network for useful answers to questions, and to make appropriate inferences about the information retrieved from long-term memory. This task of writing the parsing, inference, problem-solving, and decision programs is what will be referred to as the *interface problem* in question answering.

If one could efficiently handle both fact retrieval and interfacing, he would have a very powerful program indeed. Given the large memories that computers are coming to possess, we could simply feed into our computer the Encyclopaedia Britannica, and overnight HAM would become the most knowledgeable creature on this planet. The barrier to this goal is, of course, the interface problem. The adult who can comprehend the Encyclopaedia Britannica is a very competent speaker or reader of the language, has an enormous store of world knowledge, and is very adept at inference and problem solving. He has gained this sophistication from many long years of interaction with his world. It is that vast sophistication which must be programmed into our question-answering simulator in the form of the interface. But, of course, this is a job of unending proportions.

It is our opinion, therefore, that we should forget this Utopian goal of an all-purpose question-answer. However, we think it would be worthwhile to program a subset of the adult's sophistication into our program. Although it is infeasible to program the question-answerer with all our knowledge of the language, we could nonetheless give it sufficient knowledge to understand at least a subset of English. Although it could not solve all the problems or answer all the questions, it is of interest to see whether it handles a significant subset in a principled manner. This has been our goal in simulating HAM. Only a partial solution to the interface problem has been programmed, but enough so that we can have limited interaction with our fact-retrieval program.

A question we are sometimes asked is, Why not build up from this initial base? Why not write some more programs to increase HAM's ability to parse and comprehend sentences? Why not add some more inferential routines to increase the intelligence with which it answers questions? We started down this enticing, seductive path; but we slowly came to the realization that this was no way for experimental psychologists to proceed. Whatever is the value of such an approach for workers in artificial intelligence, from a psychological point of view it rapidly becomes fruitless and unenlightening. The end product of such an enterprise would appear to be thousands of lines of program that described the countless heuristics, procedures, tricks, and rules that the human has learned in his lifetime. We would have translated one incomprehensible mass of particulars, the human mind, into another incomprehensible mass, a computer program. But the task of a science is surely to reduce particulars to general laws rather than to translate particulars from one idiom into another.

Is there any way to study problem solving, language comprehension, or other elements of the interface problem? The answer would seem to be to look for the general principles underlying particular procedures. A good example of this strategy is the research done with the General Problem Solver, GPS (Ernst & Newell, 1969), in which an attempt was made to give a general model in which all problem solving of a well-defined sort could be understood. In particular, problem solving was viewed as searching for operators that would reduce the difference between a current state of the system and the desired goal state. However, for each problem to which GPS is applied, one must program in a characterization of the state space, the "rules of the game," and the set of permissible operators. Thus, while such research helps us understand problem solving, it does not avoid the need to separately encode each of the myriad of problem-solving heuristics into the program. We still need a seemingly endless list of characterizations of individual problem-solving tactics.

Perhaps a developmental approach would provide the needed theory of complexity. That is, one would like to characterize the initial processes and structures that permit acquisition of particular problem-solving abilities, or which permit acquisition of a language. This could be one way to obtain an efficient characterization of the adult competence. Also such a developmental theory holds out interesting prospects for research in artificial intelligence. If we could implement those structures and processes on some physical machine, we may get a self-evolving program which could eventually consume the Encyclopaedia Britannica. Our approach to describing the memory component in HAM is developmental in just this way. That is, we believe that it is simply hopeless, if not ridiculous, to try to specify all the information and procedures residing in the typical human memory. Rather we have characterized how that information and those procedures would be generated in HAM, if HAM were given the appropriate learning history.

A Sample Dialogue

To concretize our general description of the simulation program, we offer a sample dialogue we have had with it. Even though the conversation is not particularly inspiring, it does serve to illustrate some of the complexities in question answering. In the following, the symbol I references the informant who asserts facts to HAM and asks questions; likewise, H refers to HAM. To begin the discourse, the informant asserts a particular fact:

I: In a park a hippie touched a debutante.
H:

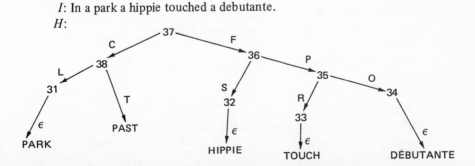

HAM's programmed response to this assertion is to parse it and then print out the above tree diagram for our inspection. Actually, a list encoding of the tree is printed out since the program has no graphic-display capabilities. This tree is the memory structure that is to represent and encode the assertion.

   I: Who was touched by the tall hippie?
   H: The tall hippie—which one?

HAM protests that it does not know of any *tall* hippies. So, we inform it that the current hippie under discussion is tall:

   I: The hippie was tall.
   H:

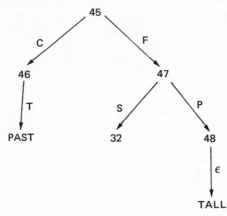

   I: Who was touched by the tall hippie?
   H: The debutante.

HAM can now generate the correct answer to this question. It should be noted that in the tree structure for "The hippie was tall," the same node (denoted here as 32) is used for hippie as was used in the previous conceptualization. This is because HAM interprets us to be talking about the same particular hippie (and we are). The next sequence illustrates HAM's procedures when it encounters a word not in its current lexicon.

   I: The sailor was kissed by the debutante.
   H: Sailor—I do not know this word—do you really mean it?
   I: Yes.
   H: What is its root form?
   I: Sailor.
   H: What type is it?
   I: A person.
   H: Would you like to talk about what it means?
   I: No.

The first possibility HAM considers is that "sailor" may be a typing error and that the informant really meant some word that it knows. Therefore, HAM asks, "Do you really mean it?" All lexical items are stored only once in the lexicon in their root form. Therefore, HAM must determine that "sailor" is the root form (e.g., instead of the plural form). Next, the parser needs to have some crude characterization of the word—whether it is a location, a person, a verb, etc. Finally, HAM asks whether the informant would like to tell it more about the meaning of this word. There are two ways for HAM to learn more about the meaning of *sailor*. First, the informant can explicitly provide such defining information. This is what HAM is requesting the informant to do in this example. Second, HAM can build up knowledge about the concept from a set of semantic contexts in which the word occurs. This is what the informant insists that HAM do in this case. The informant so insists because he knows all the programs for the former possibility have not been written and debugged.

The work by HAM to make sense of the word "sailor" turns out to be wasted in this instance because the sentence uses the definite article "the" preceding sailor. This definite article signals reference to some particular sailor, but HAM does not yet know of any particular sailor. Therefore, the sentence has to be recast using the indefinite article "a" which does not refer to a particular sailor. However, since a particular debutante has already been introduced, the definite article may be used with it.

H: The sailor—which one?
I: A sailor was kissed by the debutante.
H:

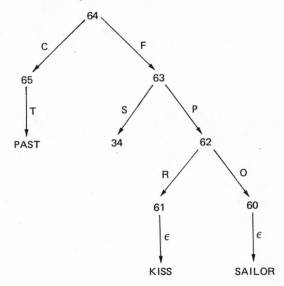

I: Who kissed the sailor?
H: The debutante.
I: Who touched the sailor?
H: I do not know the answer.

I: A prostitute who kissed the sailor was touched by the hippie.

H:

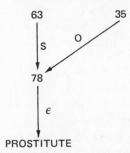

This last structure set up by HAM deserves some comment. HAM previously set up a structure to encode "A sailor was kissed by the debutante." It now uses part of that structure to encode the new proposition "The prostitute kissed the sailor." HAM adds a new subject-branch to the original structure; consequently, it now has encoded in memory "A prostitute and the debutante kissed the sailor." Similarly, HAM builds on the old structure for "In a park a hippie kissed a debutante" in order to encode the new proposition "The hippie touched a prostitute." It would then have encoded in memory a structure equivalent to "In the park the hippie touched the prostitute and the debutante." It may be noted in this regard that it was never asserted that the prostitute was touched *in the park*; but HAM's memory-matching routines conjecture that this was the location of the second act.

In essentials, the episodes described to date have the hippie touching two people and the sailor being kissed by two people. HAM maintains its memory-structure associations updated according to their recency of experience, and hence will respond with the most recent individual. This is illustrated by the following answers.

I: Who kissed the sailor?
H: The prostitute.
I: Who was touched by the hippie in the park?
H: The prostitute.
I: Who kissed the sailor in the park?
H: I do not know the answer.

The last question introduces one of the fuzzy problems in question answering. HAM has stored the fact that the sailor was kissed by the prostitute, but no mention has been made that this act occurred in any particular place. Since the query mentions a specific park, should HAM reply with "prostitute" or not? The current program balks and refuses to give an answer. Presumably an intelligent program would reply, "The sailor kissed the prostitute, but nothing was said about where that act occurred."

There is little to be gained from extending this sample dialogue because there is not much more that HAM can do that is of general interest. HAM's conversations are not so clever as those produced by some question-answering programs in artificial intelligence (e.g., Winograd, 1972) and we have not labored overmuch on developing a "smart" simulation. We shunned the many tricks known in the trade which would have made the proceeding simulation more lifelike, but which were empty of psychological significance. There are two reasons for our lack of concern about a clever-appearing simulation. First, as indicated previously, the time came when it seemed that further development of the program was only a way to exercise our skills in programming. However, the point was also quickly reached at which the simulation program became of such a size that it was beyond our limited financial resources to continue it in earnest. That is, not only was theorizing and experimentation more satisfying for us than was programming, it was also very much cheaper.

To the extent that the simulation is operative and successful, it serves to indicate that the memory system to be described in subsequent chapters meets certain sufficiency conditions for theories of human memory. To the extent that the simulation falls short of being adequately impressive, it remains uncertain whether we are just poor programmers (that has two senses!), or whether HAM is fundamentally wrong. In any event, the simulation per se has played little role in predictions and experimentation that we will be reporting. To be sure, the simulation would produce the results we predict from HAM's theoretical mechanisms, but the predictions have always been so obvious that no simulation was required to establish them. The logical status of this simulation contrasts with an earlier, less ambitious program of ours, FRAN, where the simulation really did play an essential role in generating experimental predictions. In this regard, then, HAM is rather much a "verbal theory" spelled out in the idiom of information processing which is currently popular among cognitive psychologists and comprehensible to them. Although not all aspects of our hypotheses have been programmed, the desire that we should be able to do so has kept a firm check on our flights of theoretical fancy. We offer these remarks to advise the psychologist that what he will find in the following pages is just the familiar language of current cognitive psychology, and to forewarn the computer scientist not to expect pages of code describing a snappy AI program. We now proceed to do our own thing.

5
THE STRUCTURE OF KNOWLEDGE

Let us remind ourselves that the task on which we are engaged is not merely one of English grammar; we are not school children analyzing sentences into subject, extension of subject, complement and so on, but are interested not so much in the sentences themselves, as in what they mean, from which we hope to discover the logical nature of reality.

—*F. P. Ramsey*

5.1. THE REPRESENTATION PROBLEM

The most fundamental problem confronting cognitive psychology today is how to represent theoretically the knowledge that a person has: what are the primitive symbols or concepts, how are they related, how are they to be concatenated and constructed into larger knowledge-structures, and how is this "information file" to be accessed, searched, and utilized in solving the mundane problems of daily living. The choice of a representation is central, since how one handles this issue causes widespread effects throughout the remainder of his theoretical efforts. As computer scientists working on problem solving have known for years, a good structural representation of the problem already constitutes half of its solution (see Amarel, 1968).

There are several possible ways to represent the knowledge derived from linguistic or perceptual inputs—as description-lists, analog pictures, two-dimensional arrays, attribute-value strings, trees, etc. The basic unit of knowledge in HAM will be the *proposition*, which corresponds in essentials to a complete conceptualization (i.e., an assertion or statement). The structure of these propositions will be described later in this chapter. However, before turning to that, we shall briefly indicate some of the criteria for a psychologically plausible representation of knowledge.

We wanted a standard format in which to represent incoming information, in order to store it in a retrievable form. We have searched for considerations that could motivate a particular choice for this representation and will list five that we have thought of.

1. The representation should be capable of expressing any conception which a human can formulate or understand.

2. The representation should allow for relatively efficient search for and retrieval of known information. That is, specific information should remain relatively accessible even when the data-files grow to encyclopedic proportions.

3. The representation should saliently exhibit the substantive information extracted from a given input. It should not be influenced by the peculiarities of the particular natural language in which that information was communicated. This hope for language-invariance amounts to a wish for a universal *interlingua* in which any conception in any language could be expressed, but for which the format would not be specific to a particular language. Furthermore, we would hope that sensory or perceptual information provided by "scene descriptions" would be expressible in the same formalisms. In such a manner, the system would provide a common currency in terms of which linguistic and perceptual information could be brought together to be compared, modified, combined, and coordinated in usage.

4. For reasons of parsimony, the representation should involve a minimum of formal categories. That is, it should make a minimum of *formal* (structural or syntactic) distinctions at the outset; more complex distinctions would be built up by the construction rules for concatenating primitive ideas. One motivation for minimizing the formal categories is for the sake of simplicity and elegance in the theory. Another motivation is that the fewer and simpler are the innate distinctions the mind must make, the more likely it is that the neural apparatus of a child can implement at least that much analysis of the input.

5. The representation must allow for easy expression of concatenation operations, by which "duplex ideas" can be constructed out of "simple ideas." This means, for example, that the representation should allow easy expression of conceptual hierarchies, or multiply embedded predications, or allow one to predicate new information of any old information-structure.

We believe that these five systematic considerations help delimit what is a plausible representation; they clearly are not sufficient to determine the representation uniquely. There is a considerable gap between these general specifications and a finished representational format, a gap that presently can be filled only by one's intuitions, best guesses, and biases. Because we are aware of this gap, we would therefore welcome further criteria to motivate our representation or alternative ones more satisfactory than our own.

As noted above, the proposition is the principle unit in the representation of knowledge in HAM's long-term memory. HAM's long-term memory passively records the propositional trees that it receives as input, preserving identically their structure. Therefore, our discussion here will refer indiscriminately to the structure of propositions either in long-term memory or in the input, since these exhibit identical properties.

The linguistic parser accepts a sentence and is presumed to deliver as output a set of atomic propositions related in specified ways. These atomic propositions will be represented as binary labeled trees of a particular sort to be specified. The trees will consist of a set of memory nodes linked by labeled arcs. The full set of atomic propositions and their relations within a given sentence are then represented as one large graph structure, which the memory system automatically tries to "learn" or "store." If the tree is successfully stored, the nodes and the links of the input tree will become permanent elements of long-term memory. The nodes correspond intuitively to the *ideas* of British associationism, and the links to the *associations*. Long-term memory in HAM consists of a huge network of such intersecting trees. In a later section we shall be concerned with how the total long-term memory is organized. For the moment, however, we will focus on the character of an individual tree as it is input to and stored in long-term memory.

Perhaps a word is in order regarding alternative representations for HAM's memory. We seriously considered adopting one of the linguistic representations such as Chomsky's deep-structure in *Aspects*, Fillmore's deep case structure, the generative semanticist's abyssal structure, or Schank's conceptual structure. However, with each of these representations there were some difficulties that caused us to balk. Each of these linguistic representations is concerned with explicating the structure of a single sentence, and, except for Schank's, each is aimed primarily at capturing relevant linguistic intuitions and generalities. Moreover, some of the information contained in the linguistic representations is undoubtedly specific to the peculiarities of language. For instance, some of Fillmore's case concepts, such as "instrument," appear to be motivated primarily by the fact that many languages have particular syntactic constructions for expressing instrumentality. However, we have seen no compelling argument for such a separate case distinction in a memory representation. We would argue that a memory formalism such as our own should not be designed specifically to fit the peculiarities of a given natural language, since it must also be capable of encoding *nonlinguistic* information that arises from perceptual sources like a visual scene. In contrast to the linguistic approaches, our concern has been instead with an *effective* memory representation of the information asserted by sentences. An "effective representation" would be one that is realistic and economical in terms of the memory storage requirements, that permits efficient search of its contents in carrying out various memory tasks, that facilitates the various deductions required in question answering, and so on. We felt that these linguistic formulations were rarely designed for efficiency in such enterprises. In currently popular jargon, regardless of their appeal as models of linguistic *competence*, they were not necessarily ideal as models for *performance*. Furthermore, we were not acquainted with any particular psychological data which strongly suggested that the memory structure of a proposition should take one or another linguistic form.

We will therefore propose a particular "deep-structure" of our own, one which bears a certain resemblance to Chomsky's *Aspects* grammar and also to predicate calculus. Although we will try to motivate each distinction in this deep-grammar, we confess that we are somewhat tentative about the exact details of the representation. We know that HAM's formalisms can represent any assertion or question. What is in doubt is the aptness or correctness of the representation. Although memory data will be presented to favor HAM's representation over salient alternatives, the reader should not forget the tentative nature of these proposals.

The Sensationalistic Bias

As mentioned earlier, perceptual scene-descriptions should be represented in the same sort of information structures as linguistic descriptions. In this regard, we share the sensationalist bias of past associative theories in believing that the mind has been shaped through evolution to encode perceptual information, and that all inputs to memory are basically perceptual descriptions (albeit descriptions which may sometimes be rather abstract). That is, when the memory component encounters a proposition such as "In the park the hippie touched the debutante," what it in fact encodes is a description of the perception of a scene corresponding to that sentence. Both in the evolution of man and in the development of the child, the ability to represent perceptual data in memory emerges long before the ability to represent linguistic information. We believe that language attaches itself parasitically to this underlying conceptual system designed for perception (Bever, 1970, has proposed a similar view). Indeed, it could be argued that natural languages can be learned initially only because their organization corresponds (at least in the simple cases) to the perceptual organization of the referential field.

Such speculations are made plausible by recent results reported by Moeser and Bregman (1972; 1973) on the learning of miniature "languages" by adults. The languages involved three to five phrase-structure rules involving four grammatical categories, and the terminal vocabulary was nonsense syllables. Subjects in one experiment (Moeser & Bregman, 1972) received a large amount of training (3,200 trials), being exposed to many grammatical strings exemplifying all rules, with periodic tests for recognition of novel grammatical versus ungrammatical strings. In one condition, the subjects merely saw the syllable strings alone, with no referential field. These subjects showed practically no learning of any of the syntactic rules, even after 3,200 trials. In an alternate condition, a systematic referential field (a string of geometric shapes) was presented along with the grammatical string, and the syllables in each syntactic category had a particular referential function in terms of that perceptual field (e.g., altering color, orientation, or borders of a central figure). The presence of the semantic referents alongside the grammatical string of nonsense caused a dramatic turnaround in results; all subjects now readily learned the grammatical rules, and showed productivity in distinguishing novel grammatical from ungrammatical strings even without the pictures. In commenting upon the strategy employed by subjects in this latter condition, Moeser and Bregman (1973) report:

> ... when semantic referents are present the learning strategy consists of (a) learning to associate each word with its referent, and (b) learning the specific rules of the reference field (the ways in which these referents can be organized), and then (c) learning to map words referring to relevant aspects of the visual field onto the sentence positions [p. 23] .

Such studies, then, show that the organization of the perceptual field plays a significant role in the acquisition of grammatical relations. They also make plausible the view that, in the beginning, simple syntactic organization reflects aspects of the perceptual organization of the referential field.

The interfacing of language with the memory system, even if parasitical, has important consequences. For example, it permits men to exchange their experiences verbally, to inform one another, to reinforce or punish or question one another, and generally to enjoy the many fruits of a technology for communicating with one another. Moreover, language eventually facilitates the development of abstract conceptual structures that appear far removed from a description of immediate perceptual experience. By this and other similar means, language plays a central role in our capacity for abstract thought. Abstraction of a sophisticated type would seem unlikely without some kind of language. However, the structures that develop in memory never free themselves of their origin. Even the most abstract structures seem capable of being reduced to perceptual data, and we suggested a way by which this reduction might be accomplished. The language of the mathematical grammarians seems at times to be little more than uninterpreted symbols, mere tiles shuffled about according to string-formation rules. But real languages always remain close to their perceptual base in their interpretation. The perceptual derivation of even abstract concepts is almost so obvious as to be missed. Many of these abstract concepts arise from metaphors that use perceptual terms (Asch, 1961), such as the "depth" of thought, a "piercing wit," a "heated debate," a "raging passion," a "well-tuned" car, a "stormy meeting," etc. Theoretical discourse is replete with figurative metaphors, as the quotation marks in the following passage (from Whorf, 1956) illustrate:

> I "grasp" the "thread" of another's arguments, but if its "level" is "over my head," my attention may "wander" and "lose touch" with the "drift" of it, so that when he "comes" to the "point" we differ "widely," our "views" being indeed so "far apart" that the "things" he says "appear" "much" too arbitrary or even "a lot" of nonsense [p. 146].

Of course, these sensationalist claims for our memory structure currently have the status of pure dogma—or, less pejoratively, a promissory note to be cashed in the future. We have little to say in the way of specific experimental predictions about memory for perceptual material or its relation to memory for linguistic material. We have worked exclusively with sentence analysis, and have only hinted at the nature of the interface between perceptual material and the memory component. As difficult as it is to produce a theory of the interface between language and memory, it appears far easier than constructing the necessary perceptual system. Therefore, our predictions will concern memory for linguistic material. Nonetheless, we have tried to develop a representation that would be relatively indifferent to whether it is encoding perceptual or linguistic material. In this way fundamental modifications would not be required should the theory be extended someday to perceptual material.

5.2. THE PROPOSITIONAL REPRESENTATION

In choosing a representation for propositional information we have tried to be as frugal as possible and not assume more than the bare minimum necessary. The attitude has been not to permit a further complication to the representation unless it is absolutely required. The primary concepts will be presented as a set of semantic distinctions HAM makes in its propositional trees. Each distinction will be commented upon as it is introduced.

The Subject-Predicate Distinction

To put it plainly, the purpose of long-term memory is to record facts about various things, events, and states of the world. We have chosen the subject-predicate construction as the principal structure for recording such facts in HAM. In HAM we predicate of some subject S that it has a certain property P. Consider the four example sentences in Figure 5.1 and their representations in HAM. In each case, a particular node (called the *fact* node) sprouts two links or arcs, one arc, labeled S, pointing to the subject node, and a second arc, labeled P, pointing to the predicate node. The fact node represents the idea of the fact being asserted. James Mill would have called it a *duplex* idea, formed from the complex ideas of the subject and of the predicate. It is an idea that has some of the same functional properties as the subordinate ideas to which it points. For instance, we can predicate properties of such ideas (fact nodes) just as we can predicate of simple ideas like "a balloon." To illustrate, a fact can be said to be false, or probable, or amusing, or fortunate, etc. Figure 5.2 illustrates how one may predicate a property of a fact, asserting in this case that "It is fortunate that Caesar is dead." This approach permits representation of a number of such predications embedded inside one another to arbitrary depths. For instance, one can encode and represent "It is false that it is believed that it is fortunate that Caesar is dead."

The subject-predicate distinction is an ancient and honorable one which can be traced at least as far back as Aristotle. Roughly speaking, it permits one to introduce a topic (the subject) and then to make some comment about it (the

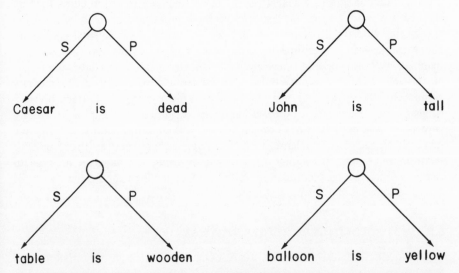

FIG. 5.1. Examples of how the subject-predicate construction may be used to express simple propositions.

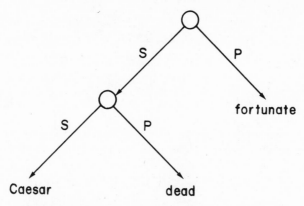

FIG. 5.2. Example of a predication about a fact node.

predicate). It is often observed that predication is the principle function of language. For instance, the "logical" subject-predicate distinction plays a very central role in Chomsky's transformational grammar (Chomsky, 1965). Furthermore, it is frequently the practice in computer science (e.g., Quillian, 1969) to represent all sorts of information in terms of a listing of object-property pairs or attribute-value pairs. But such pairs are basically just subject-predicate constructions. Philosophers have often argued that the subject-predicate distinction is more than an accident of language, that it basically reflects the way we understand reality. For instance, it has played a central role in philosophical debates regarding the distinction between universals and particulars (see Loux, 1970; Ramsey, 1931; Russell, 1911-12). Behavioristic psychologists (e.g., Mowrer, 1960; Staats, 1968) have remarked upon the similarity between stimulus-response conditioning and predication. In conditioning as in predication, one item (the response or the predicate) becomes attached to another item (the stimulus or the subject) due (in part) to temporal contiguity. So, in adopting a subject-predicate distinction, we have many prestigious precedents. However, the role of predication in HAM's representation is somewhat different from these other uses, as will become apparent.

The Relation-Object Distinction

Predication frequently involves more than ascribing a simple predicate like "wooden" or "dead" to the subject. Rather, the predication often says that the subject bears a certain relation, r, to an object, o. Examples of how such relation-object predications would be encoded in HAM are illustrated in Figure 5.3. Our representation is now even closer to the deep-structures proposed by Chomsky (1965). It may be recalled that Chomsky's grammar rewrites the sentence as a noun phrase plus a verb phrase, and rewrites the verb phrase as a verb plus a noun phrase (object). For instance, Figure 5.3b involves a verbial construction for which HAM's representation is isomorphic to the deep-structure assigned to it by Chomsky's grammar.

Earlier, in Figure 5.2, we illustrated how something can be predicated of a fact node, e.g., "It is fortunate that Caesar is dead." In a similar vein, one can predicate

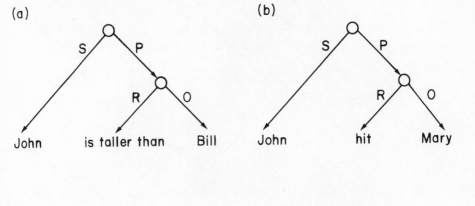

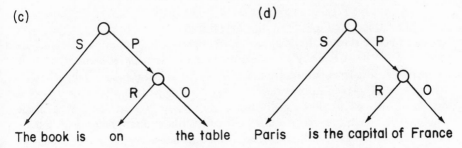

FIG. 5.3. Examples of the use of the relation-object construction.

something about a predicate node. Figure 5.4 illustrates the representation for the sentence "John cruelly hit Mary" and, for contrast, the representation of "John vigorously hit Mary." In Figure 5.4a, the predicate "cruel" modifies the predicate "the hitting of Mary," since "cruel" is a comment on the act. In contrast, in Figure 5.4b, "vigorous" just modifies the verb "hit," since "vigorously" is a so-called adverb of manner. Thus, some adverbs will modify the total predicate (the "action-object" combination), whereas others will modify just the relation (the

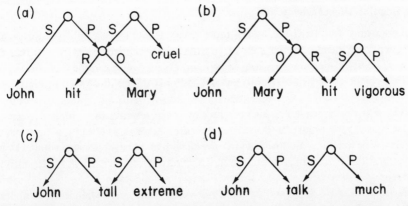

FIG. 5.4. Examples of predications about predicate and relation nodes.

"act"). For some sentences it is ambiguous whether the adverb is modifying the predicate or the relation. For instance, the sentence "John amusingly hit Mary" is ambiguous between "John hit Mary in an amusing manner" and "It was amusing of John to hit Mary."

One can, of course, predicate things of surface adjectives or properties, or of intransitive verbs, all of which will be written as S-P constructions in HAM's deep-structure. Intensifiers like *very, extremely, mildly, moderately,* etc., are typical examples. The structure assigned to "John is extremely tall" in HAM is shown in Figure 5.4*c*, whereas Figure 5.4*d* shows the structure for "John talks a lot," where an intransitive verb is modified.

The rules introduced so far represent unary relations with the subject-predicate rule, p(s), and binary relations with the subject-relation-object rule, r(s, o). It might seem that our formalism should be extended to allow for expression of general *n*-ary relations—i.e., $r(x_1, x_2, ..., x_n)$ as in the ELINOR system of Rumelhart, Lindsay, and Norman (1972). For instance, ELINOR would represent "John gave the book to Mary" in functional notation as "give (John, book, Mary)," and "John opened the door with a key" would be represented as "open (John, door, key)," where the successive noun-arguments of the verb-relation occupy distinguished case roles. In Fillmore's case grammar, many verbs typically take more than just two cases (nouns), suggesting a possible need for *n*-ary relations in a long-term memory representation. However, we believe that this use of *n*-ary relations fails to capture a certain feature of such verbs that is very important in a memory representation. Often when a verb appears with more than two cases, it turns out that the underlying proposition is really asserting a causal relation between a predicate and another atomic proposition. Roger Schank (1972), in particular, has pointed out these implicit causatives in multiple case verbs.

Figure 5.5 shows the representation that these sentences should have in HAM. In Figure 5.5*a*, "John gave the book to Mary" becomes "John transferred the book, causing Mary to possess it"; in Figure 5.5*b*, "John opened the door with a key" becomes "John turned the key, causing the door to be open." By such means, then, one would be able to express *n*-ary relations $(n > 2)$ in our binary formalisms. Moreover, unlike the formalism of Rumelhart et al., our formalism would make salient the causal connections inherent in such higher-order relations. Our representation also makes salient the so-called *presuppositional* information as contrasted to the *implicational* information in sentences such as "John gave Mary the book." The presupposition is that John previously possessed the book, whereas the implication is that Mary has it now. This expanded representation would then permit direct answers to questions such as "Who has the book now?" without requiring further inferences.

The Context-Fact Distinction

The prior distinctions provide no means for representing where and when a fact occurred. Some facts like "John is the father of Bill" or "Giraffes have long necks" are true in any context, and no stipulation of a context is needed. However, it is usually necessary to specify the context in which a fact is true. Figure 5.6 illustrates how contextual information about time and location will be represented in HAM;

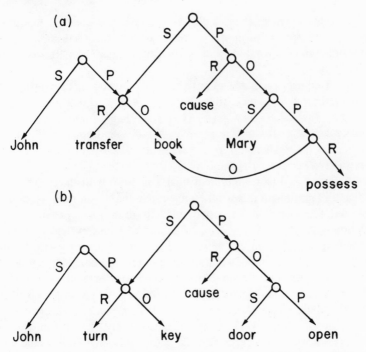

FIG. 5.5. How multicase sentences might be represented in the subject-relation-object formalism of HAM. Note that implicit causatives are often embedded in such sentences.

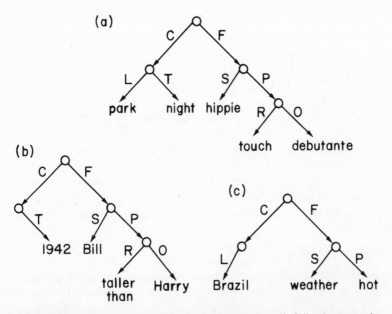

FIG. 5.6. Use of the context-fact distinction in encoding the following example propositions: (*a*) During the night in the park the hippie touched the debutante. (*b*) Bill was taller than Harry in 1942. (*c*) In Brazil the weather is hot.

two further duplex ideas are introduced into the representation to accomplish this purpose. First, we introduce the duplex idea of a context, which is composed in turn from the complex ideas of a place ("park") and a time ("night"). Second, the duplex fact-idea is combined with the duplex context-idea to construct a duplex idea of the total proposition being asserted. As mentioned above, the context modification of a fact node is optional. Also, the context node does not require expansion into both a time and a place specification. Figure 5.6b and c illustrates context ideas which are rewritten with only a time or only a location specified. Thus, Figure 5.6b may be read "John would be taller than Harry anywhere in 1942," and Figure 5.6c may be read "In Brazil the weather is hot at any time."

The context element specifies the spatiotemporal portion of reality for which a particular fact is true. This information can be very important in reasoning about the world. For instance, if we are asked whether John is now taller than Harry, it is important that our memories have recorded that it was the year 1942 when he was taller. If John was a man and Harry a child in 1942, we should hesitate to say that John is still taller. If both were grown men in 1942, we would be likely to suppose John is still taller. Thus, speci- fication of context is important to a realistic memory because of the ephem- eral nature of the particular facts about the world. Often knowledge of such facts is worthless unless we can further specify where and when they were true.

Furthermore, context information can often be called into service to resolve inconsistencies of "factual" inputs. To take a trivial example, the statement "The weather today is hot and freezing" is contradictory, whereas "The weather today is hot in Mexico and freezing in Antarctica" is perfectly acceptable. Besides time and location information, there is another contextual-like information that plays an important role in resolving inconsistencies. This is information about the source of a particular proposition. For instance, HAM may have stored "John thinks the weather is hot" and "Mary thinks the weather is freezing." Here, the contradicting assertions about the weather occur embedded as objects of propositions stating the source of the assertions (i.e., "John thinks X" and "Mary thinks Y"). The apparent contradiction can now be ascribed to the sources. Note that in this example, the source would not be given under the context branch of a proposition but rather as an embedding proposition.

A particular context node can become associated with a large number of facts. It is also possible to predicate features directly of a context. For example, Figure 5.7 illustrates how HAM would encode "San Francisco was cold, wet, and windy on Christmas." In this way, HAM could represent a lengthy description of a complex situation. Such situational descriptions prove to be very important in problem-solving applications within artificial intelligence (see McCarthy & Hayes, 1969; Raphael, 1971). Problem solving is often formulated as the task of finding a set of *operators* or *actions* that will transform one state of the world (a situational description) into a desired goal state (another situational description). Thus, our memory formalism would be well suited for use in representing "situational spaces" for problem solving.

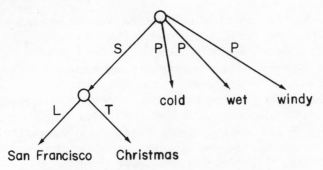

FIG. 5.7. Example of predications about a context.

Terminal Quantification

So far we have introduced four binary distinctions used in HAM's representation. In each case, a duplex idea is composed from simple ideas. Such binary trees will form the input to HAM. The trees always terminate in nodes which already exist in memory. (In this way the input trees are "anchored" or "hooked into" the existing memory structure.) For expository purposes, these nodes have been represented in Figure 5.1 through 5.7 by the corresponding English words. However, it is now time to reveal this oversimplification and to indicate the actual manner in which the trees will be linked into memory nodes.

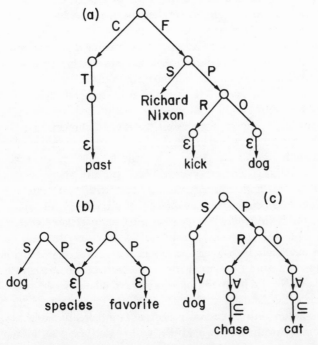

FIG. 5.8. Examples of terminal quantification.

A careful distinction is made within HAM between *concept* nodes and *individual* nodes. A concept node represents the general idea of some class concept like *dog* or *table*. It represents a set which may have individual members. In contrast, individual nodes reference the particular objects, properties, and events that fill our lives; examples are "Germany," "my dog Spot," "Richard Nixon," or "the hippie's touching of the debutante." When an input proposition is about a particular individual there are two ways of terminating the input tree, as illustrated by Figure 5.8. In one case, the node corresponding to that individual already exists in memory, as is the case with "Richard Nixon" in the proposition "Richard Nixon kicked a dog." In this case the tree (Figure 5.8a) can terminate directly with that node. However, in the case of an indefinite description like "a dog," there is no prior representation in memory of the particular individual being kicked; instead, we have only a representation of the class (e.g., dog) to which this newly designated individual belongs. In this case, then, HAM must create a new node to represent the individual in question, and connect this node by a link to the concept node. The link is labeled with the symbol ϵ for set membership. Note that in Figure 5.8a, the time "past" and the relation "kick" are similarly represented in terms of set memberships, since the proposition refers to a particular past time and a particular instance of the set of actions known as kickings.

We wish to allow for the possibility of predicating something of the concept itself. For example, Figure 5.8b shows for the concept of "dog" the predication "Dog is my favorite species." This is the one circumstance in which it is possible to use a concept node directly as the terminal node of a tree. This circumstance, in which something is predicated of the concept per se, should not be confused with the circumstance in which something is predicated of all *individuals* in the set referenced by the concept. A different representation is required, as is illustrated for "dogs" in Figure 5.8c. Here the proposition "Dogs chase cats" is rendered in HAM as "all dogs chase some cats." A node corresponding to a prototypical or generic dog is created which is connected to the dog concept by a generic link, which is labeled with the symbol for universal quantification $\forall$ (meaning "for all"). Such generic links provide HAM with the expressive power of universal quantification in a predicate calculus. Thus, if a node n_1 is related to a node n_2 by a generic link, this is to be interpreted as meaning "For every member of the set n_2, the proposition involving n_1 is true."

Figure 5.8c also illustrates how existential quantification is represented, specifically with respect to the concepts "chase" and "cat." The subset relationship is introduced here, with the label on the links in Figure 5.8c being $\subseteq$ denoting set inclusion. A subset of the total set is created (representing "some cats"), and then the generic relation branches out of that selected subset whenever something specific is to be asserted about all individuals in that subset. That is to say, while the proposition is not true of every member in the total set of cats, it is true of every member in some subset of cats. Thus, Figure 5.8c could be read "For every dog there is a subset of all cats which he chases." In predicate calculus notation, Figure 5.8c would be written as: $\forall(x)[dog(x) \rightarrow (\exists y)[cat(y) \,\&\, chase(x, y)]]$. (Later we shall take up the issue of the ambiguity in "scope" of existential and universal quantifiers.)

The Deep Grammar

We have now set forth the few structural rules of the trees that will serve as input to HAM and as "memories" in HAM. These rules are summarized by the *deep grammar* of Table 5.1, which stipulates what qualifies as well-formed input trees that will be "accepted" by HAM. The interpretation of each rule in Table 5.1 is that the label on the left of the rule can be rewritten as a node and zero, one, or two labels as specified on the right. The table indicates the constraints that a relation leading into a particular node places on the relations that lead out of that node. For instance, Rule 5.1c indicates that TIME and LOCATION links may lead from a node *n* to which a CONTEXT relation leads. Rule 5.1c may be also read as an instruction to be followed in constructing the tree: "At the bottom of a CONTEXT link, place a node *n*, and from node *n* put out a TIME link and a LOCATION link." The TIME and LOCATION links are in parentheses in rule 5.1c to indicate that they are optional; that is to say, it is possible to have just a TIME or just a LOCATION specified.

Rules 5.1a and 5.1b are special in that they start the construction of the tree. Rule 5.1a with PROPOSITION is used if the FACT is to be qualified with a context, whereas Rule 5.1b is adopted if qualification is unnecessary. In either case,

TABLE 5.1

The Deep Grammar

PROPOSITION	n CONTEXT	FACT	5.1a
FACT	n SUBJECT	PREDICATE	5.1b
CONTEXT	n (TIME)	(LOCATION)	5.1c
PREDICATE	n RELATION	OBJECT	5.1d
OBJECT	n CONTEXT	FACT	5.1e
SUBJECT	n SUBJECT	PREDICATE	5.1f
CONTEXT FACT TIME	n (ϵ $\hbar_s(t)$)		5.1g
LOCATION SUBJECT	n MEMBER		5.1h
PREDICATE RELATION	n SUBSET		5.1i
OBJECT MEMBER SUBSET GENERIC	n GENERIC		5.1j

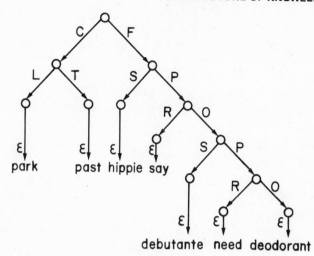

FIG. 5.9. Example of a tree structure generated by rewriting OBJECT: "In the park the hippie said the debutante needed a deodorant."

nothing is left of the start element in the resulting tree. Rules 5.1*e* and 5.1*f* deserve special notice insofar as they allow HAM to decompose OBJECT or SUBJECT as either a PROPOSITION or a FACT. Figure 5.9 provides an example of a tree structure generated by rewriting the OBJECT.

Rules 5.1*a* through 5.1*f* stipulate the branching in acceptable input trees. No more than two relations ever lead from a node. However, it is possible to have an arbitrary number of links leaving a node, each labeled with the same relation. This is the manner in which *conjunction* is expressed in HAM's memory. For instance, as in Figure 5.10, we may predicate more than one thing about a particular subject: "John hates cats but loves dogs." We have encoded this in Figure 5.10 by creating two separate predicate links leading from the fact node. However, this possibility

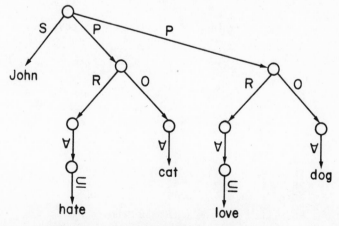

FIG. 5.10. Example of conjunction of predicates.

for conjunction should not obscure the basic *binary structure* of HAM's representation. Later we will provide a discussion of how this binary structure leads to certain efficiencies in the memory representation over other possible structures. possible structures.

So far we have confined our discussion to Rules 5.1*a* through 5.1*f*, which specify the binary structure of the input trees. Rule 5.1*g* specifies that any branch in the tree may end directly in a node from memory (the set $\mathcal{N}_s(t)$ is the set of memory nodes at time t). Finally the Rules 5.1*h* through 5.1*j* specify how we may apply the quantifiers—i.e., member (ϵ), subset ($\subseteq$), or generic ($\forall$)—to any of the terminal branches.

Intersection of Trees

The deep grammar only generates simple tree structures. But often a total proposition needs to be analyzed into an intersecting set of such trees. An intersecting tree is illustrated in Figure 5.11*a*, which encodes the proposition "In a dark alley a baby cried." Such intersecting subtrees could either be input all at once or input separately to HAM. In the separated case, first HAM would encode the subtree for "An alley was dark," as shown in Figure 5.11*b*. As a consequence of encoding this tree, node 1 of Figure 5.11*b*, which represents the particular context, would have been set up in memory. Suppose the second tree of Figure 5.11*c* is then input to the memory. Since node 1 had already been established as a memory node, it serves as a terminal node in the input tree of Figure 5.11*c*, which encodes the proposition "In context 1, a baby cried."

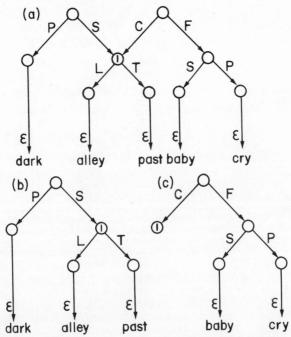

FIG. 5.11. Example of intersecting subtrees which can be separately input to HAM.

All such intersecting trees have the character that one tree is *predicating* something of a particular node in another tree. For instance, in Figure 5.11a the subject of the predication is the context node 1, and the predicate is *dark*. The input order of the two intersecting trees is immaterial to HAM's final representation of the information. That is, the same structure would develop in memory if HAM first input the proposition "In an alley a baby cried" and then input "The alley was dark." It is possible formally to make such predications about any node in the input tree. Of course, each duplex node in the tree represents a certain combination of ideas. A significant outcome of our representation is that predications are possible about only certain of the possible combinations of ideas, namely, context (time plus location), predicate (relation plus object), fact (subject plus predicate), and proposition (context plus fact). A moment's reflection will show, however, that there are many other possible combinations of ideas about which it is not possible to make direct predications, e.g., (time plus relation), (subject plus relation), (location plus object), (time plus subject plus object), and so on. In fact, there are some 26 possible combinations of two, three, four, and five elements in a five-element proposition. But our representation allows us to predicate about only four of these combinations; these are the allowable duplex ideas about which we can speak. The interesting point is that it is impossible to conceive of wanting to predicate anything of the other 22 combinations. We regard that fact as very compelling evidence for the representation that we have adopted. Our initial reasoning was that every node in memory should have a character corresponding intuitively to that of an "idea" in past associationist theories. One intuitive characteristic of an idea is that it has properties or predicates that could be true of it. Given our deep grammar, then, HAM simply will not accept any of the 22 nonpredicatable combinations as legitimate ideas. People don't seem to do so either.

Equivalence to Second-Order Predicate Calculus

Our formalism appears to have all the expressive power of the second-order predicate calculus. The predicate calculus requires several syntactic devices such as the notions of implication, falsity, the ability to compose n-place relations (where n is arbitrary), and the ability to quantify both over relations and over individuals (see Robbin, 1969). All these features are now available in HAM's deep grammar. We earlier illustrated the composition (or decomposition) of n-place predicates (e.g., the verb *give*), and have just discussed quantification over relations and individuals. Implication in our system is a relation holding between two propositions, whereas falsity is a predicate that applies to an embedded proposition. These devices are illustrated in the sentence "If John doesn't hit Mary, Bob will" (see Figure 5.12). A rephrasing of the tree structure in Figure 5.12 would be "(John hit Mary is false) implies (Bill hit Mary)."

One feature of the predicate calculus that is problematical for associative networks concerns the *scope* of existential and universal quantifiers. To illustrate the problems here, let us consider the ambiguous sentence "All dogs chase some cats." One interpretation of this sentence, which was represented previously in

Figure 5.8c, is "Each dog has a particular set of cats which he chases." This would be represented in the predicate calculus as $(\forall x)[dog(x) \rightarrow (\exists y)[cat(y) \& chase(x,y)]]$. The problem is how to represent the second, less likely, interpretation of this sentence, viz., "There is one particular set of cats which are distinguished by the fact that all dogs chase them." This is rendered in predicate calculus notation as $(\exists x)[cat(x) \& (\forall y)[dog(y) \rightarrow chase(y,x)]]$. In the first interpretation the scope of the universal quantifier $(\forall)$ is outside the expression and thus includes the scope of the existential quantifier $(\exists)$. In the second interpretation, this order of quantifier scopes is reversed.

In our representation, the scope of the subject quantifier is always interpreted as containing the scope of any quantifiers in the predicate. This subject-determination of scope appears also in people's interpretations of ambiguous sentences; in one investigation of this phenomenon, Johnson-Laird (1969) found that doubly quantified sentences were predominantly interpreted with the greater scope belonging to the quantifier on the surface subject. Thus, his judges tended to interpret "all philosophers have read some books" as meaning "some books or other" (i.e., different books for different philosophers); on the other hand, the passive transform "Some books have been read by all philosophers" tends to be interpreted as "Some books in particular." Presumably these interpretive biases for scope can be trained in or trained out according to cultural usage.

The question arises, however, whether HAM has a representation of our "dogs and cats" sentence for which the scope of the existential quantifier on the object, "cat," contains the scope of the universal quantifier on the subject, "dog." Figure 5.13 presents a possible solution within HAM's formalisms. Here, "some cats" has been made the subject of a fact, which is then related to the proposition "All dogs chase them" by the relation "are distinguished by." In this way, the scope of "cat," as subject of the main clause, contains the scope of "dog," which is the subject of the embedded object clause. Obviously, by this circumlocution it should be possible to represent arbitrarily complicated relationships of scopes. The fact that

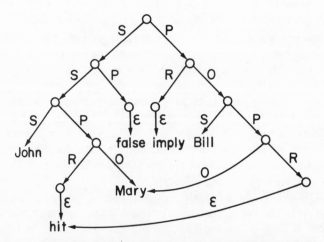

FIG. 5.12. An example of implication in HAM.

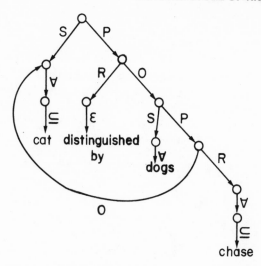

FIG. 5.13. Representation of the other interpretation
of "All dogs chase some cats." Compare with Figure
5.8c.

circumlocution is required is not necessarily an embarrassment. The full expressive
power of predicate calculus cannot be captured in natural language without much
circumlocution. It seems reasonable to suppose that neither human language nor
human memory evolved in a way that enables them to deal easily with the
expressive powers of the formal languages that have been developed only in the past
century of man's history.

The Structure of Probe Trees

The discussion so far has focused on the structure of the trees that are input to
the memory. HAM will attempt to store these trees in long-term memory by
forming associations corresponding to each of the links in the tree. This storage
process will be examined at length in Chapter 7. We will now consider the
structure of the probe trees which are sent into memory during information-
retrieval tasks. These trees correspond to questions; their function is to specify
what information is to be retrieved from memory to satisfy a particular need or
purpose. Since the structure of the input trees largely determines the structure of
the memory representation, the retrieval process will be most efficient if the
structure of the probe is as similar as possible to the structure of the input. In
deciding how the memory probes should be structured, it is important to recognize
that there are basically two ways of probing memory for information. Either we
can present a proposition and ask whether it is true (e.g., "Did the boy hit the
girl?"), or we can ask for some information that will serve to complete a
proposition ("Who hit the girl?"). The former are called *yes-no questions*
and the latter *wh-questions* (*wh* for who, what, which, when, etc.). For a

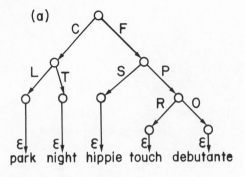

park night hippie touch debutante

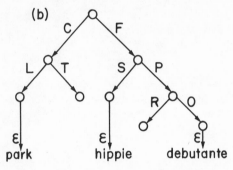

park   hippie   debutante

FIG. 5.14. Examples of probe trees: (a) for
yes-no questions, and (b) for wh-questions.

yes-no question, the structure of the probe tree is identical to that of the input tree
for the proposition whose truth is being queried. Thus, Figure 5.14a could equally
represent the input tree for "In the park during the night a hippie touched a debutante," or the probe tree for "Did a hippie touch a debutante during the night in a
park?" The difference between the question and the assertion lies in what the
processor does with the propositional trees—whether it stores it or attempts to
verify it as true or false.

In contrast, the structure of a probe tree for a wh-question differs somewhat
from the structure of the corresponding input tree. Corresponding to each queried
element of the proposition, there will be a "dummy" terminal node in the probe
tree. Unlike the terminal nodes of an input tree, these "queried terminals" of the
probe tree are not preexisting nodes in memory. For instance, Figure 5.14b
presents the probe tree for "When did the hippie do what to the debutante in the
park?" The time and relation nodes in this tree are just "dangling," not anchored to
any particular nodes in memory. When the decoding process matches the probe tree
to trees existing in memory, it will fill in these queried terminals with the memory
nodes of the matched trees. The matched memory nodes should correspond to the
right answers to the question.

This concludes the discussion of how HAM is to represent incoming inputs
(facts) and probes (questions). We have tried to indicate the various considerations
that motivated our particular choice of representation. To review, these
considerations were:

1. The representation should be capable of expressing any conception of which a human is capable. HAM's representation was shown to be at least equal to the second-order predicate calculus with respect to its expressive potential.

2. Binary-branching and labeling of links turns out to be useful in the memory matching routines to be described in succeeding chapters.

3. The representation should be designed to make salient the substantive information that is being input. It should not be influenced by the peculiarities of any natural language in which that information might have been communicated.

4. For reasons of parsimony, the representation should involve a minimum of conceptual categories.

5. It should be possible to predicate properties of any of the duplex ideas introduced by the representation, but not possible to predicate properties of any combination of ideas not represented by a node.

These five considerations go a long way in the direction of specifying what the representation should be. However, we must admit that these alone are not sufficient constraints, so that unsystematic biases and intuitions have also played a role in determining the choice of a representation. We wish it were otherwise.

6
THE RECOGNITION PROCESS

Memory is the possession of an experience potentially revivable.
—Aristotle

6.1. THE MATCH AND IDENTIFY PROCESSES

The preceding chapters were concerned with the processing and structuring of individual pieces of information as they are input into long-term memory. Chapter 5 displayed the structure of propositional trees acceptable to and recorded in HAM's memory, and referenced the parsing system by which inputs are translated into our internal representations. In the present chapter we begin to examine the matter of accessing the information stored in memory. Here the concern is with how incoming information accesses and makes contact with those portions of long-term memory which are relevant to it. This is the central problem of "recognition." It is carried out in HAM by a process called MATCH which tries to find the best matching tree in memory corresponding to an input tree. The MATCH process is used not only during decoding (i.e., in answering questions), but also in encoding (i.e., comprehending and learning new statements). In particular, the MATCH process enables HAM to distinguish already known information in an input from novel information, and so enables HAM to restrict its efforts at encoding to the new information. In this way, HAM can make use of known information to reduce the task of encoding new information.

In reusing old information (subtrees of current predications), certain difficulties arise whereby the memory system could store unintended propositions (these will be illustrated later); consequently, following the MATCH process, a further process called IDENTIFY is evoked to check on how much of the matched information is in fact useable for encoding the current input. The purpose of this first section is to describe the operation of the MATCH and IDENTIFY processes. The subsequent Section 6.2 will report some experimental tests of these processes during encoding. Chapter 8 is devoted to an experimental examination of the MATCH processes during decoding.

The MATCH Process

The function of the MATCH process is to make a correspondence between the current input or probe and some piece of the associative structure in memory. The exact details of the MATCH process are well defined and consistent. That is, there is a LISP function defined in our computer program which simulates how the MATCH process searches memory trying to bring the input or probe into contact with the appropriate memory structure. The exact details of the MATCH process will not be discussed here; a copy of the simulation program is available upon request. Here, we will emphasize those aspects of the MATCH process that are relevant to the experimental predictions to be examined.

After a sentence has been parsed, a binary-branching input structure is held in working memory on which the MATCH process operates. The MATCH process always works on only one proposition in the input at a time. If there are multiple propositions in the current input (each proposition represented by a subtree of the input network), it will attempt to match *propositional subtrees* of the total input to trees in memory. The MATCH process always begins at those terminal nodes of the tree which are also memory nodes. In an input tree all terminal nodes are memory nodes, whereas in a probe tree only a subset of the nodes are (see our discussion in Section 5.2 on this point). MATCH tries to find paths in memory that (a) connect the terminal memory nodes, and (b) correspond to paths in the input tree it is trying to match. A memory path and an input path are judged equivalent if they possess the same number of links and the same sequence of relations labeling the links. The MATCH process attempts to find the graph pattern of paths through memory that gives the maximal match (measured in terms of the number of matched links) to the input.

The MATCH process is efficient in that it only examines those paths in memory between terminal nodes that could possibly match paths in the trees. It does so by use of labels on links. For instance, if a terminal node in the input tree is "dog" and it is linked in the input tree to a dominating node by a *member* relation ϵ, the MATCH process will not consider any links with $\subseteq^{-1}$ or $\forall^{-1}$ leading out of the "dog" node in memory; only ϵ^{-1} links giving "dog-instances" will be considered. This is one way that HAM uses the relational information on links to guide its search of memory. Of course, there could be a great many ϵ^{-1} associations to "dog." That is, the list returned by the function GET(dog, ϵ^{-1}) could be very long. (The function GET(dog, ϵ^{-1}) is a primitive in HAM that will retrieve a list of all elements b such that <dog ϵ^{-1} b> is a long-term memory association.) This ordered list of nodes is referred to as the *GET-list*. The associates on this list are constantly updated according to their recency of mention. Since a recently mentioned instance of a dog is likely to be the instance HAM is searching for, HAM is likely to find the appropriate associate early in its search of the GET-list. Of course, none of the ϵ^{-1}

associations on the GET-list may match the input. To prevent many long and fruit-less searches of GET-lists, it is assumed that HAM will only search a GET-list to a probabilistically determined depth.

The fact that only a probabilistically determined portion is examined turns out to be very significant. This is the sole mechanism in HAM that produces forgetting. That is, old unused associations will tend to descend relatively far down in the GET-list and will hence become effectively inaccessible. We will expand upon this mechanism in Chapter 10, where we will discuss how the literature on interference and forgetting can be accommodated by this mechanism. It is important to realize that its motivation is not to produce forgetting but to make the MATCH function more efficient by preventing protracted but fruitless searches.

To explore the mechanics of how the MATCH process operates, it will be useful to trace through an example of how an input is matched to memory. A plausible search theory, we believe, involves a quasi-parallel simultaneous search from all terminal nodes of the input tree, possibly with the earlier elements in the left-to-right processing of the input getting started ahead of the later elements. From each node a search proceeds forth trying to find a match in memory to the input tree. This simultaneous search process is similar to one proposed earlier by Quillian (1968), but there are some notable differences. First, the searchers from different terminal nodes are independent of one another. Thus, an input proposition is not considered matched to memory until one of the MATCH processes, searching from a terminal node, achieves a complete match by itself. There can be no intersection or "meeting in the middle" of a number of search processes as there is in Quillian's model. Quillian seems to have only concerned himself with intersections of two searches in conceptual hierarchies. Here it is relatively easy to define how an executive routine should respond to an intersection. However, when one has more than two MATCH processes searching propositional tree structures, as is the case with HAM, it is very complicated to define an executive routine that will appropri-ately respond to all possible patterns of intersection. It was so complicated that we decided it was implausible psychologically to have HAM attempt to use these intersections.

A second difference between HAM and Quillian's model is that in HAM each MATCH process searches memory in a serial fashion rather than parallel. In fact, MATCH time is linearly related (the precise model is developed in Chapter 8) to the number of associations searched during the attempted match. As a consequence, any associative fanning encountered at a particular node during the search (e.g., multiple ϵ^{-1} associations leading from a terminal node) will increase the mean MATCH time. This is because each of the fanning associative links will have to be considered sequentially to see if it leads to the best matching proposition. Thus, each fanning association can result in further associations to search and an increase in search time.

An Example

Despite our commitment in theory to this simultaneous search from all nodes, we will present an example where the MATCH process is only proceeding from one terminal node at a time. This is the actual routine programmed in the MATCH function. We will consider how the input tree in Figure 6.1*a* would be matched to the memory structure in Figure 6.1*b*. The input is an encoding of the sentence "In the park a hippie sang." The current MATCH program will select the leftmost terminal, *park*, at which to begin its search process. Since *park* is linked into the input tree by an ϵ relation, MATCH evokes the process GET(park, ϵ^{-1}) to obtain the list of all park instances that it knows. This list is ordered with instances to be called *a, b, c, ...* Suppose that instances *a* and *b* will not lead to substantial matches with the memory structure. Consequently, the MATCH process will search the memory structures accessible from these two nodes, and it will not recover any substantial matches. After attempting these two nodes, it then attempts the node *c*—provided three nodes does not exceed the probabilistically determined depth for searching the GET(park, ϵ^{-1})-list.

The MATCH process is a *recursive mental operation* in that, having matched the input node 1 to memory node *c*, linkages emanating from node *c* are similarly matched to the linkages in the input emanating from node 1. Node 1 in the input is connected by an L-link to node 2. Therefore, the MATCH routine evokes GET(*c*, L^{-1}) from node *c* in the memory tree, and returns with node *e*. Now the MATCH function attempts to match the associative structures from nodes 2 and *e*. There are two differently labeled links in the input tree leading from node 2. Suppose MATCH searches the *time* construction first. It will match the input link <2 T 3> to the memory association <*e* T *d*> and <3 ϵ past> to <*d* ϵ past>.

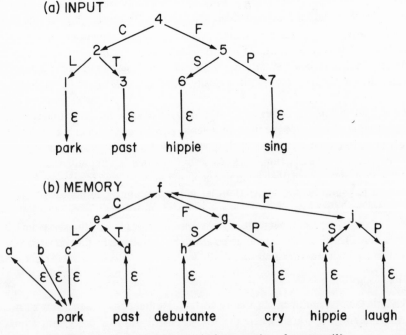

FIG. 6.1. An input (*a*) is matched to a portion of memory (*b*).

At this point it has arrived at a terminal node in the input tree, *past*, and that terminal node matches the memory node. Therefore, it has found a tentative path through memory that matches a path between two of the elements in the input tree. MATCH files away on a temporary "matching candidates" list this particular match, between the memory structure $[<e\ L\ c>,\ <c\ \epsilon\ \text{park}>,\ <e\ T\ d>,\ <d\ \epsilon\ \text{past}>]$ and the input structure $[<2\ L\ 1>,\ <1\ \epsilon\ \text{park}>,\ <2\ T\ 3>,\ <3\ \epsilon\ \text{past}>]$.

There may be a great many ϵ^{-1} associations leading from *past*, but they do not affect search time in this example. On the other hand, search time was affected by the number of ϵ^{-1} associations leading from *park*, since HAM had to consider each one separately. With respect to *past*, however, the MATCH process had only to consider the possible ϵ associations leading from node d, and there was only one. If the MATCH process works as currently programmed, that is, selecting one terminal node of the input tree at a time and searching memory from it, then it becomes crucial which memory node is selected first. For instance, if there is little ϵ^{-1} fanning from *park* but much from *past*, it is clearly advantageous to begin at *park*. In contrast, if, as we really believe, search begins simultaneously from all terminal nodes, search time would be largely determined by the terminal node from which there was least fanning. There would be no need for HAM to concern itself with problems of selecting the best starter node.

The reader will note in this example that initially HAM wasted a lot of time searching for the appropriate ϵ^{-1} association, but now the search is proceeding much more expeditiously. In general, most of the wasted search time is due to fanning of associations at the bottom nodes in the input tree where many associations like ϵ are likely to be found. Once MATCH gets up into the duplex nodes, it is less likely to encounter many identically labeled associations, and hence the overall search will proceed faster through these higher portions of the tree.

To return to our example, we have matched the context subtree in the input to a corresponding piece of memory. The match process will now attempt to match the $<4\ C\ 2>$ link of the input with a link from memory connected to node e. It will evoke GET(e, C), obtain the node f, and recursively apply the MATCH process to the memory node f and input node 4. In attempting to match the fact subtree from 4, it will first consider the *fact* subtree in memory, encoding "A debutante cried," which gives a complete mismatch to the input. It is informative to see how MATCH rejects this subtree of memory. It makes a tentative match between the input link $<4\ F\ 5>$ and the memory link $<f\ F\ g>$. Subsequently, MATCH assigns $<5\ S\ 6>$ to match the link $<g\ S\ h>$. Then it will attempt to match $<6\ \epsilon\ \text{hippie}>$ to $<h\ \epsilon\ \text{debutante}>$. But it now has arrived at two terminal memory nodes, *hippie* and *debutante*, that fail to match. Therefore, it concludes that the *subject* branch it is currently examining is not an appropriate match, and it withdraws the tentative assignment of $<5\ S\ 6>$ in the input to $<g\ S\ h>$ in memory. It then attempts to match the *predicate* branches from nodes 5 and g, but is similarly frustrated. Since the MATCH process can assign none of the memory structure from node g to the input tree from node 5, it also withdraws the tentative correspondence made earlier between $<4\ F\ 5>$ and $<f\ F\ g>$. The MATCH process thus retreats back to the nodes 4 and f, which is its last still-matching nodes, and tries to find another fact subtree in memory.

The second node on the list returned when GET(*f*, F) was evoked is node *j*. MATCH tries to match *j* to node 5 in the input. It will succeed in matching the subject branch from node *j* to the corresponding input branch, since both branches terminate in the *hippie* memory node. MATCH has now found a second path in memory that corresponds to an input path and therefore adds to its stored match the correspondence between the input path [<4 C 2>, <4 F 5>, <5 S 6>, <6 ∈ hippie>] and the memory path [<*f* C *e*>, <*f* F *j*>, <*j* S *k*>, <*k* ∈ hippie>]. The MATCH process will then fail to find a match between the predicate branch from node 5 in the input and the predicate branch from node *j* in memory, because the first terminates in *sing* and the second in *laugh*. Since the match is not perfect, the MATCH process may continue to search to see if it can find a better match. The search will eventually be terminated by a "cutoff" time (see our discussion in Chapter 10). If MATCH cannot find a better match, it will accept this partial one. Remember that MATCH processes are also proceeding from the other terminal nodes in the tree. One of these other MATCH processes may have found a better partial match or a perfect match. HAM accepts the most complete match returned by any MATCH process.

Encoding upon Partial Matches

It should be noted that the MATCH process has made a strong and possibly incorrect claim in this illustration. It is claiming that the hippie who sang in the park is the same hippie recorded earlier in memory as laughing. Moreover, it is making this claim solely on the basis that they both were in a park at some time in the past. Given that hippies frequent parks, we should realize that the MATCH process is quite possibly wrong in this particular claim. The doubtful veracity of this match makes it problematical whether HAM should use the matched memory structure to reduce its encoding task. That is, HAM could encode the input in Figure 6.1*a* by simply adding another predicate branch to the memory structure in Figure 6.1*b*. This encoding of the input is illustrated by the memory structure in Figure 6.2. It should be noted that in this melding of the input tree of Figure 6.1*a* with the memory tree of Figure 6.1*b*, all the nodes 1 through 6 of the input tree have disappeared, being replaced by memory nodes *c* through *l*, and only node 7 of the input tree was encoded into memory. Thus node 7 is "new information" that has been added onto the preexisting information in memory.

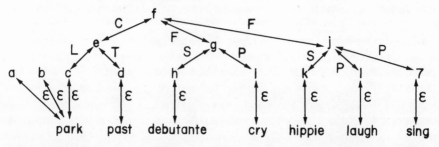

FIG. 6.2. The input in Figure 6.1*a* has been built onto the memory structure of Figure 6.1*b*.

However, it is unclear whether HAM should endorse all the implications of this modified memory structure in Figure 6.2. That is, it may not really be the same hippie, the same time, or the same park for the two acts of laughing and singing. An easy solution to this issue would be never to build an input upon a partially matched memory structure. However, there are good reasons not to go to this extreme either. After all, if it really were the same place, time, and hippie, then we do not want HAM to miss this fact. We do not want to have the same person, place, or time represented by two different instance nodes in memory. Moreover, there are clear advantages to HAM if it takes advantage of the redundancy (correspondences) between input and memory. That is, less time and fewer associations will be required to encode the input. As the information input to the typical human memory is probably highly redundant, it is important that the memory take pains not to reduplicate knowledge. No matter how efficiently HAM's memory is structured, to build up a normal adult memory will require nodes and associations numbering at least in the hundreds of thousands and probably in higher orders of magnitude. If maximum efficiency is not attempted in the representation, HAM will lose credibility simply because of the sheer vastness of the memory structure hypothesized.

So the question is, how is HAM to decide when it can "chance it" and attach partially matched input onto some corresponding memory structure? How would *we* react if someone informed us "A hippie sang in the park," and we remembered "A hippie laughed in the park"? Quite possibly we would set out to determine whether or not this partial correspondence was accidental. Suppose we knew that the hippie of our memory was Jerry Rubin and that the park was New York's Central Park. Then we might ask of our informant, "Was that Jerry Rubin who was in Central Park last Saturday?" If our informant assented, we would be fairly confident that the match obtained was not accidental. This is how we would like HAM to react to a partial match—by asking a question regarding its conjecture. That is, it should intelligently set out to determine whether or not to endorse the proposed identification.

In the simulation of HAM, where its interaction with the world takes the form of a teletype dialogue with its informant, one could have HAM, whenever it encounters a match, to announce that fact and request of the informant whether or not the match is spurious. Of course, this simply transfers the burden of decision from HAM to the informant. Nonetheless, we are seriously contemplating programming such a strategy because we make no pretense of having captured all of human intelligence. Rather, the goal is to simulate certain aspects of human memory. But all this is hypothetical; such informant-program interaction is not yet programmed. As the simulation currently operates, either it will accept any partial match between memory and input, or (if a parameter is changed) it will only accept perfect matches.

The IDENTIFY Process

When HAM does encode input trees using partially matched memory structures, there occur certain logical problems that have forced the postulation of a second mental process, IDENTIFY, which determines whether any unwarranted conceptualizations would occur if HAM built upon the partially matched memory structure. To establish that building on partial matches can have unwarranted and unwanted outcomes, consider the following example: Suppose HAM first hears the proposition "In a park a hippie touched a debutante" and then later hears "In a park a hippie touched a prostitute." In the mode in which partial matches are permitted, HAM would encode these two inputs into the memory structure illustrated in Figure 6.3a. That is, the second input would be encoded by simply

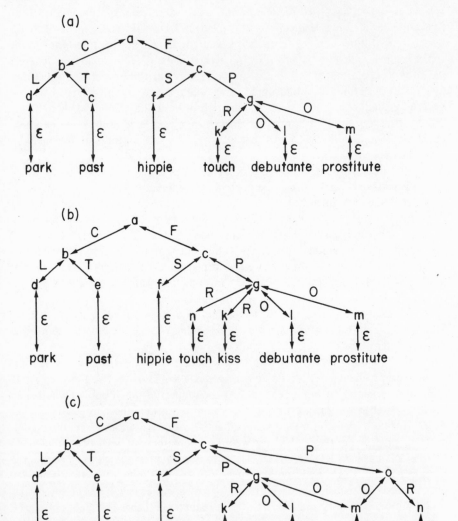

FIG. 6.3. The encoding of an additional relation branch to (*a*) leads to unwanted multiplication of meanings in (*b*). The structure in (*c*) illustrates a satisfactory representation that avoids multiplication of meanings.

adding an object branch to the memory structure that was constructed to encode the first proposition about the *debutante*. Incidentally, the same memory structure would be established if HAM were to encode the single proposition "In a park a hippie touched a debutante and a prostitute." Consequently, in Figure 6.3*a* HAM would be unable to determine later whether it had encoded two separate assertions or a single one. This, of course, suggests an experiment in human memory.

In any case, there is no logical problem with the memory structure set up in Figure 6.3*a*. Difficulties arise when HAM is asked to encode a third related proposition such as "In the park a hippie kissed a prostitute." The input tree for this proposition mismatches the memory structure in Figure 6.3*a* only at the relation (R) association. Therefore, at first thought, it might appear that the memory structure in Figure 6.3*b* would successfully encode the input. It differs from the old memory structure in Figure 6.3*a* only by the addition of a new relation association. But the error in Figure 6.3*b* is that HAM can now infer from it that "In a park a hippie kissed a debutante," which is a proposition it never encoded and which is probably false. The problem basically is that the two *relation* links and the two *object* links have *multiplied* together to yield four possible propositions, whereas only three of these are intended. Thus, HAM has overused the redundancy in the input or overgeneralized. Rather than the erroneous memory structure in Figure 6.3*b*, it should have produced a memory structure more like that in Figure 6.3*c*. Some of the input links and nodes, although assigned by MATCH to memory nodes, were nevertheless encoded in Figure 6.3*c* rather than replaced. The purpose of the IDENTIFY process is to identify which matched input links can be used (replaced by memory associations) and which will have to be encoded as new differentiating information.

The first step to understanding IDENTIFY is to understand the exact class of memory structures which will yield the unwanted multiplication of propositions that was illustrated in Figure 6.3*c*. In characterizing these to-be-avoided memory structures, it will be helpful to introduce the concept of a *conjunction* in a memory structure. A conjunction refers to a group of two or more identically labeled associations leading from a node. For instance, in Figure 6.3*b* there is a *relation* conjunction (node g is connected to the two *relation* nodes n and k) and an *object* conjunction (node g is also connected to the two *object* nodes, l and m). When there are two or more conjunctions in the memory structure, the propositions can "multiply" and yield undesired interpretations, as is the case for Figure 6.3*b*. However, multiple conjunctions in the memory structure do not always result in disaster, as testified by the structure in Figure 6.3*c*. In that figure there is both a *predicate* and an *object* conjunction, yet there is no unwanted multiplication.

Multiple conjunctions in the memory structure imply difficulties if there are two *distinct* sequences, $X_1, X_2, ..., X_n$ and $Y_1, Y_2, ..., Y_N$, that lead from one node in memory through two conjunctions. This condition may be illustrated by Figure 6.3*b*. From node g, the relation R leads into one conjunction and the relation O leads into a second conjunction. Two conjunctions need not be at the same memory node in order to have multiplication of meanings, as Figure 6.4 illustrates. Here the sequence C, L leads from the proposition node a to two locations, and the

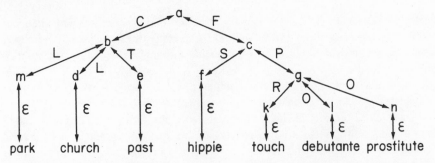

FIG. 6.4. The object and location conjunctions multiply in this memory structure.

sequence F, P, O leads to two objects. In general, according to sequence $X_1, X_2, ...,$ X_n one will have i $(i > 1)$ interpretations, and according to sequence $Y_1, Y_2, ...,$ Y_N, j $(j > 1)$ interpretations. When these two distinct paths are accessible from the root node, there are at least i-times-j possible interpretations of the propositional structure. In the encoding of inputs to partially matched structures, this multiplication of meanings is rarely if ever intended.

But now consider the situation in Figure 6.3c. This has two conjunctions, but they are both on the path P, O; consequently, interpretations do not multiply. It is necessary that the conjunctions be on two distinct paths to have multiplication of meanings.

IDENTIFY uses the list of matched memory links returned by the MATCH process to replace links in the input tree. It starts at the root node and proceeds through the input tree in a depth-first, left-to-right order, replacing paths in the input tree by memory paths. After IDENTIFY has replaced one path with a memory path that has a conjunction, it will replace no more input paths by conjoining memory paths. In this way it is guaranteed that the encoding process will never generate unwanted multiplication of conjunctions. (The exact details of the IDENTIFY process are contained in the LISP function that simulates this process. Copies are available upon request.) IDENTIFY returns to HAM the list of links it was not able to replace. These links HAM will have to store in memory as new information.

The Utility of Binary Branching

It was promised in Chapter 5 that we would have something to say about the utility of binary branching in the input tree. The time has come to make good on that promise. Clearly, some branching is needed if HAM is to connect a number of elements into a single proposition. A disadvantage of greater than binary branching is that it tends to reduce the amount of match obtained between the memory structure and the input tree. If both of these claims are accepted, it follows that binary branching is optimal in one sense. However, the second claim, that binary branching optimizes the amount of matching, is not obvious, so we will prove it. Towards that goal, it will be useful first to prove the following lemma:

Lemma. Suppose some node a in the input tree having n differently labeled downward links (i.e., labels from the set $\mathfrak{R}$) is to be matched to a memory node b which has n like-labeled associations. Then at least $n-1$ of these links must be matched if the memory structure is to be utilized in encoding the input.

Proof. Mismatching two links out of node b would simply mean that two conjunctions would have to be created from b to encode the input tree. But then two conjunctions would be accessible via different paths from memory node b. Therefore, the memory structure could not be used to encode the input because of the unwanted multiplication of meanings. This proves the lemma.

This proof depends only upon the multiplication of meanings caused by conjunctions within a proposition. It does not depend upon any special properties of our MATCH or IDENTIFY routines. Therefore, it is a general result that should be applicable to a variety of associative structures. The consequence of the lemma is that one is less likely to get useable matches between input trees and memory trees when the branching is of higher order because there is a greater likelihood of having two mismatches from a particular node.

As a further argument for HAM, its binary trees have an advantage over other binary constructions in that elements which would tend to be repeated together are close together in HAM's tree structure. For instance, *time* and *location*, which are close together in the tree structure, will often be repeated as providing the context for a number of different facts. HAM would just encode the context subtree once while storing the many facts about that context. The *proposition* node in each proposition could be associated to the same context node. In this manner, HAM can take advantage of repetitions of just pairs of elements like *time* and *location* which are close together in the input tree. However, it cannot take advantage of repetitions of just pairs of elements that are far apart in the tree, such as *time* and *object*. Intuitively, pairs of elements like *time* and *object* seem unlikely to be the only parts of an input tree that will be repeated.

However, there is a disadvantage with binary branching that somewhat cancels out this efficient utilization of known information. Lower degrees of branching tend to require more associative links to be formed to represent the proposition in memory. If there are n elements to be connected into a binary tree structure, $2(n-1)$ associative links will be required. However, if all n elements were permitted to branch directly from the root node, only n links would be required. This means that at least $n-2$ links must be matched in a binary tree if it is to require as few links as an n-ary structure. Thus, it does not seem likely that binary structures will result in substantial savings in memory requirements. The real motivation for HAM's binary representation is that it permits memory to organize itself around cooccurring elements like a particular time and location which may form the context for a large set of facts.

6.2. EXPERIMENTAL TESTS OF THE MATCH PROCESS

The proposed operation of the MATCH process suggests many psychological experiments. This section reports some of the research that we have done to test the MATCH process.

Proper Names versus Definite Descriptions

One of the more interesting features of our simulation program is the way in which it treats definite descriptions. Suppose that the parser encountered an input sentence such as "The first president of the United States was a good husband." It would take the definite description "X was the first president of the United States," match that to memory, determine that X is George Washington, and then encode in memory that "George Washington was a good husband." Thus, no record would be left in HAM's memory to the effect that the assertion had been made using a definite description rather than a proper name. HAM would only know that it was true of a particular individual node that the person referenced by the node was a good husband. It would already know that the name corresponding to that node was George Washington and that the individual was the first president of the United States; but there would be no trace left of whether the proper name or the definite description had been paired with the "good husband" predicate. Hence, we would expect HAM as well as human subjects to false alarm to "George Washington was a good husband." Our first experiment was designed to test this prediction, that there should be recognition confusions in sentence memory between proper names and definite descriptions.

This prediction is interesting for a number of reasons. First, the synonymy between definite descriptions and proper names is not a case of *conceptual synonymy*—that is, synonymy resulting from knowledge of the language. Someone may be a perfectly competent speaker of the English language, know the meanings of the words of the language, but not know that George Washington was the first president of the United States. Rather, this is a case of *referential synonymy*. It is a consequence of our general world knowledge that we know the proper name and the definite description *refer* to the same historical individual. Before we dealt with conceptual synonymy and reviewed the ample evidence that subjects make memorial confusions between sentences on this basis. No one, however, has yet researched the question of referential synonymy.

Second, the matter of definite descriptions is interesting because it is a particularly well-formulated case of the phenomena of recognition memory in HAM. That is, what HAM is really doing when it replaces the definite description by the appropriate memory node is *recognizing* that description as the individual referenced by that node. We would argue that all manners of recognition (e.g., recognition of faces, patterns, contexts, etc.) have the identical procedure underlying them. That is, a description is taken of the object to be recognized, the MATCH process determines the best match in memory, and this best match constitutes the basis for the recognition decision.

Now the experiment will be described in greater detail: The experimental subjects (Stanford students) studied 60 sentences that had been generated from 15 *sentence-sets.* For each sentence-set a pair of proper names was selected, such as the pair George Washington and Abraham Lincoln. Appropriate definite descriptions were selected that would uniquely reference these individuals—e.g., "The first president of the United States" and "The president who freed the slaves." Then two predicates were selected for these individuals. These predicates were chosen to be plausible, but also such that their truth value with respect to the individual was probably unknown to the subjects, e.g., "was a good husband" and "had good health." Two further predicates were created from these two by introducing slight changes in the wording that produced major reversals in the semantic import of the sentences, e.g., "was a bad husband" and "had bad health."

Fifteen such sets of two proper names, two definite descriptions, and four predicates were the ingredients that went into the construction of a recognition experiment identical in logic to the J. R. Anderson (unpublished data, 1972) and Tieman (1971) experiments. From each sentence-set, four study sentences were created, one having each of the proper names and definite descriptions as subject and one having each of the four possible predicates. Thus a subject might hear the following four sentences distributed randomly throughout a study list:

> George Washington had good health.
> The first president of the United States was a bad husband.
> The president who freed the slaves had bad health.
> Abraham Lincoln was a good husband.

In this way, the subject heard each of the proper names, definite descriptions, and predicates in some sentence. His later task would be to remember which subjects went with which predicates. Semantically converse predicates were never asserted of the same individual, but rather of the other individual of a pair. For instance, we did not claim the same individual was both a good and a bad husband. In this manner 60 base sentences were constructed. Two sets of 60 sentences were created by randomly re-pairing individuals with predicates. Twenty subjects listened to each set. The sentences were presented auditorily by a tape recorder at the rate of one every 10 seconds. In the 10-second interval for each sentence, it was read twice.

After studying all 60 sentences, the subjects were tested for their recognition memory of the sentences by a four-alternative forced-choice procedure. The subject might see the following four test sentences and would be asked to indicate which was the original he had heard:

> Abraham Lincoln had good health.
> The president who freed the slaves had good health.
> The president who freed the slaves had bad health.
> Abraham Lincoln had bad health.

That is, the definite description and the proper name for a particular individual would be paired with the two semantically converse forms of one predicate in the four possible ways. Always, the subject would have heard only one of the four possible combinations. Subjects were asked to rate the sentences numerically from 1 to 4 according to their subjective likelihood of having heard each sentence, with 1 indicating the most likely sentence. Although we only analyzed data for sentences rated 1, subjects were instructed to rate all four sentences to insure that they carefully considered all four possibilities before making their choice. The subjects worked at their own pace through a recognition booklet that contained 60 four-alternative forced-choice tests, one for each of the 60 sentences heard during study. The sentences were tested in the same order that they had been studied. The total experiment, including the reading of the preliminary instructions and the filling out of a subsequent questionnaire, took about 45 minutes.

Tieman's experiment has shown the importance of instructions on the type of results one obtains from such experiments. Therefore, the following instructions were used in the hope that they would induce the subjects to analyze the sentences in as natural a manner as possible:

We are going to tell you a large number of facts about certain people and places you have heard of. Some of these facts you will already know, most you will not. Some of the facts you will find surprising and a few you will disagree with. Your task is to try to remember all the information that is stated. After hearing all these facts, you will be given a task that requires knowledge of them.

On a postexperimental questionnaire, about two-thirds of the subjects indicated that, upon hearing proper names and definite descriptions for the same individuals intermixed in the study sentences, they began to suspect that the purpose of the experiment was to test their memory for definite descriptions versus proper names. Undoubtedly, this affected the way they processed the sentences. Some subjects reported adopting deliberate strategies to keep the definite descriptions separate in memory from the proper names. For instance, some subjects refused to think of the definite description as referring to the appropriate individual—e.g., the first president of the United States as being George Washington. Due to the intervention of such deliberate encoding strategies, we cannot expect subjects to false alarm to the referentially synonymous sentence as often as they identify the correct sentence. However, they should false alarm to the referentially synonymous sentence much more frequently than to either of the other two alternatives. This is because these other two alternatives have predicates that are not conceptually synonymous with the original statement.

The results are summarized in Table 6.1, which classifies 2,400 observations according to whether the original sentence studied involved a definite description (D) or a proper name (N), and whether the subject selected the test alternative involving the definite description and correct predicate (+D), the proper name and correct predicate (+N), the definite description and wrong predicate (-D), or the proper name and wrong predicate (-N). Subjects selected the correct alternative much more frequently than the referentially synonymous alternative (.624 vs. .217). Importantly, however, they also false alarmed to the referentially

TABLE 6.1

Classification of Subjects' Responses in Definite Description
Experiment—Proportion of Responses

Original	Subjects' choice			
sentence	+D	+N	–D	–N
D	.652	.214	.072	.063
N	.222	.596	.093	.090

synonymous alternative much more frequently than to one of the sentences that had the wrong predicate (.217 vs. .080). For 14 of the 15 sentence sets, the referentially synonymous alternative was more frequently chosen than the conceptually distinct alternatives; hence, one can be quite confident in the result. Overall, there was a small and insignificant bias to select definite descriptions (51.9%) over the proper names (48.1%).

This experiment clearly establishes that there is considerable confusion in memory between definite descriptions and proper names, as is predicted from the use of the MATCH process by HAM's parser. This is an example of how the MATCH process can function to make difficult the recording of certain kinds of information in memory. However, this was not the intended purpose of the MATCH process. Rather, its motivation partly was to ease the recording of information by using known information to reduce the amount that needs to be stored. There are many trivial examples to demonstrate that people do use past knowledge to help reduce their storage task. For instance, American adults would presumably remember a sentence like "George Washington was the first president of the United States" much better than a sentence like "John McDonald was the first prime minister of Canada." HAM expects this trivial result because the first proposition would be matched to an existing memory structure while the second would not. Therefore, the encoding process would not need to form any new associations in the first case, but would have to form a great many in the second case. We presume that this outcome is so obvious that no experimentation is required to establish it. It clearly indicates the need for some kind of memory matching routine. However, such an outcome could be predicted by models with very different memory structures and different match routines than those embodied in HAM. The next experiment will be concerned with obtaining more discriminating evidence in favor of both the representation and the match routine employed in HAM.

Repetition of Relative Clauses

In this experiment, we will be interested in what happens when subjects study related pairs of sentences that repeat a relative clause such as Sentences (1) and (2). We will contrast these results with what happens with pairs of sentences such as (3) and (4).

The *hippie* who was *tall* touched the debutante.   (1)
The *hippie* who was *tall* kissed the prostitute.   (2)
The hippie who was *tall* touched the *debutante.*   (3)
The captain who was *tall* kissed the *debutante.*   (4)

In both sentence pairs a noun and an adjective (italicized) are repeated. Moreover, both cases are superficially very similar. However, the important difference is that the elements in the first pair—Sentences (1) and (2)—are repeated within the same proposition, whereas the repeated elements in the second case—Sentences (3) and (4)—arise out of different propositions. In fact, in the first case the entire embedded proposition "The hippie was tall" is repeated. The MATCH routine defined in HAM can take advantage of the repetition of an entire proposition in the first case, but it is unable to take advantage of the repetition of "unrelated elements" in the second case. This is because the MATCH process only works with a single proposition at one time. Therefore, it cannot detect repetition between propositions. As a consequence, after storing Sentence (1), when HAM came to Sentence (2), it could use the associative structure established for Sentence (1) to store the embedded proposition in Sentence (2) and would need only to build associations to store the embedding proposition. Therefore, HAM would require fewer associations to store the pair of Sentences (1) and (2) than the pair of Sentences (3) and (4), and so recall should be higher for the first pair than for the second pair.

In the following experiment to test this prediction, each subject studied eight successive lists of 16 sentences with recall test immediately following each study list. In each list, four of the sentences represented each of the following four conditions:

Control—Sentences were composed from new words never before encountered by the subjects in the experiment.

ASR (Across-Sentence Repetition)—The two nouns and the adjective were repeated from different sentences in the past list. Thus, the words had been studied previously, but never in that combination. This was a control for the effect of sheer repetition of the words.

APR (Across-Proposition Repetition)—This is the condition exemplified by the pair of Sentences (3) and (4). That is, the adjective and the object noun were repeated from a single sentence of the past list. The subject noun was also repeated but taken from a different sentence. So this condition differs from ASR, because in that condition the adjective and object had not appeared in the same sentences before.

WPR (Within-Proposition Repetition)—This is the condition exemplified by Sentences (1) and (2). That is, the subject and adjective had occurred in the relative clause construction of a sentence from the preceding list. The object was taken from a sentence in the past list, but had not appeared before with the subject-adjective pair.

All repetition of element pairs was between lists. Within a particular list of 16 sentences there was no repetition of any content words. So all the sentences on list 1 were equivalent because each presented a novel configuration of words. It is only on later trials that we expect differences between conditions. The words that were repeated in conditions ASR, APR, and WPR occurred once on each of the eight lists. Also, the particular pairings that were repeated in conditions APR or WPR were repeated in all eight lists. Hence, in condition WPR, by the eighth study-list the subject would have heard the phrase "The hippie who was tall . . ." eight times in the experiment. The one word that was never repeated in any of the conditions was the verb. Thus it could serve to uniquely cue the recall of a particular sentence.

A total of 35 subjects were tested in this experiment. A different set of sentences was randomly generated for each subject. The subjects studied the sentences one at a time on IBM cards at a 15-second rate. After studying the 16 sentences in a list, the subjects received a cued recall test of the sentences in the same order as they had been studied. This involved presenting on IBM cards the adjective and the verb as cues in a sentence frame such as the following:

THE   WHO WAS TALL TOUCHED THE

The subject's task was to recall by filling in the missing two nouns. Subjects were given 15 seconds to make their recall for each sentence. Sentences were tested in the same order as they were studied, thereby insuring a constant lag between study and test. After completing this procedure for one list of 16 sentences, the procedure was immediately repeated for the next list, and so on through the eight successive lists. Including instructions, the experimental session lasted about 75 minutes.

Figure 6.5 displays the results of this experiment in terms of the mean number of words correctly recalled in each condition. Figure 6.5a shows the recall of the first noun in the sentence, N_1, which was the subject (i.e., *hippie*). This is the word that was constantly paired with the same adjective in condition WPR. As can be seen, recall of this subject-noun continuously improves across trials in condition WPR as it is re-paired again and again with the same adjective. In contrast, recall of N_1 for the other conditions is relatively constant, showing little in the way of reliable trends. So, we have clear evidence that subjects are able to take advantage of within-proposition repetition and hence use the memory structure established for the subject-adjective proposition in one sentence to help record it in a subsequent sentence. Overall, 66% of the N_1 words were recalled in condition WPR. This contrasts with 40% in condition APR, 41% in ASR, and 46% in the control condition. None of these latter three conditions are significantly different from one another, but all are very significantly worse than condition WPR (statistics by a Duncan's range test).

Figure 6.5b shows the results for recall of N_2, the object in the sentence (i.e., *debutante*). There seems to be little improvement across trials in any of the conditions and little difference among the conditions. Overall, 45% of the N_2 words

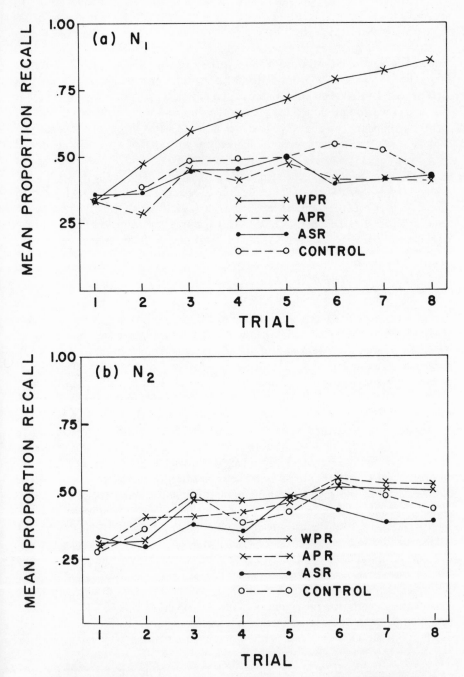

FIG. 6.5. Recall of sentences of the form: "The N_1 who was ADJ VERBED the N_2."

were recalled in condition WPR, 45% in condition APR, 38% in condition ASR, and 42% in the control condition. According to a Duncan's range test, the conditions WPR and APR show significantly more recall than ASR ($p < .05$), but no other differences are significant. So, it appears that the subject derives at least some benefit in condition APR from the repetition of the adjective with N_2, despite their being in different propositions within the same sentence; this mild advantage only appears in a comparison to condition ASR in which elements were repeated from different sentences. Moreover, the improvement is not nearly so marked as the improvement in condition WPR of N_1 recall as a consequence of the repetition of N_1 with the adjective within a single atomic proposition. Also, the level of N_2 recall in condition APR is no different than N_2 recall in WPR. In condition WPR the N_2 element, although repeated, had not cooccurred previously with any other element in the sentence. The improvement of N_2 recall in condition WPR may be a consequence of the fact that subjects are able to focus on the proposition in which N_2 occurs because they already have encoded from past lists the other proposition in which N_1 occurs.

Repetition of Major Clause

To summarize the results of the last experiment, repetition of elements *within* a proposition in a sentence greatly improved recall, whereas repetition of elements *between* propositions had hardly any effect. We decided to pursue this repetition phenomena in a second experiment to further establish its generality and strength. Again we were principally concerned with contrasting within- versus between-proposition repetition of elements. However, this time we tried to load the surface sentences against the within-proposition condition and more in favor of the between-proposition condition. We contrasted the within-proposition repetition exemplified by Sentences (5) and (6) with the between-proposition repetition exemplified by Sentences (7) and (8).

The *hippie* who touched the debutante was *tall*.   (5)
The *hippie* who kissed the prostitute was *tall*.   (6)
The hippie who touched the *debutante* was *tall*.   (7)
The captain who kissed the *debutante* was *tall*.   (8)

In Sentences (5) and (6), although *hippie* and *tall* are repeated from the same underlying proposition, they occur at a considerable physical distance in the surface sentence because a relative clause intervenes between the elements. In contrast, in Sentences (7) and (8), although *debutante* and *tall* are taken from different propositions, they occur in close physical proximity in the surface sentence. Thus, the between-proposition repetition is being made very salient physically, while at the same time the within-proposition repetition is made physically obscure. It will be recalled that in the previous experiment, the cooccurring elements were at approximately equal physical distances in the two pairs of sentences.

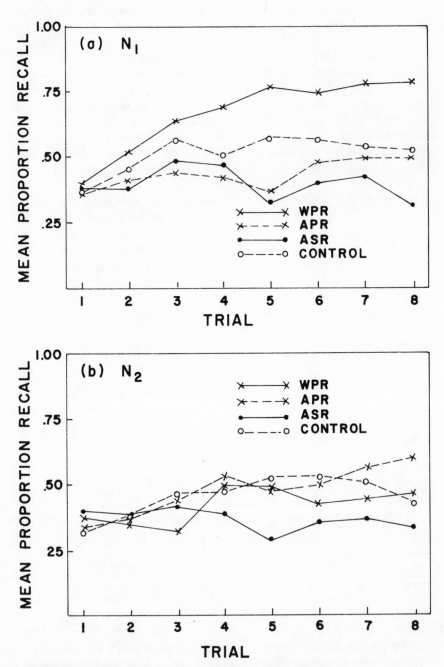

FIG. 6.6. Recall of sentences of the form: "The N_1 who VERBED the N_2 was ADJ."

Except for the surface structure of the sentences studied, this experiment was identical in design and procedure to the previous experiment. A total of 46 subjects were run. The results, displayed in Figure 6.6, appear quite similar to those in Figure 6.5. With respect to N_1 recall, there was the expected increase across trials in the WPR condition. The overall levels of N_1 recall were nearly identical to those of the previous experiment: 67% for condition WPR (66% in the previous experiment), 44% for condition APR (40% in the previous experiment), 40% for condition ASR (41% previously), and 51% for the control condition (46% previously). Again, recall in the WPR condition was much superior to all others. However, in this experiment recall in the control condition is significantly superior to both conditions APR and ASR ($p < .05$). In the previous experiment, this difference was in the same direction but did not reach statistical significance. The difference may indicate negative transfer in conditions APR and ASR because the adjective is constantly being re-paired with a new N_1 term. There were no other significant differences with respect to N_1 recall.

Again there appears to be little effect in N_2 recall (see Figure 6.6b) either in terms of changes across trials or differences among the conditions. The overall levels of N_2 recall in this experiment were quite similar to the previous: For condition WPR, 42% in this experiment (45% in the previous), for condition APR 48% (versus 45%), for condition ASR 36% (versus 38%), and for the control condition 45% (versus 42%). However, more of the small differences between conditions achieved marginal significance (.05 level) than in the previous experiment. A Duncan's range test finds all conditions superior to the ASR condition, suggesting considerable negative transfer in this case. Condition APR is also superior to WPR, suggesting some slight benefit of the across-proposition repetition of N_2 with the adjective. However, neither condition APR or WPR is significantly different from the control condition.

So, it seems that our attempt to manipulate perceptual saliency of the repeating elements has had relatively little effect on the character of the results. The one substantial effect in the data is still the across-trials increase in N_1 recall in condition WPR. Although there was a slight improvement in the amount of N_2 recall in condition APR, it was not so much as to become a clear-cut effect statistically. Thus, we must conclude that, as predicted by the MATCH process, human memory appears to be set up in such a way that it can only easily detect and take advantage of repetition of elements within an atomic proposition.

Rosenberg's Results

We would like to relate our theory to some experiments by Sheldon Rosenberg (1968a, 1968b, 1969, 1970) that seem to establish some of the same points that we have been making in our research, but using somewhat different procedures. His 1969 experiment is rather similar in logic to our last two. He compared subjects' recall of sentences like Sentence (9) with their recall of sentences like Sentence (10).

The doctor who fired the janitor cured the patient.   (9)
The doctor who fired the janitor shook the author.   (10)

The important difference between these two is that in Sentence (9) the main clause
"The doctor cured the patient" is likely to be already recorded in the subject's
memory, probably many times over, since we all know of many different doctors
having cured many different patients. In contrast, the main clause in Sentence (10),
"The doctor shook the author," is likely to be a novel assertion for most subjects.
Rosenberg also examined subjects' recall of sentences like Sentences (11) and (12)
in which the relative clause might contain the well-known proposition.

The doctor who cured the patient fired the janitor.   (11)
The doctor who shook the author fired the janitor.   (12)

The subjects in Rosenberg's experiment studied lists of 10 such sentences and
then were asked to free-recall the sentences. The results he obtained are entirely
consonant with our own. Recall of the well-known proposition in one sentence was
higher than of the corresponding unknown proposition in another sentence.
Rosenberg also examined recall of the second, novel proposition in the sentence
(i.e., "The doctor fired the janitor"). Recall of this novel proposition was higher
when it occurred with a well-known proposition, as in Sentence (11), than with
another novel proposition, as in Sentence (12). This accords with our finding that
N_2 recall was higher in the Within-Proposition Repetition condition (WPR) than in
the Across-Sentence Repetition condition (ASR), although in neither condition had
N_2 been repeated with an element from the sentence.

In another experiment, Rosenberg (1968b) contrasted the recall of highly
interassociated sentences like Sentence (13) with sentences like Sentence (14).

The old king ruled wisely.   (13)
The poor king dined gravely.   (14)

Of course, sentences like Sentence (13) are more likely to be already partially or
totally recorded in memory and hence are better recalled. The more interesting
finding was that these highly interassociated sentences were recalled largely in an
all-or-none manner. They did not show the same word-to-word transitional error
probabilities that are found with unfamiliar sentences. The *transition error
probability* denotes the probability of *not* recalling the $(n+1)$st word, given that the
nth word in the sentence is recalled. In unfamiliar sentences, these transition error
probabilities were high across major syntactic boundaries such as the
subject-predicate boundary (see also Johnson, 1968). In contrast, higher interphrase
transition error probabilities were not found with the highly interassociated
sentences. Rosenberg concluded that these sentences must have been "recoded into
units that transcend the phrase boundary." The unitary memory for such sentences

is just what HAM would predict. Since the propositions are largely or entirely recorded in memory already, HAM only needs to tag these preexisting propositions as to-be-recalled material. In contrast, as will be shown in Chapter 7, fragmentary recall occurs in abundance when HAM must encode all the associations in a novel input sentence like Sentence (14).

On the Mnemonic Structure of SVO Propositions

The earlier experiments on the MATCH function used repetition of complete atomic propositions (e.g., "The *hippie* who is *tall* touched the debutante"). In those cases, the MATCH process was able to locate and reuse a complete propositional tree while encoding the "partially repeated" sentence. But what about repetition of subparts of a single proposition? Which subpart repetitions will HAM be able to recognize and reuse?

Consider first a pair repetition using simple SVO propositions. Let $S_1 V_1 O_1$ denote the first proposition studied. Its later mate can be either $S_1 V_1 O_2$, $S_1 V_2 O_1$, or $S_2 V_1 O_1$, where the repeated pairs have the same subscript. The MATCH and IDENTIFY processes within HAM see all these as symmetrical. In each case, HAM should recognize the cooccurring pair and reuse any old memory structure involving that pair in order to encode the new sentence. For example, in the case of a subject-object repetition, input of the second sentence $S_1 V_2 O_1$ should match up with the old memory structure $S_1 V_1 O_1$ and result in the encoding of a verb conjunction of the form $S_1 (V_1 \text{ } and \text{ } V_2) O_1$. Significantly, the associative path in the tree from S_1 to O_1 is strengthened just as much by a partial SO repetition with a changed verb $(S_1 V_2 O_1)$ as it would be by a complete repetition of the full proposition.

This prediction has been tested twice in our laboratory, once 6 years ago by Samuel Bobrow and again last year by Michael Fehling. The results both times were strictly in accord with the model's prediction. To describe Bobrow's earlier experiment, the subjects studied a list of 45 SVO sentences exemplifying various control and repetition conditions within the study list. For our purposes here, the conditions of relevance were: the "once-presented" control ($S_1 V_1 O_1$ once), the "twice-presented" control ($S_1 V_1 O_1$ twice), and the "changed verb" condition ($S_1 V_1 O_1$, then $S_1 V_2 O_1$).

The sentence which repeated the critical elements occurred in the input list at least 10 sentences after its initial mate. After studying all the sentences, the subjects were tested by being presented with the subject noun and were asked to recall the object noun. The average lag or number of intervening items from the last study of an item to its test trial was the same for the three conditions.

The comparison of interest is the probability of correct object recall to the subject cue. For the once-presented sentences, this probability was .33; for the twice-presented sentences (with the same verb), it was .67; for the condition with SO repetition (but different verbs), this probability was .68. So clearly, there is a pairwise repetition effect (within the repeated pair); and clearly it is about the same magnitude whether the third content element is kept the same or is changed. This is all in accord with HAM's predictions.

Consider a further prediction along these general lines. In this case, we change the object noun paired with a given subject, and we do this either keeping the same verb or changing the verb as well as the object. The case with SV (same-verb) repetition is symbolized as "$S_1 V_1 O_1$ then $S_1 V_1 O_2$," whereas with changing verb the symbols are "$S_1 V_1 O_1$ then $S_1 V_2 O_2$." Bobrow compared these conditions in a second part of his experiment. Following study of the list, the subject was given the subject-noun as a cue and was asked to recall *both* objects that had been paired with that subject. The probabilities of recall of O_1 and O_2 for the SV repetition condition were .56 and .39, respectively, with a mean of .48. For the changed-verb condition, O_1 and O_2 recall probabilities were .47 and .30, respectively, with a mean of .38. There is a "primacy" effect in these data; it is a frequent result in such within-list comparisons and is perhaps comprehensible in terms of the subject, at the time of the repetition, retrieving and rehearsing the earlier proposition (see our discussion of "negative transfer" in Chapter 10).

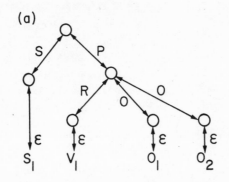

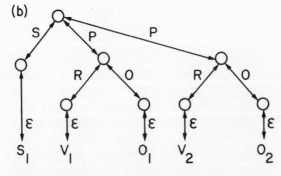

FIG. 6.7. HAM's representation of the sentence pairs from the Bobrow experiment: (*a*) Same verb conditions; and (*b*) Different verb condition.

Disregarding that auxiliary effect, what does HAM predict for object recall in this experiment? In terms of reuseable memory structure, the condition which uses the same verb should produce a simple object conjunction (see Figure 6.7a), reusing the same links up to the predicate node. However, when a new verb is used, $S_1 V_2 O_2$, more new structure has to be built, because this new verb causes a predicate conjunction (see Figure 6.7b). The "sentence-to-predicate" link is reused in the structure in Figure 6.7a, but not in the structure shown in Figure 6.7b. For this reason, w' would expect recall of either object to be somewhat higher in the same-verb condition than in the changed-verb condition. This was true, as shown by the proportions reported above.

A further, more refined prediction concerns the *correlation* between recall of O_1 and O_2 in these two cases. In the same-verb case (Figure 6.7a), recall of O_1 to S means that the path from S up to the predicate node is intact, so therefore further recall of O_2 requires just the two links from this predicate node to the O_2 word. On the other hand, for the changed-verb case (Figure 6.7b), recall of O_1 to S insures only that the path from S to the fact node is intact, so that further recall of O_2 would require three links (P, O, ϵ) to have been established and retained. For these reasons, one expects recall of O_1 and O_2 to the S cue to be more highly correlated in the same-verb case than in the changed-verb case. This is just what Bobrow found: tabulating recall and nonrecall of O_1 and O_2 in a 2×2 matrix (pooling across items and subjects), there was a significant positive correlation in O_1 and O_2 recall for the same-verb condition, but virtually no correlation for the changed-verb condition. So that detail is also in line with the sentence representations and MATCH processes used by HAM.

6.3. STIMULUS RECOGNITION

Having described the MATCH process by which HAM accesses propositions stored in its memory, and having described some relevant evidence from sentence-memory experiments, it is appropriate to turn now to a somewhat more general discussion of stimulus recognition. In the following, the terms "stimulus recognition," "pattern recognition," "pattern classification," and "stimulus identification" will all be used interchangeably as equivalent terms. The issue under consideration is how the processes and structures of HAM's memory might be applied to pattern (or concept) learning and pattern identification.

In everyday parlance, we commonly distinguish between several different types of recognition performance. The first and major distinction is that between class recognition versus individual identification. In cases of class recognition, the stimulus object or event is assigned to one of several categories or classes; for instance, handwritten As, zebras, pencils, and human faces. While it is possible to talk about recognition of abstract concepts such as "male chauvinism" or "morality," we will confine our discussion to recognition of more or less perceptual concepts.

Recognition of an individual, the second major type of recognition performance, differs from concept recognition in that we do not recognize the object as a member of a class or set, but rather as an entity that shares a spatiotemporal continuity with an entity previously encountered. Namely, we conceive of the two entities as identical, independent of whether they share the same attributes or not. Thus, Joe Krud is still recognized as the same individual after he (she?) undergoes a sex change and becomes Josephine Krud. Individual identification, as a set of performances, can be subdivided into judgments of familiarity and retrieval of associated contextual facts. Examples of the first are judgments that we have or have not experienced a particular stimulus pattern before; of the second, that we can remember the context in which we last (or first) experienced this pattern.

An Overview of the Recognition Process

We have now classified the several types of recognition performance: recognition of classes, of individuals, and of familiar patterns, with or without retrieval of context. Examples would be, respectively, that I can recognize dogs, that one is Spot, and I first met Spot last week at a friend's house, or the dog is familiar but I cannot recall anything about him. In each of these cases we suppose that the "perceptual parser" has extracted a relevant description of the critical features of the stimulus pattern and their interrelations. This description corresponds to a (possibly large) network of propositions and also constitutes the input to HAM. A "concept" or "perceptual category" corresponds, in HAM, to a stored description network. As a consequence of exposure to many variable instances, the original network has been modified, certain features have been dropped or added, some relations have been made mandatory, others optional, and so on. The concept network thus summarizes the information regarding class membership criteria abstracted from HAM's encounters with a series of instances of the class.

The description network of particular concepts is stored in memory, and the input network describing the current scene is sent to memory to find the best matching concept. The MATCH process described earlier in this chapter would be used for carrying out this memory search. The current program would report out the most specific or detailed concept giving the greatest degree of match to the input tree. Thus, given a clear perceptual description, it would say that a given pattern is "Spot" rather than saying "dog" or "hairy quadruped." Of course, the system could answer affirmatively to the question "Is the following a picture of a dog?" when shown a picture of Spot. In principle, this could be done either by identifying the individual *Spot*, then evoking the ϵ link to the concept *dog*; or the MATCH function itself, comparing the dog-template to the Spot-description, could be set to return a yes whenever a sufficient number of template features were matched, ignoring the extra features in the input that distinguish Spot from other dogs. This latter strategy is effective only when the test stimulus (Spot) is a subset of the question stimulus (dog).

As an incidental but relevant point here, it is obvious that with multiobject scenes, the question which is posed will itself direct the focus of attention. If the question is about a dog, the perceptual parser should not concentrate on encoding the mountains in the background of the picture. The question determines the way in which the picture will be processed. For the question "Is the black man tall?", a crowd scene would first be scanned to find a black man, and then check to see whether he is tall. But for the question "Is the tall man black?", the scanning would look first for a tall man, then check to see whether he is black.

To return to our comparison of recognitive types, all of these forms—class or individual recognition with or without retrieval of context—can be represented and implemented in HAM in exactly the same way. Basically, the "concept" or "event" in memory is a description network; the input is a description network; HAM's MATCH process brings them together.

The MATCH process reports out a measure of the maximal "degree of match," and we presume that this measure corresponds to the feeling of familiarity which we experience in recognition. The perceptual description may also have further information attached to its collection node—facts known about the pattern, such as its context of acquisition. This link to the context is what is accessed in the typical laboratory studies of "recognition memory" using familiar stimuli. HAM would first access the memory node corresponding to the test item CAT, and then it would check to see whether the most recent context associated to that node is a prototype of the relevant experimental context (e.g., LIST-1). This suggests that if the test stimulus itself is degraded, somewhat altered, or just poorly learned, the feeling of familiarity might be enhanced by supplying an acquisition context as an additional cue. For example, we may not fully recognize a person until he reminds us of where we had met before and of other events associated with that meeting. These extra bits of information increase the overall matching score and our sense of familiarity with the person's appearance.

A topic not specifically discussed in this last section is recognition of sentences and propositions, but our treatment of such matters is detailed in earlier sections of this chapter. It is with respect to these materials that our theory of recognition is most explicitly formulated. It is also with these materials that we have attempted careful empirical tests of this theory. In this section we have been trying to outline how the theory would generalize to the nonlinguistic domain. In summary, the associative theory embodied in HAM would seem capable in principle of dealing with all the more salient forms of recognition we have discussed. What is lacking in our efforts is an explicit development of a "perceptual parser," that wondrous machine which will sort out the relevant information from the noise in the stimulus array and deliver up to HAM a well-formed description-tree of just the critical variables and relations. Those working on scene-analysis programs know that *that* is the really tough problem. We have not worked on it at all, since our main concern has been with sentence memory. Our discussion therefore relies very heavily on the scene-analysis programs of Guzman (1968) and Winston (1970), and their logical extensions, and we have shown how the scene descriptions output by their programs could serve as the input to HAM's memory. Within the purview of that discussion, HAM seems to provide a reasonable hypothesis for understanding how recognition performances come about.

7
MODEL FOR SENTENCE LEARNING

In thus deriving memory from association, it is never to be forgotten that every concrete memory-process is by no means a simple process, but is made up of a large number of elementary processes.

—Wilhelm Wundt

7.1. THE MATHEMATICAL FORMULATION

In this chapter we will develop our theory regarding the encoding of sentences into memory, provide an explicit mathematical (probabilistic) model of the process, and report several experimental tests of this explicit model. Memory for sentences has been one of the favored ways to study their mental representation. The general working premise has been that contingencies in recall of sentential elements reflect proximities of the elements in the underlying mnemonic representation of the sentence. We shall not review here the research of others using this strategy, but will refer the interested reader to reviews by Fillenbaum (1971) or Wanner (1968).

Past research efforts generally have lacked an explicit model of how a particular mnemonic representation is derived from the input, how it is stored, and how it is retrieved—all of which processes result in a particular pattern of recall probabilities of various sentential fragments. HAM provides just such a possible theory, which we will now explicate.

When HAM hears a sentence such as our standard "In a park a hippie touched a debutante," it has direct access to the word nodes in memory; it also has in working memory the parsed tree structure shown in Figure 7.1, in which lowercase letters denote newly created memory nodes which serve to group together lower elements in the labeled graph structure. The concepts or ideas are also connected to the actual words of the sentence by the relations labeled W. The concept nodes and their word associations already exist in memory. All the structure above the concept nodes in Figure 7.1 is new and is recording the novel information in the

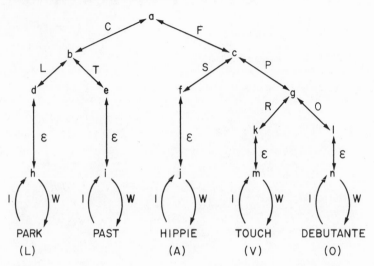

FIG. 7.1. An example of a propositional representation generated by HAM.

sentence. To encode this sentence into memory, each of the 13 links above the concept nodes must be transformed into long-term memory associations. Once a link is encoded as an association, it may be evoked in the future to retrieve information about the sentence. In later chapters (Chapters 9 and 10), an extensive discussion is given about matters such as guessing and deductive strategies evoked by the subject when he is asked about a proposition not explicitly recorded in memory, about implicit elaborations a subject will make when hearing the overtly stated propositions, and about interference between propositions and consequent forgetting of information. All these matters serve to enrich and complicate the study of human memory. However, in the verbatim memory tests used in the research under immediate discussion, we hope that such complicating factors have been kept to a minimum. The principal determinant of recall patterns should be the stochastic process by which links in an input tree like Figure 7.1 are converted into long-term memory associations.

We assume that the linkages between nodes in memory mechanistically determine what the subject can recall. Thus in Figure 7.1, for the subject to recall L to A there must be an intact associative path between the concept node for L and the concept node for A. If any association is missing in the path, recall will fail. In addition, for successful recall the I connection from the word A must be intact as must the W connection to the word L. For the subject to recall A to L, the same interidea associative path must be intact as well as the W connection to A and the I connection from L. By use of these W and I connections we will be able to capture the role of response availability and stimulus effectiveness in recall. The effects of the sentential representation will be reflected by the interidea associations. In this way, we hope to separate three factors that have been confounded in past research on sentence memory.

The Encoding of Associations

This conception of sentence memory may be converted into a stochastic model that delivers detailed predictions about patterns in sentence recall. All predictions will depend on the simple assumption that the probability of encoding an input link into long-term memory will depend solely on how long that link resides in working memory. In particular, this probability is assumed to be independent of how many other links are being encoded from working memory, and it is independent of how many of these links or which ones are successfully encoded.

Thus, there is no process-versus-capacity tradeoff such that the more links to be stored, the less effort devoted to the formation of any particular one link. There is only one limitation on the formation of associations, and that is the number of links that can be held in working memory. This number of active links in turn is determined by the number of long-term memory nodes that must be recruited to support the input structure. We place only this one restriction on encoding input simply in the interest of parsimony. There is no need to assume multiple restrictions until data can be marshalled to justify their postulation. We shall assume a simple relationship between the time t an input link resides in memory and the probability that it is encoded into memory as an association; namely, there is an exponential distribution of times at which the encoding will succeed. The mean of the distribution will be denoted as a. Thus, letting $f(t)$ represent the probability density for forming an association, the following equation holds:

$$f(t) = \frac{1}{a}\, e^{-t/a} \tag{1}$$

Letting $p(t)$ denote the probability of forming an association by time t, Equation (2) follows by integrating Equation (1):

$$p(t) = 1 - e^{-t/a} \tag{2}$$

For reasons of parsimony, it is assumed that for a particular input tree, the parameter a is constant for all associations in that input.

Given these assumptions, some interesting facts may be derived about the encoding of an input that has n associative links. First, consider how many associations would be established if the input were studied for t seconds. The number of associations formed, k, is binomially distributed with parameters $(1 - e^{-t/a})$ and n:

$$p(k = i) = \binom{n}{i}(1 - e^{-t/a})^i (e^{-t/a})^{n-i} \tag{3}$$

The mean number of associations formed, $E(k)$, is:

$$E(k) = n(1 - e^{-t/a}) \qquad (4)$$

A related question is how long it will take to encode an input with n associations. Let T_n be the time to encode n associations. Interesting properties of the probability density of T_n depend upon three facts: (a) the time between the formation of the ith and $(i+1)$st association (out of n) will be exponentially distributed with parameter $a/(n-i)$; (b) the "interarrival" times in (a) are independent; and (c) T_n is the sum of these n interarrival times. It follows from these facts that T_n has a generalized gamma distribution (see McGill, 1963) with mean and variance as follows:

$$E(T_n) = a \sum_{L=1}^{n} \frac{1}{L} \qquad (5)$$

$$Var(T_n) = a^2 \sum_{L=1}^{n} \frac{1}{L^2} \qquad (6)$$

The Central-Limit Theorem applies to T_n since it is a sum of independently distributed random variables. Therefore, as n becomes large, the distribution of T_n will tend to a normal distribution with the mean and variance given by Equations (5) and (6).

With this as background, let us now consider what might happen when a subject is asked to remember the sentence "In a park a hippie touched a debutante." The input structure of Figure 7.1 would be set up temporarily in working memory, and the subject would attempt to encode all 13 interidea links in the input tree. For illustration, let us suppose that he succeeds in encoding 11 of the 13 associations during the study trial and is left with the memory structure of Figure 7.2 as his record of the sentence. When we later probe his memory for the sentence with the word "hippie," the subject would recall, "I remember the hippie did something to the debutante, but I can't remember what or where."

This example illustrates the basic experimental paradigm that will concern us in this chapter. That is, after studying a sequence of unrelated sentences, a subject is presented with parts of the sentences he has studied and is asked to recall the remainder. The structural assumptions of the theory plus its encoding assumptions deliver interesting predictions about the patterns of recall that should be obtained in such experiments. For instance, consider the structure of the input in Figure 7.1. Note that V is closer in number of links to O than it is to L or A. Therefore, V should be a better cue for O simply because fewer associative links have to be established to connect the two. These are the sort of phenomena that are to be captured in the mathematical predictions derived from the model. Unfortunately, the mathematical model that will generate empirically viable predictions must be more complicated than indicated so far. Let us therefore begin to uncover these mathematical complications.

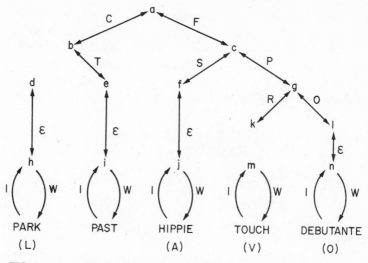

FIG. 7.2. A partial encoding of the sentence "In the park the hippie touched the debutante."

Subject and Item Differences

A first problem concerns the fact that the model, as presented so far, only describes what would happen for a single subject for a single sentence. However, the data to be predicted is average data taken from many subjects studying many different sentences. Individual subjects vary enormously in the ability they display in learning. Also, an individual subject will vary in how well he remembers different sentences. His mind will wander during the study of one sentence, whereas he may concentrate very hard while studying another sentence. The problem, then, is that while it may be reasonable to assume that the learning paramater a is constant across all associations to be formed within a sentence, it is completely implausible to assume that the parameter will be the same across sentences in a pool of observations taken from many subjects.

If we ignored this problem and fit the model to average data, assuming a constant parameter a for all sentences, what would be the consequences? Basically, the model would underpredict the frequency with which subjects recall the total sentence or recall nothing at all. The parameter a estimated from average data would be approximately the mean of the distribution of the parameter a across individual sentences and subjects in the sample. For sentences from the pool with a less than the mean we would observe more complete failures to recall than predicted, whereas for sentences with a higher than the mean we would observe much more total recall than predicted. In fact, when we tried to predict recall data with an average parameter a we consistently underpredicted the amount of all-or-none recall.

What is needed to rigorously apply the model to average data is information about the distribution of the parameter a across individual sentences in the observation pool. We will hypothesize a particular probability density of the parameter a over the sentences for the typical experiment. This hypothesis has only two things to commend it: It does not seem unreasonable a priori, and it leads to mathematically tractable results. Our hypothesis concerns the probability density of the reciprocal of a, which gives us the *speed* or *rate* at which associations are formed. We will assume that the probability density of the rate, $1/a$, is itself an exponential distribution with mean b:

$$f\left(\frac{1}{a}\right) = \frac{1}{b} e^{-1/ba} \tag{7}$$

The probability density of a can now be determined by a simple change of variable, viz.,

$$f(a) = \frac{1}{ba^2} e^{-1/ba} \tag{8}$$

One is really interested in the probability distribution of $p(t)$, the probability of forming an association in t seconds. It can be computed by another change of variable using Equations (2) and (8):

$$f[p(t)] = \frac{1}{tb} [1 - p(t)]^{-(tb-1)/tb} \tag{9}$$

This is a special case of the beta distribution which is defined as:

$$f(x) = \frac{\Gamma(\alpha + \beta)}{\Gamma(\alpha)\Gamma(\beta)} x^{\alpha-1}(1 - x)^{\beta-1} \tag{10}$$

where Γ denotes the gamma function. Our distribution has the parameter $\alpha = 1$ and $\beta = 1/tb$. The mean of this distribution, $E[p(t)]$, is

$$E[p(t)] = \frac{tb}{tb + 1} \tag{11}$$

and its variance is

$$Var[p(t)] = \frac{1}{2tb + 1}\left[\frac{tb}{tb + 1}\right]^2 \tag{12}$$

The effective parameter in this probability density is tb, which is the product of the time available for encoding, t, and the overall mean rate of encoding, b. Figure 7.3 illustrates how the probability density, $f[p(t)]$, will vary with the parameter tb. The densities are well behaved in that they shift towards 1 as tb increases. That is, the probability of forming an association will increase both with increases in the encoding time, t, and with increases in the mean encoding rate for the population of sentences, b.

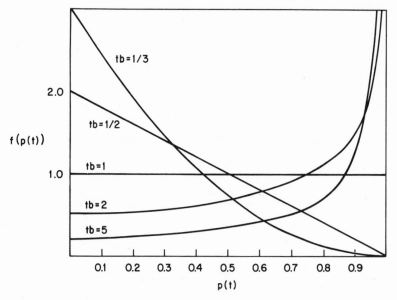

FIG. 7.3. The probability density $f[p(t)]$ for various values of tb.

To derive predictions about the average recall patterns of sentences, we need to determine the value of $Q(k, n)$, which is the probability of encoding a particular k of the n associations that are in working memory. Its value is given by the following integral:

$$Q(k, n) = \int_0^1 p(t)^k [1 - p(t)]^{n-k} f[p(t)] \, dp(t) \tag{13}$$

To explain this equation, we first are determining the probability, $p(t)^k [1 - p(t)]^{n-k}$ of forming a particular k association in the input for each value of $p(t)$, weighting this by the probability density $f[p(t)]$ at that value, and integrating this over the 0 to 1 domain of $f[p(t)]$. This integration gives the following:

$$Q(k, n) = \frac{1}{tbn + 1} \prod_{i=1}^{k} \frac{tbi}{tb(n - 1) + 1} \tag{14}$$

Again, the effective parameter is tb. To illustrate $Q(k, n)$, Table 7.1 shows it for n up to 12 when $tb = 1$. When $tb = 1$, $E[p(t)] = tb/(tb+1) = .5$. Note that although the mean probability of forming a single association is .5, the probability of forming n out of n associations is much higher than $.5^n$ and the probability of forming 0 out of n associations is similarly much higher than $.5^n$. The function $Q(k, n)$ thus shows a marked deviation in the direction of all-or-none encoding of

TABLE 7.1

Values of $Q(k, n)$, the Likelihood of Forming k Out of n Possible Associations. The Parameter tb is 1.

						n						
k	1	2	3	4	5	6	7	8	9	10	11	12
0	.500	.333	.250	.200	.167	.143	.1250	.1111	.1000	.0909	.0833	.0769
1	.500	.167	.083	.050	.033	.024	.0179	.0139	.0111	.0091	.0076	.0064
2		.333	.083	.033	.017	.010	.0060	.0040	.0028	.0020	.0015	.0012
3			.250	.050	.017	.007	.0036	.0020	.0012	.0008	.0005	.0003
4				.200	.033	.010	.0036	.0016	.0008	.0004	.0003	.0002
5					.167	.024	.0060	.0020	.0008	.0004	.0002	.0001
6						.143	.0179	.0040	.0012	.0004	.0002	.0001
7							.1250	.0139	.0028	.0008	.0003	.0001
8								.1111	.0111	.0020	.0005	.0002
9									.1000	.0091	.0015	.0003
10										.0909	.0076	.0012
11											.0833	.0064
12												.0769

the associations. The function $Q(k, n)$ represents how the probabilities of individual associations covary across sentences in the data pool.

Response Availability Parameters

In fitting this model to data, a grid search will be performed over the values of tb to find a minimum chi-square estimate. However, in fitting this model to data it is necessary to estimate more parameters than just tb. The problem is that the parameter tb only governs the formation of *interidea* associations, but these associations in themselves will not permit recall of the words in the sentence. One needs to get from these ideas to the appropriate words. For instance, even if the subject perfectly encoded the input of Figure 7.1, he would not be guaranteed verbatim recall of the words "park," "hippie," "touch," and "debutante." The subject would still have to be able to get from the terminal concept nodes in the encoding of the sentence to the corresponding word nodes. The process by which one moves from a concept to a word is not well worked out in the model, but it is clear that the transition will not always be perfect. An illustration of the difficulty is the common experience of not being able to "find the words" to express an idea. A second problem involves word synonymy. That is, if more than one word expresses the same concept (e.g., postman and mailman), how does the subject remember which was the correct word he heard? We are not able to offer any enlightening solutions to these matters. We sidestep the matter by merely noting that *on the average* there will be some probability, r, of getting from the concept to the verbatim correct word and that this probability will, in general, be less than one. This probability will serve to reflect the availability of the particular word as a response to the concept.

In this research a different value of r has been estimated for each type of word in the sentence that must be recalled. There are two reasons for doing this. First, it is not unreasonable to suppose that the difficulty in getting from the concept to an appropriate word will be different for different classes of words (e.g., locations versus verbs). Second, the value of r tends to reflect biases in the encoding process. For example, the subject might focus on the first or last word in the sentence at the expense of others. One consequence of this focusing might be that the probability of getting from concept to word would be higher. Of course, it is also possible that focusing may affect the parameter a which governs the probability of forming a particular association, rather than just response availability. If focusing does have this effect, then permitting different values of r helps protect the model from disconfirmation because of that failure of assumption. A constant value of a had been assumed only for purposes of simplicity and tractability. So it would not be an interesting failure of the model in any case.

Covariation of the r_i

For each sentence, then, there is a set of parameters r_i. Presumably, the probability r_i will vary across sentences just as the probability, $p(t)$, of forming interidea associations. We previously introduced a hypothesis of how the probabilities, $p(t)$, of forming individual idea-to-idea associations within a sentence covaried across sentences. For similar reasons, the parameters r_i for different responses within a sentence may be expected to covary across sentences—that is, for some sentences in the pool these parameters will all be high, and for other sentences they will all be low. The task of producing a model of this covariance is more difficult than the previous covariance for two reasons. First, the different r_i's have different means and distributions, whereas we could assume one distribution $f[p(t)]$ for all the associative links in a sentence. Secondly, we have no clear idea of what the mechanisms are that permit the idea-to-word transitions. Therefore it is difficult to justify any probabilistic model of their effect.

Our solution to the second problem was to adopt, arbitrarily, the probability density adopted for $p(t)$. So, adapting Equation (9) we have:

$$f(r_i) = \frac{1}{\alpha_i} (1 - r_i)^{-(\alpha_i - 1)/\alpha_i} \qquad (15)$$

This gives the distribution of r_i across sentences in the observation pool. There was no strong justification for this probability density of r_i except that it was well behaved and served us well in the past. In equation (15) α_i plays the same role as tb in Equation (9). We will also assume that $\alpha_i = tb_i$, where t is study time and b_i is the rate parameter. Hence, α_i should increase with study time or the mean encoding rate for word i, b_i.

Let us now turn to the difficult problem of how to express the covariance of these different distributions of r_i. With respect to the associations, it was assumed that $p(t)$ for each association within a sentence was identical. We cannot assume that different parameters r_i and r_j are identical for each sentence because r_i and r_j have different densities across sentences. Rather, we will assume that within a single sentence r_i and r_j will be associated with the same cumulative probability in the population. That is, for a particular sentence, r_i may be .7 and r_j may be .9, but the

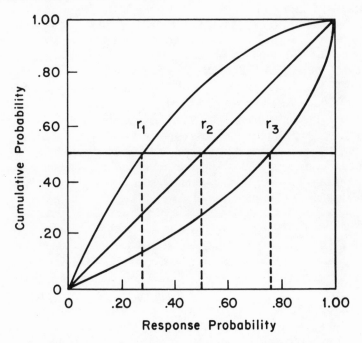

FIG. 7.4. Cumulative distributions of response probabilities.

area of the probability density to the left of r_i will be identical to the probability area to the left of r_j. That is to say, r_i and r_j for a particular sentence have the same "percentile scores" in their respective distributions.

Figure 7.4 illustrates what is being assumed. Three cumulative distributions of response probabilities are shown—for response 1 with $\alpha_1 = .5$; for response 2 with $\alpha_2 = 1.0$; and for response 3 with $\alpha_3 = 2.0$. The horizontal line intersecting the ordinate at .5 represents a sentence at the 50th percentile. The abscissa value at which it intersects the ith cumulative distribution gives the value of r_i for that sentence. In this case, we have $r_1 = .29$; $r_2 = .50$; and $r_3 = .75$ for this sentence.

Probabilities of Response Availability Patterns

We want eventually to derive the probability that a specific k out of n idea-to-word associations are intact. In order to begin this computation we will need the cumulative distribution, F, for r_i, which is:

$$F(r_i) = 1 - (1 - r_i)^{1/\alpha_i} \qquad (16)$$

From Equation (16) r_i can be expressed as a function of $F(r_i)$:

$$r_i = 1 - [1 - F(r_i)]^{\alpha_i} \qquad (17)$$

Letting $q_i = 1 - r_i$ denote the probability that the idea-to-word connection fails, and letting $X = 1 - F(r_i)$, the following simple equation obtains from Equation

(17):

$$q_i = X^{\alpha_i} \tag{18}$$

The variable $X = 1 - F(r_i)$ is just the converse of the cumulative probability. For any i (i indexes a particular word), X has a simple density

$$f(X) = 1 \qquad 0 \leqslant X \leqslant 1 \tag{19}$$

Since all response probabilities for a single sentence have the same cumulative probability, all q_i will be functions of the same random variable, X. Therefore, to find the probability that *no* idea-to-word connections are established out of n, we need only to solve the following integral:

$$q_{12...n} = \int_0^1 \prod_i^n X^{\alpha_i} dX \tag{20}$$

On the left-hand side of Equation (20), we are using $q_{12...n}$ to denote that the idea-to-word connections are not established for words 1 through n. On the right-hand side of Equation (20), i indexes the n words. Equation (20) is derived from Equation (18), which expresses each q_i as a function of the common variable X, and from Equation (19), which gives the probability density of X. Equation (20) is weighting the value of the product Πq_i at each value of X by the probability density of X. Integrating, we find:

$$q_{12...n} = \frac{1}{\left(\sum_i^n \alpha_i + 1 \right)} \tag{21}$$

Equation (21) gives the probability of having no responses available, assuming the probability of priming any response within a single sentence is identical in "percentile score" to any other response probability.

We need to be able to calculate the probability of each possible combination of availability and nonavailability of the individual responses (idea-word links). Equation (21) is sufficient for this purpose. The notation $r_{ab...c} q_{xy...z}$ will be used to denote the probability that responses $a, b, ...,$ and c are available but responses x, $y, ...,$ and z are not. We will illustrate its use with a simple example where we are concerned with two responses, word 1 and word 2. From Equation (20) the probability that both words are unavailable, q_{12}, is $1/(\alpha_1 + \alpha_2 + 1)$. We can also calculate from Equation (20) the marginal probability $r_1 q_2$, that response 1 is available and response 2 is not: $r_1 q_2 = q_2 - q_{12}$. Similarly, we can calculate the probability that response 2 is available, but response 1 is not: $r_2 q_1 = q_1 - q_{12}$. Finally, we can calculate the probability that both responses are available: $r_{12} = 1 - r_1 q_2 - r_2 q_1 - q_{12}$. These provide the probability of all four combinations

TABLE 7.2

Example Computation of Response Probabilities

	Available	Not available	
Response 2 — Available	$r_{12} = \dfrac{\alpha_1 \alpha_2 (\alpha_1 + \alpha_2 + 2)}{(\alpha_1 + 1)(\alpha_2 + 1)(\alpha_1 + \alpha_2 + 1)}$	$r_2 q_1 = \dfrac{\alpha_2}{(\alpha_1 + \alpha_2 + 1)(\alpha_1 + 1)}$	$\dfrac{\alpha_2}{\alpha_2 + 1}$
Response 2 — Not available	$r_2 q_1 = \dfrac{\alpha_1}{(\alpha_1 + \alpha_2 + 1)(\alpha_2 + 1)}$	$q_{12} = \dfrac{1}{(\alpha_1 + \alpha_2 + 1)}$	$\dfrac{1}{\alpha_2 + 1}$
Total	$\dfrac{\alpha_1}{(\alpha_1 + 1)}$	$\dfrac{1}{(\alpha_1 + 1)}$	1

of availability and nonavailability of the two responses. These calculations are summarized in Table 7.2. This method can be generalized to any number of responses. That is, with Equation (21) one can calculate the probability of any combination of available and unavailable responses.

This, then, is the method by which the availability of various combinations of responses will be determined. Note that while the availability of one response covaries with that of another, these probabilities of responses, r_i, do not covary with the probability, $p(t)$, of establishing idea-to-idea associations. Different processes underlie these two mechanisms, and there is no reason to suppose that they will covary.

Stimulus-Cueing Parameters

One issue remains before turning to the experimental data. Just as it is not certain that the subject can get from a concept to a word, it is uncertain that he can get from the cue word to the concept. Words are notorious for their multiple meanings, and it is unclear how the subject manages to revive the appropriate interpretation of the word when he is cued. We have finessed this problem of how a cue word contacts a concept in the same way we finessed the problem of how a concept contacted a word. That is, we introduce a parameter, s_i, that is the probability that the cue word i makes contact with its appropriate concept. Just as with the response probabilities, a separate stimulus-cueing probability will be estimated for each word type in the sentence. These parameters tend to reflect varying stimulus effectiveness. In addition, the probabilities s_i will tend to reflect focusing and encoding biases just as had the probabilities r_i. We have not bothered to worry about possible covariances among these s_i parameters.

Summary

The mathematical complications are now at an end, and we are ready to apply our model to experimental data. We should emphasize how we have separately identified three components that have been confounded in past experimentation: The parameters r_i represent varying response availability; the parameters s_i the varying stimulus effectiveness, and the configuration of interidea associations the effects of sentential representation. Not surprisingly, to obtain separate estimates of all these factors will require an experimental design much more complicated than previous research efforts.

Our principle motivation in the experimentation will be to confirm hypotheses about the exact details of the sentential representation. One source of support for this representation will be reasonably satisfactory fits of our predictions to average data. However, as just seen, we have been forced to make a number of rather arbitrary assumptions to generate a quantitative model that yields satisfactory predictions. These assumptions were made to take account of the indisputable facts that subjects do differ a great deal in their ability, that they will favor one sentence over another in amount of processing, and that some words are more effective cues or better responses than others. Since these arbitrary assumptions play an important role in generating quantitative predictions, it would be a mistake to attach too much concern to the exact quantitative predictions of the model. Equal importance should be assigned to the qualitative predictions about ordinal trends in the data; these follow fairly directly from the sentential representation without the intercession of the mathematical model. In the analysis of the experiments, we will devote equal attention to both the qualitative and the quantitative predictions.

7.2. LOCATION-AGENT-VERB-OBJECT

This experiment was the simplest of the four originally reported. The sentences learned had the structure of location-agent-verb-object (L, A, V, O) constructions as illustrated in Figure 7.1; that is, all sentences were of the paradigmatic form "In the park the hippie touched the debutante." Each subject studied a different set of 72 sentences constructed by randomly selecting locations, agents, verbs, and objects from sets of 72 words for each function. These 72 sentences were randomly divided into three lists of 24 sentences. Each list of 24 sentences was studied twice in succession in the same order at a 10-second rate. This pair of study trials was followed by one cued recall test for that list of 24 sentences. The sentences were tested in the same order that they had been studied, and verbatim recall was requested.

Memory for the sentences in this experiment was tested by the method of incremental cueing. This involves testing each sentence with three successive cues, with each additional cue providing further information about the sentence. The first of the three cues presented just one of the four content words (L, A, V, or O), and the subject was given 30 seconds to recall (in writing) the missing three content words. The second cue followed immediately and contained the content word of the first plus an additional content word; the subject had 20 seconds to try to recall the two missing words. The third cue which then followed added another content word to the second cue, and the subject had 10 seconds to recall the one content word that was still missing from the original sentence. Thus, a subject might see the following sequence of cues:

IN THE	THE HIPPIE	THE
IN THE PARK THE HIPPIE		THE
IN THE PARK THE HIPPIE		THE DEBUTANTE.

There are 24 possible ways to create a set of three cues in this manner (4 content words to choose from for the first cue, 3 content words left to choose from for the second cue; and then 2 content words for the third cue, which is $4 \times 3 \times 2 = 24$). Each possible sequence of cues was randomly assigned to one of the 24 sentences in each list.

After going through the first list of 24 sentences in this manner, the subjects went through the other two lists of 24 sentences in the identical manner. The study sentences and test cues were presented to the subjects on IBM cards. Before the experiment began, the exact nature of the experiment and the types of recall cues were described in considerable detail to the subjects. The total experimental session lasted about 100 minutes. A total of 41 subjects were run in the experiment.

Qualitative Results

All of the qualitative predictions for this experiment rely on the assumption that V and O are closer together in the input tree (see Figure 7.1) than either one is to either L or A. The predictions concern which words are better cues for which others, and which words tend to be recalled together. The only data that is informative on these issues comes from sentences that are partially recalled. If the sentence is perfectly recalled or not recalled at all, then there is no information about the proximity of elements in the sentence. Unfortunately, in this experiment there was a considerable portion of total recall (12%) or complete nonrecall (50%). Therefore, these predictions will be concerned with the trends in only the 38% of the data where partial sentence recall was obtained.

The first prediction is a particularly intriguing one. To illustrate it, consider this hypothetical situation: suppose the subject is cued with L and recalls V but nothing else. Then he is cued with L plus A. According to the tree structure in Figure 7.1, adding A in this case should never lead to recall of the O. If the subject were able to recall V to the first cue of the L then he must have retrieved the predicate node. In theory, the reason that he failed to recall O to the L cue must have been due to a fault in the path from the predicate node to the O response. Therefore, he should not be able to recall O to the later L-plus-A cue because O recall to this cue still demands an intact path from the predicate node to O.

The structural basis for such predictions can be made more salient by simplifying the graph structure of Figure 7.1, aggregating together nodes and links of no interest at the moment. This simplified structure is shown in Figure 7.5; the critical nodes F (fact) and P (predicate) from Figure 7.1 are preserved here, whereas all other links and nodes connecting these to the L, A, V, and O elements have been collapsed. In this diagram the prediction above is clearer: if L causes recall of V but not O, then the associative path F to P is intact, while the P-to-O path is missing; therefore, adding an A-plus-L cue cannot cause recall of O.

In contrast to the above prediction, consider this scenario: The subject is cued with L and can only recall A. Then, if he is cued with L-plus-V, it should be possible (according to Figure 7.5) for him to recall both A and O. This recall pattern could happen if the predicate link were not established from the fact node to the predicate node whereas all other links were formed. Thus, when given the L-only cue, the subject could retrieve A, but would be unable to retrieve the predicate node to recall either V or O. But when cued with V, he could reach the

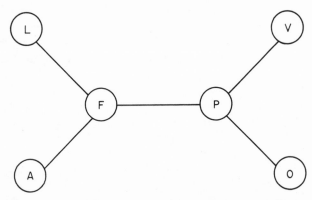

FIG. 7.5. Simplified graph of the memory structure in Figure 7.1, collapsing over nonessential nodes and links.

predicate node and so retrieve O. To summarize the significance of these two examples, when one word is recalled to a first cue, the possibility of further recall to a later cue depends upon the identity of the first word recalled.

So we eagerly went to the data to determine if this prediction would be confirmed. The results were rather disappointing. We averaged together all those situations when the model predicts the possibility of a second recall and all those when it does not. The former are called *predicted second recalls* and the latter *unpredicted second recalls*. There were 5.9% (14 of 239 opportunities) unpredicted second recalls. In the situation where recall was expected, there were only slightly more—6.5% (10 of 155 opportunities). However, there are complications in the data that make this outcome difficult to interpret. To illustrate, consider the following scenario: The subject is cued with L and recalls A. Then he is cued with L and A. Certainly, on almost any theory, he should not recall anything further. However, the data showed such further recall in 4.1% of such circumstances. Such events will be referred to as *recalls to inadequate stimuli*. It is easy to imagine conditions that might underlie these 4.1% of the cases. The subject may have been very unsure even about his recall of one word and may have inhibited his recall of another. However, upon learning that his recall of the first word was correct, he might gain the confidence to venture a second. The subject may have been in a tip-of-the-tongue state with respect to a word and only retrieved it when the second cue was presented. There are innumerable such possible explanations for these recalls to inadequate stimuli.

The point is, of course, that many of the unpredicted second recalls may be due to the same sources as the recalls to inadequate stimuli. The real test of our theory would seem to be the difference between the predicted and the unpredicted second recalls. This difference was only slightly in favor of the model—6.5% versus 5.9%. However, it should be pointed out that the model does not expect a large difference. According to the mathematical model fitted to the data and presented later, there should only be 4.8% predicted second recalls and, of course, 0% unpredicted second recalls. So, while this prediction about second recalls is intriguing in principle, it turned out to be rather indecisive in this experiment. It proved a more informative statistic in other experiments where there was more partial recall.

We now examine two qualitative statistics that were more informative. The first statistic concerns recall of one word to the first cue *conditional* upon recall of a second word to that cue. We will illustrate these predictions again with respect to Figure 7.5. Suppose that the subject is cued with L and he recalls A. What is the probability that he will also recall O to this cue? For successful recall of A, the theory says that there must have been an intact associative path from L to the fact node F. Therefore, conditional on recall of A, the probability of O is the probability that there is an intact link from node F to the predicate node P *and* an intact path from the predicate node P to the object word O. Now, contrast this situation to a second situation in which we conditionalize upon V recall to the L-only cue. The theory infers that there is an intact path from the L to the predicate node P, and hence the conditional probability of O recall is just the probability of an intact path from the predicate node to O. Therefore, the conditional probability of O recall in this situation is higher than in the former, because only in this circumstance is it known that the predicate link between the fact node and the predicate node is intact.

So, conditional on which words are recalled, we can sometimes only know that the S has access to the fact node (e.g., recall of A to L), sometimes only that he has access to the predicate node (e.g., recall of V to O), and sometimes that he has access to both (e.g., recall of L to O). When it is known conditionally that the subject can access the predicate node, recall of V or O should be higher than when its access is uncertain. Similarly, the probability of L or A recall should be higher when it is assured that the subject has access to the fact node.

Table 7.3a presents the data relevant to these contrasts. In this table, $P(X|Y)$ denotes the probability of recall of word X in those conditional situations where the theory tells us that the subject must have access to the Y node, whereas $P(X|\bar{Y})$ denotes the comparable probability in those situations where the theory is uncertain. Observations from a number of separate cases have been pooled to give each conditional probability in Table 7.3a. We have only conditionalized on that subset of the data where there is partial recall because that is the only portion of the data which is informative. That is, we have examined recall of a third word conditional on recall of just one of the other two to-be-recalled words. For instance, contributing to $P(L|fact)$ are the probabilities of L recall, given that (a) O and not V has been recalled to A, (b) V and not O has been recalled to A, (c) A and not O has been recalled to V, and (d) A and not V has been recalled to O. (Note that symmetry of these cases in the structure of Figure 7.5.) In all these cases the model says that there has been access to the fact node. Similarly, contributing to $P(L|\overline{fact})$ are the probability of L recall, given that (a) O and not A has been recalled to V, and (b) V and not A has been recalled to O. Table 7.3a also lists the theoretical differences predicted by the mathematical model to be introduced later.

Except for L recall, the differences in Table 7.3a match the expectations of the theory. The differences in V and O recall are significant and in the predicted direction. The average difference in recall between the favored conditions and the unfavored is .083. Given that the theory only predicts a difference of .066, this

TABLE 7.3

Recall Probabilities Conditional on Node
Accessibility—Experiment 1

Conditional probability	Observed	Theoretical	n	$\chi^2(1)$
(a) First cue				
$P(L\mid\text{fact})$	.528	.535	212	
$P(L\mid\overline{\text{fact}})$	.538	.465	132	.03
$P(A\mid\text{fact})$	.459	.484	231	
$P(A\mid\overline{\text{fact}})$	.413	.393	104	.61
$P(V\mid\text{predicate})$	.458	.442	264	
$P(V\mid\overline{\text{predicate}})$	.306	.373	121	7.92
$P(O\mid\text{predicate})$	.594	.557	202	
$P(O\mid\overline{\text{predicate}})$	.451	.524	153	7.15
(b) Second cue				
$P(L\mid\overline{\text{fact}})$	.583	.652	60	
$P(L\mid\text{fact})$	.400	.592	40	3.22
$P(A\mid\overline{\text{fact}})$	.553	.627	85	
$P(A\mid\text{fact})$	.405	.523	37	2.26
$P(V\mid\overline{\text{predicate}})$	.492	.590	65	
$P(V\mid\text{predicate})$	.500	.547	36	.00
$P(O\mid\text{predicate})$	.488	.696	43	
$P(O\mid\text{predicate})$	.425	.667	47	.36

result is quite satisfactory. The chi-square values listed to the right of the probabilities provide a measure of the significance of the difference between recall in the favored and unfavored conditions.

Subjects failed to recall anything to 64.2% of the first cues. For this subset of the data, a similar analysis was performed on the recall to the second cue. For the second cue there are only two words that the subject can recall. So, we examined recall of one word conditional on the recall of the second. The important variable was whether one could infer that the subject had access to the fact or predicate nodes on the basis of his recall of the first word. Table 7.3b presents the result of this analysis. The mean difference between favored and unfavored conditions is .098; the theory expects .059. The sample sizes are not large enough to make any of the differences significant, but the results are encouraging. The theoretical values are all much larger than the observed probabilities of recall. Plausible reasons for this discrepancy will be discussed later in examining the details of the fit of the model to the data.

Model Fitting

The qualitative details of data seem consistent with the theory, though hardly overwhelming. The next question is whether we can get a reasonable quantitative fit of the model to the data. The procedure of fitting the model will be discussed in some detail now. There are 11 links in Figure 7.1 that are important to the model's predictions. The two links on the time branch are not important since the time marker was held constant (at *past*) throughout the experiment. It is necessary to compute the probabilities of all possible (2^{11}) combinations of success and failure at forming the 11 associations. These probabilities depend only upon the number of associations and not upon the particular configuration of associations (see Equation (14)).

Then we compute the probabilities p_{ij} that there was a path from the ith concept to the jth. This requires summing the probabilities of those of the 2^{11} configurations for which i and j are connected. This leads to the symmetric Theoretical Matrix given in Table 7.4b, where i indexes the rows and j the columns. The values in the Theoretical Matrix come from the best fit of the theory to these data. The value of the parameter tb, which governs the formation of associations, was estimated to be 3.9 for this best fit.

Table 7.4b is to be compared with the actual probabilities of recall of a response j to a stimulus i as the first cue. These probabilities are given in Table 7.4a, which will be called the *Data Matrix*. Letting r_{ij} represent the entries of the Data Matrix, the following relation obtains among p_{ij}, the cells of the Theoretical Matrix, r_j, the probability of a transition from the jth concept to the jth word, and

TABLE 7.4

Matrices and Parameter Estimates—Experiment 1

		(a) Data Matrix Response						(b) Theoretical Matrix Response			
		L	A	V	O			L	A	V	O
Stimulus	L		.253	.225	.266		L		.557	.537	.537
	A	.255		.220	.264		A	.557		.581	.581
	V	.203	.180		.221		V	.537	.581		.611
	O	.276	.248	.243			O	.537	.581	.611	

		(c) Residual Matrix						(d) Logarithms			
		L	A	V	O			L	A	V	O
Stimulus	L		.454	.418	.495		L		-.79	-.87	-.70
	A	.458		.379	.454		A	-.78		-.97	-.79
	V	.378	.310		.362		V	-.97	-1.17		-1.02
	O	.514	.429	.398			O	-.67	-.85	-.92	

(e) Parameter Estimates

$tb = 3.9$

$s_L = .833$	$r_L = .631$
$s_A = .743$	$r_A = .534$
$s_V = .592$	$r_V = .503$
$s_O = .802$	$r_O = .606$

s_i, the probability of a transition from the ith word to the ith concept:

$$r_{ij} = p_{ij} \times s_i \times r_j \tag{22}$$

Therefore, a matrix of the values of the products $s_i \times r_j$ can be obtained by dividing the entries of the Data Matrix by the entries of the Theoretical Matrix. This yields the matrix in Table 7.4c, which will be called the *Residual Matrix*. From that matrix, estimates of $\log s_i + \log r_j$ can be obtained by taking logarithms of the entries. Table 7.4d displays these logarithms. It is a simple matter to use Table 7.4d to obtain separate estimates of $\log s_i$ and of $\log r_j$ by maximum-likelihood estimation procedures. Actually these estimates are obtained with one degree of freedom. Thus, the estimates are of the form: $\log s_i = x_i + z$ and $\log r_j = y_j - z$, where z is variable and the x_i's and y_j's are estimates obtained by the maximum-likelihood procedure. Converting from logarithms, we have $s_i = e^{x_i + z}$ and $r_j = e^{y_j - z}$. Substituting into Equation (22) yields $r_{ij} = p_{ij} e^{x_i + y_j}$.

The mechanics of the estimation procedure may be summarized as follows: We select a value of tb, compute a theoretical matrix (e.g., Table 7.4b), and from that a residual matrix (e.g., Table 7.4c). From that we estimate the four parameters s_i and the four parameters r_j by the maximum-likelihood method. These maximum-likelihood estimates have one degree of freedom, expressed by parameter z. A grid search is computed over the possible values of z, searching for the one that gives a minimum chi-square fit to the original data. Then this whole procedure is repeated with a new value of tb. This continues until a value of tb is obtained that gives the minimum chi-square. So, grid searches are conducted over the parameters tb and z, seeking minimum chi-square estimates. Given a particular value of z, the parameters s_i and r_j are determined by maximum-likelihood procedures. The estimates of these various parameters are given in Table 7.4e.

From these parameters the theoretical frequencies of various experimental events can now be estimated. Consider, for instance, the event in which the subject recalls L and A but not O to the first cue of V (which event will be abbreviated as V → LAŌ). There are two configurations of idea-to-idea associations for which this could happen—either all n associations are intact (prob. = .482) but response O is not available, or the object branch is missing one or both of its links (prob. = .024). The total probability of this event is the sum of the probabilities of this event when either of these two underlying configurations of associations holds; i.e.,

$$P(\text{V} \rightarrow \text{LA}\bar{\text{O}}) = .482 \cdot s_\text{V} \cdot r_{\text{LA}}q_\text{O} + .024 \cdot s_\text{V} \cdot (r_{\text{LA}}q_\text{O} + r_{\text{LAO}}) \tag{23}$$

In Equation (23), $r_{\text{LA}}q_\text{O}$ is the probability of the responses L and A being available but not O, and r_{LAO} is the probability that all three responses are available. Remember that response probabilities covary, so that $r_{\text{LAO}} > r_\text{L} \cdot r_\text{A} \cdot r_\text{O}$. The value of $r_{\text{LA}}q_\text{O}$ is .073, and of r_{LAO} is .352. Substituting into Equation (23), it is found that $P(\text{V} \rightarrow \text{LA}\bar{\text{O}}) = .027$. Given that there were 738 observations of recall when the subject was cued with V, the expected frequency of this event is 19.77. The observed frequency was 18.

It will be informative to consider a second example of how event probabilities are predicted. What is the probability that when the subject is first cued with O, he recalls nothing, but then when cued with O plus A he recalls both L and V? This event (denoted $O \rightarrow : A \rightarrow LV$) can happen with either of two underlying configurations of associations: either all associations are intact and O was not an effective cue (it will not be effective with probability $1 - s_O$), or the object branch is missing one or both associations. These are the same two underlying configurations as in the previous example. Again, the probability of this event is just the sum of the probabilities of the event for either of these configurations; i.e.,

$$P(O \rightarrow : S \rightarrow AV) = .482 \cdot (1-s_O) \cdot s_A \cdot r_{LV} + .024 \cdot s_A \cdot r_{LV} \qquad (24)$$

Given that $r_{LV} = .403$, the probability in Equation (24) is .036. There are 246 circumstances in which the first cue is O and the second A. Therefore, 8.8 such events are predicted. The observed frequency was 5.

Table 7.5 provides the details of the fit of the model to the data. This is a very long table because overall there were 82 events that can be predicted. Because 9 parameters were estimated from the data and the probabilities must sum to 1, 72 degrees of freedom are associated with the chi-square measure of goodness of fit. This chi-square sum was 79.44, which is nonsignificant. Therefore, we may conclude that the model has captured most of the nonrandom variance in the data.

The event notation used in Table 7.5 requires some explanation. The first 28 events are those circumstances in which the first cue evoked some recall and the later two cues did not. The symbol to the left of the arrow provides the cue and the symbols to the right describe the recall. If the letter has a bar above it, the word was not recalled; if it has no bar, the word was recalled. So, $L \rightarrow \overline{A}V\overline{O}$ means that cue L evoked the recall of V but not A or O. The reader will note that there is a strong tendency for total recall in these data, although there is considerable partial recall as well. The model adequately predicts the relative proportions of total versus partial recall.

Events (29) and (30) summarize the circumstances in which one word was recalled to the first cue and another word to a later cue. A number of separate events have been pooled to obtain large enough expected values for these two events. In (29) are all such events where the first cue was L and the word recalled to it was A, or vice versa. The second recall in (29) involves recall of V to O or vice versa. Line (30) pools those events with V and O as the first cue and response, or vice versa. The second recall in (30) involved L and A. These are the only first-cue sequences that should permit later recall according to the theory.

Events (31) through (66) summarize those events in which the first cue evoked no recall but the second cue did. The first cue X that produced no recall is indicated by the notation $X \rightarrow :$. Events (67) through (78) summarize those circumstances in which the first two cues evoked no recall, but the third did. We have pooled over two events for each of these observations. That is, the notation XY there denotes either the case where X was the first cue and Y was added to it as the second cue, or the reverse order. In either case, the compound cue contained both X and Y, and evoked no recall. The theory predicts little difference between

TABLE 7.5

Fit of Model to Data—Experiment 1

Event	Observed	Expected	Chi-square
1) L→AVO	93	89.0	.18
2) L→AV$\bar{O}$	17	21.2	.83
3) L→A$\bar{V}$O	33	39.2	.98
4) L→A$\bar{V}\bar{O}$	41	35.1	.98
5) L→$\bar{A}$VO	33	32.6	.00
6) L→$\bar{A}$V$\bar{O}$	23	23.4	.00
7) L→$\bar{A}\bar{V}$O	37	39.4	.15
8) A→LVO	87	88.8	.04
9) A→LV$\bar{O}$	20	23.0	.40
10) A→L$\bar{V}$O	36	42.4	.97
11) A→L$\bar{V}\bar{O}$	43	39.1	.39
12) A→$\bar{L}$VO	36	26.3	3.61
13) A→$\bar{L}$V$\bar{O}$	19	22.0	.42
14) A→$\bar{L}\bar{V}$O	36	35.5	.00
15) V→LAO	78	74.2	.19
16) V→LA$\bar{O}$	18	19.8	.16
17) V→L$\bar{A}$O	30	30.3	.00
18) V→L$\bar{A}\bar{O}$	24	24.0	.00
19) V→$\bar{L}$AO	21	22.4	.09
20) V→$\bar{L}$A$\bar{O}$	16	19.2	.53
21) V→$\bar{L}\bar{A}$O	30	34.9	.68
22) O→LAV	95	87.8	.58
23) O→LA$\bar{V}$	38	39.6	.06
24) O→L$\bar{A}$V	30	32.9	.26
25) O→L$\bar{A}\bar{V}$	41	40.7	.00
26) O→$\bar{L}$AV	22	24.7	.30
27) O→$\bar{L}$A$\bar{V}$	29	31.7	.23
28) O→$\bar{L}\bar{A}$V	31	37.7	1.18
29) Recall after L→A$\bar{V}\bar{O}$ or A→L$\bar{V}\bar{O}$	5	3.7	.47
30) Recall after V→$\bar{L}\bar{A}$O or O→$\bar{L}\bar{A}$V	5	3.7	.47
31) L→:A→VO	6	9.7	1.39
32) L→:A→V$\bar{O}$	6	4.9	.22
33) L→:A→$\bar{V}$O	11	7.7	1.46
34) L→:V→AO	4	8.1	2.09
35) L→:V→A$\bar{O}$	5	4.3	.13
36) L→:V→$\bar{A}$O	11	7.7	1.40
37) L→:O→AV	11	9.5	.25
38) L→:O→A$\bar{V}$	8	7.3	.06
39) L→:O→$\bar{A}$V	11	8.4	.84
40) A→:L→VO	6	11.9	2.89
41) A→:L→V$\bar{O}$	4	4.8	.13
42) A→:L→$\bar{V}$O	4	8.2	2.15
43) A→:V→LO	5	10.2	2.64
44) A→:V→L$\bar{O}$	7	4.7	1.18
45) A→:V→$\bar{L}$O	13	7.7	3.58

TABLE 7.5

Fit of Model to Data—Experiment 1 (*Continued*)

Event	Observed	Expected	Chi-square
46) A→:O→LV	9	11.8	.65
47) A→:O→L$\bar{\text{V}}$	10	8.4	.33
48) A→:O→$\bar{\text{L}}$V	13	8.4	2.52
49) V→:L→AO	12	18.6	2.36
50) V→:L→A$\bar{\text{O}}$	14	8.8	3.01
51) V→:L→$\bar{\text{A}}$O	11	10.9	.00
52) V→:A→LO	8	19.1	6.42
53) V→:A→L$\bar{\text{O}}$	13	9.9	.99
54) V→:A→$\bar{\text{L}}$O	7	10.0	.91
55) V→:O→LA	14	18.0	.89
56) V→:O→L$\bar{\text{A}}$	14	10.9	.90
57) V→:O→$\bar{\text{L}}$A	11	9.1	.41
58) O→:L→AV	13	8.7	2.19
59) O→:L→A$\bar{\text{V}}$	8	6.9	.18
60) O→:L→$\bar{\text{A}}$V	4	4.9	.16
61) O→:A→LV	5	8.8	1.63
62) O→:A→L$\bar{\text{V}}$	10	7.6	.76
63) O→:A→$\bar{\text{L}}$V	3	5.0	.79
64) O→:V→LA	8	7.4	.05
65) O→:V→L$\bar{\text{A}}$	9	4.7	3.96
66) O→:V→$\bar{\text{L}}$A	4	4.3	.02
67) LA→:V→O	7	7.0	.00
68) LA→:O→V	7	7.9	.10
69) LV→:A→O	7	8.7	.34
70) LV→:O→A	8	8.3	.01
71) LO→:A→V	11	4.6	8.78
72) LO→:V→A	5	3.9	.30
73) AV→:L→O	9	9.2	.00
74) AV→:O→L	10	9.2	.07
75) AO→:L→V	7	4.4	1.54
76) AO→:V→L	7	3.9	2.42
77) VO→:L→A	7	7.9	.11
78) VO→:A→L	11	8.4	.83
79) AVO→:	386	366.2	1.08
80) LVO→:	368	370.2	.01
81) LAO→:	358	363.8	.09
82) LAV→:	365	367.2	.01
Total	2952	2952.0	79.44

these two events. Finally, events (79) through (82) summarize those circumstances in which no cue provoked any recall. The symbol $XYZ \rightarrow$: indicates that the three unsuccessful cues were words X, Y, and Z. All the six possible sequences of first, second, and third cues have been pooled because the theory predicts very little difference among them.

A few "data-smoothing" operations were performed in obtaining the observed frequencies in Table 7.5. For instance, there are those cases of recall to "inadequate stimuli" where the subject's recall to an initial cue will include X, and then when we augment a later cue with X he is able to recall a new word Y. The few events of this kind were reclassified as events where both X and Y were recalled to the first cue. There were also the unpredicted second recalls where the subject recalls X to U and then $X + Y$ to $U + Z$, but the theory predicts no second recall. These were reclassified in the same manner as the recalls to inadequate stimuli. The supposition in either case is that the subject knew Y all along, but was not recalling it. There were also some examples of what might be called *omissions*, in which the subject recalls X to one cue and then inhibits it in recall to the next cue. We count such events as if X had been recalled all along and not later inhibited. The principle in reclassifying all such aberrant data was always to give the subject the benefit of the doubt. Altogether, 2.5% of the data had to be reclassified for one of the reasons listed above. This seems a tolerable level of experimental "noise."

While the overall fit to the model is quite satisfactory, there is one point of systematic misfit which deserves comment. This involves recall to the second cue when nothing was recalled to the first cue (events 31 through 66). It is clear from inspection that the model predicts more total recall and less partial recall than was in fact occurring. That is, subjects were recalling both of the remaining two words with less than expected frequency (9 of 12 comparisons) and just one of the two with greater than expected frequency. Overall, the model expected 141.8 total recalls and 175.5 partial recalls to the second cue, but the observed frequencies were 101 total recalls and 211 partial recalls. The reason the model predicts such high total recall is because of the high covariance of response probabilities. This high covariance served us well in predicting recall to the first cue. However, it seems that, conditional on failure to recall to the first cue, the response probabilities do not covary so strongly. This suggests some covariance between the stimulus probabilities s_i and response probabilities r_j. However, it would have exceeded the powers of the estimation procedure to capture this further source of covariance. In any case, this systematic deviation from prediction on second-cue recall is the source of the discrepancies between data and theory back in Table 7.3b where we were examining conditional probabilities of recall to the second cue.

The outcome of the various analyses has been generally favorable to the model. It seems that the model is able to capture both the qualitative and the quantitative details of the data obtained from this cued recall experiment. The only disappointing feature was that the qualitative differences were rather marginal.

8
FACT RETRIEVAL

It is better to confine it (memory) to ideal revival, so far as ideal revival is merely reproductive, and does not involve transformation of what is revived in accordance with present conditions.

—G. F. Stout

8.1. FACT RETRIEVAL

An elementary distinction that can be made in the artificial intelligence literature is between "fact-retrieval" systems and "question-answering" systems. In fact-retrieval systems, the user wishes to store vast quantities of data (e.g., indexing key words of abstracts of papers on organic chemistry) and then retrieve relevant parts of the information by sending a few key words into the system. In such systems, there is almost no inference to be done, no deduction, no subtle semantic interpretation of the question itself. The user is usually restricted to a small vocabulary of specified key words, and the syntax of his retrieval requests is usually restricted to only a few standard syntactic frames, with no possibility of complex embeddings or the like. The issue in such systems is efficiency of a given coding (keying) and organization of the information files, so that the user obtains rapid and maximum return of documents or facts relevant to his request, with a minimum of irrelevant information that must be scanned for significance. These are "fact-retrieval" or "document-retrieval" systems.

Question-answering (QA) systems have as one of their principal aims the generation of as many "correct" answers to questions as is logically possible, given a particularly *economic and efficient* organization of the data files, and given a particular set of *inference heuristics* that permit deduction or indirect calculation of an answer from the facts known. QA systems emphasize the information which is *implicit* in the data base, which is not directly stated but which is deducible from what is known. Although some questions can be answered by direct look-up (e.g., 9 times 3 equals ?), the QA system builders have been much more interested in those cases where direct look-up fails, and answer-search and inference heuristics must be invoked. It is at this point that QA research makes contact with problem-solving and theorem-proving programs; an answer to be deduced from the known facts is viewed much like a theorem in mathematics which is to be proved by applying admissible rules of inference to the axioms; and formal methods for theorem proving, using so-called "resolution techniques," are quite advanced now in the artificial intelligence field (see Nilsson, 1971). However, the relevance of these theorem-proving techniques to elucidating how people actually answer inferential questions is problematic.

Experimental psychologists working on memory have almost always investigated fact retrieval (e.g., what syllable occurred beside JIR?). Our model HAM has been developed specifically for this task. Our ideas about question answering are much more programmatic. In the current chapter, we will discuss the mechanisms of fact retrieval in HAM. Since our conception of fact retrieval is much the more articulated, we will be able to bring experimental data to bear in much more detail on our hypotheses.

In describing HAM's mechanisms for fact retrieval, we will be restating several points made earlier in Chapter 6, which discussed how the MATCH process was employed in stimulus recognition. The same MATCH process will be employed here to describe how HAM searches memory for an answer appropriate to a particular probe or query. To review, there are two types of probes that HAM deals with. First, yes-no questions which query whether a particular proposition is true (e.g., "Did the hippie touch the debutante in the park?"). The probe tree for such a query is a complete encoding of the proposition. HAM attempts to match the probe tree to memory, returns as output the best match, and determines whether there are any negations attached to the proposition (e.g., "It is false that the hippie touched the debutante in the park" would yield a perfect match to the probe, but an outer negation is attached). From this yield HAM must intelligently compute an answer to the question. The second class of questions are the wh-questions that interrogate specific elements within a proposition (e.g., "Who touched the debutante?"). Their probe trees are identical to the yes-no probes, except that "dummy" elements exist at each of the terminals which have been queried. Identical mechanisms search the memory as in the yes-no case. This section reviews the mechanisms that intervene between the stating of the question and HAM's output of the answer. First is the linguistic analysis of the question.

The Question Grammar of HAM

The surface grammar accepted by HAM operates in conjunction with the parsing system. There is a subset of six rules (Rules a to f) for writing questions, permitting expression of most of the significant ways of querying particular elements in a complex question. To show this, consider as an example the sentence "Yesterday, in the zoo a topless dancer fed the lions." Rule a is used to query the context: "Where and when did the dancer feed the lions?"; Rule b queries the agent: "Who fed the lions yesterday in the zoo?"; Rule c queries the action: "What did the dancer do to the lions?"; Rule *d* queries the object: "What was fed by the dancer?"; Rule *e* asks a yes-no question: "Did the topless dancer feed the lions yesterday in the zoo?"; Rule *f* queries an adverb of manner: "How did the dancer feed the lions?" Only the last question, querying an adverb of manner (or the instrument by which the action will be done), has no answer stipulated by the example sentence. Relevant information, for example, would be that "she fed them *hurriedly*" or "*with a ten-foot pole*," answering the foregoing questions by giving an action modifier or an instrument for the act.

As indicated, HAM's parser accepts English sentences and rewrites them in terms of a "deep grammar," as a binary tree of associations. When analyzing questions, the parser produces as output an incomplete tree with a "dummy element" at the specific information slot which is being queried and into which the answer is to be inserted, when (and if) it is found. Figure 8.1*a* and *b* shows question trees querying the subject and the predicate nodes of the sentence "The dancer fed the lions at the zoo." The question mark in the diagrams indicates the dummy node which is to be filled by the answer. The answer is defined only in terms of what constants can fill these variables (slots) so as to make the filled-in sentence true or at least consistent with the beliefs of the question-answerer. Obviously, there will be several dummy nodes if several parts of a proposition are being queried.

In the idiom of the human-memory literature, a question is a "retrieval cue," or rather, a compound of retrieval cues. Almost all psychological theories of memory

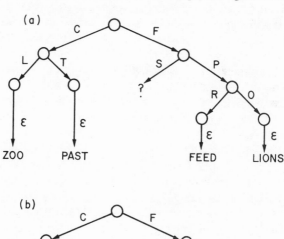

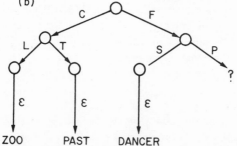

FIG. 8.1. Examples of probe trees: (*a*) "Who fed the lions in the zoo?" and (*b*) "What did the dancer do in the zoo?"

suppose that access of a retrieval cue to a stored memory trace occurs on some basis of "similarity" or "resonance" between the two information structures. This principle is true for HAM, too, except that the "similarity" between the initial study string and the later test string is not determinable from the surface features of the two strings. Rather, similarity will depend upon the deep-grammar propositions extracted from the two strings by HAM. If propositions were encoded and remembered perfectly, then the overlap of deep-structure propositional concepts and of the relations among them would be an accurate metric of similarity for HAM's retrieval mechanisms.

The MATCH Process

Once the probe tree has been set up by the parser, the MATCH process is evoked to interface the probe with memory. To briefly recapitulate how the MATCH process works, HAM always matches the terminal nodes of the input tree to nodes in memory (dummy nodes in wh-questions are not matched initially to anything). This match to the nodes of the input tree can always be done, since it is assumed that HAM can access the nodes directly from the words in the sentence (the assumption of content-addressability). If an unfamiliar word is input to HAM, it will be accepted as such, but a new node will be created to begin collecting information about that unit, such as how it is spelled and what predicates have been associated to it in input trees.

Once the terminal nodes in memory have been accessed, HAM then tries to find paths through the memory structure which connect terminal nodes of the input tree and which correspond to paths in the input tree. An associative path in the memory structure corresponds to a path in the input tree if and only if the following two conditions are satisfied: (a) they connect the identical terminal nodes, and (b) the labels or relations on the path segments occur in an identical sequence for the two paths. To illustrate, predicating that someone "hit Bill," we would have stored in memory the links labeled ϵ^{-1}, R^{-1}, O in that order from *hit* to *Bill*. Then a later "X hit Bill" would match memory as would "X struck William." But "Bill hit X" would not match the prior "hit Bill" memory structure because the paths from *hit* to *Bill* would be different in the two cases.

By these graph-searching techniques the MATCH process attempts to obtain the maximum MATCH between the current input pattern and the patterns stored in memory. Of all HAM's theoretical mechanisms, this MATCH process is the one that has figured most centrally in our experimental predictions. And it is clear that something like the MATCH process is central to human intelligence, since it brings past knowledge to bear in interpreting current experience.

Reducing Search Time

When a probe sentence is given (e.g., "A dog bit Bill"), what is to guide the search for its matching structure in a vast memory network that contains many thousands of facts? Even confining the search to tokens of *dog, Bill,* and *bite* may not restrict the search sufficiently, since the system might know many facts about dogs, many facts about Bill (or many Bills), and also be able to access many episodes involving biting. How can the search process be curtailed?

In HAM there are two devices which shorten the search. First, it uses the labeled relations of the input tree (the probe) to search selectively from the memory nodes accessed by the input words. Thus, if the node dominating *dog* in the input tree is labeled with the ϵ relation, then HAM will consider only ϵ^{-1} links leading out of the *dog* node, and thus not search from the node any links labeled with $\forall^{-1}$ (which tell universal facts about all *dogs*) or with $\subseteq$ (which list supersets of *dog*) or $\subseteq^{-1}$ (which list kinds of *dogs*). This is one way that relational information attached to links is used to guide the search through memory.

There will probably be a large number of ϵ^{-1} associations from *dog*, corresponding roughly to some facts one can remember about particular instances of dogs. That is, the list of memory nodes returned by the function GET (dog, ϵ^{-1}) could be very long. In Chapter 6 it was assumed that the entries on a given "GET-list" were being constantly updated according to their recency of being experienced. This mechanism of recency updating of a GET-list has been used as a heuristic solution to the problem of determining anaphoric reference. Problems of anaphoric reference arise whenever pronouns, definite articles ("The dog---"), and definite descriptions ("The brown dog who likes ice cream---") are used to refer to specific concepts introduced earlier in the text or dialogue. HAM selects as the referent the most recent node on a concept's GET-list for the ϵ^{-1} relation. This heuristic usually works because an anaphoric referent is almost always the most recently mentioned instance of a given concept in a particular dialogue.

To return to our description of the MATCH process for "A dog bit Bill," the GET-list for ϵ^{-1} of *dog* may be quite long; moreover, the particular dog who bit Bill may not even be on this list. To forestall possibly fruitless and lengthy searches, HAM will search a GET-list to only a probabilistically determined depth (the exact rules are given in Chapter 10). As a consequence, very old associations that have not been recently revived will tend to be low in the GET-list, and so are unlikely to be searched. This is the main mechanism in HAM for "forgetting" of information that was once encoded into long-term memory.

On Incomplete Matches

The discussion so far has focused on the simple case where the test probe finds a perfect match in memory, leading to a fully confident yes or confident filling in of the dummy elements in the probe tree. Alas, life is not always so simple. Much of the time the probe tree will not be matched perfectly, either because the question is probing for slightly different information than the system knows or because some original information was never encoded or has been forgotten. We will deal here with the issue of matching fragmentary material.

HAM will retrieve the best-matching tree it can find which does not contradict information in the probe question. To a recall probe, HAM will recall those parts of a full proposition it can retrieve, but will remain vaguely neutral about the forgotten remainder. For example, if we input the proposition and then later ask "Did a hippie touch a debutante in the park?" but HAM had forgotten the context, it would answer something like "I know a hippie touched a debutante, but I don't know where or when." The system admits its ignorance about appropriate elements. If it had forgotten the verb then to the recall cue "What did the hippie do?", HAM would output "The hippie did something involving the debutante in the park, but I forget exactly what it was."

In principle, there could be a conflict between which of two partial structures provide the better or more important match to the probe. However, HAM gives equal importance to all elements of the probe. For example, consider a query stipulating a SUBJECT, RELATION, OBJECT, and LOCATION. Suppose memory structure M_1 matches the probe on the SUBJECT, RELATION, and LOCATION (and has no contradictory elements for the remaining elements), whereas memory structure M_2 matches the SUBJECT, RELATION, OBJECT. Then these two matches are equally valid, and HAM would arbitrarily select the first one it encountered in its memory search. In fact, in conducting its search, HAM keeps track of the most successful matching M_i found so far. Unless a new partial match M_j exceeds M_i in the number of content elements matched, M_i just maintains its preferred position as the best match found so far. Since the M_i will be accessed in the order of their relative recency of predications involving the elements of the probe, this arbitrary heuristic gives preference to more recent rather than distant fragmentary matches.

Response or Decision Rules

In the abstract, the retrieval probe specifies k propositional elements explicitly; wh-queries stipulate some d further dummy cases to be filled in by memory. In wh-questions, HAM will select the best-matching memory structure to the k elements of the probe, and use whatever this memory structure contains to fill in whatever it can of the d dummy elements being queried. For those elements it cannot fill in, it admits its ignorance. In case only a partial match can be found for the k retrieval cues of the probe, say j (when $j < k$), then depending on how an adjustable "recall threshold" is set, HAM will either (a) output nothing in case j is below the recall threshold, or (b) in case j exceeds the criterion, output what it is able to of the d queried dummies, with the qualification that it is not sure of the unmatched elements of the question probe. If one follows through what this strategy means, it seems to accord intuitively with the patterns of vagaries and confidences that characterize human memories of complex propositions.

If the probe is a yes-no question, akin to a recognition memory test, with k cues specified, then the system may match j ($j \leqslant k$) elements, mismatch on none or some, and it must decide whether the test sentence is true. Here, decision criteria enter very heavily; how the subject should respond to this matching-mismatching evidence will be strongly influenced by strategies, general knowledge about the test conditions, and payoff contingencies for correct and incorrect True and False responses. The factors influencing this criterion for saying "Yes" or "True" are summarized in statistical decision theory. Given the maximal match of j elements in memory to a k-element probe with no contradictions, and given that some i elements of the memory structure were not stipulated in the probe, how confident should HAM (or the human) be that the test query is true? Such questions have been addressed in the multicomponent theory of the memory trace (see Bower, 1967). In general, if one supposes that the number of matches (j) is probabilistically distributed (say, binomial) for both True and False probes, but with a lower average number of matches for False sentences, then the theory will predict the proper kind of memory operating characteristic (or "MOC curve") that has been observed in recognition memory experiments (see Wickelgren & Norman, 1966). We will not pursue this discussion of decision criteria further here, because it is really ancillary to the theory of memory structures under test. We turn now to some empirical evidence for the search heuristics of HAM, where the scan is over a data base which one can be reasonably confident that it knows.

8.2. EVIDENCE FOR HAM'S SEARCH STRATEGIES

This section reports the results of several experiments performed at Stanford to test HAM's search strategies for propositional materials. Under consideration is the sequential manner in which associations on various GET-lists are searched. This process leads to strong predictions about how reaction times (abbreviated RTs) should increase as the associative branching in a memory structure is varied.

The experiments below first teach the subject a set of artificial facts such as "A hippie is in the park," or "The miner helped the judge," and so forth. Following learning of these facts, the person receives a series of true-false questions about these facts, and we measure his reaction time. We then try to relate these RTs to the structural interrelations of the fact base and to our hypotheses regarding search over that data base. We are sometimes asked why we use artificial facts rather than making use of the common stock of facts which most college students (our subjects) would know. The difficulty with using commonly known facts (e.g., "Chicago is in Illinois") is that one does not know exactly how they are stored and interrelated in the person's memory, nor does one know the recency of the subject's having thought about the various facts. With artificial facts, we know not only the exact interrelations among the facts but also the subject's methods of learning and rehearsal, and his relative recency of having experienced the various facts. In the model, all of these factors are expected to be potent determinants of RTs. So these factors must be controlled in experimental tests of the model. Later, in Section 8.3, we will review the search done on "natural" facts, and the problems inherent in such research.

Thorndyke's Experiment

An experiment by Perry Thorndyke, a colleague at Stanford University, provides the first test of HAM's strategies. He was interested in simple subject-verb-object propositions like "The boy saw the girl." Figure 8.2 shows HAM's representation for such sentences. The contextual element specifying the time (past) has been omitted as it is not a factor in the experiment. Subjects studied lists of nine sentences (see Table 8.1), three sentences of which contributed to each of three experimental conditions: (a) the "1-1" propositions, which used a single subject and verb with three different objects; (b) the "3-3" propositions, which used a unique subject, verb, and object in each proposition; and (c) the "3-1" propositions, which used three distinct subject-object pairs all linked by the same verb. The numbers identifying the condition refer to the number of distinct subjects and verbs in each condition. Table 8.1 illustrates a sample list from

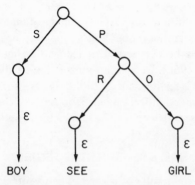

FIG. 8.2. HAM's representation for the sentences used in the Thorndyke experiment.

Thorndyke's experiment. That table also lists the false sentences created by recombining subject, verb, and object from the nine true sentences.

After the subject had memorized the nine target sentences (as judged by two successful free recalls), his memory was tested by presenting the nine Trues and nine Falses and requesting truth judgments. Presentation was done with a tachistoscope, and the subjects indicated their decision by pressing a button. The mean verification time for the true sentences in the 1-1 condition was 1,488 msec.,

TABLE 8.1

Sample List

Condition	Mnemonics	Sentence
1-1	$S_1 - V_1 \begin{matrix} -O_1 \\ -O_2 \\ -O_3 \end{matrix}$	The queen rescued the professor. The queen rescued the grocer. The queen rescued the hunter.
3-3	$S_2 - V_2 - O_4$ $S_3 - V_3 - O_5$ $S_4 - V_4 - O_6$	The thief tackled the singer. The miner helped the judge. The addict scolded the infant.
3-1	$S_5 \begin{matrix} \\ \end{matrix} -O_7$ $S_6 \rangle V_5 \langle -O_8$ $S_7 \begin{matrix} \\ \end{matrix} -O_9$	The gentleman watched the poet. The priest watched the officer. The father watched the miser.

The nine "true" sentences comprise the study list. The test list is composed of the nine true sentences plus the following "false" sentences:

F1	$S_1 - V_2 - O_5$	The queen tackled the judge.
F2	$S_2 - V_3 - O_6$	The thief helped the infant.
F3	$S_7 - V_1 - O_6$	The father rescued the infant.
F4	$S_1 - V_2 - O_4$	The queen tackled the singer.
F5	$S_4 - V_4 - O_1$	The addict scolded the professor.
F6	$S_1 - V_1 - O_7$	The queen rescued the poet.
F7	$S_5 - V_5 - O_2$	The gentleman watched the grocer.
F8	$S_1 - V_5 - O_4$	The queen watched the officer.
F9	$S_3 - V_5 - O_4$	The miner watched the singer.

in the 3-3 condition 1,386 msec., and in the 3-1 condition 1,488 msec. So in the two conditions where elements were repeated in multiple propositions, longer reaction times occurred. This is as expected by HAM, since the repetition of an element results in multiple propositions leading from that element's node in memory. Figure 8.3 illustrates the memory structures that are set up in each of the experimental conditions. In the 1-1 condition, associative fanning (multiple paths with the same label) occurs at the object branches leading out of the predicate node; in the 3-1 condition, the fanning occurs with respect to the member branches leading from the verb concept. At each point of fanning the subject would often have to search multiple branches before he found the appropriate one resulting in verification of the proposition. This is the main cause of the longer RTs in these cases.

(a)   1-1

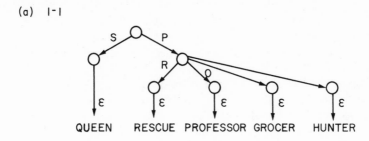

(b) 3-3

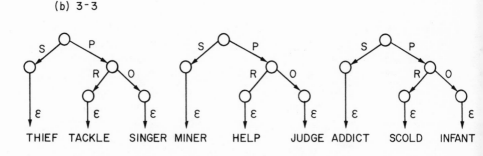

(c) 3-1

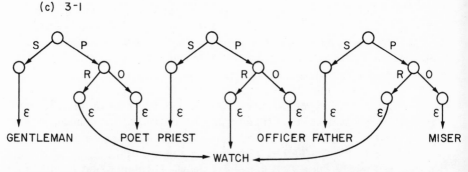

FIG. 8.3. The memory structures HAM would set up in the three conditions of the Thorndyke experiment: (a) 1-1 condition; (b) 3-3 condition; (c) 3-1 condition.

A Model for Verification Times

An interesting question is whether we can predict the result obtained of near-identical verification times in the 1-1 and 3-1 conditions. To answer this question and to make predictions for later experiments in this chapter, an explicit model for predicting verification times will be required. One hypothesis would be that there is linear relation between computation time for the MATCH function to run in the computer program and the corresponding reaction times in a verification task. However, this would be to attribute unjustifiable significance to many of the programming details in HAM. Rather, we propose a simple but plausible hypothesis: Reaction time should be proportional to the number of associative links that must be examined to obtain a MATCH.

To illustrate, let us consider verifying one of the 3-3 examples in Figure 8.3b. To obtain a complete match of the whole tree starting from the subject node, seven associative links must be examined. Thus the mean reaction time for path-tracing, starting from the subject node, should be $7a$, where a represents the time per link. However, a critical and significant part of our search hypothesis must now be added; we assume that a parallel search process occurs, with the MATCH process being *simultaneously* evoked from all the content words of probe. In Thorndyke's experiment, that means that three independent search processes are initiated simultaneously from the subject, verb, and object of the probe. The verification time will be determined by whichever process first succeeds in obtaining a complete match. Thus, in this case there will be a race between three processes, each with mean time $7a$.

To determine the mean verification time for the *fastest* of three searches, one needs to first characterize the distributions of verification times from each entry point considered in isolation. For purposes solely of mathematical tractability, we will assume that this distribution of completion times is exponential with mean na, where n is the number of links searched before completion. Equivalently, we may assume that the rate parameter of the distribution is the reciprocal, $1/na$. The advantage of the exponential distribution is that the distribution of the fastest of k exponentials, with rate parameters $r_1, r_2, ..., r_k$ is easily characterized. The fastest has another exponential distribution, with a rate parameter equal to $r_1 + r_2 + ... + r_k$ and a mean which is the reciprocal of this summated rate.

Initially we considered it more reasonable to assume that the time to examine *each* link would be exponentially distributed with mean a. If so, then the time to examine n associative links would have a gamma distribution with parameters n and a. But this is intractable since there is no simple characterization for the fastest of several gamma-distributed random variables.

With these assumptions, the expected verification times for the 3-3 condition may now be derived. For verifying any single S-V-O proposition in this condition, there will be three parallel MATCH processes, each proceeding simultaneously with rate $1/(7a)$. Therefore, the rate parameter for the distribution of the fastest of the three is $1/(7a) + 1/(7a) + 1/(7a) = 3/(7a)$, and its mean time is the reciprocal, $2.33a$. This gives us the mean time for the memory match. But time is also required for analysis of the sentence, for word look-up, for response generation, and so on.

Since these processes do not involve the MATCH process, their times are assumed to be identical for all true conditions (i.e., 1-1, 3-3, and 3-1) and to be independent of the time for the MATCH process. These non-MATCH times will be assigned a mean value K_T (subscript T for True). Hence, the predicted mean verification time for true sentences in the 3-3 condition is $K_T + 2.33a$.

Consider now the prediction for the 1-1 condition in Figure 8.3a. Here the scanning rate starting from the object of the probe will still be $1/(7a)$ because only seven links must be examined to match the memory structure from the object. The situation is more complicated for MATCH processes that begin from the subject and the verb. When a MATCH process starting from subject or verb attempts to access the object association from the predicate node, it will retrieve via the GET function an ordered list of three object associates which it will have to search *serially*. We will assume that the search will terminate when the association to the desired object (of the test probe) is obtained. That is, the search of a GET-list is self-terminating (see Sternberg, 1969). If the desired association is the first on the GET-list, the subject will have to search seven links; if it is second, he will have searched nine links; if third, eleven links. We can assume each possibility is equally likely (since all three propositions in the 1-1 case were tested). For the present illustration, then, with probability 1/3, the search rates from subject and verb will each be $1/(7a)$; with probability 1/3, these search rates will be $1/(9a)$; and with probability 1/3, $1/(11a)$. Therefore, the following distribution of rate parameters is predicted for the fastest of the three MATCH processes:

$$\text{rate} = 1/(7a) + 1/(7a) + 1/(7a) = .429/a \qquad \text{with probability } 1/3$$
$$\text{rate} = 1/(9a) + 1/(9a) + 1/(7a) = .365/a \qquad \text{with probability } 1/3$$
$$\text{rate} = 1/(11a) + 1/(11a) + 1/(7a) = .325/a \qquad \text{with probability } 1/3$$

The average MATCH time may be obtained by weighting the mean times (reciprocals of the above rates) in each of these cases by their one-third probability: mean MATCH time = $1/3\ (a/.429) + 1/3\ (a/.365) + 1/3\ (a/.325) = 2.716a$. So, adding the constant for encoding and true responses, the predicted verification time for the 1-1 condition is $K_T + 2.716a$.

Finally, predictions for the 3-1 condition will be derived. Referring to Figure 8.3c, it may be verified that seven links must be searched to obtain a MATCH from either the subject or the object. The complications are produced by the verb from which three ϵ^{-1} associations lead. These links will be returned as a list when the function GET (verb, ϵ^{-1}) is evoked at the beginning of the search. The number of links to be searched depends on where the desired association (tree) is on this verb-instance list. If it is the first verb-instance, then only seven links will have to be considered. However if it is second, the MATCH process will then have to examine 14 associations: 7 involving the first incorrect proposition (to which the first ϵ^{-1} association led), and 7 more for the correct proposition. Finally, if the association leading to the correct response is the last on the GET (verb, ϵ^{-1}) list, then 21 associations will have to be searched. Thus, the distribution of rates for the fastest of the three MATCH processes is:

rate $= 1/(7a) + 1/(7a) + 1/(7a) = .429/a$ with probability 1/3
rate $= 1/(7a) + 1/(7a) + 1/(14a) = .354/a$ with probability 1/3
rate $= 1/(7a) + 1/(7a) + 1/(21a) = .331/a$ with probability 1/3

From these, the mean MATCH time for the fastest of the three is found:

Mean MATCH time $= 1/3 \ (a/.429) + 1/3 \ (a/.354) + 1/3 \ (a/.331) = 2.693a$

Therefore, the expected verification time in the 3-1 condition is $K_T + 2.693a$.

To summarize, the theory predicts the verification time in the 1-1 condition $(K_T + 2.716a)$ to be very close to that in the 3-1 condition $(K_T + 2.693a)$, but both would be longer than in the 3-3 condition $(K_T + 2.333a)$. This is precisely what Thorndyke observed, with the reaction times of 1,488.2 in the 1-1 condition, 1,487.6 in the 3-1 condition, and 1,386.3 in the 3-3 condition. It is worth emphasizing why the 1-1 and 3-1 conditions are so similar. The MATCH process can become slowed down in searching multiple object paths starting both from the subject and from the verb in the 1-1 condition, while it encounters multiple paths only from the verb in the 3-1 condition. However, this tends to be balanced by the fact that the MATCH process requires much longer to explore the rejected propositions in the 3-1 case.

From Thorndyke's data we may compute an estimate of the parameters a and K_T, which will be useful for comparisons with other experiments. The estimate of a is 273 msec. and of K_T is 748 msec.

The Person-Location Experiment

The next experiment was performed to obtain data more discriminative regarding two matters: (a) the parallel (or simultaneous) application of the MATCH process to each memory node in the probe; and (b) the serial scanning of associations leading from the memory nodes. All of the facts taught to the subjects were of the type "A PERSON is in the LOCATION." Examples are "A hippie is in the park" and "A policeman is in the store." What was varied was the number of locations a particular person could be in (1, 2, or 3) and the number of people who could be in a particular location (1, 2, or 3). Thus, "hippie" might occur in two propositions: the one above, and "A hippie is in the church." The item "park" might occur in three propositions: the one above, "A policeman is in the park," and "A sailor is in the park." If so, the sentence "A hippie is in the park" would represent what we shall call a "2-3" proposition, since the person of the probe occurred in two locations and the location of the probe contains three people. These two factors were varied orthogonally over the fact base, yielding $3 \times 3 = 9$ conditions. All these conditions were exemplified in a list of 26 sentences which the subject studied until he could recall all of them perfectly. Recall was tested by asking him to enumerate to the questions "*Where* are the hippies?" and "*Who* are the people in the park?" For some subjects, recall was accessed equally often from the person and from the location; for others, just from the person (i.e., "Where are the hippies?"); and for still others, just from the location. No reliable differences appeared as a function of the questions used in the recall test. Therefore, only the pooled data will be presented.

Once the facts could be perfectly recited, the verification RT phase of the experiment began. The subject was shown a declarative sentence, "A PERSON is in the LOCATION" and had to judge it as True or False, pressing one of two buttons. The sentences were back-projected on a screen before the subject by a Carousel slide projector with an electronic shutter. Reaction times were measured from the opening of the shutter (projecting the sentence) to depression of the correct response button. The tests may be conceived as six replications of a basic block of 50 tests, or 300 trials in all. First, nine basic sentences were selected as critical targets, one exemplifying each of the 3×3 experimental conditions. (The exact sentences exemplifying particular conditions were completely counterbalanced over subjects.) In each block of 50 tests, these nine basic sentences were tested as True twice each. Also, a set of 18 False sentences were composed by mispairing these nine basic sentences; these 18 false sentences occurred once in each block of 50. Just as the Trues, the Falses represented the nine experimental conditions depending on how many places the person of the false probe was in (1, 2, or 3) and how many people were in the location. The remaining 14 tests in each block were "filler tests" constructed from the other $26 - 9 = 17$ sentences of the training list. About half of these tests were Trues and half were Falses. Although data from these filler items were not analyzed, the tests were included to keep active in the subject's memory the "nonbasic" propositions in the training list. If this had not been done, the target propositions might have risen to the top positions in the "GET-lists" of ϵ associations leading from each of the terminal nodes in the probe tree. We needed to keep all relevant predications "active" rather than letting only the nine basic propositions work their way into the top-priority ("most recent") positions in the GET-lists. If that were to happen, then the predictions below would have to be altered. The predictions presuppose that the elements of the test sentence are located at some random position in the GET-lists corresponding to the person and location conditions of the test elements. Eighteen subjects were selected from a pool of subjects in the introductory psychology course at Stanford. The total experimental session, including the learning of the 26 sentences and the 300 RT trials, lasted about 2 hours.

Figure 8.4 illustrates four possible representations that HAM might generate for the 2-3 example of "A hippie is in the park." In Figure 8.4a, HAM has taken advantage of the fact that "hippie" occurs with two locations and has thus produced multiple object branches from the predicate node to these locations. In contrast, in Figure 8.4b HAM has taken advantage of the fact that "park" occurs with three people by building multiple subject branches from the fact node. Now, such subject and object conjunctions cannot be combined within a single proposition, since that will produce unwanted multiplication of meanings as discussed earlier in Section 6.1. In Figure 8.4a the subject may have to search up to 9 associations from "hippie" to obtain a match, and up to 21 associations from "park." In contrast, in Figure 8.4b there is a maximum of 14 associations from hippie and only 11 from park. So in Figure 8.4a search is faster from "hippie," but in Figure 8.4b it is faster from "park." It is also possible for HAM to partially

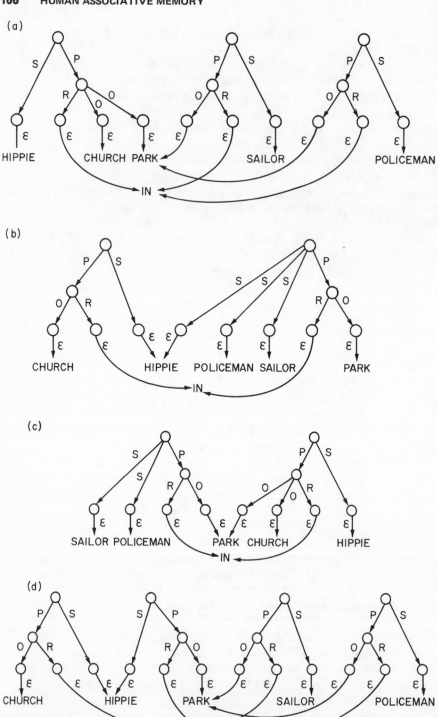

FIG. 8.4. Possible memory structures that might be set up in HAM for the 2-3 condition.

use the object branching and partially the subject branching, as Figure 8.4c illustrates. We will be unable to obtain precise reaction-time predictions if we must worry about all these and other possible overlappings of redundant trees. Therefore, in our work here, we shall adopt the representation shown in Figure 8.4d, in which each proposition is encoded separately and there is no attempt to take advantage of redundancy among the 26 propositions input to HAM. As discussed in Section 6.1, the current simulation of HAM has the option of either attempting to take advantage of partial overlap, as in Figure 8.4a to c, or not so doing, as in Figure 8.4d.

In Figure 8.4d, then, the maximum number of associations to be searched from the person and location will vary from 7 to 14 to 21 as the items appear in 1, 2, or 3 propositions. The maximum number of links that must be searched from the relational element "in" is $26 \times 7 = 182$. We will ignore the contribution of successful searches from "in" to the overall reaction time as it is relatively negligible. The reaction times will be usually determined by the MATCH processes starting from the person or location. So we shall be considering a simple race between these two MATCH processes in deriving the predictions.

In this experiment both the False and the True reaction times will be predicted. (In Thorndyke's experiment, insufficient observations were collected for false-item types to obtain reliable data.) To falsify a particular probe, HAM must examine either all the stored propositions accessible from the person or all from the location given in the probe. Since all seven associations in each proposition will be examined by HAM, to falsify a probe HAM must exhaustively search $7n$ associations from the person and from the location, where n is the number of propositions in which the person or location is involved. The subject can respond "False" as soon as the fastest one of these searches is exhausted without verifying the probe question. Hence, the following is the expected value for $F_{i,j}$ the time to respond "False" to a false proposition in which the stated person is involved in i true propositions stored in memory and the location in j propositions:

$$F_{i,j} = K_F + a/(1/7i + 1/7j) = K_F + 7aij/(i+j) \qquad (1)$$

In this equation, K_F is the constant associated with encoding and response execution for False sentences. This function $F_{i,j}$ increases continuously with i or j, and it is symmetric with respect to i and j. Figure 8.5 illustrates this function for various values of i and j. A distinctive feature of the function $F_{i,j}$ is that if j is held constant and i varied (or vice versa), the increments in $F_{i,j}$ decrease with equal increments in i. Thus, the curves in Figure 8.5 are negatively accelerated. This is because the value of $F_{i,j}$ is always bounded above by $K_F + 7ja$, which is the mean time for successful verification from a single entry node with n propositions. That is, the value of $7ja$ would be the MATCH time if there were no race. The expected value for the winner of the race cannot be slower than this bound, but will approximate it as i becomes large.

To falsify a proposition, the MATCH process must exhaustively search all the propositions retrieved by the GET process at a particular entry node. To verify a proposition, however, it is only necessary for HAM to search until it finds the

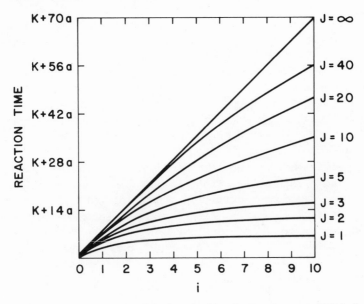

FIG. 8.5.   Possible values of the function $F_{i,j}$—the time to respond "False" to a probe in which the person is in i propositions and the location is in j propositions.

proposition to match the probe, at which time it may terminate the search. This option has been denoted a "self-terminating" search by Sternberg (1969). The expected time of a self-terminating search is determined by the location of the target proposition on the GET-list of associations that leads from the entry node. As before, it is assumed that all positions on the GET-list are equally likely to hold the sought-after item. Thus, if the person is involved in ℓ propositions and the location is involved in m propositions, there are $\ell \times m$ equally likely configurations of the target proposition on the two GET-lists. If the target proposition is at the ith position on the person GET-list and at the jth position on the location GET-list, the MATCH time should be the same as that to falsify an i, j proposition, namely, the fastest of two exponentials which proceed at rates a/i and a/j. Letting K_T denote the constant time associated with the non-MATCH processes for true propositions, the following equation for $T_{\ell,m}$ describes the time to verify an ℓ, m proposition:

$$T_{\ell,m} = K_T + 1/(\ell \times m) \sum_{i}^{\ell} \sum_{j}^{m} 7aij/(i+j) \tag{2}$$

With the theory explicated, we are now prepared to deal with the data from this experiment; this is presented in Table 8.2 for correct responses only (errors were less than 4%) for Trues in the left half and for Falses in the right half of the table. About 200 observations contribute to each entry. Progressing across any row or down any column, HAM expects a monotonic increase in RTs as the person or location appears in more propositions. For the True data this is nearly always the case:

TABLE 8.2

Verification Times for the Person-Location Experiment

		Trues No. props. person in						Falses No. props. person in			
		1	2	3	Mean			1	2	3	Mean
No. props. location in	1	1.022	1.068	1.076	1.055	No. props. location in	1	1.110	1.112	1.149	1.124
	2	1.040	1.068	1.159	1.089		2	1.128	1.298	1.170	1.199
	3	1.075	1.116	1.271	1.154		3	1.139	1.379	1.441	1.320
Mean		1.046	1.084	1.169	1.100	Mean		1.126	1.263	1.253	1.214

the only discrepancy is a tie between the 2,1 and 2,2 cells. For the False data there is one reversal: that between the 2,2 and 3,2 cells. Altogether there are 36 pairwise comparisons along rows and columns. Of these only 2 (or 6%) fail to conform to the monotonicity predictions. So at the level of ordinal predictions, HAM's search mechanisms are clearly supported. The orderliness of the RT functions reduces the credibility of those models (e.g., Quillian's, 1968, intersection search) which suppose that search proceeds in parallel along all possible paths leading out from an entry word, and that speed of search is not affected by the number of paths. However, the data are consistent with a "parallel" model whose search rate is slower in proportion to the number of paths that must be searched (see Townsend, 1971).

Model Fitting

The search model will be fit separately to the True data and then to the False data. The reason for this separate treatment will soon be apparent. The model's predictions for the True data, assuming a self-terminating search, are given in the "self-terminating" column of Table 8.3. An independent fit of the model to the False data is given under the column labeled "exhaustive." For the True data the additive constant, K_T, was estimated to be 712 msec., and the rate per association, a, was estimated to be 81 msec. For the False data, K_F was estimated at 900 msec. and a at 49 msec. The discrepancy between the two estimates of a suggests that the search for the True propositions may have been exhaustive rather than self-terminating. That is, the MATCH process may have continued searching past the target proposition and proceeded to the end of the GET-list. A model with such an exhaustive search would result in a lower estimate of a. Fitting an exhaustive search model to the True data (in the column labeled "exhaustive search" under Trues), the estimate of K_T is 902 msec. and of a is 31 msec. Thus, when we assume a pure exhaustive search, the estimate of a is now less than the estimate based on the False data. The self-terminating model's predictions have an average discrepancy of 21 msec., whereas the exhaustive model has an average discrepancy of 22 msec. So, there is little basis to choose between the two search strategies for the True data. In fact, it would seem that the truth lies somewhere

TABLE 8.3

Fit of Model to Data

Condition	Observed	Self-terminating	Exhaustive	Single-access
		Trues		
1-1	1.022	.996	1.011	1.089
2.1	1.068	1.043	1.047	1.045
3-1	1.076	1.074	1.065	1.100
1-2	1.040	1.043	1.047	1.045
2-2	1.068	1.114	1.119	1.100
3-2	1.159	1.164	1.162	1.156
1-3	1.075	1.074	1.065	1.100
2-3	1.116	1.164	1.162	1.156
3-3	1.271	1.231	1.228	1.211
		Falses		
1-1	1.110		1.072	1.053
2-1	1.112		1.129	1.134
3-1	1.149		1.157	1.214
1-2	1.128		1.129	1.134
2-2	1.298		1.243	1.214
3-2	1.170		1.312	1.295
1-3	1.139		1.157	1.214
2-3	1.379		1.312	1.295
3-3	1.441		1.415	1.375

between a pure exhaustive search and pure self-terminating search. That is, subjects would appear to self-terminate only some of the time.

Parallel or Single Access?

One assumption makes our model difficult to simulate, namely, that the MATCH process proceeds simultaneously in parallel from every entry node in the probe. Is this assumption really necessary? Would it not be simpler to assume that the subject randomly accessed one of the nodes, in this case either the person or the location, each with 50% probability, and then searched for the full tree from only that one entry node? We call this the "single-access" model, and it differs from the parallel model in the curves predicted for Figure 8.5. The single-access model predicts the following relation between verification time for Falses and the variables i and j:

$$F_{i,j} = K_F + 7a(i+j)/2 \qquad (3)$$

That is, for each value of j, reaction time should increase linearly as a function of i with a slope of $7a/2$. Similar linear functions are predicted for the True data. Thus, the increment in verification time as i varies from 1 to 3 should be independent of j. Since $F_{i,j}$ is symmetric in i and j, the single-access model similarly predicts that the effect of increasing j should be independent of i. In contrast, the parallel-access model predicts that the effect of manipulating one variable will be more pronounced for larger values of the other variable. The data in Table 8.2 clearly support the parallel model. The mean effect associated with varying i or j from 1 to 3, when the other variable has value 1, is 44 msec.; when the other has value 2, it is 119 msec.; and when the other has value 3, it is 246 msec.

The last column in Table 8.3 gives for the Trues and Falses the best fit of the linear, single-access model (estimating different slopes for True and False data). The single-access model is off by a mean of 27 msec. for the True data, compared to 21 and 22 msec. for the two versions of the parallel model. It is off a mean of 65 msec. for the False data, compared to 41 msec. for the parallel model.

Comparison with Thorndyke's Experiment

It is interesting to compare the present parameter estimates with those obtained in Thorndyke's experiment. Using the estimates obtained with the self-terminating parallel model applied in the True data, which was the model fit to Thorndyke's data, the estimate of a is 81 msec. and of K_T is 712 msec. The estimates for Thorndyke's experiment were 273 msec. and 748 msec. Several reasons may be cited for the large discrepancy in a between the two experiments. First, a tends to decrease as the subject becomes more practiced. In the first 150 trials in the person-location experiment, a was estimated to be 100 msec.; in the second 150 trials, a was 62 msec. Since Thorndyke tested his subjects for only 18 trials on a particular propositional base (they learned nine such bases), his data should yield much higher estimates than in the agent-location experiment which involved 300 trials of continuous testing. Another reason for the lower estimate of a is that in our representation of the person-location experiment, we have supposed that there was no redundancy of encoding as there was in the 1-1 conditions of Thorndyke's experiment. As a consequence, in fitting HAM to the person-location experiment, each additional proposition to be searched was presumed to require an additional seven links. In contrast, in Thorndyke's 1-1 condition each additional proposition merely added an object branch (or two more links). The net effect of this difference is that the same reaction-time differences would result in a higher estimate of a in Thorndyke's experiment.

8.3. SEMANTIC MEMORY

Partly in response to Quillian's memory model and partly for autonomous reasons, there has been a recent spate of research studying the search processes that operate on natural memories rather than on some artificial memory structure created for experimental purposes. That is, subjects are interrogated about facts which are presumably part of their everyday world knowledge, and interest centers on how fast various types of questions can be answered. Such research is fraught with experimental dangers due to the confounding of experimental manipulations with inherent characteristics of the materials. The experimenter is not totally free to choose his experimental materials. He must select from what has been provided by the whims and quirks of natural language and culture. When the experimenter assigns material to conditions on the basis of some semantic criterion, he is also probably producing differences between conditions on the basis of word frequency, conjoint propositional frequency and recency, concreteness, or some other dimension. It thus becomes very difficult to assess the significance of a difference in RT between the conditions. Is it due to the specified change in the semantic variable, or is it some unspecified variable that happens to correlate with the semantic variable? For an extensive discussion of these methodological problems, the reader is directed to a paper by Landauer and Meyer (1972). Despite these inherent problems, many researchers have moved to natural materials. The principal motivation is the suspicion that the search processes that operate on the highly over-learned natural knowledge structures may be different from those that operate on memories acquired only briefly and imperfectly for the purposes of a psychological experiment.

Much excitement was created by a seminal paper by Collins and Quillian (1969) which proposed that the organization of semantic memory could be revealed by the time subjects needed to answer queries which required some inferences. Specifically, Quillian (1968) had postulated that concepts were hierarchically organized into logically nested subset-superset chains, and that particular predicates or properties would be attached directly only to that node designating the most general class to which that property applied. Thus, the superset of *pekinese* was presumed not to be *animal*, but rather was first *dog*, which has superset *mammal*, which then has superset *animal*. Thus, to verify that a *pekinese* is an *animal* would require three deductive steps, whereas to verify that a pekinese is a dog would require but one deductive step, and so less time to respond. The further assumption, that properties are attached to the most general concept to which they could possibly apply, leads to similar predictions regarding reaction time to verify subject-property conjectures. Thus, if *sings* is a property stored directly with the concept *canary*, whereas *has skin* or *breathes* are properties stored only at the superordinate category *animal*, then it will take less time to verify that "A canary can sing" than "A canary has skin." Presumably, to verify that "A canary has skin" the subject must search through superset chains to get from *canary* to *animal*, and thence to the fact that all animals *have skin*.

The Collins and Quillian proposal was really concerned with how a certain type of deduction would be made in memory. That is, if we know A is a subset of B, and B a subset of C, then we may properly conclude that A is a subset of C. Similarly, if we know A is a subset of B and that B has property P, we may correctly deduce that A has property P. What is novel and intriguing about the Collins and Quillian proposal is their claim that these deductions can be largely effected by simple search routines defined on a hierarchical memory structure. The important predictor of reaction time is the number of superset chains that must be searched to accomplish the inference. Collins and Quillian interpret their data not as evidence about the character of human deduction, but rather as evidence about how memory is structured and searched.

Their basic claim is that reaction time should increase with the number of nodes to be traversed; this claim is perfectly compatible with the inference processes in HAM. Where we differ from Collins and Quillian is in regard to the degree to which memory is hierarchically organized and the degree to which properties are only stored with supersets. We think that when we assent to the fact "Canaries can fly" it is probably because the "can-fly" predicate is stored directly with *canary* rather than inferred from *bird*. It is only for rare subject-predicate combinations (e.g., "Spinoza had an elbow") that inferences are likely to occur and that the Collins and Quillian predictions should hold. In fact, Collins and Quillian chose their experimental items so that the subject-predicate combinations used were rare and likely to require inference making (e.g., "A birch has seeds").

The initial data reported by Collins and Quillian on these issues confirmed their hypotheses both for subset questions ("A canary is an animal?") and for property questions ("A canary can breathe?"). Statements requiring longer pathways to be traced out to connect them in the alleged hierarchy were also found to take longer to verify. However, given the selection of stimulus materials, it remained unclear whether all property information was stored in the hierarchical, nonredundant manner proposed by Quillian. Later research concerned itself more directly with this question.

Effects of Associative Strength

A first complication in the results was shown by Wilkins (1971), who found that reaction times to verify subset relations such as, "An A is a B," depend strikingly upon the preestablished "associative strength" between instance A and category B. Wilkins measured the subject's time to decide whether a particular word belonged to a given category. Sample sentences would be "Is the following an instance of a *bird:* . . . *robin?* . . . *flamingo?* . . . *ostrich?* . . . ." The RT to verify that "A *robin* is a *bird*" was correlated with the relative frequency with which a normative group of English speakers gave *robin* as a categorical associate to the concept *bird*. This associative strength is presumed to index the frequency with which the two terms occur conjointly in discourse.

This result is easily accounted for with the ordered GET-list of bird instances that would be delivered when HAM evoked GET (bird, $\subseteq^{-1}$). The position of a particular bird subset on this GET-list is determined by the recency of its experience. In the absence of specific recency information, a good predictor of an item's position in the GET-list is its frequency of occurrence in contexts in which the category is under discussion; this amounts to saying that category-instance cooccurrence frequency is the critical variable. These simple mechanisms, of recency and frequency effects on an item's location on a GET-list, would thus account for Wilkin's verification latencies. Rips, Shoben, and Smith (1973) have observed similar effects of "associative strength" on verification latencies for instance-category questions.

It is also plausible that a similar ordering influenced by recency and conjoint frequency of supersets on a GET-supersets list would account for much of the so-called "distance" effect on verification latencies with superset statements. If one asks for superordinates of *sparrow, bird* is the most frequent, and *animal* is less frequent; *aves*, which is technically near *bird*, does not occur (Loftus & Scheff, 1971). Similarly, to *collie* as a cue, the listing of categorical associates supersets come out in the order *dog*, then *animal*, with *mammal* (which is logically intermediate) following far behind in the listing. In HAM this would clearly be simulated by the order of categories on the list returned by GET (*pekinese, superset*); this order would be determined primarily by conjoint frequency. The farther down in the ranking a given superset is, the longer HAM must search to find it. Since supersets that are semantically far removed from the subject-word tend to have low rankings, they would tend to take a longer time to verify. This simple notion would seem to account for the "superset distance" results in the literature without necessitating the assumption of a hierarchy of nested sets. The above discussion assumes that single links to the various supersets of a given concept are stored directly at a given node. This is, of course, a procedure that is wasteful of "storage space," since the system could infer (from subset relations) much of what it thus stores redundantly. Quillian (1968) in particular offers this spacesaving as an argument for eliminating all redundant facts stored in semantic memory. Quillian's position in the extreme claims that if the system learns that all dogs have fleas, it should *erase* the prior information it had stored about Fido having fleas, because that old fact would now be derivable from the new fact plus the fact that Fido is a dog.

We disagree fundamentally with this space-saving assumption and with the erasure idea to which it leads. There is no compelling reason to believe that human memory cannot retain many redundant facts; there is no strong need for erasure or "garbage collection" of redundant facts just to "clean up" the memory system. We handle forgetting in HAM by essentially making a certain fact very difficult to retrieve from particular concepts, by its gradually settling far down in the GET-lists associated with these concepts through its disuse but multiple uses of the concepts with other interpolated, interfering facts. Quillian's hypothesis, that predicates are erased from specific instances and attached as a generalization about the class of instances, is simply implausible.

Let us enumerate a few of the problems with the Quillian model: First, subjects do not have stored in logical order the various supersets to which each concept belongs. As Collins and Quillian (1969) point out themselves, *mammal* is technically between *dog* and *animal*, so therefore *mammal* should be closer to *dog* in a semantic hierarchy than *animal* is to *dog*. However, animal is a more frequent associate of dog than is mammal. The reaction time to verify "A dog is a mammal" is found to be much longer than for "A dog is an animal" (see Rips, et al., 1973). This is true even for adult subjects who know the logical nesting relations among these three concepts. Therefore, when we pit associative frequency against logical nesting, it is the former variable that is the effective predictor of categorization times.

Second, Conrad (1972) has shown that RTs to verify property statements like "A canary has skin" are predicted more accurately by association norms than by one's intuitions about the highest level in the hierarchy at which a given property generalization would be attached. For example, Quillian has proposed that a predicate like "has wings" would be attached directly to the *bird* concept since it applies generically to all birds, while "has skin" would be attached to the *animal* node. Conrad (1972) collected property-association norms to each concept (noun) in a typical hierarchy used by Collins and Quillian; that is, subjects would be asked to describe a *canary*, or a *bird*, or an *animal*, and so forth. These norms showed clearly that high associates of *canary* tended to be those properties presumed by Collins and Quillian to be stored directly with *canary*, whereas the properties used by Collins and Quillian for testing more distant subject-predicate constructions tended to be of much lower associative frequency. This confound, of alleged hierarchical distance with associative frequency, is not necessarily damning to the hierarchical viewpoint, since distance in the logical concept hierarchy may itself be determining the association data.

To assess such confounds, Conrad ran several experiments to factor out the effects on verification latencies of associative frequency versus alleged hierarchical distance. In each case, the associative probability of a property to the subject of a True statement (or to a superordinate of the subject) strongly determined reaction times (with more probable properties being verified faster), whereas logical distance in the hierarchy between the subject and predicate gave inconsistent effects overall. For example, in her Experiment II, Conrad used high- versus low-frequency predicates of the highest-level concepts like *animal*, and used subjects (nouns) which were logically either zero, one, or two hierarchical levels removed from the predicate (e.g., *animal, bird*, or *canary*). She found that predicate frequency (to *animal*) had a large effect on RT (approximately 250 msec. difference), whereas hierarchical distance did not contribute significantly to the variation in RTs.

One would not wish to give up entirely on the Collins and Quillian idea of superset chaining, but the various negative results suggest caution in exactly how the process is to be formulated and when it is to be activated. In HAM, we envision essentially two mechanisms for verifying property statements—either a direct associative link or, if that fails, a chaining through supersets. Conjoint frequency of experiencing a particular concept-predicate pair would determine the probability that the association can be directly retrieved. This means, of course, that a given predicate may be duplicated redundantly and many times all over the network. This violates Quillian's assumption of cognitive economy. As Conrad (1972) says:

> Thus, there seems to be little evidence to support the hypothesis that all properties are stored only once in memory and must be retrieved through a series of inferences for all words except those that they most directly define [p. 153].
>
> ... it was shown that the Collins and Quillian data which supported this hypothesis could be attributed to a failure to control for the frequency with which a property is stored with its assumed superordinate in memory. In addition, a somewhat stronger test of the hypothesis [Experiment II reviewed above] failed to provide supportive data. This suggests that properties are stored in memory with every word which they define and can be retrieved directly rather than through a process of inference [p. 154].

Some recent research at Stanford by S. M. Kosslyn and K. E. Nelson (personal communication, 1972) adds a final blow to the Collins and Quillian proposal. They used individual subject's ratings of the "saliency" and conjoint frequency of the subject-predicate combination. These various ratings were highly intercorrelated; more importantly, they were much better predictors of verification reaction times for subject-predicate test probes than was the logical node distance in a Quillian hierarchy. As we have assumed for HAM, Kosslyn and Nelson interpret their results in terms of a serial self-terminating search of a property list associated with the subject noun. More "salient" properties are simply ones that are higher on these lists.

To place some perspective on the issue, however, it is clear that something like superset chaining must be used to answer the thousands of queries a person encounters which require some inference. Let us call these the queries with an "almost-zero" conjoint frequency between the subject and predicate. Some examples would be: "Did Leibnitz have a four-chambered heart?", "Did Martha Washington have a mouth?", or "Is the climate of Yucatan hot?" No one has probably heard precisely those predications, yet they are inferred directly (in two-steps) by moving up to a superset (*is a person* or *is in Mexico*) and finding the property. This sort of inference would take more time than the direct association. However, it is not clear that there is much need for very lengthy chains of deductions. Each of the above bizarre examples used exactly one "superset" link. We doubt that people frequently carry through inferential chains of much greater length.

Effects of Category Size

We have argued that propositions like "A canary is an animal" are stored directly, even though they could be inferred from pairs of propositions like "A canary is a bird" and "A bird is an animal." Also more remote superset relations will lead to longer verification times insofar as the more remote superset is less accessible on the GET-list. For the above example it would be claimed that the GET (*canary, superset*) list would tend to be ordered "bird, animal, living thing, physical object, etc." However, another factor would predict the same result. The proposition "An A is a B" can be verified in two ways: either B is found on the superset list of A, or A can be found on the subset list of B. As in the previous discussions, one may conceive of a race between these two search processes, with the fastest determining the verification time. If B is logically a second-order superset of A (as *animal* is of *canary*), its subset list will be much longer than if it is a first-order superset (as *bird* is of *canary*). Consequently, it will probably take longer to find A among the many B subsets. Therefore, first-order superset statements may be faster to verify simply because more often an A is found on the GET (*B, subset*) list, thus "beating out" the search process operating on the GET (*A, superset*) list.

In fact, Wilkins (1971) found that the time to verify categorical statements of the form "An A is a B" was slightly faster for smaller B categories. Unlike other researchers (e.g., Landauer & Freedman, 1968), Wilkins' smaller B categories were not nested within larger B categories (e.g., as *bird* is in *animal*). Therefore, his category-size effect is not confounded with node distance. A second example comes from an experiment by Meyer and Ellis (1970) who found that the time to determine that a nonword was not a member of a specified category (e.g., "A Mafer is a bird") increased with category size. Since nonwords cannot enter into semantic hierarchies, Meyer and Ellis argue that their effect cannot reflect node distance.

Rather, they argue for a sequential search of the category which can sometimes exhaust small categories before the determination is made that the item is a nonword. This is approximately what happens when HAM evokes its GET (*bird, subset*) function while simultaneously searching for associations to Mafer.

Freedman and Loftus (1971) reported an experiment which is sometimes interpreted as evidence that category size does not affect verification time. They had subjects generate instances of categories that satisfied a certain criterion—for instance, an animal whose name begins with the letter Z or a season that was hot. Response latencies were only slightly and negatively related to the rated size of category. However, there is no reason to expect an effect of category size in such a task. If it is assumed that a subject scans a serial list of category instances, what should determine his response time is how far down the list is an instance that satisfies the criterion, rather than how long the list is. There is no reason to suppose the required instance will be further down a longer list. Assuming that the position of the instance is related to its frequency in the language or the frequency with which it is given as an instance to the category (see Battig & Montague, 1969), then reaction time should display a strong negative relation to such frequency measures. In fact, this is just what Freedman and Loftus (1971) found.

A recent experiment by Loftus (1973) is very encouraging with respect to HAM's race model for categorization judgments. Loftus had her subjects judge whether an instance belonged to a category. Either the instance was presented one second before the category or the order of presentation was reversed. By presenting instance or category first, Loftus was giving a "head start" to the search process proceeding from that member of the pair. That is, HAM could access that word and ready it for a search that would begin immediately with the presentation of the other member of the pair. Therefore, the effective predictor of RT should be how quickly the search process from the initially presented member would find the target association. This is just what Loftus found. When the instance preceded the category, the effective predictor of RT was how dominant the category was as an associate to the instance. When the category preceded, the effective predictor was how dominant the instance was as an associate to the category.

Thus, most of the evidence seems consistent with the claim of HAM's search model: namely, that search processes in long-term memory will be slowed down in proportion to the number of competing associations that must be examined to retrieve the desired information, but that several such search processes (beginning from the separate elements of a compound probe) race against one another in the attempt to verify a test proposition. On the other hand, the assumption of Quillian's search model was that activation (the search) spreads out in parallel from a node, down all paths, and that the speed of this radiation was independent of the number of associative paths leading from the node. This assumption should be laid to rest, for it appears to be incorrect.

The denial of Quillian's memory-search assumptions has serious consequences. These may be illustrated by propositions of the form "A has relation R to B." The time to verify this proposition should vary with the number of propositions stored individually about A, R, and B, and should be very long when the number of propositions is very large for all three elements. Does this claim coincide with the everyday facts of memory? Is it not the case that we can quickly verify propositions involving much-used concepts and individuals? For instance, consider the proposition "Nixon is the president of the U.S.A." We immediately recognize it as true (in 1973), but how many facts do we know about "Nixon," about the relation "is-president-of," and about the "U.S.A."? Many hundreds, so how can we verify this one quickly? HAM's answer to this query rests upon the saliency of the test proposition. While these items are indeed involved in a great many propositions, it seems likely that this particular proposition would be near the top of any GET-list leading from "Nixon," "is-president-of," or "U.S.A."

But let us consider a less salient proposition about Richard Nixon, such as "Richard Nixon consults with Billy Graham." Many of us can quickly affirm the truth of this, but for most of us it is not a very salient feature of Richard Nixon. HAM's mechanisms nonetheless predict relatively rapid verification in this case because the proposition is a relatively salient fact about Billy Graham. Recall that for rapid verification, it suffices if just one of the racing MATCH processes obtains a quick result.

Finally, consider a proposition that is not only nonsalient with respect to Nixon, but also with respect to the other elements of the proposition. Understandably, it is difficult to come up with such propositions, but consider this one: "In 1964 Richard Nixon supported Barry Goldwater." Presumably, for most of us, the proposition is not a very salient fact about 1964, Nixon, "supports," or Barry Goldwater. Yet it was well reported in the news media at the time and presumably was deposited firmly in our long-term memory. Most people cannot even recall whether this particular fact is true. A typical response is "Well, I know Nixon was a loyal Republican, and loyal Republicans supported Goldwater in 1964, so I suppose that Nixon did too." HAM interprets this failure of memory by supposing that the proposition had become "buried" far down on all GET-lists so that it was practically unavailable. Chapter 10 gives a thorough discussion of such interference effects; but basically it is assumed that there is a "cutoff" time after which a MATCH process ceases to search memory anymore. If the desired proposition is not found by that time, the system gives up and believes that it does not know (or has forgotten) the proposition.

So, perhaps, what at first seems an unpalatable assumption may be viable after all. In the absence of countervailing evidence, we will continue with the claim that the time to verify a proposition should vary with the saliency of the proposition for its various elements. Moreover, the principal determinant of verification time will be the highest saliency it has for some element. The lower saliencies it has for other elements will be less important. This certainly suggests a systematic research program on semantic memory.

The Mysterious Case of Negatives

Some data on "False" judgments appear to upset the consistent picture developed so far. Schaeffer and Wallace (1970) examined the time required to verify that two instances came from the same category. The possible categories were *tree, flower, mammal,* and *bird.* The striking result concerned the time to decide that the two instances were not from the same one of these categories. This "different" judgment was over 100 msec. longer when the two instances were similar (i.e., both were plants, one being a tree and the other a flower) than when they were dissimilar (i.e., one was a tree and the other a bird). A simple prediction from Quillian's hierarchical model would have been that reaction time would be less for similar "differents" because the node distance between the two items is less (i.e., *tree* and *flower* intersect at *plant*, but *tree* and *bird* only at *living thing*). Therefore, it would take longer for dissimilar "differents" to find the path that justified a different response. Meyer (1970) and Collins and Quillian (1972a) report similar findings in terms of subjects' speed of rejecting subset statements like "All *A* are *B*." When the sets overlap (e.g., "All mothers are writers"), it takes approximately 100 msec. longer to reject these statements than when the sets are disjoint (e.g., "All typhoons are wheat").

The way HAM should handle these distance effects with false statements is not obvious. Consider falsifying statements like "All women are writers." A first pass by HAM would not find "writers" among the supersets of "women." A second pass might evoke GET (ϵ^{-1}, woman), yielding a list of known individual women. These exemplars may then be checked for being writers. The first failure found would disconfirm the universal test probe. The more overlapping are the two concepts (e.g., "All women are students"), the longer would be this expected scan over exemplars before a disconfirming instance would be found, causing a judgment of False. This hypothesis, which Meyer (1970) called "exemplar searching," would explain part of the semantic-distance effect. For even more distant, almost bizarre, probes like "All typhoons are wheat," these superset and exemplar checking procedures seem counterintuitive; rather it would seem that people note the incompatibility of one or more of the inalienable properties of the two concepts, and so exit "False" without further ado. Such restricted search strategies *could be* programmed into HAM, of course, if we felt there were sufficient rationale for doing so.

Both Schaeffer and Wallace (1970) and Meyer (1970) propose two-stage models to explain their results. Schaeffer and Wallace propose that in the first stage the meaning of the two words are compared. If the two words have little in common semantically, the threshold is lowered for making a different response in the second stage. Meyer argues that the first stage determines if the concepts have any overlap. If not, the subject can give a fast No response. If they do overlap, the subject must move to a second stage in which information is retrieved to determine if S is a B-subset.

Several comments are in order regarding these developments. A first complaint is that these results typically are based upon very restricted sampling of different item types, despite the fact that there are usually large item-specific effects. If different items had been included as a variable factor contributing to the variance among RTs, then it is doubtful whether the observed mean differences would have been statistically significant. This is to argue that use of just a few exemplars of given material conditions limits one's ability to generalize from the observed results to the entire population of such exemplars. H. Clark (personal communication, 1972) has forcefully advanced this argument of "inadequate design" against many of the experiments on "semantic memory," including those by Meyer (1970) and by Schaeffer and Wallace (1970).

A second problem with the two-stage models, particularly that of Meyer (1970), is that they assume that true "Some A are B" statements are always verified faster than corresponding true "All A are B" statements. But we now have evidence that this generalization is incorrect. Under many circumstances, true "All" statements can be faster than true "Some" statements—a fact which leaves the evidential status of the two-stage models somewhat in limbo.

A further problem with the search models of Meyer and of Schaeffer and Wallace is that they appear usable only for deciding whether subset conjectures are true or false, and they do not extend in any obvious way to searching fact bases for more complex predications (e.g., a four-case proposition), nor for filling in the missing parts of a complex retrieval query. In brief, their search models are rather "task-specific," and reflect more on the decision components of a verification task than upon retrieval from long-term memory.

Despite these detracting comments, we feel that the phenomenon is important; if there is a reliable semantic-distance effect with false subset statements, then it is not obviously explained by the current memory structures and search processes now present in HAM.

9
VERBAL LEARNING

> *The domain of psychological research known today under the title of verbal learning has suffered through a long and dull history.*
> —*Tulving and Madigan*

9.1. A PROPOSITIONAL ANALYSIS OF VERBAL LEARNING

In this chapter we wish to interpret some of the more salient procedures and results of verbal learning research in terms of our theory. Although HAM is really a theory about learning and retrieval of propositions rather than lists of single items, we nonetheless think it advisable to try to link up the theory with the verbal learning research. This is because most of the laboratory studies of human memory have been done in the verbal learning tradition, and it is from these that we have our most reliable findings. It is clear too that if HAM is to initiate very many experimental tests of its claims, they will come largely from the members who comprise this "human-memory" group rather than from the linguists or computer scientists. Although this chapter attempts to interpret or "translate" some of the verbal learning results in terms of the theoretical mechanisms of HAM, we should emphasize that HAM was not specifically designed for this interpretive task, we have not invested as much time as we should have liked in these thoughts, nor should the model stand or fall on the strength of these interpretations.

This chapter is organized into three sections. The first section will introduce HAM's propositional interpretation of verbal learning—an interpretation which is both novel and, we think, quite important. The next section will apply HAM's propositional representations to interpret one principle verbal learning paradigm—paired associates. The last section will argue for HAM's propositional system as the representation of information during mental imagery. This analysis of imagery is even more radical than our propositional interpretation of verbal learning. A discussion of mental imagery is included in the verbal learning chapter because much of the research on imagery has used verbal learning paradigms.

Most research in verbal learning has not taken the proposition as the basic unit of analysis, as we have done for HAM. Rather, the traditional units in verbal learning studies have been the single nonsense syllable or the single word. Behind the bias for the nonsense syllable was the desire to study learning in the raw, beginning from scratch, with unorganized materials to which no prior knowledge or meaningful associations were relevant. The nonsense syllable was supposed to catch the learner at ground zero and enable the psychologist to study the learning process as the subject slowly memorized the material by the sheer heave of the will. Although this assumption of "rote learning" of nonsense materials is sometimes justified, it is just as frequent that subjects learn nonsense by use of linguistic coding strategies which convert a nonsense unit into a meaningful word or phrase (e.g., Prytulak, 1971). The use of such encoding strategies varies considerably across subjects and items, making the results somewhat variable and erratic—in fact, defeating the original purpose for which nonsense syllables were designed, viz., to homogenize the process of learning across subjects and materials.

The use of single words as learning materials was partially motivated by the belief that propositional thoughts or sentences were decomposable into word-to-word associations. This *associative chain hypothesis* is refuted by many lines of data (e.g., the sentence memory data reviewed earlier) and is clearly inept for explaining any interesting linguistic performance. The associative chain hypothesis is denied by HAM. In HAM, words are not directly associated together. They become connected one to another only in that the ideas which they reference can be terminal nodes in the tree structures that encode a sequence of propositions.

However, for many theoretical analyses of verbal learning paradigms, the important fact is that two words are or are not connected together. It is irrelevant whether the connecting bond is a single unanalyzable link, a propositional structure as in HAM, or the emergent relation as proposed by the Gestalters. Indeed, in many of our subsequent analyses, we will proceed as if words were connected by single labeled associations rather than propositional tree structures. However, the reader should always keep in mind that this is just a "shorthand" to facilitate explication, and we remain firmly committed to the tree structures that were used in the representation of memory in earlier chapters.

Since HAM only learns complete propositions, it is clear that in order to learn single words or a list of single letters (a nonsense trigram), HAM must "propositionalize" the single-term information to be learned. It is a relatively easy matter to convert most single-term learning tasks into tasks requiring encoding of a corresponding proposition. Plausible propositions would be: "In the list, I was presented with word X," or "... I thought of word X, then thought of word Y," or "... idea X occurred before idea Y." These essentially encode autobiographic events—what Tulving (1972) has called "episodic" memories. If such propositions are learned, then presentation of appropriate cues would cause retrieval of the propositional memory structures. In other words, when presented with the context query "What items were presented in the list?", this probe would access propositions like "In the list, I thought of ideas $X, Y, \ldots$" Similarly, the query "What item followed or was paired with item X?" could access a proposition enabling paired-associate recall.

A basic problem with this approach is that there is an abundance of propositions that could be formulated surrounding presentation of a single unit in a learning list—depending on how the person encodes that item in relation to other items and other things he knows. The theory embedded in HAM does not provide any magical truths about the encoding strategies used by subjects on isolated verbal units presented for memorization. In this regard, we confront the same issues as do other verbal learning theories concerning the encoding variability injected into the acquisition process by virtue of different strategies used by subjects. Therefore, in what follows we identify one or another propositional encoding of material as "probable" in a given situation, doing this to get on with our analysis of paired associates or serial learning or free-recall learning. But these propositional encodings are to be viewed as suggestive rather than as ironclad premises of the analysis.

On Encoding Nonsense

Nowhere is this propositional variability more apparent than with nonsense syllables like CHP. At a primitive level, HAM has "idea nodes" corresponding to the individual letters, $C, H,$ and P. One proposition exemplifying learning of the trigram is illustrated in Figure 9.1a: "Within a CHP, a C precedes an H which precedes a P." Note that, although the context node has been denoted "CHP" in Figure 9.1a, it is an unanalyzable idea node in memory. We have labeled that node CHP only for expository purposes, to indicate what concept it represents; we cannot "explode" that node itself into the letters $C, H,$ and P. Such orthographic information is only retrievable from the fact subtrees to which this context had been attached. For shorthand purposes, we will have occasion to rewrite the structure in Figure 9.1a as that in Figure 9.1b. The dominating node in Figure 9.1b represents the concept of the nonsense syllable.

The compound proposition in Figure 9.1a involves a goodly number of associative links. The number of links would, of course, increase as we increased the length of the nonsense syllable. It is easy to imagine that in a brief study period, HAM would only encode enough of the associative structure to retrieve part of the nonsense syllable. This partial learning would lead to later partial recall of fragments, and to confusions with similar trigrams during retrieval. For instance, if Ham had only learned C-P, then it would yield the same match and ensuing behavioral result whether CQP or CHP were the test stimulus.

The coding above might be classed as "rote memorizing" of the trigram since each letter of the trigram corresponds to a distinct memory-node, and the relations were only ones characterizing spatial or temporal contiguity of elements. But there are alternate ways to proceed. One coding possibility recognizes that two-letter pairs (digrams) may already exist as units, that is, as regular or familiar spelling patterns. Thus, ZAT could be coded as "Z followed by AT-node" and BEQ as "BE-node followed by Q." In this case, the memory already contains the digram as

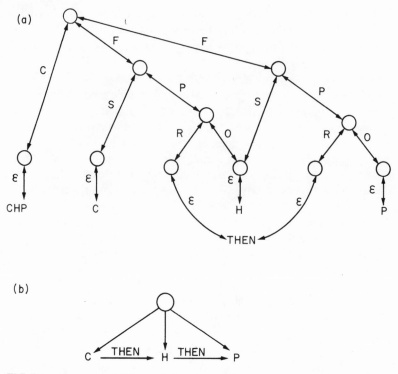

FIG. 9.1.   Two representations of the rote encoding of a nonsense syllable: (*a*) long-hand, and (*b*) shorthand.

a familiar spelling pattern or word, so a *token* of that digram is referenced in the tree encoding ZAT, BEQ, or similar syllables. An implication of this encoding style is that trigrams containing digram spelling patterns should be easier to learn than trigrams which do not. One rough index of whether a digram forms a spelling pattern is the relative frequency of the digram in words randomly sampled from text. This was the measure used by Underwood and Schultz (1960) in scoring a set of digrams. These digrams were then used as response terms in a paired-associate learning task. As expected, the more frequent digrams were easier to learn, even though none of them were actual words.

A third alternative encoding of a nonsense trigram is in terms of a word or phrase that it suggests. This tends to be done when the presentation rate is slow enough. In the literature, these transformed codes are called "natural language mediators" (NLMs), and we shall use that term in our discussions. A quite extensive analysis of NLM selection and use was given by Prytulak (1971), and we have little to add to his analysis. He enumerates many of the transformations which adults can and do use to convert a nonsense syllable into a word or phrase. What happens in encoding a particular trigram depends on what it is as well as on which of an ordered set of transformation rules first succeeds in converting it into a word. From various sources, Prytulak hypothesized a modal rank ordering of the most frequent transformations he observed, called the transformation-stack (or T-stack). For instance, the first "transformation" of the trigram was "identity," which just checks memory to see whether the trigram is a known word. If not, then the next transformation to be tried is to "add a suffix." For instance, this converts LOV to LOVE, and GOL to GOLF or GOLLY or GOLD, etc. If a high-frequency word can not be found in this manner (e.g., ROF would fail), then the next transformation on the T-stack would be tried. This might be something like inserting an additional letter at a particular place (e.g., ROF to ROOF, HIN to SHIN) or replacing a letter by a substitute (e.g., ROF to ROT, HIN to HIT or SIN or HEN).

HAM's MATCH process would identify potential transformations out of partial matches it obtained with memory. For instance, ROOF would be encoded in memory (see Figure 9.2a) or "R-THEN-O-THEN-O-THEN-F." The encoding of ROF would be "R-THEN-O-THEN-F" (see Figure 9.2b). The MATCH process would discover the substantial overlap between the two structures. HAM could then encode this new stimulus as "ROOF without an O" (see Figure 9.2c). This is the schema-plus-correction notion. Prytulak's "transformations" are just various classes of "corrections" that can be applied to the schema. Prytulak's ordering of transformations in the T-stack would essentially correspond to a priority ordering on the acceptability of (a) different partial matches recovered by HAM's MATCH process, and (b) the corrections applied to these partial matches. For instance, the "add suffix" transformation corresponds to finding a memory tree (e.g., for GOLLY) which matches the stimulus (e.g., GOL) exactly except it has more elements to the right. The second transformation mentioned above, insertion of a new letter in the middle (ROF → ROOF), would find as the best match (according to the priority rules) the word which adds a middle element. Replacing a letter, signaled by a positive mismatch between the input and the best-matching memory tree, would be of even less priority because a lesser match would be obtained to memory. Even less acceptable transformations in Prytulak's scheme were those involving two or more alterations of the trigram to get a word. For example, PYM might go to PAYMENT, having a middle-letter insertion plus a heavy suffix added.

The importance of Prytulak's T-stack theory is that it provides an explanation for why trigrams of low meaningfulness are harder to learn than trigrams of high meaningfulness. The idea is that the harder it is to convert a trigram into a word—the further one has to search the T-stack for a successful transformation of the trigram—the less study time there will be left to actually encode the trigram after the transformation is uncovered. Moreover, if the transformation is a very low priority one, it might not be uncovered in the available study time (being at a lower T-stack depth). Even if a successful transformation is found, it will probably contain two or more elementary operations. Each detail of a transformation rule (e.g., "PAYMENT except delete A and delete the suffix") adds further associations to be learned by HAM, creating greater likelihood of a recall failure.

9.2. PAIRED-ASSOCIATE LEARNING

Paired-associate learning (PAL) appears to fit the "stimulus-response association" paradigm of behaviorism almost exactly. The learner acquires a list of

(a)

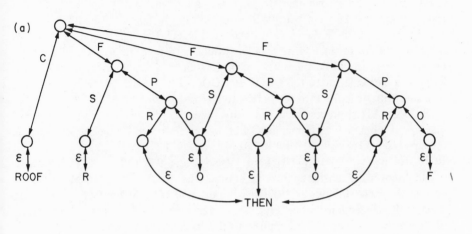

(b)

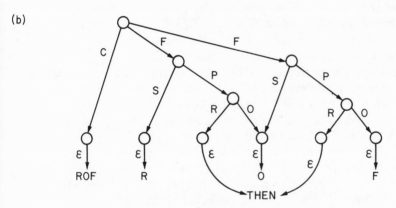

(c)

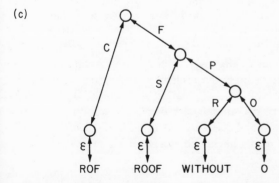

FIG. 9.2.   (a) The representation of ROOF in memory; (b) the immediate representation of ROF; and (c) the schema-plus-correction encoding of ROF with respect to ROOF.

artificial pairs of items; the first or left-hand member of the pair is the nominal "stimulus" term used as a retrieval cue for the pair; the second or right-hand member is the "response" term which is to be recalled to the appropriate stimulus cue. The stimulus and response terms can be any type of material—words, digits, syllables, pictures, sounds—and they are typically paired together arbitrarily, and the subject learns concurrently a list of, say, 10 to 20 of such pairs.

From the time of McGuire's classic paper (1961), it has been widely recognized that paired-associate learning is conceptually analyzable into three components: stimulus discrimination, response learning, and stimulus-response association. To illustrate, in order to learn a pairing such as BEQ-713, the subject must discriminate the stimulus BEQ from similar trigrams in the list, learn the three-digit response 713 as a unit, and learn that 713 goes with BEQ. The heart of our propositional analysis of PAL concerns the association phase. Our claim is that stimulus and response will become associated if and only if a proposition is formed to link them. So given a pair like "cow-lawyer," the subject might form and learn the proposition "*Cow* is next to *lawyer*" or the mnemonic elaboration "The cow kicked the lawyer." But before we develop the propositional connecting further, it is necessary to consider the logically prior stimulus and response learning.

Stimulus and Response Learning

If the stimuli and responses are common words, then HAM does not have to bother learning them since they are already represented by word nodes in memory. However, when they are nonsense syllables, a major portion of HAM's learning task will be to construct representations of the stimulus and response terms. In the past section we outlined various means for representing nonsense syllables in memory. Using the rote encoding option and the shorthand introduced in Figure 9.1, the paired associate "BEQ-713" has been encoded in Figure 9.3. Given this information structure, the query "What is paired with BEQ?" will match and retrieve the stimulus subtree in the usual fashion, and the response subtree will be output.

The major difference between response and stimulus learning is that the response has to be entirely encoded so the subject can generate it, but the stimulus need be only sufficiently encoded to discriminate it from the other stimulus members. Thus, if BEQ were the only stimulus beginning with B, it would be sufficient for HAM to encode "B is paired with 713." The general reasoning here is the same as in EPAM or in E. J. Gibson's (1940) original analysis of PAL in terms of stimulus differentiation. Such analyses predict that PAL becomes harder as the stimuli are more similar and that more of a stimulus structure must be encoded to permit discrimination from other stimuli. Such similarity effects with nonsense syllables are well documented, and HAM predicts them for the same reasons the other analyses do.

However, unlike the earlier analyses, HAM also explains why semantic similarity interferes with learning when words are used as stimuli. To understand HAM's explanation, consider how HAM would deal with lists that contained semantically similar words such as *dog, mutt, hound,* and *canine*. When one of these words is used in PAL, an idea node connected to that word is selected by HAM for use in a

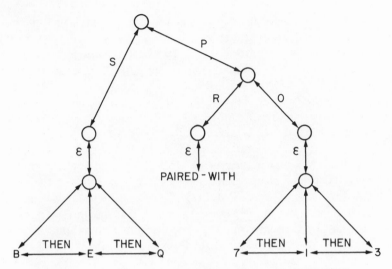

FIG. 9.3.   A rote encoding of the paired-associate pair "BEQ-713."

proposition conjoining the "stimulus word" to the "response word" of the pair. A given word is usually associated to several different idea nodes, representing the differing "meanings" to which that word is associated. These idea nodes correspond intuitively to the different nuances of meaning people have for one word. For example, comparing *dog* and *hound*, in a primary meaning *hound* is a subset of *dog* (poodles are dogs but not hounds); in particular, hounds are hunting dogs. But *dog* as a word also references other meanings, such as metaphorical extensions (e.g., to refer to a homely woman, or a low-quality performance, or persistent following). *Hound* also has metaphorical extensions, being used frequently as a verb (e.g., "He was hounded by the tax man").

In the abstract, then, we may conceive of a set of idea nodes in HAM accessed by a given word; the sets corresponding to two words may overlap with shared concepts. For instance, *hound*, just as *dog*, can refer to the general species of canines. The greater the degree of overlap of the two sets of idea nodes, the greater the "semantic similarity" of the two words. A few word pairs like *mailman* and *postman* are almost complete synonyms in the sense that they seem to be connected to the same set of idea nodes. The word nodes themselves might have different predications attached to them—for instance, "The word *postman* is used more frequently in England but *mailman* more frequently in America."

From the above characterization of the similarity of meaningful words within HAM, it should be apparent how we explain the effect of semantic similarity on paired-associate learning. Two pairs like *boy*-R_1 and *lad*-R_2 will be confused with one another in case the idea node primed for use in the *boy*-R_1 association is the same as the one used by the *lad*-R_2 association. These confusion errors will continue until a distinct idea node is referenced by at least one word of the confusing pair. Thus, although both *boy* and *lad* reference the idea node "young male human," in a particular person's lexicon *boy* might also reference "big bully boy," whereas *lad* does not. This "big bully boy" concept node thus provides a distinct, potentially useful idea node for reducing confusions during the learning of the *boy* and *lad* pairs. The more semantically similar are the stimulus members of the list of pairs, the more overlap there will be in idea nodes referenced by the different words, and the more difficult will be the subject's task of selecting a distinct, discriminating idea node to represent each word in the list to be learned. Much as in "hypothesis-testing" models of discrimination learning, HAM would try out one idea node after another for a given stimulus word on the list, searching for a successful discriminator. The current idea node being used for a given word would be the top item (most recent one) returned by the GET (word, IDEA) function called from the stimulus word. Thus, once a distinct idea node was found, it would thereafter be immediately accessible from the word, at least until that word were used in different, interfering contexts. In those rare cases where two words are complete synonyms, so that no distinct idea nodes exist for the two words, HAM would have to resort to learning a rote proposition about the words qua words rather than ideas. HAM would learn something like "The input to word node X occurred next to the input to word node Y."

Stimulus-Response Association Learning

The crux of the paired-associate task, of course, is associating the cue term appropriately to the response term. We suppose that this is always done by propositionalizing the relationship—either finding a preexisting relationship between the two concepts corresponding to the stimulus and response terms, or confabulating an "artificial" relationship (such as "is paired with") to deal with the exigencies of the learning task itself.

This analysis of PAL leads to an interest in preexperimental association norms that characterize the availability of associations issuing from a particular stimulus word. We do not interpret free-association norms as indicating direct connections between ideas. While some associations reflect phonetic or orthographic relationships, those of a "semantic" variety are to be interpreted as indicating some propositional connection between the two words. Thus, the pair "cow-milk" may reflect the underlying proposition "Cows give milk"; "cat-dog" the proposition "Cats are chased by dogs"; and "oak-tree" the proposition "An oak is a tree."

If a proposition already exists in memory connecting stimulus and response, HAM is saved the need to form a new one. If idea S has *any* association to idea R, then that (or an equivalent) connection would probably be located in the PDS on Trial 1 (of the S-R pairing) and tagged as usable for later trials. This means, in effect, that the connection from S to R has, after a single trial, been primed into dominance when S is presented as a recall cue. A clear implication is that rate of "association learning" of an S-R pair will not be dependent on where the response occurs in the rank-ordering of the associate in the norms for the S-term; rather, learning rate will depend on whether or not any preexperimental association is available from the S-concept to the R-concept. This implication seems to accord with the facts of the case. Postman (1962) found that there was little or no difference between high and low associates; but Postman, Frazer, and Burns (1968) did find a difference between associates and completely unrelated pairs.

The Propositional Structure

We have supposed that in learning an arbitrary word pair, the subject locates in memory or constructs a new relation between the two concepts and tries to learn a proposition using this relation. If it is a pair of nouns, then probably a verb or preposition would be found to relate them; if a pair of adjectives, then probably a noun having both properties would be found; if a noun-adjective pair, then the adjective may be predicated of the noun, or if that fails, the adjective may be applied to a new noun dredged up to form an association to the initial noun. To illustrate this last case: to learn an arbitrary pair like *horse-icy*, the adjective is difficult to predicate directly of horse, but we could apply it to, say, the horse's drinking trough or the horse's hair or his breath, etc.

Figure 9.4 illustrates the kind of proposition HAM might find to relate the noun pair *cow-lawyer*. The basic relation which HAM might find to connect these concepts is the transitive verb *kick*, so the proposition would be "A cow kicked a lawyer." Further information is also predicated about various parts of this structure. For instance, HAM learns that *cow* is the first word of the pair and *lawyer* is the second. It also learns that the "cow-kick-lawyer" proposition is something it thought of in the context of the experiment. Of course, these auxiliary propositions are attached to each of the pairs being learned in the list. Because they are used repeatedly, these auxiliaries are easily attached to each new propositionalized pair.

There are good reasons for encoding these auxiliary propositions around each pair. First, they enable the subject to discriminate between list words versus nonlist

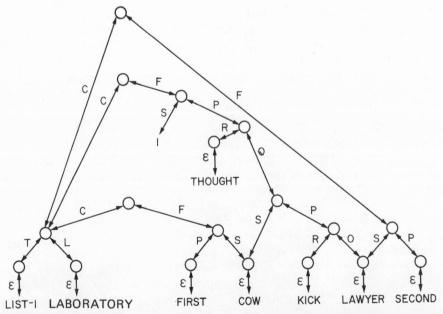

FIG. 9.4. The total memory structure underlying the paired associate "cow-lawyer."

additives (like *kick*). Second, they enable him to discriminate first words or "stimuli" from second words or "responses" in the list of pairs. This prevents the subject from using stimulus words as possible guesses for response terms. Such intrusions are known to be quite rare in such experiments.

The "second word" node in Figure 9.4 also provides the list of responses from which guesses can be made in case the stimulus word *cow* fails to access its response term directly. HAM could implement various sophisticated guessing strategies, provided time is available on the retention test. A particularly good strategy uses backward associations when the forward association fails, trying thus to weed out unlikely guesses. The prescription of the strategy is to scan through the "second word" response list looking for one having a backward association to the current test stimulus; if one is found, to give that as the response to the test stimulus; if the backpath for a response leads to a stimulus word differing from the test cue, then to eliminate that response as a possible guess; and when all list responses have been so scanned, to guess from the set not eliminated by the above backpath-scanning strategy. This is the kind of guessing strategy which permits success at a greater than chance level even before the forward associations from S to R are fully formed and accessible. Execution of that guessing strategy takes a lot of time, however, so the subject could not complete it in a fast-paced retention test.

The context tag in Figure 9.4, "In the experiment I thought of . . . ," is necessary because we do not want the subject to leave the experiment with various mistaken beliefs. He knows that the event, of a cow kicking a lawyer, did not really happen. He only thought of it for purposes of the experiment. Thus, the context is a sort of tag marking the embedded proposition as a hypothetical.

A few psychologists to whom we have shown propositional structures such as Figure 9.4 have exclaimed at the number and complexity of associations required by our theory. Why not, they urge, simple associate *cow* to *lawyer* directly with one link? The answer, of course, is that *cow-lawyer* is not a proposition, and we believe that human memory only stores propositions. The simple associative link conception also does not begin to deal with all the auxiliary knowledge which we can demonstrate that the subject has about the pair (e.g., recalling the list of stimuli separately or the responses). Also as mentioned before, the auxiliary predications are used so frequently throughout a list that they are overlearned subtrees which are easily attached to a new pair-proposition with relatively little cognitive strain. Such considerations therefore make our propositional theory of PA learning not so unwieldly in comparison to the "direct link" hypothesis.

Backward Associations

Our theory supposes that associations are always formed in a bidirectional manner. Thus, the associative path in Figure 9.4 leading from *cow* to *lawyer* can also be traversed backwards from *lawyer* to *cow*. This forms the basis for "backward recall" of the stimulus word when cued with the response word. A strong qualification on all this, however, is that the accessibility of the forward path may be greater than that of the backwards path. Specifically, from the node representing the lawyer-instance in Figure 9.4, there is a single "is a member of" link to the concept *lawyer*. However, if the MATCH process begins at the concept node *lawyer* (as it does in a backwards-recall test) and evokes GET (lawyer, ϵ^{-1}), the particular instance-node in question may not be the first element on the GET-list. The general principle is that for the triple $<A \text{ R } B>$, B may be on the top of the GET(A,R) list, whereas A need not be on the top of the GET (B, R^{-1}) list. The principle applies to our present case where R is the relation ϵ, A is the instance-node for a particular individual, and B is the concept-node *lawyer*. The upshot of these considerations is that backwards recall could fail despite the ability to do forward recall.

These backward associations reveal themselves indirectly in causing slow learning of "double function" lists. In double-function lists, a given item appears as a stimulus of one pair and a response of another pair. An example would be the list *A-B, B-C, C-D, D-A*. In such lists, when the person is cued with item *C* he is supposed to give only the forward association, *C-D*. However, the backward association from *C* to *B* (from the *B-C* pair) intrudes and interferes with recall of *D* to *C*. HAM would have exactly the same difficulties as do people, as is illustrated by Figure 9.5. This shows two propositions, one linking the pair *cow-lawyer*, the other linking the pair *lawyer-butcher*. The auxiliary propositions in Figure 9.5 are deleted to reduced clutter and in any case are of no use here, since *lawyer* (as well as *cow* and *butcher*) is a first word in one pair and a second word in another, and there is no simple, direct way to encode in which pair it is first and in which pair it is second. This is the cause of the confusion and interference when *lawyer* is the test cue. How does the person (or HAM) know whether to recall "The *lawyer* was kicked by the *cow*" or "The *lawyer* sued the *butcher*"? He might use a fact such as that the stimulus and response of a given pair generally fill the subject and object positions in the propositional constructions, but that is not a perfectly reliable cue. The alternative is to encode a rote proposition regarding cooccurrence of the words. That is, the subject would learn propositions similar to "Word *A* was to the left of Word *B*," "Word *B* was to the left of Word *C*," and so forth. This would solve the confusions, but it also considerably slows down the learning because predications about words qua objects are always more difficult to learn than meaningful predications involving the ideas and concepts associated to the words.

Rote versus Meaningful Learning

That "rote" learning should be harder than "meaningful" learning is one of those transparent facts which everyone readily accepts, but which turns out to be

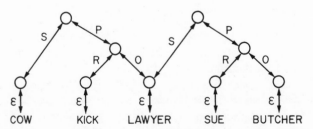

FIG. 9.5. The word *lawyer* encoded both as stimulus and response in a double-function list.

very difficult to explain with any cogency. After all, "Word *cow* next to word *lawyer*" is a perfectly decent proposition. Yet subjects who encode all pairs in terms of relationships between items qua physical words will in general learn much more slowly than subjects who concoct "meaningful" relationships among the conceptual ideas. But why? We suspect that the outcome depends on the fact that predications about ideas can be expanded and elaborated into a large set of related propositions, whereas predications relating words as objects cannot be expanded into anything other than what they already are. The proposition "The cow kicked the lawyer" can lead to some mental imagery or propositions regarding what parts of the cow and lawyer got contacted, what this caused the lawyer to do, and so on and on, to a rather full-blown description of the scenario, its setting and sequel. These subsidiary propositions provide multiple connecting pathways between the two concepts which are to be associated together for the paired-associate task. Consequently, there are just many more opportunities for at least one pathway to be learned and retrieved at the time of the later recall test. On the other hand, in the "rote" proposition, a spatially static (nonaction) predicate (x to the left of y, x beside y, etc.) provides for no elaborate unpacking of its underlying semantics. Also, the objects "Word A" and "Word B" can support no particular elaborations in their own right. Therefore, the rote proposition "Word A beside Word B" is likely to be encoded alone, without elaboration and embellishment.

According to this view, then, pairs leading to meaningful propositions are learned more rapidly than pairs leading to "rote" propositions because of redundant, multiple pathways elaborated in the former but not in the latter case. This characterizes the meaningful-rote difference as a quantitative difference. What differs in the two cases is the way that our semantic memories are primed to elaborate and process the two classes of propositions.

Type of Connectives in PA Learning

A set of experiments in paired-associate learning, with noun-noun pairs, has investigated learning rate when a connective of some kind is placed between the two nouns. Rohwer (1966) reported, for example, that when the connective between two nouns is a verb ("*cow* kicked *lawyer*"), PA learning is facilitated relative to a condition in which the connective is a simple conjunction ("*cow* and *lawyer*"). Prepositions like *in, outside, beside, near* (as in "*cow* near *lawyer*") produce variable results, sometimes yielding recall as high as verb-connectives, and in other experiments producing recall comparable to that of conjunctions.

HAM can explain the basic differences observed by Rohwer. Verb-connectives produce better subject-object learning than do conjunctions (and, or) because an "S-V-O" combination constitutes a complete proposition whereas "S and O" is not a proposition at all; nothing is yet predicated of the S and O conjunction. HAM stores only complete propositions, so the subject must find or supply some predicate in the noun conjunction case. Since subjects may not do the necessary search for a predicate, or the search may fail, pairs linked by the conjunction will be acquired more slowly than pairs presented with a verb, yielding a complete proposition.

As the foregoing indicates, a subject may attend in only a cursory manner to a paired associate without trying to find and tag a meaningful linkage from the stimulus term to the response term. Perhaps no linking proposition is formed at all, or perhaps only the "rote" proposition referring to coocurrence of the two physical symbols is encoded. In any event, learning or long-term remembering is unlikely to result from such cognitive processing of the pair. Different individuals will vary in their strategies for the paired-associate task; there will be those who predominantly search for meaningful relationships to learn the pairs, and those who try to learn primarily by rote. These individual differences in strategies create corresponding differences in learning rate; subjects who search for meaningful relational mnemonics learn faster than those who do not (see Bean, 1971). But instructing the poorer subjects to always search for and remember meaningful relations for the pairs enhances their learning appreciably, so that individual differences in learning are reduced, though not eliminated. We suspect that this result is the general rule: subjects who learn and remember a lot do so because they use more efficient and powerful encoding strategies. If mnemonic strategies are equated by instruction and tutoring, the individual differences are expected to be reduced, if not eliminated.

9.3. IMAGERY

In recent years, there has been a renewed interest in nonverbal imagery and the role it plays in verbal learning. The research surrounding this issue has been amply summarized in Allen Paivio's book *Imagery and Verbal Processes* (1971), and we will not attempt a competing summary here. Suffice it to say that visual imagery seems subjectively to be a principal representation of the meaning of words and propositions. It is particularly relevant to the referential function of language. It is also our principal way of thinking about or processing spatially organized information.

An example task used by Paivio (1971, p. 34) to illustrate imaginal processes is to have the person visually image a large block letter (e.g., an E) and, beginning at an arbitrary place and proceeding in any specified direction, to have him begin counting the interior angles or corners of the figure. Most people can do this comfortably with any figure, starting anywhere and proceeding in either a clockwise or counterclockwise direction. The example illustrates several significant points. First, the internal symbolic structure which describes the block letter is not "directionally specific"; we can "focus" our information processor (attention?) on any part of the structure, and proceed in any direction. Second, the task of counting angles is a verbal process, performed sequentially under the control of a sequential "internal scan" of the corners of the figure. Third, we proceed systematically in one direction around the corners of the imagined figure, not because we must scan in that order but because it simplifies keeping track of where on the figure we began our count. We could have our internal scan "leap" erratically from one corner to any other, but we would soon lose track of which corners had or had not been counted.

Given the sensationalist basis of HAM's concepts, and given our acceptance of something like Winston's (1970) program as an adequate beginning for describing scenes, we have at least the rudiments for representing such performances. The block-letter E would be described by the perceptual parser in terms of the connectivity relations between lines, angles, etc. A "counting" program called by the executive could then scan systematically through the elements of this description tree counting angles, much as a person would proceed if he had the block letter before him. Such programs are not at all beyond implementation. For example, Baylor (1971) has developed a detailed information-processing model to characterize how people might solve visual puzzles in imagery. His program works on "cube-dicing" problems such as the following: "Take a 3-inch white solid cube, paint all six sides red, then dice it into 1-inch cubes by making six slices (two slices in each of three dimensions); now, how many cubes have three red faces, how many two, how many one, and how many have zero red faces?" This performance too can be represented in terms of problem-solving maneuvers operating over a symbolic graph structure.

The *subjective* counterpart of processing these symbolic descriptions of spatial information is that we are "seeing images" of successive parts of the puzzle, much as we would see an actual cube that we were dicing. There is no denying the validity of such subjective reports. What is to be cautioned against is the common view that the subjective imagery *explains* the performance in any acceptable sense. Pylyshyn (1973) has argued, correctly we think, that even granting the subjective validity of having images, one still needs an information-processing analysis of (*a*) what is the symbol structure that represents spatially distributed information, and (*b*) what executive processes can operate on that information. The preceding discussion shows our bias to have HAM represent spatial information as in Winston's (1970) program, as a description-tree of elementary perceptual properties, objects, and spatial relations connecting them.

It is clear that man's perceptual and linguistic systems are very closely linked together; for instance, we can describe our perceptual experiences to someone else, and he can in turn "understand" and be somewhat in contact with our experience. But in order to describe perceptual scenes, we must first interpret them; and this interpretation is itself strongly controlled by a preceding context, established particularly by language as well as by pragmatic considerations regarding the actors, objects, and actions in a given episode. The effect of a prior sentence on the interpretation of a perceptual event has been extensively documented in a paper by Clark, Carpenter, and Just (1972). The effect is most obvious with ambiguous figures, such as the duck-rabbit figure, or the wife–mother-in-law picture (see Figure 9.6), etc. If, before showing the subject the picture, he is asked to "Find the duck," he will practically never see the opposite interpretation. In this instance, he would store his "duck description," noting, for example, which way it was oriented, etc. But he would suppose there to be little or no information left over in this instance for HAM to later reimage that picture in memory and reinterpret it as a rabbit. The perceptual descriptions stored are inferential conclusions; the raw texture of appearance which initially supported those conclusions are rarely stored in any detail.

Verbal Learning and Imagery

In recent years considerable research has investigated the role of mental imagery in verbal learning. As the mnemonic experts have been saying since ancient times,

FIG. 9.6. Famous ambiguous figures: (*a*) the duck-rabbit figure; and (*b*) the wife–mother-in-law picture.

the explicit use of mental images or pictures to represent verbal materials enhances people's memory for the material. What is currently a controversial issue is the exact interpretation of that fact. There are three main lines of evidence to indicate that mental imagery aids verbal learning. First, words which have concrete referents and which elicit vivid imagery are learned faster in almost all situations than are words which are abstract and which arouse little imagery; second, subjects report spontaneous use of mental pictures to learn particular paired-associate word pairs, and these tend to be the pairs that they learn the quickest; and third, instructing subjects to form mental pictures of imaginal interactions among the referents of the words of a pair greatly enhances paired-associate learning of nouns. A fourth fact that is frequently cited in such discussions is that actual pictures of objects are easier to remember than are the names of the objects. Logically, however, that fact is not strictly relevant to whether *verbal* materials are aided by evocation of imagery.

There have been essentially three theoretical postures taken in interpreting such results. We will call them the "radical imagery" hypothesis, the "conceptual-propositional" hypothesis and the "dual-coding" hypothesis. The radical imagery hypothesis (e.g., Bugelski, 1970) supposes that subjects convert the verbal materials to mental pictures, store these pictures away in memory, then revive and describe these pictures at the time of the retention test for learning. At the other extreme is the conceptual-propositional hypothesis of HAM which supposes that knowledge—even knowledge that is derived from pictures or that is used in generating images—is always represented in the form of abstract propositions about properties of objects and relations between objects. According to this view, concrete words are more easily learned than abstract words because of the lexical complexity of the items themselves and because concrete concepts are more easily related by way of the exceptionally rich set of *spatial* predicates that exist for binding together concepts.

Finally, there is the "dual-coding" hypothesis that was advocated vigorously by Paivio (1969, 1971) and was subscribed to earlier by the second author (Bower, 1972). In rough outline, the hypothesis supposes that there are two distinct representational and storage systems—the verbal and the imaginal. They are richly interconnected and often operate in conjunction in encoding and recording experiences. The two systems are presumed to be specialized for handling somewhat different tasks and have somewhat different capabilities. For example, Paivio (1971) mentions that the verbal system is specialized for representing and processing sequentially presented information, whereas the imaginal system is specialized for representing simultaneous arrays of information, the parts of which may be processed in parallel. The dual-coding hypothesis supposes that when a person tries to memorize concrete verbal materials using mental imagery, he establishes two distinct memory traces, one in the verbal-associative store, and a second, redundant one in the imagery store. The redundancy of the traces makes for better memory of concrete materials, since the learning event can presumably be reconstructed later on the basis of either memory trace. Abstract materials suffer because they are naturally encoded primarily in just the verbal-associative store, establishing but one trace. Therefore, memory for abstract materials is more vulnerable to disruption, more likely to be forgotten, than for concrete materials.

It is proven difficult to achieve any clear-cut differentiation and testing among these several points of view. Part of the problem of distinguishing the hypotheses is that the denotations of the "verbal" and "imagery" systems change in the theoretician's hands according to the explanatory demands of the situation. Imagery refers not only to our detailed memory of pictures and melodies, but also to vague, schematic memory for such stimuli, as well as to memory for the *meaning* of a sentence. On the other hand, the verbal medium is taken variously not only to denote words as acoustical stimuli, but also to denote semantic interpretations and rich, meaningful relationships among concepts. The terminology in this nether world has just become exceedingly imprecise. Paivio (1971) offers a similar opinion on the distinction between verbal and imaginal systems:

> Our goal of differentiating these two symbolic processes is an extraordinarily difficult empirical problem at best, but is especially so when the theoretical goal is the explanation of verbal behavior, for here it is difficult to rule out verbal mediation as the most parsimonious interpretation and at the same time isolate whatever contribution may have been made by imagery [p. 9].

The problem, as we see it, involves confusions regarding theoretical representations of knowledge. And until those representations are made sufficiently explicit in theoretical detail, we can do little but thrash about with the vagaries of the layman's terms.

We have said that HAM comes down on the side of the conceptual propositional hypothesis regarding the role of imagery in verbal learning. Our principal point of disagreement with both the radical imagery and the dual-coding hypotheses is that they are too "peripheral" in their conception of the memory trace. The radical imagery hypothesis only permits raw sensory information; the dual-coding hypothesis augments this with memory for exact lexical items. We insist that the principal representation in memory is neutral with respect to the question of modality and that information is represented in abstracted, conceptual, propositional structures. Therefore, our arguments for the conceptual hypothesis will largely take the form of an attack on peripheral encoding as a viable memory system.

Against the Mental-Picture Metaphor

Our first arguments are simply that it is not scientifically viable to suppose that memories, or other sorts of knowledge, are carried about in a form like an internal photograph, videotape, or tape recording, which we can reactivate and replay in remembering an image. This is not to deny the subjective experience of imagery; we mean to distinguish, however, between that subjective experience and a scientific account of the symbolic structures and information-processing components which underlie our competence in carrying out imaging tasks.

We would argue that people store perceptual interpretations of scenes rather than "raw, unanalyzed, textured details" of such scenes. (The one exception known to us is an incredible eidetiker of Stromeyer, 1970). The visual scene is filtered, abstracted, summarized—in something like the propositional descriptions we would hope to have as output from HAM's perceptual parser. The abstract character of images shows up in the typical vagueness and sketchiness of memory images; they are frequently very schematic, categorical, and focused on only salient features. If one thinks on the matter for a moment, storage of textured details in all their minutiae would require gigantically large storage and retrieval capabilities.

Furthermore, it would be ultimately useless to store full pictures of scenes, because they could never support any usable performance. It is well known that pattern recognition cannot be explained by comparing an external scene to an internal picture (or template). Some intelligent device would still be needed to decide which are the relevant features and which are irrelevant for a particular classification or purpose. Also, if thinking is to be conceptualized as a kaleidoscope of mental pictures like a videotape, what is the homunculus that sits inside our head and "reads" and interprets these internal pictures? Doesn't he have to do the perceptual interpretations? If so, then why not do them neat, at input, rather than storing a passive videotape, which is then interpreted only upon later reruns?

It is perfectly clear, too, that in recognition memory for pictures, subjects are in fact recollecting their earlier interpretations of the pictures rather than comparing a raw, textured template of the initial study patterns and later test patterns. This is shown most clearly, perhaps, in an experiment by Wiseman and Neisser (1971) on recognition memory using the Mooney pictures, which are relatively unstructured blobs and snatches of ink scattered about (actually obtained by deletion of contours from a naturalistic scene). The concealed figures were difficult to find, and many of the subjects of Wiseman and Neisser failed to "construct" an interpretation of a given Mooney picture. The picture series was shown a second time, with some old (previously shown) pictures and some new (distractor) pictures. For each test pattern, the subject was to (a) try to "see" some object in the jumbled ink patches and say what he saw, and (b) judge whether or not he had seen this exact stimulus pattern before in the training series.

Wiseman and Neisser found that complex visual patterns will be stored and recognized only if (a) they yield a familiar interpretation—the subject "sees" something in the picture—and (b) upon re-presentation, he "sees" the same interpretation of the test pattern, in which case he recognizes it as one seen before. If the visual pattern remains uninterpreted (e.g., not "seen" as a dog) either at study or at the test trial, then the raw, uninterpreted textured visual stimulus will hardly be recognized at all from memory. Such results argue that what is stored in memory from an encounter with a visual scene is dependent upon the interpretation "projected" onto that scene by the perceptual parser.

A related argument that fits in here is that people can comprehend and remember conceptual distinctions that would appear very difficult to represent, at least in naive imagery. We argued this point earlier with respect to confusions in recognition memory for sentences. Some examples which appear difficult to distinguish in imagery involve judgments of mental traits ("He speaks *dishonestly*" or "He *forged* a name to the check"), negations of all varieties ("John isn't present" or "Only a few babies are unloved"), causality versus temporal precedence ("John's arrival made Mary cry" versus "Soon after John arrived, Mary began to cry"), different temporal locations ("John thought" versus "John will think"), and different anchor reference points for measuring an event ("The glass is half empty" or "half full"; "Stephen's hair is long because he let it grow" or "because he didn't cut it"), and so on. One can multiply such examples ad infinitum in which there is a perfectly clear conceptual distinction between two propositions, but no compelling distinction between the *static* images aroused in the two cases. And although such pairs of propositions will be confused somewhat in a recognition memory experiment, the significant point is that the particular proposition studied is remembered and discriminated quite well from its "imaginally similar" alternative.

Representing visual scenes as unanalyzed pictures in all their textured detail is also useless for doing any kind of visual search or visual problem solving. A simple illustration is solution of visual analogy problems, such as those shown in Figure 9.7. The analogy question is: "Figure A is to Figure B as Figure C is to which: one, two, three, four, or five?" Representation and storage of these line drawings as

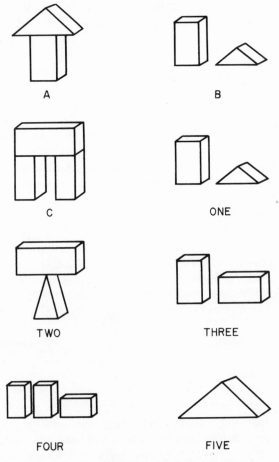

FIG. 9.7.   Examples of visual analogy problems.

just pictures is of no help at all. We need interpretations and descriptions of objects, parts, and relations within a figure as well as the ability to describe the difference between Figures A and B, and the ability to apply that difference description to Figure C to generate a plausible answer figure. The computer programs of Evans (1968) and Winston (1970) perform these feats but only by first interpreting each figure and representing it as a relational graph structure.

A further note here regarding the "mental-picture" metaphor is that it will not suffice really to deal with the referential interaction between language and the external world. We have already seen earlier how a prior linguistic context biases how we interpret and encode a visual scene, e.g., the duck-rabbit ambiguous figure. But to even verify propositions about a scene, such as "The wedge is above the block," it is necessary that the scene be converted into something like a proposition. Chase and Clark (1972), in their many studies of subjects' reaction times to verify sentences against pictures have repeatedly shown the necessity for assuming that the sentence and picture are coded into a common format for comparison, and that this format must be propositional in character rather than imagistic. For example, negated sentences or negated predicates are readily verified against a picture, yet they lead to no particular images (i.e., no particular image encodes "The ball isn't present").

On Imagery Effects in Verbal Learning

We would suppose that the so-called "imagery effects" found in memory for verbal materials are not primarily due to the subjective experience of mental pictures (or because such images are "remembered better"—which explains nothing), but rather are due to a combination of factors, some due to the mnemonic coding strategies engendered in subjects given imagery instructions, and some due to the encoding of propositions using spatial relationships, which can be very efficient for storage.

It was mentioned earlier that learning of word-word paired associates can be greatly enhanced by instructing the subject to concoct mental images of the two referents (of the word pair) interacting in some vivid way. It is clear, however, that at the least this induces subjects to search out and activate sensible conceptual-semantic relationships between the two concepts. Practically the same benefits can be produced in PA recall of noun pairs by simply instructing subjects during the study trial to find and report sensible sentences connecting the concepts of a pair (see Bobrow & Bower, 1969; Bower & Winzenz, 1970). Typically the sentence-generation subjects will learn just as well as the imagery subjects, and both will far exceed control subjects instructed to learn by overt rote repetition of the word pairs.

Moreover, in an experiment by Bower, Munoz, and Arnold (1972), it was shown that subjects instructed at the time of study to learn some pairs (designated at random) by imagery and some other pairs by sentence generation could not remember very well later which mnemonic method they had used for a given pair, even though they could recall the pair itself. Although they correctly identified the mnemonic used 70% of the time (chance was 50%), in a control condition where they used the same mnemonic for all pairs but where half were presented on the left and half on the right edge of the study card, they remembered the location of presentation (which was the cue for the other subjects to image or not) at the same 70% level. In short, subjects could not remember for each pair whether they had been told to generate a sentence or an image to learn it, any better than they could remember whether it was presented on the left or right. If subjects were following instructions, to image or generate sentences, then one must conclude that not much distinguishable residue of the two activities was left behind. Such negative results are inconclusive, however, since subjects might not have been following instructions.

Somewhat more convincing evidence that imaging and propositional relating share common features arises when we constrain via presented materials or instructions the kinds of relations between items that the person tries to learn. If the subject uses a verb or locative preposition to make up a phrase relating two nouns, then he associates the two items together better than if he uses a simple conjunction (and, or). Similarly, one can show pictures of two objects interacting in some action photograph or show the two objects as static, standing singly side by side without interaction. In such cases, the interactive picture promotes better associative learning of the object pairs than does the noninteractive picture. As a third point in this comparison, consider a paired-associate experiment by Bower (1970c) in which subjects were told to learn the pairs either by use of interaction imagery or separation imagery. In the former case, subjects were to image the referents of the to-be-learned word pairs and to image some interaction between them. In the latter case, subjects given separation-imagery instructions were told to imagine the two objects of a pair as two separate noninteracting pictures, as though they were two still pictures hanging on opposite walls of a room, with the contents of one "picture" not being influenced in any way by the contents of the other. This kind of separation imagery resulted in very poor *associative* recall compared to the interactive imagery condition. That is, when cued with one word of the pair, the separation-imagery subjects could not recall the other word of the paired associate nearly so well as the interaction-imagery subjects; in fact, subjects doing separation imagery recalled at the same level as control subjects instructed to learn by rote repetition of the word pairs.

If one examines the verbalizations or descriptions of the images generated by these subjects, the interaction-imagery subjects invariably use verbs or locatives, as in agent-action-object constructions (e.g., "Cow *kicked* lawyer") or agent-preposition-object constructions ("lawyer *on top of* cow"). On the other hand, separation-imagery subjects invariably use simple *conjunctions* to describe the two objects: "A picture of a *cow* over here and a picture of a *lawyer* over there." There might be many adjectival embellishments of each object singly, but the primary connective between the two objects was the simple conjunction *and*.

We believe that all these results are showing the same thing. Sentences, pictures, or images which lead to propositions relating the two terms produce greater associative learning than do stimuli that lead merely to coordinate conjunctions or simple static predicates of the kind "*X* beside *Y*." Coordinate conjunctions by themselves do not provide any propositional structure at all, and the static predicates are not much better. Such static relations as *next to* place virtually no semantic constraints whatsoever on X and Y. Therefore, if a subject is cued with X and retrieves the predicate *next to*, he has done little to narrow down the possible alternatives for the object. Thus, if the object association to Y is not intact, there will be little avail in guessing strategies of various sophistication. For instance, consider the contrast between "Cowboy beside steer" and "Cowboy ropes steer." Given "Cowboy beside . . .," it is unlikely that steer will be provided as a guess to complete the phrase, whereas such a guess is very likely to "Cowboy ropes . . . ." Moreover, the static relation permits little elaboration, whereas other relations permit elaboration into new propositions interconnecting X and Y. Thus, "Cowboy ropes steer" suggests such additional facts as "Cowboy chases steer," "Cowboy bulldogs steer," "Cowboy brands steer." Moreover, each of these episodes can be expanded into its microstructure, providing further interconnections. For instance, "Cowboy ropes steer" expands into the cowboy taking aim, letting go of the rope, the rope encircling the steer, the rope becoming taut, the steer tripping, the cowboy's look of accomplishment, etc. This sort of expansion is much less readily accomplished with a predicate like "Cowboy beside steer."

Concreteness-Abstractness of Verbal Materials

It was mentioned earlier that learning is usually faster with concrete words than with abstract words. How might the conceptual-propositional hypothesis explain that abstract-concrete difference? At least part of the usual effects result from other attributes of the words that are typically confounded with concreteness-abstractness. One of these confounded attributes is the complexity of the lexical item as an English word, which determines the complexity of its entry in our internal lexicon. Frequently, abstract nouns are derived morphemically by adding prefixes or suffixes to verbs or adjectives, whereas concrete nouns tend to be lexically simple and not derived. This is how we get the abstract nouns *explanation, interpretation,* and *liberation* from the transitive verbs *explain, interpret,* and *liberate,* or how we derive *ability* and *difficulty* from the adjectives *able* and *difficult.* In fact, Kintsch (1972) has shown that lexically complex words are learned more slowly in a paired-associate task than are lexically simple words, even when the words were equated on imagery value.

A second overlooked contaminant in the comparison of abstract versus concrete words is the number of different semantic senses or dictionary meanings which a word has. In a paired-associate task, Schnorr and Atkinson (1970) found that words with many dictionary meanings were learned more slowly than words with fewer meanings, perhaps due to greater variability in encoding of the former items. This effect held for words equated on their imagery value. Furthermore, there is known to be a positive correlation between the average abstractness of a word and its number of dictionary entries—which may be why it is so difficult for people to communicate their exact meanings in abstract discussions.

There may be other confounding "linguistic" attributes correlated with the concreteness-abstractness ratings of words. The reason for mentioning these confounding factors is to illustrate that one should exercise extreme caution in basing major conclusions on the correlation between word abstractness and verbal learning rates. The correlation might be substantially reduced when various possible confounding word attributes are controlled.

Modality-Specific Interference?

There was a short-lived hope that the imaginal versus semantic representation of the memory trace could be distinguished by so-called "modality-specific interference" effects, an idea adapted from earlier work by Lee Brooks (1968). The basic notion is that if visual imagery involves some specifically visual process, then it must engage some of the same brain mechanisms as are engaged in visual perception. If this is true and if these visual mechanisms have a limited processing capacity, the visualization should suffer if the subject tries to visualize learning materials at the same time as he is required to do a visual perception task. On the other hand, according to this hypothesis, the subject's visualization should not be reduced nearly so much by having visualized learning material while he is doing a nonvisual distraction task. In brief, according to this hypothesis, it should be hard to do two visual things at once, even when one of the things is only visually imagining; the outer eye should compete with the inner eye.

This idea, based on Brooks' (1968) performance results, was tried out in the context of a memory experiment by Atwood (1971) with apparently positive results. He found that a *visual* distractor task (given during study of a paired-associate list) reduced later recall of concrete, imageable material more than it reduced recall of abstract material. On the other hand, a comparable *auditory* distractor task had the reverse effect, reducing recall of abstract verbal material more than recall of concrete material. This was the "modality-specific interference" effect that was being sought.

The interpretive problem is that the Atwood results have not stood up under systematic replication (Bower, Munoz, & Arnold, 1972; Lee Brooks, personal communication, 1972). Thus it appears best not to rely too heavily on that result for drawing theoretical conclusions. Moreover, later experiments by Brian Byrnne (reported in Brooks, 1970) have cast an entirely new light on the interpretation of Brooks' original results. In brief, Byrnne showed that in order to scan in memory over a spatially distributed array of information (e.g., an image of words in a 3 × 3 matrix), the person must be permitted to move his eyes in a homologous sequence. If his reporting task requires him to carry out completely conflicting eye movements (e.g., to report the serial order of the words in the matrix by finding them in a scrambled list), then his memory scan suffers. If the report task requires eye movements in a serial order that is spatially compatible with the spatial array of memory information the subject is scanning, then there is no conflict between visual perception and remembering in visual imagery. So, the conflict is not between imaging and visual perception, as originally supposed, but rather is between the motor (eye movement) scanning of sensory arrays and the scanning of mnemonic information structures encoding spatial information (e.g., about the location of words in a 3 × 3 matrix).

The upshot of these various considerations is that we cannot rely on the "modality-specific interference" effect to dictate our memory representation in favor of imagery versus a propositional base. Quite the contrary, the present results appear particularly insufficient to support a firm conclusion on such a major matter.

HAM's View of Imagery

In concluding, we would like to emphasize that we are not downgrading the importance of imagery. Rather, we are disputing one interpretation frequently given to the effects of imagery in memory. We have been arguing that the representation of an image should be in terms of the abstract propositional system of HAM and neither in terms of internal "pictures" nor in terms of verbal associations. In fact, as we argued in Chapter 5, we think such a propositional system initially evolved to deal effectively with perceptual material, and that language attached itself parasitically onto this propositional base. As a consequence, most of the primitives in HAM's base set of simple ideas correspond to elementary sensations.

The only difference between the internal representation for a linguistic input and a memory image is detail of information. A moment's reflection will reveal that most of what we say is very abstract and quite removed from a complete description of the causal microstructure of the concrete happenings. The listener either can be content to comprehend at this abstract level what we are saying, or he may choose to form an image of what we are asserting. If he chooses the latter, he will *unpack* each of our concepts into its more primitive terms.

Our words spoken to a listener are like the cryptic directions a playwright provides for a play director, from which a competent director is expected to construct an entire setting, an expressive mood, or an action episode in a drama. To illustrate, in the course of reading a story, you might read the sentence "James Bond ran to his car and drove to the casino." As you read, you can concretize that sentence by bringing to bear all sorts of facts and sensory images about running, about getting into cars, about driving, and so forth. These "fill-ins" would be called upon, for example, if you were to be asked simple questions like "Did James Bond sit in a car? Did he start its motor? Did he move the steering wheel?" Such trivial implications seem immediately available from the referential semantics of the verb phrase "drive a car." What the sentence does is merely mention a couple of signposts (source, instrument, goal) along the way in the description of an event sequence; the listener interpolates or fills in all the interstitial events between the mentioned signposts. Of course, at a later time, the listener is hardly able to say exactly what he heard as compared to what he filled in; if he is asked to tell the story "in his own words," he will probably select slightly different descriptions or signposts to mention in reconstructing the salient episodes.

All this can be represented in the structures of HAM, although we make no pretense to having programmed all the processes necessary to effect the unpacking of concepts. Note also that, in this view, the difference between abstract comprehension and imagery is one of degree. That is, the unpacking need not go all the way to the visual primitives, but can stop at some intermediate level. To the extent that the level of unpacking remains removed from the primitives, to that extent the image will be described as schematic and incomplete. We would suppose that such expansion goes progressively deeper the more time a person is allowed to think about or image the meaning of the sentence.

Summing-up

We have presented a very strong version of the conceptual-propositional hypothesis, arguing that HAM's representation is sufficient to handle all information processing associated with visual imagery. We are aware that this is probably too strongly stated, that there are imaginal processes that seem to require a representation of a mental object that is isomorphic to the structure of the physical object, rather than a propositional representation. Particularly striking evidence for the former representation comes from Shepard and Metzler (1971), who showed that the time to recognize that two perspective line drawings portray objects of the same three-dimensional shape is a linear increasing function of the angular difference in the orientation of the objects. Thus, figures which were 180° apart took the longest to identify. In contrast, network models like Winston's find 180° equivalences quite easy to identify. Such recognitions only require a switching of right and left relations in one description and a test whether the transformed description matches the other. Network models would find harder the recognition of equivalences between objects at less than 180° rotation. The introspections of Shepard and Metzler's subjects is that, unlike Winston's program, they mentally rotate one object into the other. In general, it would seem difficult for network systems like Winston's or like HAM to deal with continuously varying visual attributes such as degree of rotation, size, shape, and color. Presumably, the mind processes such information in analog fashion while the information is in a rather raw, textured form.

However, there are important limitations on the usefulness of such an information representation. As Posner (1969) has demonstrated, it appears to be very fragile and does not last well in the absence of the physical stimulus. Certainly, it is completely useless in reasoning tasks such as reported by Clark, Carpenter, and Just (1972). Finally and most important, whatever its value as an immediate representation for visual information, our preceding arguments still hold in implying that it cannot serve as a basis of representation in long-term memory.

We have now covered the main points we wished to make regarding imagery, the conceptual-proposition hypothesis, the relation between them, and their relation to verbal learning studies. We have devoted considerable space to the topic because it concerns a fundamental issue in current-day cognitive psychology, namely, how to represent theoretically our knowledge of the world. Also, mental imagery is currently a very fashionable topic for psychologists to study, and any newly proposed theory dealing with a representation of cognitions must confront and come to grips with the expanding experimental literature on imagery and cognition. Although there are many further details we have skipped concerning our views on imagery, the main points have been stated, and it is time to conclude our general review of verbal learning. The next chapter will be devoted to a detailed analysis of the topic of interference and forgetting, which has received extensive investigation in the verbal learning literature.

10
INTERFERENCE AND FORGETTING

Interference theory occupies an unchallenged position as the major significant analysis of the process of forgetting.

—Leo Postman

10.1. FORGETTING IN HAM

A fault found in most of the current stock of computer simulations of human memory is that they have forgotten that people forget. In the few programs that do forget (e.g., Reitman, 1965), information loss is viewed as simple decay of the strength of past memories. The research on EPAM and SAL (Feigenbaum, 1963, 1970; Hintzman, 1968; Simon & Feigenbaum, 1964) has been the only attempt to produce simulation models that make contact with the basic facts of forgetting from long-term memory. However, these conceptions of memory are not adequate for the task of expressing the propositional character of memory.

In contrast, experimental psychologists have developed an impressive body of data and theory surrounding the process of forgetting. This, the work of the interference theorists, has been the major substantive accomplishment of American associationism. However, these efforts suffer from difficulties similar to those of EPAM and SAL. That is, the interference research has been conducted within the framework of an inadequate conception of the character of human memory. The basic unit of knowledge has pretty much still been taken to be the S-R habit, undifferentiated according to the relations among the terms; human knowledge is equated with just a list of habits. Recent papers by Underwood (1969) and Wickens (1970) recognize several different "attributes" of memories but do not go beyond cataloging some of the evidence that people can remember all sorts of things about past events. What is lacking in these efforts is an attempt to characterize the associative organization of long-term memory and how the "mind" brings that to bear in recording new facts and events, while forgetting others. Another aspect that has been conspicuously lacking is the study of interference and forgetting of sentences and textual materials. Interference theorists are probably uncomfortable analyzing the learning and forgetting of propositional materials because they have not developed any viable ideas regarding the structure of sentences (they are obviously not serial lists of words), nor any specific ideas regarding how the person brings his cognitive equipment to bear upon comprehending, storing, retrieving, and using propositional information.

In past chapters we have outlined the beginnings of a more adequate conception of human memory. In this chapter we will try to indicate how forgetting would occur in such a memory. This section discusses the basic mechanism that produces forgetting in HAM. We will illustrate how it accounts for some of the salient facts of forgetting. In Section 10.2 this theoretical conception is compared with others, and we will note how HAM can account for data previously thought to be solely favorable to other theories. However, in reviewing the recent evidence for "response-set suppression," we will find ourselves forced to make some kind of concession to the notion of a generalized loss of response availability.

The basic facts of forgetting that demand explanation are now fairly well documented. The learning of laboratory materials tends to interfere with memory for other laboratory material that precedes or follows it. In serial learning, this interference increases with the similarity of the two lists of items. In paired-associate learning, increasing similarity of the stimuli in the successive lists of materials increases the interfering effect, but increasing the similarity of the responses has inconsistent effects and may actually facilitate memory. Retroactive interference (RI) refers to the effect of later learned material on retention of earlier material; proactive interference (PI) refers to the effect of learning earlier material upon retention of later learned material. In this section we will focus on how HAM would handle RI. The next section considers, among other things, the problem of how HAM could be extended to deal with PI and the related matter of negative transfer.

Stimulus-Specific Interference in HAM

The mechanism for stimulus-specific interference lies in HAM's search of the GET-lists when the MATCH process is evoked to search memory for information which will match an input or probe tree. When HAM searches from a node a for associations having relation Y to a, it must serially search the list (the GET-list) of all nodes b such that $<a\ Y\ b>$ is an associative link. This list may contain many members, and HAM will search only a probabilistically determined portion of the list for an association to match the input probe. HAM always searches the GET-list from the beginning and moves down the list examining member after member, to a randomly determined depth. This serial search process was used in explaining the search-time data for Chapter 8. Since the GET-list of a given relation out of a given node is constantly updated to reflect the most recently used associations, this search routine guarantees that the most recent associations are the most likely to be examined. Consequently, the acquisition of new associations will tend to "bury" old associations and make them inaccessible when the GET-list is searched. That is, the probabilistic retrieval mechanism may not search far enough down the GET-list to find the desired association. In barest terms, this is the mechanism for retroactive inhibition in HAM.

An important feature of this search process is that it was originally motivated solely to provide for an efficient search of memory, not to fit the interference data. Since the GET-lists that must be searched can become inordinately long, it is necessary to have some mechanism to inhibit long and fruitless searches that would result in excessive verification times.

The Stop Rule

Let us consider a simple model of how the search from a memory node is terminated. The model is tentative, and little in this chapter rests on this specific formulation. However, we prefer to have something explicit to reference in later discussions of interference. Basically, it is assumed that the MATCH process will terminate after T seconds of search. Thus, the mechanisms developed in Chapter 8 may be used to give a precise characterization of the amount of memory that will be searched from a particular entry node. In that chapter we assumed that there was an exponential distribution of search times for completely examining N memory associations from a terminal node in a probe tree. This distribution had mean aN:

$$f(t) = \frac{e^{-t/aN}}{aN} \tag{1}$$

Using Equation (1) we can derive the probability that N associations will be searched by time T:

$$\text{Prob(Completing } N \text{ associations in time } T) = 1 - e^{-T/aN} \tag{2}$$

This model may be applied to particular examples to compute the probability that a particular fact will be retrieved. As an example, consider the case of a sentence in the "3-3 true" condition in the agent-location experiment described in Section 8.2. To refresh the reader's memory, that experiment varied the number of places a particular class of people (e.g., hippies) were and the number of people in a particular location (e.g., park). Thus, if "A hippie is in the park" is a "3-3 true" sentence, then hippies were in two other locations, and the park had two other people in it.

Thus, from the "hippie" node in memory, three ϵ^{-1} associations would lead to three separate propositions; similarly, three ϵ^{-1} associations would fan out from "park." Retrieval of the "hippie in park" proposition would be particularly difficult when it is the last proposition leading out of both the "hippie" node and the "park" node (as in Section 8.2, we will just ignore the contribution of search from the "in" node). Suppose, then, that when the subject calls the function GET (hippie, ϵ^{-1}), the ϵ^{-1} association leading to the proposition "A hippie is in the park" happens to be the last on the GET-list. Suppose that similar misfortunes arise when the system evokes the function GET(park, ϵ^{-1}). In this set of disastrous circumstances, HAM would have to search 21 associations from either entry node in order to verify the test assertion. We wish to calculate the probability that the subject will fail to retrieve this proposition if we fix time for retrieval, T, at, say, 2 seconds. Having estimated a to be 81 msec. for that experiment, we can determine the probability that a MATCH process will not succeed in examining 21 necessary associations in 2 seconds from Equation (2); it is Prob(failure) = $e^{-2,000/(81 \times 21)}$ = .31. Since the two MATCH processes from the two entry nodes are independent, the probability of failure of search from both is the product of the two identical values above, or .095.

Now, compare this unfortunate case with the favorable case where the "hippie in park" proposition is on the top of the two GET-lists leading from "hippie" and "park." Again, we compute the probability that the MATCH process fails from both nodes in 2 seconds, but this time the MATCH process need only consider seven associations from each node. Again, using Equation (2) we find for either node, Prob(failure) = $e^{-2000/(81 \times 7)}$ = .029. The joint probability of the failure of both MATCH processes is the product, which is .001. Comparing these two cases, the probability of successfully retrieving a proposition depends markedly upon how far down it is on the appropriate GET-lists of associations.

Assuming the "stop rule" above means that the distribution of MATCH times will be truncated at time T. Consequently, the model fit to the RT data in Chapter 8 was only approximate because it assumed that the exponential distribution of MATCH times had positive probability for values beyond any cutoff point T.

An intuitively satisfying feature of this interference mechanism is that it offers a partial explanation of the fluctuating availability of information in long-term memory. It is a common experience to try to retrieve a particular fact but to fail, only to have it later "come to mind." According to HAM, the interpretation is that a later activation of the MATCH process has scanned through long-term memory at a more rapid rate and has come to the criterion information before the cutoff time T.

This fluctuating availability not only holds over days, but also occurs from moment to moment. Upon hearing "The president hurt the dog," we might initially fail to match this to memory. That is, in searching GET-lists from "president," "hurt," and "dog," we might initially retrieve nothing appropriate. However, the probe could be reentered again and again into memory, rematched and rematched, and eventually the GET(president, ϵ^{-1}) list would be searched to the instance "Lyndon Johnson," and the GET(Johnson, S^{-1}) list would be searched to the proposition referring to that occasion when Johnson tugged on the ears of a beagle for the national news media (see Figure 10.1). In this eventuality, the proposition would be recognized. Most experimenters have observed subjects that "strain" at a memory for a while and then recall it successfully. How often a subject will reenter memory with the same probe, trying to find a match, is presumably affected by such factors as motivation, expected reward for recall, and how sure the subject is

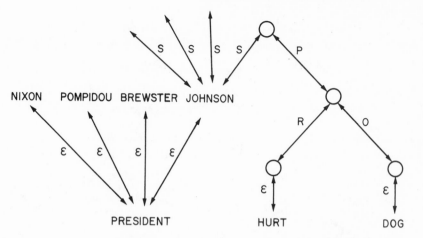

FIG. 10.1. An example of how multiple-branching associations make it difficult to verify the proposition "The president hurt the dog."

that he knows the answer. Shiffrin (1970), p. 434) has reported evidence that requiring subjects to "search memory" again after an initial failure to recall may dredge up some more information.

Comparison with the Data of Retroactive Interference

The mechanism proposed above accounts for the gross fact of interference, i.e., that new information will tend to interfere with recall of old learning. What needs to be examined is the extent to which this mechanism can explain some further details of retroactive interference (abbreviated as RI). This discussion will be confined principally to the literature on the paired-associate learning (PA) of words, since most of the careful research on the topic of interference has been done in this context. We will use the same mechanisms for paired-associate learning as were developed in Section 9.2. That is, HAM will learn by embedding the two members of a paired associate into some proposition. The tree structure encoding this proposition will contain a pathway interlinking the stimulus and response of the paired-associate pair.

Stimulus Similarity

First, we examine the effects on RI of stimulus similarity. HAM clearly predicts maximal interference when the stimuli of the two lists are identical, i.e., in the so-called *A-B, A-C* paradigm. A detailed examination of how HAM produces RI in this paradigm will be informative. HAM initially established an associative path from word *A* to word *B*. During the course of second-list learning the path from *A* to *C* will have to branch off from the former *A*-to-*B* path. The *A-B* and the *A-C* paths could branch immediately at the word *A*. In this case, the *A-C* path may involve a different word-to-idea link than the *A-B* path, a circumstance illustrated in Figure 10.2*a*. In this case, word *A* is being used in two different semantic senses in the two PA pairings. Figure 10.2*a* illustrates two senses of the word "crab." As another alternative, if both propositions used the same word-to-idea link, then the

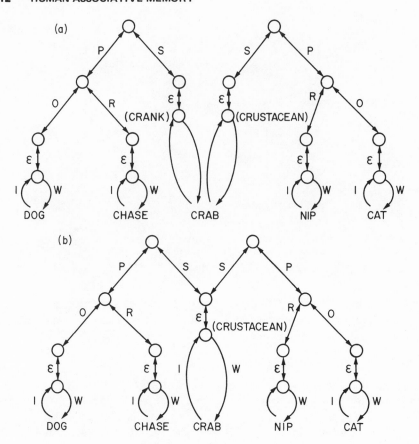

FIG. 10.2. Two alternate memory structures that encode the *A-B* pair "crab-cat" and the *A-C* pair "crab-dog."

point of branching would occur at one of the idea-to-idea associations. The illustration in Figure 10.2*b* has the branch point at the S^{-1} (subject) associations leading from the crab-instance node; other illustrations would have the branch points at somewhat different places in the tree depending on the nature of the *A-B* and *A-C* propositions the subject composes. But the important point is that the two paths from word *A must* branch at some point before they arrive at the words *B* and *C*.

The *A-C* path will interfere with the *A-B* path at the point of branching if that branching introduces a *conjunction* in the memory structure. To review Section 6.2, a conjunction occurs when two identically labeled associations are attached to one node. The *A-B* and *A-C* paths may branch in this identically labeled manner, or they may branch by the *A-B* path leaving the branch node *a* via one label ℓ_1 and by the *A-C* via a different label ℓ_2. These two distinct cases are illustrated in Figure 10.3*a* and *b*. In Figure 10.3*a*, an S^{-1} conjunction occurs since both associations leaving the hippie-instance have an S^{-1} label; on the other hand, in Figure 10.3*b*, one association leaves the hippie-instance node via an S^{-1} association and the other via an O^{-1} association. The theory expects RI to occur only in the former case where there is a conjunction. In the conjunctive case both the B associate and the C associate will be on the list returned when $GET(a, \ell_1)$ is evoked, and the C associate will be the first on the list. If HAM searches this GET-list to only a depth of 1 (which event will happen with some probability), then HAM will not be able to recall in A-B retest. We would have thus observed RI in this case. Note that it is by no means "complete" or a "massive" forgetting effect.

Let us now consider the A-B, A'-C paradigm, where the stimuli in the two lists are semantically similar (e.g., "boy-lad") and the responses different. HAM predicts RI in this circumstance, although not as much as in the A-B, A-C paradigm; and this is found. HAM predicts this finding because, with semantically similar stimuli, the A-B and the A'-C paths are likely to converge at some point. That is, the two paths which start at different word nodes A and A' are likely to contain idea nodes in common. If they do converge, then they must branch at a later point in order to accommodate the new A-C proposition. For those A-B and A'-C paths that do converge, the same mechanism will produce interference as in the A-B, A-C case. That the A-B and A-C paths will often converge is easily argued for pairs of stimuli such as "boy" and "lad." Although both words are likely to lead to the same idea node, the two paths may diverge by selection of a different instance (ϵ) for the two paired associates. Figure 10.4 illustrates how the two paired associates "boy-dog" and "lad-chair" might be encoded. Note the divergence from the idea node for boy. This is the point in this memory structure where interference would occur during retrieval.

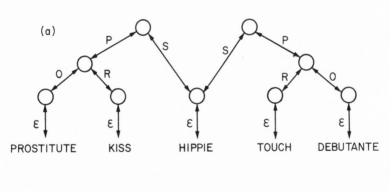

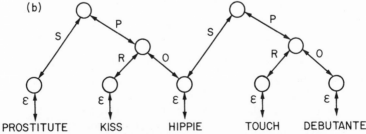

FIG. 10.3. Two alternate memory structures that encode the A-B pair "hippie-prostitute" and the A-C pair "hippie-debutante." HAM only expects RI in panel (a), where there is competition of identically labeled relations.

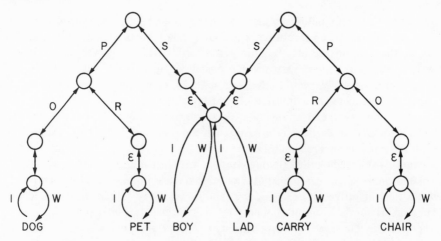

FIG. 10.4. Example of how learning the A'-C pair "lad-chair" may interfere with retention of the A-B pair "boy-dog."

Now consider the question of how HAM performs in an A-B, C-D paradigm—that is, when the stimuli for the two lists are dissimilar. While there is less interference in this paradigm than with similar or identical stimuli, it is known that A-B, C-D conditions produce reliably more interference than rest-control conditions where some unrelated activity like solving jigsaw puzzles is substituted for learning of the interpolated C-D list. Since the A and C stimuli are not related, there seems little possibility for a convergence of the C-D path with the A-B, as there was in the A-B, A'-C condition. It seems rather that forgetting in this situation results from a general loss of the availability of the B responses as a consequence of the interpolated C-D learning. This is an example of interference that is not stimulus-specific; it is difficult to produce from the mechanisms of HAM. The research regarding this general loss of response availability will be reviewed in Section 10.2 and evaluated alongside the mechanism of response-set suppression advanced by prominent interference theorists. At that point we will also consider how such data might be accommodated within HAM.

Number of Trials

Let us continue applying HAM to the basic findings in RI. The basic effects on forgetting of the number of trials of original and interpolated learning (see Slamecka & Ceraso, 1960, for a review) can be handled within HAM. We will briefly indicate how these effects would be predicted. First, it is known that RI for the A-B list increases with the number of interpolated trials on A-C. Two mechanisms would combine to produce this effect in HAM. First, with more A-C trials, there is a greater probability that the subject will successfully construct an A-C path to compete with the A-B path. Furthermore, as noted in Section 9.2, subjects in paired-associates experiments tend to form multiple redundant paths to interlink stimulus and response terms. With more A-C trials, then, more A-C paths should be formed that would compete with the original A-B path. Wherever this competition resulted in conjunctions, the A-B path would fall to less and less accessible regions of a GET-list.

It seems reasonable that, on the later trials of an A-C list, the subject is more likely to rehearse old connections than to form new ones. Consequently, later A-C trials should produce lesser increments in RI. It is generally observed that amount of RI does asymptote with large numbers of A-C trials. It has also been shown a number of times (e.g., Underwood, 1945; Postman, 1965) that it is more effective to have a number of distinct interpolated lists (i.e., A-C, A-D, etc.) than just one list, even though the same total number of IL (interpolated learning) trials are administered. That is, m trials on each of n IL lists causes more forgetting of A-B than $m \times n$ trials on one interpolated list. This is as it should be. With each new list HAM must learn, it will be forced to add new associative paths to compete with the originally learned paths. If those trials learning more interpolated lists had been spent overlearning the first interpolated list, then HAM might just rehearse the same A-C associative paths rather than construct new ones.

Consider further details of RI as the number of interpolated-learning trials on A-C is increased. As IL increases, the amount of RI (as measured by recall errors of A-B) increases monotonically, whereas the number of intrusions of A-C first increases, reaches a maximum at intermediate degrees of IL, then decreases with further learning of the A-C list. These details can be produced within HAM by using the "list discrimination tags" that are part of our representation for paired-associate learning (see especially Figure 9.4). As A-C training commences, a branch point in the A-B structure will have to be found to fit in the required A-C association. The increasing success in doing this accounts for the general rise in RI. However, with increasing trials on A-C, it becomes increasingly likely that response C will be tagged with an association to a "List 2" marker. If, in attempting recall of the first list associate (A-B), the executive monitor checks for the list membership of the retrieved association, then the "C-List 2" association would prevent intrusions of C. Thus, C intrusions in A-B recall would rise, then decline as A-C trials are extended, despite the fact that total RI increased. This is the standard explanation of this result (e.g., Thune & Underwood, 1943); our discussion demonstrates that the standard explanation in terms of list discrimination has a natural formulation in the mechanisms of HAM.

Another well-documented fact is that resistance to interference increases with the number of trials on the original A-B list. With extra A-B trials, HAM could form multiple paths interlinking A and B. The example in Figure 10.5 will serve to illustrate that this multiple pathing would produce in HAM greater resistance to interference. Here, "hippie" and "debutante" have been linked during A-B learning by two propositions: "The hippie touched the debutante" and "The debutante slapped the hippie." In A-C learning, "hippie" is paired with "sailor," and the subject encodes the proposition "The hippie kicked the sailor." This new proposition interferes with the "hippie touch debutante" proposition leading from the hippie-instance; but not with the "debutante slap hippie" proposition. The second proposition is not interfered with because it is a subject (S) branch that leaves the hippie-instance in the A-C proposition, and this branch will interfere only with earlier propositions in which that hippie-instance was the subject. In this case,

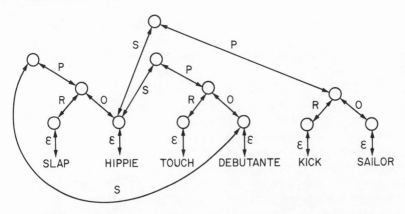

FIG. 10.5. An example of how forming two associations to encode the *A-B* pair "hippie-debutante" protects from interference by the *A-C* pair "hippie-sailor."

by encoding two original *A-B* propositions, HAM has protected itself from interference in *A-C* learning. However, the reduction in RI depends upon having at least one of the *A-B* propositions relate *A* and *B* by a different *sequence* of syntactic links than occurs for the *A-C* proposition. Of course, on later trials of original learning the subject may rehearse old *A-B* paths rather than form redundant new ones. Hence, the effect of number of original-learning trials in reducing RI should asymptote. This is clearly the case (e.g., Briggs, 1957).

In HAM, the *A-B* path is not destroyed by *A-C* learning; rather the *A-C* path (or paths) competes with it for availability. Even though HAM can no longer recall *A-B*, the path remains between *A* and *B*. Therefore, it is not surprising that the interfering effect of *A-C* quickly dissipates with one or two relearning trials on *A-B* (e.g., Osgood, 1948; Underwood, 1945). The interpretation within HAM is that these relearning trials update the "recency" of the *A-B* path, making it once again available by raising its position on the GET-list at which the branch with *A-C* paths had occurred.

One point of interest in this analysis of retroactive inhibition is that it identifies the theoretical communality between the mechanisms contributing to the increases in times to search memory in fact retrieval (reviewed in Chapter 8) and the interference mechanism. That is, the reaction times reflect the time to search particular connections on the GET-list, while the phenomenon of interference in recall occurs when the GET-list becomes longer than can be searched before a preset cutoff time. An experiment by Postman and Kaplan (1947) is particularly interesting in relating these measures. They examined the latencies with which subjects could retrieve their correct responses in the *A-B* retest. Subjects in the *A-B*, *A-C* paradigm showed consistently longer latencies than in the control condition. Moreover, although the difference in recall scores between the control and experimental subjects quickly dissipated after a few relearning trials, the latency difference was maintained. These findings suggest that even when the *A-B* path remained or became accessible on the GET-list, the interfering *A-C* connection still made its presence felt in terms of the time to search the GET-list and retrieve the *A-B* association.

Recall that in the person-location RT experiment of Section 8.2, we found that subjects had relatively little difficulty in searching through three propositions. Given this result, we have been asked why it is we postulate considerable interference between just a pair of elements, A-B and A-C. A number of technical points need to be made in response to this question. First, because of the possibility that the subject encodes multiple propositions in learning A-C, more than two propositions may have to be searched to arrive at the A-B proposition. Second, in the person-location experiment, subjects had two points from which they searched memory, whereas in the paired-associate experiment there is only one entry point, the stimulus A. If the subject has a probability p of not retrieving the proposition when one entry point is available, the probability is reduced to p^2 with two entry points. Finally, we should point out a third fact for which HAM has no compelling explanation: As propositions are more practiced, they are searched more rapidly. For instance, in our person-location experiment, the search rate parameter a was 100 msec. for the first 150 trials and only 62 msec. for the second 150 trials. Moreover, subjects in our person-location experiment already had a half hour's practice with the material before the experiment began. Thus, it would be expected that their memory structures are being searched more rapidly than in the typical paired-associates experiment where the material is only imperfectly learned. Consequently, in the person-location experiment the memory structures could be searched to a greater depth. So for these three reasons, we may expect moderate interference in the typical A-B, A-C paired-associates paradigm.

10.2. COMPARISON TO OTHER INTERFERENCE THEORIES

To use the terms of the interference literature, the mechanism that produces RI in HAM is a hybrid combination of *response competition* and *unlearning*. Like McGeoch's (1936) original notion of response competition, it is assumed that the A-B connection fails because it is overcome by one or more competing A-C connections. It is often assumed in the response-competition hypothesis that the subject must either overtly or covertly recall the competing C responses during the A-B retest. These recalled C responses compete with and hinder the subject's recall of the appropriate B responses. There are a number of well-known empirical embarrassments to this version of the response-competition hypothesis. It has been shown that most of the forgetting in A-B retest does not manifest itself as intrusions of the competing C responses, but rather as total failures to recall (e.g., Melton & Irwin, 1940; Thune & Underwood, 1943). Moreover, at high levels of IL where RI is maximal, the number of overt intrusions is very negligible. If the C responses were competing with and displacing the B responses, we would expect to see an increase in overt intrusions. Earlier, we indicated how such results can be explained by "list-discrimination" factors in HAM.

The modified–modified free recall (MMFR) experiment reported by Barnes and Underwood (1959) is another classic demonstration of the deficiencies of a simple response-competition hypothesis. Barnes and Underwood asked their subjects to recall both the B and the C responses to the A stimulus, during the retention test following A-B, A-C learning. They found that as their subjects had more A-C trials, their ability to recall the B terms decreased. It was argued that the loss of the first-list responses in this case could not be due to response competition because the subject was free to recall both responses, and in fact was even instructed to do so.

While such data embarrass the traditional response-competition mechanism, they are as expected from the interference mechanism in HAM. In HAM, even though A-C paths compete with and make A-B paths unavailable, it is not the case that C responses will be intruded in the A-B retest. Through the list-discrimination mechanism discussed earlier, HAM can inhibit C responses to A stimuli when first-list recall is requested. As noted earlier, HAM expects fewer C intrusions in A-B retest with greater IL training, which is what Melton and Irwin (1940) found.

Of course, when list discrimination fails, HAM will incorrectly recall the C response (although B was available) because C is more accessible than B. Such cases exemplify overt competition of responses, with C dominating B, which was the original response-competition thesis regarding forgetting. However, in HAM associative paths also compete for availability on the GET-lists. This means that even if HAM is urged to recall both responses as in the Barnes and Underwood MMFR experiment, it still may fail to "get at" the B response.

In this way the mechanism of interference in HAM is like the unlearning mechanism that has been traditionally advanced to account for findings such as those of Melton and Irwin or Barnes and Underwood. The unlearning postulate claims that A-C learning produces unlearning of the prior A-B associations. Underwood (1948a, 1948b) suggested that this unlearning may be similar to the phenomenon of "experimental extinction" seen in classical and instrumental conditioning; i.e., B responses are extinguished because they are evoked but not reinforced during A-C learning. (A curious paradox is that prominent contemporary accounts of experimental extinction in the animal conditioning area—e.g., Amsel, 1967; Logan, 1960; Spence, 1960—attribute extinction to response-competition-like factors such as avoidance of frustrative nonreward.) Underwood found evidence that RI decreases over the retention interval. This was attributed to "spontaneous recovery" over time of the unlearned A-B associations. Spontaneous recovery of an extinguished response is usually found in classical and instrumental conditioning paradigms. Much research has investigated the "spontaneous recovery" of verbal responses in interference paradigms. Absolute recovery of A-B is sometimes found, sometimes not, depending on a variety of circumstances such as the degree of original learning of A-B, the retention interval, and so on. Recent reviews are contained in papers by Postman, Stark, and Fraser (1968) and by Postman, Stark, and Henschel (1969).

The unlearning and the response-competition hypotheses are generally considered complementary (e.g., Keppel, 1968). Proactive interference (PI) was thought to reflect only response competition, whereas retroactive interference was assumed to reflect a combination of both factors. Unlearning was presumed to be absent in PI because the interfered-with material is learned last, so it cannot suffer from unlearning due to a subsequent interpolated task. An embarrassment for this analysis is evidence that PI is not solely a result of response competition. For instance, in an MMFR retention test the subject is asked to recall both responses to the stimulus, one from each list (i.e., both B and C). This should eliminate any interfering effects of response competition since the subject is free to give both responses. However, PI has been found in MMFR tests (e.g., Koppenaal, 1963; Koppenaal, Krull, & Katz,1965), contrary to the early prediction. But how can previous learning cause later-learned material to be unlearned? We shall return later to this issue of PI.

At this point it will be instructive to note the differences between our interference mechanism and the unlearning mechanism. The major difference is that there is no committment in our theory to notions of reinforcement and extinctive inhibition. Unlearning is often conceived of as caused by the unreinforced evocation of the B responses during A-C learning. As Melton (1961) noted, this implies that "there is some correlation between the specific responses that are unavailable in specific subjects and the specific nonreinforced intrusions of these same responses during IL [p. 184]." But there is no evidence for such a correlation. In fact, in an experiment that manipulated IL intrusion rate by guessing instructions, Keppel and Rauch (1966), found no relation between RI and intrusion rate. HAM does not require this dependence of RI on the overt elicitation of the B response. The A-B path will tend to be buried by the A-C path purely as a function of acquiring A-C. One way to keep the A-B path from sinking too far below the A-C paths on GET-lists is to require the subject to explicitly recall both the B and C responses throughout interpolated learning of A-C. Postman and Parker (1970) found, in fact, that simple instructions to maintain B responses during IL did reduce (although not eliminate) RI.

Spontaneous Recovery

One of the more persuasive pieces of evidence for the inhibitory conception of unlearning has been the demonstration of spontaneous recovery from RI. Sometimes, the number of A-B items that can be recalled actually increases over a short interval between A-C learning and retest. This is referred to as *absolute spontaneous recovery*. Sometimes, however, there is only *relative spontaneous recovery*, in which loss of A-B items is less rapid relative to their loss rate in a control condition. For instance, immediately after IL, recall of A-B items may be 70% for subjects who have had A-C interpolation but 90% for subjects without any interpolation. However, at a 24-hour delay these recall percentages may become, respectively, 60% and 70%. Thus, subjects in the A-C group have lost only 10% of the items over the 24-hour retention interval, relative to the 20% loss for the control group.

It might seem that HAM would not produce spontaneous recovery, particularly of the absolute variety. Once the A-B had been buried by the A-C path, how could it ever become available again? A possible solution to this dilemma lies in the observation that while the A-B path may not be any longer available, the B-A path may be. Recall that the branch that causes interference occurs along the path from A to B. In contrast, there is no such branching on the path from B to A. With respect to the backpath, the A-B, A-C paradigm is actually a retroactive facilitation paradigm (i.e., B-A, C-A). Therefore, should HAM in its random mental wanderings, ever generate the B responses during the interval between A-C learning and retest, it is likely to revive its memory of the B-A backpath. As a consequence of reactivating that connection, the forward A-B path would rise to the top of the GET-list at that point where the branch occurred with the A-C paths. Hence, B would become once again available as a response to A. Of course, the probability that the subject will think about the B response and its backpath to A, and thus revive the forepath, will increase with the interval between A-C learning and the retention test. Hence we would have the phenomena of spontaneous recovery.

There are two lines of evidence which suggest this "backpath" analysis of so-called spontaneous recovery. First, no spontaneous recovery can be found with "associative matching" tests under comparable conditions which produce recovery in the case of PA recall (L. Postman, personal communication, 1972). In associative matching tests, the stimuli and responses of the A-B list are given in scrambled sets, and the subject must pair them according to the A-B pairings learned. This is a kind of "pair-recognition" test. HAM can perform pair recognition on the basis of either the A to B path or the B to A path (see also Wolford, 1971); so A-C learning should not seriously degrade pair recognition. But more importantly, since pair-recognition tests already tap both A-B and B-A, there can be no evidence of "spontaneous recovery" over time due to the B-A path inadvertently making the A-B path more available than the A-C path.

A second bit of positive evidence has been provided by Merryman and Merryman (1972). They considered the increase in A-B recall (following A-C interpolation) which accompanies repeated nonreinforced test trials with the subject trying to recall A-B. HAM expects some improvement in A-B recall over repeated test trials for two reasons: first, successive retrievals at the branching point out of the A stimulus are independent, and a low A-B associate which is not retrieved on initial trials may be retrieved at later opportunities, recognized as the first-list response, and so updated to the top position in the GET-list. The second reason for improved test performance is the backpath argument given above: repeated tests provide more opportunities for the subject to scan the list of B responses retrievable from the context cues (i.e., "LIST 1 contains responses B_1, B_2, ..., B_m"), and to recognize the backpath from a B to its appropriate A stimulus. This then reinstates that A-B forepath to have priority over the A-C forepath, thus appearing to be "spontaneous recovery" of the unlearned A-B pair.

Merryman and Merryman (1972) tried to eliminate this second source of recovery. To do this, they arranged the interpolated learning so that both forward and backward associations were "unlearned." Following A-B learning, the interpolated list contained D-B pairs as well as A-C pairs—the former to lower the availability of the B-A path, and the latter to lower the availability of the A-B path. The series of 10 nonreinforced tests for A-B retention which followed showed considerably less "recovery" in this condition of double unlearning than in the condition of just A-C forward unlearning only. The result is relevant to HAM's interpretation of "spontaneous recovery" of A-B over time if it is supposed that the multiple test trials in the Merrymans' experiment are simply measuring explicitly what is implicitly occurring over an "unfilled rest interval" when the A-B associations recover.

This analysis also suggests why subjects display progressively increasing proactive inhibition with the interval between A-C learning and retest. The subject is ruminating over old *A-B* connections and reviving them so that they have a degree of availability greater than *A-C*. Of course, on the traditional two-factor theory, the reason for increasing PI was the recovery of the *A-B* associations. What is novel in our account is the belief that the subject's conscious ruminations are an important causal factor. Houston (1969) has performed an interesting experiment relevant to this issue. He supposed that PI was particularly marked in the normal laboratory experiment because subjects were expecting to be retested. Therefore, in the retention interval they would rehearse *A-B* pairs, making the *A-C* pairs less available. Houston's experiment tested this possibility by using four groups of subjects, two learning only a single *A-C* list, and two learning *A-B* and then *A-C* lists. Within each condition, one group was told that it should return to the lab in 7 days for a retention test for what had been learned, whereas the other group was told (falsely) that the experiment was completely finished. Six days later, the experimenter unexpectedly telephoned each subject and administered the MMFR retention test over the telephone. The recall results were entirely consistent with the implicit-rehearsal hypothesis; that is, (*a*) subjects expecting to receive a retention test showed significant PI, comparing recall by the double-list group to that by the single-list group, whereas (*b*) subjects not expecting to be tested did not show significant PI on the MMFR test, the double-list group recalling the *A-C* pairs just as well as did the single-list controls. In addition, those subjects expecting to be tested reported that they had consciously rehearsed the test lists several times throughout the retention interval. Such results (which have been replicated— Houston, 1971) provide a plausible interpretation of PI in the usual MMFR tests—a result that could not be accommodated by the two-factor theory that attributed PI to response competition.

The Differentiation Hypothesis

Another dimension of complexity was added to interference theory by Underwood (1945) when he proposed the *differentiation* hypothesis. The basic idea is that in *A-B*, *A-C* learning the subject requires some means to distinguish when to respond with *B* and when with *C*. Underwood supposed that subjects use various temporal and contextual cues to differentiate between Lists 1 and 2 but that the discriminative power of these cues would deteriorate as the retention interval increased. Birnbaum (1965) has shown that in an MMFR test, the subject's ability to identify the list membership of a response does deteriorate from about 99% immediately, down to about 78% at one week's delay. So clearly, list discrimination may be another factor promoting both PI and RI in non–MMFR recall tests.

HAM contains a reasonably satisfactory analysis of list discrimination and the causes of its deterioration over time. This mechanism was developed more fully elsewhere (Anderson & Bower, 1972), and only its basic characteristics will be indicated here. List discrimination occurs by means of retrieval of contextual information stored with the elements of the list (the stimuli and/or responses). This contextual information constitutes basically a description of the situation in which the responses occurred. On the basis of the contextual information, the subject makes a decision about whether the word appeared in List 1 or 2. With the passage of time, the word will occur in additional contexts, and new context descriptions will be stored with it. These will tend to interfere with and make less available the old contextual descriptions. The mechanism of interference among contextual descriptions is the same as our mechanism for interference among responses to the same stimuli in PA, namely, loss of availability of associative paths. So, HAM's basic interference mechanism is responsible for the loss of list discrimination over time and for the consequent misidentification of B and C responses in a paired-associates paradigm.

Response Set Suppression

The basic notion of list differentiation and its role in retention is an important addition to interference theory. We use the idea in HAM, and try to suggest the bases for list identification. We are somewhat less sympathetic to the use of list-differentiation principles to bolster the theory of response-set suppression (see Postman, Stark, & Fraser, 1968), an approach that has become somewhat popular in the recent literature of interference theory.

The hypothesis is that during A-C learning following A-B learning, the subject soon comes to confine his response selections to the C response set and to avoid or "suppress" the B response set (which produces intrusions). The response-suppression mechanism is assumed to show "inertia," so that once it is set to select from the C responses, this setting persists willy-nilly for a while, causing difficulty in recalling the B responses on an MMFR retention test. Such assumptions predict RI, especially on tests that require the B responses to be recalled (rather than recognizing A-B pairs presented for test); the assumptions also imply that RI will appear strongly in the A-B, C-D paradigm despite the absence in this design of stimulus-specific interference. It is further hypothesized that the set to select C responses and suppress B responses "spontaneously dissipates" over the retention interval, so that eventually neither response set will be dominant. This hypothesis of the dissipation of response-set suppression predicts, correctly, the A-B recall will recover from RI in the A-B, A-C paradigm; it also predicts, correctly again, that just as much recovery of A-B occurs in the A-B, C-D paradigm as in the A-B, A-C paradigm (see Postman, Stark, and Henschel, 1969).

We personally find this notion of *response-set suppression* unattractive. The mechanism is unexplained, it seems disturbingly ad hoc, and its theoretical properties are not yet fully developed. To postulate that the subject is a helpless victim of a perseverating tendency to suppress B responses runs counter to the increasing acceptance of the importance of cognitive control and the speed with which people can switch their "cognitive set" or search strategies. But our theoretical biases are not at issue here. Let us examine the empirical evidence for response-set suppression. It is useful to discriminate and examine separately three empirical claims that have been made by its promoters: (a) there is a generalized competition between B and C responses for availability; (b) the mechanism underlying this competition is the conscious or unconscious *suppression* of one entire set of responses; and (c) all RI observed in the A-B, A-C paradigm is a consequence of this generalized response loss—there is no stimulus-specific interference as postulated in HAM. The available evidence forces acceptance of claim (a), is rather weak with respect to claim (b), but clearly refutes claim (c). We now review this evidence.

Generalized Response Loss

It seems clear that as interpolated learning progresses, the subject's ability to access the original responses deteriorates, while the interpolated responses become ever more available. After IL, the originally learned responses gradually recover in strength at the expense of the availability of the IL responses. The facts in this case evoke metaphorical imagery of an army of OL responses and an army of IL responses battling for control of the high ground of response availability. Using the A-B, A-C paradigm Ceraso and Henderson (1965, 1966) have shown that the B responses become more available over a 24-hour interval after A-C learning, but that C responses become less available as measured in either MMFR or free recall.

Postman and Warren (1972) have examined the effect of the temporal point of the interpolated learning in the interval between original learning and its relearning. They found that the point of maximal interference was just before relearning, and this was true for both A-B, A-C and A-B, C-D designs. Newton and Wickens (1956) had reported similar results. The interpretation is that the B responses recover their availability in the interval between A-C learning and before retest. Lehr, Frank, and Mattison (1972) have shown that interpolation of free-recall learning can also have an interfering effect on A-B retention, although the interference is not as strong as that caused by new paired-associate learning. Thus, simply requiring the subject to learn and make available a new set of responses interferes with A-B recall. Moreover, the spontaneous recovery of the A-B list over the retention interval was about the same for either source of interference. This suggests that spontaneous recovery may be largely a matter of recovery of response availability.

There is also some evidence that requiring the subjects to free-recall the B responses after interpolated A-C learning will reduce the interfering effect. Postman, Burns, and Hasher (1970) found that reexposure to the B responses had a beneficial effect for the weak A-B pairs (i.e., those correctly anticipated only a few times in acquisition), but there was no effect of free recall on the strong A-B pairs. Cofer, Faile, and Horton (1971) report extensive research on the effect of interpolated study and free recall of B responses. Free-recall tests on the B responses were given either during or after learning of the interpolated list. Either procedure reduced A-B forgetting in the A-B, A-C paradigm. However, none of their various manipulations were able to completely eliminate RI in the A-B, A-C paradigm, nor to eliminate the greater RI in this paradigm than in the A-B, C-D paradigm, Thus, while response availability is clearly one factor in RI, there appears to also be a role left for stimulus-specific interference.

Evidence for the Suppression Mechanism

The research reviewed shows that general loss of response availability is one factor contributing to forgetting. But what is the evidence for a response-set suppression mechanism? Need we believe that a selector mechanism, "suffering from inertia," is withholding the B responses? The evidence for such a mechanism is presently not very compelling.

Some of the existing evidence derives from the assumption that the subject will show more inertia in repressing B responses the more difficulty these B responses produce in retarding A-C acquisition. Postman, Keppel, and Stark (1965), Friedman and Reynold (1967), Birnbaum (1968), and Shulman and Martin (1970) have examined the effect of manipulating the similarity between the B and C sets of responses. The consistent finding is that there is more RI when the B and C responses come from the same class (e.g., words of the same conceptual category in the Shulman and Martin study). It is argued that since the response classes are similar to one another, the responses would tend to compete more during A-C learning, the selector mechanism would have to become even more discriminating to keep out B responses during A-C learning, and would consequently show more inertia in the A-B retest. The logic of this argument is not unassailable.

Postman, Stark, and Fraser (1968) have shown that, when the subject is presented with A and its second-list response C and asked to recall its first-list response B, RI is greater than when the subject is asked either to recall just B or to recall both B and C to the stimulus of A alone. They suggest that this greater interference is because presentation of the C response maintains the bias of the selector mechanism in favor of the C response over the B response.

Unfortunately, manipulations designed to bias the selector mechanism do not always have their intended effect. Postman and Stark (1965) reexposed subjects at the end of IL to the B responses by means of an incidental task. The hope was to increase the dominance of the B responses. The tactic succeeded in that the B responses were more likely to be given first before the C responses in MMFR. However, the amount of RI was unchanged. That is, the B response was no more likely to be recalled, despite the fact it was more likely to be emitted first when it was recalled. So, a manipulation that should have reduced the RI due to the inappropriate suppression failed.

To summarize, then, the evidence reviewed does not provide a conclusive case for the concept of response-set suppression.

Evidence for Stimulus-Specific Interference

A question asked in the recent interference literature is whether there is any evidence for the loss of specific A-B associations in the A-B, A-C paradigm, as opposed to the hypothesis that all RI is a matter of general loss of response availability. If one tries to explain all forgetting in terms of generalized response loss, it becomes problematical why there is more RI in the A-B, A-C paradigm, where there is opportunity for stimulus-specific interference, than in the A-B, C-D paradigm, where this opportunity does not exist. It has been suggested (e.g., Postman & Stark, 1969) that the response-set suppression may be more severe and more persistent with A-C interpolation because the occurrence of explicit B intrusions early during A-C learning calls forth greater efforts to suppress B terms, or efforts to find more bases for distinguishing B and C responses and thus to edit out and suppress the B terms.

Postman and Stark attempted to test this notion with a multiple-choice PA retention test that would negate the effects of response-set suppression. That is, instead of having to recall the B responses to the A stimuli, the subject was given a set of possible responses and asked to select the correct one. They argued that in this circumstance, since the subject was given the correct B response along with the irrelevant distractors (incorrect B responses), there was no way to suppress the set of B responses. Consequently, they predicted and found no RI with such tests in the A-B, A-C paradigm relative to a rest control. There was also no RI in the A-B, C-D paradigm with the multiple-choice recognition procedure. Thus, it would appear that in an associative matching test that eliminates the factor of response availability, there is no RI for either paradigm.

Several objections can be advanced regarding the conclusions from the Postman and Stark experiment. First, other researchers (Delprato, 1971; Garskof, 1968; Garskof & Sandak, 1964) have found some RI in a response-matching task. Second, a model like HAM does not predict much RI in the A-B, A-C paradigm when retest involves response matching. As noted before, if HAM were given the B response as one choice in a set of alternatives, it could determine that B was the correct one either by (a) finding a path from A to B, or by (b) finding a path from B to A. The possibility of using this second path, or backpath, is what is distinctive about the multiple-choice task, and it is the reason HAM predicts little or no RI (see Wolford, 1971). The only standard PA paradigm which HAM expects to produce large RI in a multiple-choice test is the A-B, A-Br paradigm—that is, when the responses and stimuli are kept in the interpolated list but are just re-paired in new ways. There should be considerable RI in this circumstance because there will be branching on both forward and backward paths of the old A-B structure. In fact, Postman and Stark did find quite large RI in this circumstance, even in a multiple-choice test, just as HAM would predict.

Several recent experiments support this analysis of the Postman and Stark experiment. Anderson and Watts (1971) tested first-list retention using one of three types of unpaced multiple-choice tests. When each multiple-choice test for A-B included the specific competing response, C, from the second list, there was a substantial amount of RI, whereas no RI appeared when the multiple-choice tests contained only first-list responses or noncompeting second-list responses. Recent experiments by Merryman (1971) and by Greenberg and Wickens (1972) are particularly enlightening on this issue. They guaranteed that backward associations were unlearned by having the subjects learn both A-D and B-E during interpolated learning after originally learning A-B. They found significant RI in a multiple-choice test when the backward associations were selectively interfered with. Postman and Stark (1972) have criticized the design of these experiments, but have replicated this result, although their effect was not statistically significant.

Another line of evidence commonly given against stimulus-specific interference comes from the apparent independence of A-B and A-C recall in MMFR tests (see Greeno, 1969; Martin, 1971). That is, the probability of retrieving the B response to the A stimulus in MMFR appears to be independent of whether or not the C response is retrieved—i.e., $P(B) = P(B|C)$. This would appear to provide a substantial embarrassment to a model like HAM, since it predicts that the availability of the B response decreases as a consequence of competing A-C paths. Hence, one might expect that, conditional on recall of C, the number of A-C paths displacing the original A-B paths would be greater, so that recall of B would be less likely.

However, a serious problem in interpreting the data indicating independence of associations is that it is average data pooled over many subjects and items (i.e., A terms). As Hintzman (1972) has recently observed:

Thus, quite apart from any theoretical prediction, one should expect to find a positive relation between recall of B and C. Good subjects will tend to recall both B and C while poor subjects will recall neither, and easily encoded stimuli will tend to elicit both responses while hard to encode stimuli will not [p. 261].

Thus, Hintzman's argument is that the positive relation due to subject and item differences may be cancelling out the negative relation due to item-specific interference. Martin and Greeno (1972) countered Hintzman's criticisms by presenting data that showed that independence held for good and poor subjects, for easy and difficult items, and for any combination of these two factors. Basically, the variance in subject ability or item differences was not sufficiently large to introduce a substantial positive relation between the average recall of B and C items. Nonetheless, Hintzman's argument might hold if there were strong subject-by-item interactions in that some stimuli are easily encoded for some subjects and other stimuli for other subjects. This variance in the effectiveness of particular stimuli for particular subjects could be very large and hide a negative relation due to the stimulus-specific interference. Unfortunately, it is difficult to estimate empirically the magnitude of subject-by-item interactions. But because of this point, the empirical phenomena of independence of associations is at best inconclusive evidence against stimulus-specific interference. There are several plausible sources of strong positive covariance in B and C availability which makes the failure to find a negative covariance uninterpretable.

The most clearly devastating evidence against the hypothesis that all RI is due to general response competition comes from demonstrations of interference with mixed-list designs. That is, some of the items in the interpolated list are A-C pairs with respect to certain first-list A-B pairs, whereas other second-list pairs are functionally C-D pairs. If RI is greater for those A-B pairs whose stimuli are paired with new responses in IL, such evidence would indicate that particular A-C associations interfere with particular A-B associations. Birnbaum (1970) has reported weak and nonsignificant effects in this direction. Ceraso (1964) found evidence for specific interference in a mixed-list design but only when OL items were well learned. Merryman (1971), Weaver, Duncan, and Bird (1972), and Wichawut and Martin (1971) have also reported evidence for stimulus-specific interference of varying magnitudes. Very impressive evidence for stimulus-specific interference in a mixed-list design comes from our research reported in the original version of this book. Deliberate and concerted efforts were made to produce massive stimulus-specific interference; A-B retention when followed by C-D items was 84%, whereas only about 50% retention was obtained with A-C interpolation. In light of these many results, there can be no doubt that there is stimulus-specific interference in the A-B, A-C paradigm.

In conclusion, most of the forgetting in the A-B, C-D paradigm appears to be a matter of loss of general response availability, but stimulus-specific interference also plays an important role in the *A-B, A-C* paradigm. This explains why manipulations reinstating *B* responses improve recall in both paradigms, but do not eliminate the difference between the two paradigms (e.g., Cofer, Faile, & Horton, 1971). It also explains why there is little difference between *A-C* and *C-D* interpolation in terms of reducing free recall of the old *B* responses, while there is a considerable difference in terms of cued recall of old *A-B* associates (e.g., Delprato & Garskof, 1969; Keppel, Henschel, & Zavortink, 1969).

A Mechanism for Generalized Response Competition

We clearly have to admit generalized response competition as a fact of life. The theoretical question is how to conceive of it. One approach would be to assign strengths or availability measures to each response, and to make the probability of recall in a paired-associates paradigm a function of both the response strength and the intactness of an associative path. In Chapter 7 we were forced to assume a similar response-availability factor to account for the detailed characteristics of the recall data from sentence-memory experiments. We could assume that these response availabilities behave in an appropriate manner, increasing with repeated exposure to the response, but decreasing with exposure to other responses. Thus, the response strength of any particular item is both a function of the total time spent studying it and the time devoted to making other responses available. This viewpoint is similar to Slamecka's (1969) hypothesis which supposes that the probability of recall of an item is a function of both the absolute time spent studying it and the relative amount of the total study time devoted to that item as opposed to others. Slamecka shows that this hypothesis predicts the basic interference effects associated with temporal manipulations. The problem with the hypothesis, of course, is that it is not really a mechanism at all, but rather only a compact description of the results. We will attempt an alternative formulation that is compatible with the mechanisms of HAM.

The formulation we shall propose is very similar to McGovern's (1964) analysis of the role of contextual stimuli in paired-associate learning. We shall identify the concept of "response availability" with the association of a response to the contextual stimuli of the experimental situation. In FRAN (Anderson, 1972) there is an explicit model of how the responses in a list can become connected to the contextual stimuli. It will be remembered that FRAN succeeded in free-recalling responses by building and tagging associative paths that permit access to the responses from the list-marker, which was FRAN's concept of the list context. In the following discussion, *X* will denote the list-marker or contextual cues. Thus, in learning the first list of *A-B* pairs, the subject is conceived to be simultaneously learning the *X-A* and *X-B* pairs. That is, associative paths would develop to connect the items *A* and *B* to *X*. In learning an interpolated *C-D* list, *X-C* and *X-D* paths would be learned, thus to compete with and to make less available the old *X-A*, and *X-B* paths. Moreover, by the same mechanism as outlined above for spontaneous recovery of the *A-B* connection, the *X-A* and *X-B* paths should recover over the retention interval. These statements correspond substantially to the assumptions regarding the buildup and dissipation of suppression of List 1 responses during List 2 learning.

Although this proposed contextual unlearning notion appears plausible, some further thought is required to show its relevance for RI. The question, in brief, is why should loss of the X-B connection seriously affect recall of the A-B connection? This issue has not received a detailed analysis in the interference literature. In the following we therefore construct a plausible explanation for how X-B unlearning could affect A-B recall.

Basically, the idea is that recall of response B to stimulus A can occur either if there is an intact *forward* association leading from A to B, or if there is an intact *backward* association from B to A and the subject can generate the B response (and possible others in List 1) from an intact X-B association (see Wolford, 1971). We may conceive of performance within an A-B recall trial to proceed as follows:

1. Check for a forward path from cue A: if one exists, give the response to which it leads; if none exists, go to step 2.

2. Retrieve List 1 responses at random from the list of X-B connections; for each response generated, check if it has a backward path to the current stimulus.

3. If so, give that as the overt response.

4. If the candidate response has a backward path to a different stimulus than the current test cue, then eliminate that response from the current "guessing pool" to that test cue.

5. If the candidate response has no backward association, then put it into the guessing pool.

6. Return to X and try to generate a new List 1 response (i.e., go back to step 2).

If the correct response has not been found by either a forward or a backward association by the end of a certain time, then the person either omits giving any answer, or he guesses randomly from the reduced set of alternatives in his guessing pool. These are plausible guesses, since they are known to be on List 1 but are not known to belong to other stimuli.

The foregoing outlines a very rational guessing strategy for a subject to use if he has forgotten (or not yet learned) the forward connection from A to B. In conjunction with the notion of loss of availability of specific connections (backward or forward), this analysis has a number of implications regarding different interference paradigms. For example, the A-B, C-D paradigm will exhibit RI to the extent that X-B associations are unlearned during C-D and consequently the B response is not available to be considered as a guess or examined for a backpath to cue A. This assumes that there will be some base-level forgetting of forward associations in the rest-control group (for a variety of reasons). Roughly speaking, the probability (P) of B recall to the A cue will be:

$$P = f + (1 - f)bc \qquad (3)$$

where f is the probability of retrieving the correct forward path, c is the probability that response B is retrieved from the X-B connection, and b is the likelihood that it has a backward path to A. Compared to the A-B rest controls, subjects learning in the A-B, C-D paradigm will have a lower value of c in Equation (3) due to unlearning of X-B. But the magnitude of variation in P with c depends on $(1 - f)$—that is, some substantial loss of forward but not backward associations is required to cause an appreciable difference.

It seems reasonable to suppose that the parameter c, giving the probability that the B response is retrieved from X, should increase with the time the subject has to respond. That is, if the subject is given more time to respond, he has longer to search for and access the appropriate B response from X. This implies that the effects of manipulating response availability should be stronger with unpaced retention tests when the subject has unlimited time to make his recall. There is some evidence that this is the case. For instance, Cofer, Faile, and Horton (1971) found that reinstatement of first-list responses by free recall reduced RI in an unpaced recall test, but not in a paced test. In fact, most of the experiments cited as evidence for the importance of response availability used unpaced retention tests.

Let us summarize HAM's analysis of interference in a paired-associate task. Four sets of associative paths must be considered: the A-B paths that are particularly prominent in forward recall, the B-A paths that become very important in backward recall and in recognition tests, the B-X paths that permit list discrimination, and the X-B paths that determine response availability (and, partly, free-recall performance). Forgetting is both a matter of new paths being encoded and displacing old paths, and of old paths being revived and displacing new paths. It seems that this analysis of the associative connections underlying paired-associate learning and this displacement mechanism will handle many of the facts of retroactive and proactive inhibition.

Negative Transfer

A remaining problem is to provide some analysis of the phenomena of negative transfer. That is, after learning A-B, it is frequently found that it is harder to learn A-C than to learn a new pair C-D. In part, this can be viewed as an instance of proactive interference. That is, in A-C learning each pair must be retained over the interval from when it was acquired on trial $n-1$ until the time it is tested on trial n. This is a retention interval over which the mechanisms of PI may operate to reduce the probability of successful reproduction of C to A on trial n. However, PI over such short intervals is typically weak, whereas the amount of negative transfer relative to the C-D group can be considerable. Therefore, it seems unlikely that one can successfully account for negative transfer by identifying it as solely proactive interference. Moreover, we have conjectured that PI is a consequence of the subject's conscious ruminations about old A-B associations. But during the retention interval defined by one trial to the next of A-C learning, the subject is unlikely to have much time for leisurely thinking over his old associations.

Subjects' introspections in such an experiment suggest a slightly different mechanism that might be important for producing negative transfer. They frequently say that when seeing the pair A-C, they will call to mind the old A-B pair. Thus, time and effort are expended wastefully reminiscing over the old A-B memories, time that is more profitably spent learning the new pairs in the C-D case. This conception of negative transfer is testable. Subjects could be asked to introspect out loud during second-list acquisition. It should be found that probability of recall of a second-list pair is a positive function of the amount of time spent considering it rather than other matters. It should be the same function of rehearsal time for A-C as for C-D pairs. However, the amount of time given to rehearsing the C-D pairs should be greater than for the A-C pairs. We would expect to observe A-B reminiscences creeping into the introspections and taking time away from A-C rehearsal.

Possibly as important as its effect on A-C study time is the fact that "stolen" A-B rehearsals would alter the relative availability of A-B and A-C paths. In such cases, A-B paths may come to temporarily dominate the A-C paths on the relevant GET-lists. So, in this way, this suggested mechanism of negative transfer is like that for proactive interference. The only difference is that revival of A-B paths is not the result of a random free association occurring sometime in a rather long interval; rather, it occurs in response to the stimulus of A-C presentations.

11
PROBLEMS AND NEW ISSUES

Some substantial problems with the HAM theory have come to light, and several new issues have been raised. This chapter reviews these problems and issues. They fall under three major categories: representation, learning, and retrieval. One motivation of Anderson's (1976) ACT theory was to address these issues and problems.

11.1 REPRESENTATION

We claimed we could represent any declarative fact in HAM's propositional network. We have now come to the conclusion that either this claim was wrong or at least imprecise. The most serious difficulties with HAM concerned its inability to properly represent the complexities of quantification. Numerous criticisms of network models have contended that they do not properly represent quantification (Anderson, 1976; Hendrix, 1975; Martin, 1975; Schubert, 1974; Woods, 1975). Often the contrast is made between the success of predicate calculus in representing quantificational concepts versus the difficulties of many of the semantic networks. Predicate calculus uses a combination of scope plus variables to deal with quantification. Scope is not naturally represented in a network, although many of the critics have suggested satisfactory ways of introducing it into a network. HAM had no means of representing variables or scope. The closest thing in HAM to a variable was the prototypical concept node indicated by the generic ($\forall$) link.

Consider the following sentence:

All philosophers read some books.

This has two meanings, which would be rendered in predicate calculus as:

1. $(\forall x) (\exists y)$ (philosopher $(x) \supset$ (book (y) + read (x, y))))
2. $(\exists y) (\forall x)$ (philosopher $(x) \supset$ (book (y) + read (x, y))))

The first would be rendered in English as:

1. ′ For all x there exist y such that if x is a philosopher then y is a book and x reads y.

while the second would be rendered as:

2. ′ There exist y such that for all x if x is a philosopher then y is a book and x reads y.

The two differ in the order of the universal quantifier ($\forall x$) and the existential quantifier ($\exists y$). In (1), the scope of the variable x includes y while this is reversed in (2). The consequence for interpretation is that in (2) a specific set of books is being discussed for all philosophers, while in (1) each philosopher may be reading a different set of books. We claimed (see Fig. 5.13, p. 97) that we could represent this difference in scope by particular circumlocutions. However, it has subsequently become clear that it is impossible to evaluate whether the circumlocutions do actually represent the distinction. The problem is that, in contrast to the predicate calculus, HAM's network representations do not have a formal semantics. Therefore, it is not possible to decide what meaning a representation has simply by inspecting it. As Anderson (1976) notes, this is a problem with almost all propositional representations in psychology.

Probably, for any quantification concept, it would have been possible to invent some circumlocution, and we could claim that this circumlocution in HAM represented the concept. However, there are a number of examples for which there is no known representation and which Anderson (1976) claimed could not be represented in HAM. We mention two here. One is the distinction between:

3. All black dogs are faithful,

and

4. All faithful dogs are black.

Figure 11.1 shows the most natural HAM representation for these sentences. Note that the same representation is being assigned to both sentences and that HAM is not distinguishing between their meaning representations. In fact, the correct translation of Fig. 11.1 is probably:

5. All dogs are black and faithful,

which is not the same as either (3) or (4). These three sentences would be rendered in predicate calculus as:

3. ′ $(\forall x)$ $((\text{black}(x) + \text{dog}(x)) \supset \text{faithful}(x))$
4. ′ $(\forall x)$ $((\text{faithful}(x) + \text{dog}(x)) \supset \text{black}(x))$
5. ′ $(\forall x)$ $((\text{dog}(x) \supset (\text{black}(x) \text{ and faithful}(x)))$

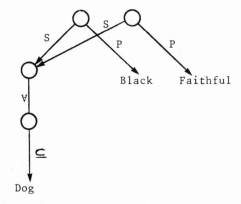

FIG. 11.1.   Example of HAM's use of terminal quantification, attempting to represent "All black dogs are faithful."

Another sentence that HAM had difficulty representing was:

6. The defenders of the Alamo were heros,

which would be rendered in predicate calculus as:

6.'' (∀ x) (defend (x, Alamo) ⊃ hero (x)).

Figure 11.2 illustrates the closest HAM representation possible, which would
probably be interpreted as:

7. Some defenders of the Alamo were heros

or in predicate calculus:

7.' (∃x) (defend (x, Alamo) ⊃ hero (x))

FIG. 11.2.   An (inadequate) attempt to represent in HAM the expression "The
defenders of the Alamo were heroes."

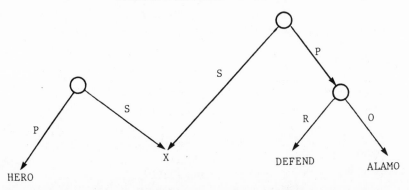

The other major difficulty with the HAM representation concerned the issue of the psychological reality of the network structures. In developing the HAM representation, we were led by the notion that there would be a direct correlation between complexity in the network structure and memory performance. A number of experiments in excised portions of this book found at best equivocal evidence for this prediction.

We think that a fundamental mistake in the HAM theory was the idea that there should be a direct connection between network representation and memory performance. It has been argued subsequently (Anderson, 1976, 1978) that there is a considerable tradeoff between representations and the processes that operate on them. Quite different representations can be made to yield the same predictions by interfacing them with different process assumptions. With respect to representing quantificational and other semantic distinctions, the real issue is not what the representation looks like but rather how the various processes of interpretation, inference, or reasoning use the representation. If the processes treat a representation as if it encodes a particular semantic distinction, then it does. If the processes do not so treat the representation, then it does not contain the information. Similarly, whether there is a direct mapping between network complexity and memory complexity is a question of how memory processes respond to the network complexities. Given the processes assumed in HAM, there was a direct relationship between complexity and memory process. However, in the ACT model, Anderson was able to take a very similar memory representation but not be committed to the same predictions about complexity.

One aspect of the HAM network that led to unacceptable complexities was our insistence that all structure be binary branching. This created considerable complexity in trying to represent relations with more than two arguments. Figure 5.5 (p. 88) illustrates the complexities created by these argument structures. Things get yet more complicated with four- and five-argument relations, like:

8. John drove the car from New Haven to New York,
9. Mary pushed the ball to Jane with a broom,
10. John carried the egg from Fred to Dick with a spoon.

Figure 11.3 illustrates how the third, five-argument sentence would have been represented in HAM. Note that its representation is five times as complex as a two argument subject-verb-object sentence. While such five-argument sentences are undoubtedly more complex, we hardly think they are five times more complex.

In general, our feeling is that the exact distinctions encoded in the HAM network have proven to be less important than the idea of a propositional network. The propositional character of the network predicts that what will be retained from a linguistic communication is its meaning content and not its exact wording. The exact status of this prediction is somewhat in dispute (eg., Anderson, 1976; Clark & Clark, 1977; Kolers, 1978), but right or wrong, this is an important claim about memory. The network character of the representation, in conjunction with a set of encoding and retrieval assumptions, also leads to an important set of predictions about memory, which we discuss in more detail shortly.

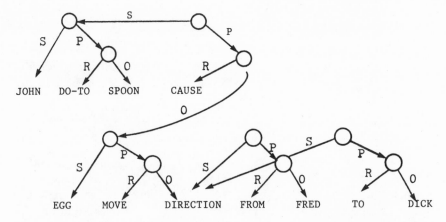

FIG. 11.3.   HAM'S complex manner of decomposing a five-argument verb into binary branching trees.

In concluding our retrospective discussion of the representation issue, it is useful to return to the five considerations set forth in Section 5.1, which were the motivations for the HAM representation. We still feel that these are important considerations for a theory of representation. Except for the first issue of completeness on which there is uncertainty, we feel that the HAM representation satisfied these considerations. However, as we noted then, these considerations in themselves were not enough to specify a working representation. The difficulties that arose in the HAM representation concerned our attempts to fill in the details needed for a working representation and to develop some psychological correlates of these details.

11.2   LEARNING

The learning model introduced in Chapter 7 was one in which the various associations underlying a sentence's structure were independently and probabilistically encoded. There have been two lines of criticisms of these assumptions. One argument alleges that propositions are not composed from independent components but rather are encoded as complete, all-or-none units. Second, there have been criticisms of the particular structural assumptions used and the relationship between these assumptions and fragmentary recall.

R. C. Anderson (1974; Goetz, Anderson, & Schallert, 1978) attacked the fragmentary character of HAM's encoding assumptions as has Graesser (1978). In our defense, we found 24% partial recall of propositions in the experiment in Section 7.2. This would seem to confirm the partial encoding assumption of HAM. However, R. C. Anderson has argued that this may be an artifact of the methodology and scoring procedure. He argues that subjects either recall nothing or else recall all the concepts in a simple sentence but sometimes label them imprecisely. For instance, a subject might remember that the subject of the sentence was a laborer but not be able to recall whether he heard *lumberjack, miner,* or *gardener.* In face of this uncertainty, the subject may inhibit his recall. Anderson has used procedures in which he encourages subjects to venture such guesses, and he uses a liberalized scoring procedure in which a large range of variations are accepted as correct. So, for instance, *lumberjack* would be accepted as correct when *gardener* was what was studied. He is able to find as much as 95% all-or-none recall of subject-verb-object sentences with such scoring procedures.

Frankly, it is hard to know what to make of these results. One would expect less partial recall with 3-term sentences than the 4-term sentences reported in Section 7.2. Although all aspects of the procedures in scoring have not been equated, the finding of all-or-none recall for SVO sentences has not been universal even with attempts at gist scoring (Anderson, 1976; Jones, in press). There is also the question of why 5% partial recall is not enough to justify a theory that allows fragmentary recall. Finally, there is the fact that relatively successful mathematical theories have been developed for fragmentary recall. One is hesitant to call a phenomenon an illusion if there are successful and systematic theories of the phenomenon.

The issue of an all-or-none theory versus fragmentary theory has become all the more muddied with the development of the elaboration notions in Anderson (1976). Consider the prototypical (but, alas, dated) HAM sentence:

In the park a hippie touched the debutante.

Anderson suggests that a subject might elaborate the sentence as follows:

The *hippie* was at a love-in in the *park*. The *debutante* was attending a classical concert in the *park*. The attenders at the love-in were running about *touching* people in the park. The *hippie* was *touching* everyone. The *hippie* saw the *debutante* in her beautiful gown. The *hippie* ran up to the *debutante* and *touched* her. The *debutante* was upset because she did not want to have her gown *touched*.

Suppose that the subject does not commit the individual sentence to memory but rather this elaboration. Consider the implications for the all-or-none vs. fragmentary issue. Suppose that each proposition could be encoded in fragmentary manner. Because of the extreme redundancy of such an elaboration, recall of the target proposition might appear much more all-or-none than it actually is. Even if some portion of the original proposition was not remembered, it might be possible to fill it in with one of these redundant elaborations. On the other hand, suppose memory for propositions was all-or-none. If the original proposition was not recalled but one of the elaborations was, memory might appear fragmentary. For instance, retrieving the first elaborative proposition above would allow the subject to retrieve the hippie-park fragment but nothing about the debutante or touching.

Another line of criticism (Graesser, 1978; Jones, 1976, 1978; Wender & Glowalla, 1979) of the HAM learning model has focused on the exact assumptions about encoding. We find the fragmentation theory of Jones to be the most extensively developed and probably the best suited to deal with the elaboration difficulties just noted. His theory ignores the internal structure of propositions and simply considers a sentence or other stimulus unit to be a bundle of elements. The bundle starts out with everything interconnected. Jones assumes that within an interconnected bundle one has access from every element in the bundle to every other element. This means that immediately after study a subject should be able to recall the entire sentence if cued with any element of the sentence.

However, over time, the representation of a sentence breaks apart or fragments. For instance, an LSVO (location-subject-verb-object) sentence might fragment into LS and VO fragments. If so, the subject should be able to recall L if cued with S, and vice versa; similarly, he should be able to recall V when cued with O, and vice versa; however, there would be no cross cueing between the LS and the VO fragments in this case. To fit his model to the data, Jones simply estimates the probability of every possible pattern of fragmentation. Some of the predictive power of the theory comes from its assumption of symmetry. For instance, it predicts that the probability of recalling LS but not O to V as a cue, of recalling LV but not O to S as a cue, and SV but not O to L as a cue will all be the same. All reflect the probability of an LSV fragment.

Jones' theory displays a better job than any other in accounting for patterns of sentence recall. Certainly it does better than the original HAM model. This is because it is not constrained by the HAM representation but rather can assume any degree of contingency among elements that the data require. Given the complexities introduced by subject elaborations, this seems like the only way to model a probabilistic, fragmentary memory.

While we think Jones' theory is in many ways an improvement, we point out two aspects of the Jones' model that seem like problems to us. The powerful symmetry assumption claims that items are just as potent as stimuli and as responses. We think there are clear exceptions to this rule. For instance, it is well known in the paired-associate literature that abstract words make better responses than stimuli (eg., Paivio, 1971) but that for concrete words this is reversed. So a concrete-abstract pair will display higher recall than an abstract-concrete pair. In our sentence data, there is some evidence that some words are better responses than stimuli. For instance, in Section 7.2, nouns evoke recall of verbs 23% of the time, while verbs evoke nouns 20% of the time. The effect was much larger involving the time element in an experiment deleted from this edition. Here the nouns evoked 24% recall of the time element, but the time element evoked 18% recall of the noun. Jones comments that this is an aspect of our data that his fragmentary model cannot explain.

A second difficulty with the Jones model is that it does not have any provision for variation in subject and item difficulty. As a consequence, Jones makes certain predictions that prove to be false. For instance, consider the LSVO experiment of Section 7.2. Jones predicts that the following three events will have equal frequency:

1. Subject is cued with L, recalls only S, is subsequently cued with V and O and recalls no more;
2. Subject is cued with V, recalls nothing, is cued with L recalls S, is cued with O and recalls nothing more;

3. Subject is cued with V and then O, recalls nothing to either, then is cued with L and recalls S.

All three events reflect the same probability of a LS fragment. It turns out that there is a difference in the number of cueing sequences like (1) that would reflect a LS fragment on first cue, versus sequences like (2) that reflect the fragment on second cue, versus sequences like (3) that reflect the fragment on third cue. The 12 cueing sequences LSV, LSO, LVS, LVO, LOS, LOV, SLV, SLO, SVL, SVO, SOL, SOV all can show a LS fragment on cue 1. The eight sequences VLS, VLO, OLS, OLV, VSL, VSO, OSL, OSV all can show a LS fragment on second cue. (The sequences LSV, LSO, SLV, SLO cannot because they give both L and S by the second cue.) The four sequences VOS, OVS, VOL, OVL all can show the LS fragment on the third cue. Given that all sequences are equally frequent, the fragment model predicts that the number of LS fragments should occur in the ratio 3-2-1 for first, second, and third cue. More generally, the fragment model makes this 3-2-1 prediction for all 2 element fragments.

The actual frequencies of these 2-element-fragment events are 370 for first cue, 211 for second cue, and 97 for third cue, implying a ratio of 3.76-2.20-1. This deviation from the predicted ratios is significant ($\chi^2_{(2)}$ = 6.82; p < .01). This deviation is expected on the HAM model of variation on items and subjects (pp. 133-140). Failure of recall on early trials is indicative of a bad item or subject and so is predictive of failure of recall on a later trial. Thus, the frequency ratio should be less than the 3-2-1 ratio in the fragment model.

In conclusion, we think that Jones was right in abandoning the HAM network for predicting patterns of recall. On the other hand, we see no reason to abandon the two other aspects of the model in Chapter 7—namely, the potential for asymmetry of a word as a stimulus versus response and the idea that there will be variation in the goodness of items and abilities of subjects.

The HAM, R. C. Anderson, and Jones theories differ on whether there can be fragmentary memory for individual propositions and, if there can, whether there is an internal propositional structure to predict these patterns of fragmentary recall. However, in contrast to this intrapropositional level, there is greater consensus regarding storage at the interproposition level. Here, all psychologists (and most data) agree that there should be a considerable amount of partial recall. A model like Jones' is also probably quite apt for describing recall at this level.

11.3   RETRIEVAL

In HAM, retrieval from long-term memory was conceived of as a search of a semantic network. We are still in basic agreement with this conception of retrieval as a network search. However, many specifics of that search process have proven to be wrong. HAM conceived of this search as serial in nature, exploiting the semantic labels (relations) on links to guide the search. The associations bearing a particular relationship to a concept were ordered on a GET-list, with the most recent association on top of the list. The search assumptions in HAM corresponded closely to the actual LISP implementation of the associative retrieval mechanism.

We have now been convinced by a wealth of experimental data that the true retrieval picture is rather different. Search of memory now appears to take place by means of a limited-capacity parallel process of spreading activation. The idea of spreading activation comes from Quillian and his colleagues (Collins & Loftus, 1975; Collins & Quillian, 1972; Quillian, 1968), although we inferred its limited capacity character from our data. Anderson's (1976) ACT theory assumes that each link emanating from a node has a strength associated with it. The speed at which activation spreads down a link is a function of the strength of that link relative to the strength of all other links from that node. The relative strength of a link will decrease the more other competing links there are. This strength mechanism implies the fan effect noted in Chapter 8 as well as several semantic memory results noted in the chapter. The fact that a parallel model can explain many of the phenomena we attributed to the serial HAM model is another instance of the general equivalence between parallel and serial models (Townsend, 1974).

A number of phenomena can be explained by the spreading activation theory but not by the original HAM theory. Some of these are reviewed in chapter 8 of Anderson (1976). For instance, it happens that the most rapidly available association out of a concept is not always the most recent but rather is the most frequently used association. This goes against the serial ordering of items on HAM's GET-list but fits well with ACT's strength notion. Related to this are the phenomena of negative transfer and proactive interference (see our discussion in Section 10.2). It was difficult to explain how the most recent association (on top of the GET-list) would suffer interference from less recent associations (lower on the GET-list). Our attempt in HAM to explain negative transfer in terms of rehearsal pattern proved to be incorrect. On the other hand, these proactive interfering effects can be explained with strength mechanisms.

Another finding was that the logical relation of a link did not affect the amount of interference (Anderson, 1975). This was impossible to explain with the HAM search mechanism (which exploited link labels) but seemed a natural consequence of diffuse spreading activation.

This new conception of the retrieval process was incorporated into the ACT theory. Another important and documented aspect of that theory concerned the sensitivity of the system to an intersection of activation from two or more sources. One implication of this was that subjects should have difficulty rejecting probes that can lead to spurious (logically incorrect) intersections of activation. For instance, consider the experiment by King and Anderson (1976). They had subjects learn related sentences like:

The hippie touched the debutante.
The hippie shot the lawyer.

Later, subjects were presented with probes like "touched lawyer" and had to decide whether this verb-object pair had occurred in some single sentence they had studied. Subjects were slower at rejecting pairs like this, where the verb and object shared a common subject, than when they did not. Similar effects of spurious intersections prove to be the key to explaining similarity effects for negative semantic memory probes (see "The Mysterious Case of the Negatives" in Section 8.3). Basically, similar negatives are difficult to reject because they lead to spurious intersections. Recently, Anderson and Ross (in preparation) were able to increase time to reject such statements by introducing spurious connections experimentally.

This notion of intersection of activation is important for understanding several memory phenomena that appear to violate HAM's associative analysis. For instance, Foss and Harwood (1975) showed that subjects displayed better recall of the object noun, when cued with subject and verb of an SVO sentence, than would be predicted by recall to the subject alone or the verb alone. Thus, subject and verb were "superadditive" in a way that could not easily be explained by the HAM model. However, the phenomenon has an easy explanation within a spreading activation model. Activation will summate from the subject and verb. This combined level of activation may be enough to exceed the threshold for recall, whereas activation from either source individually is not enough.

HAM has a related difficulty in accounting for the effects of encoding specificity (see Tulving & Thompson, 1973; Watkins & Tulving, 1976). Basically, encoding specificity refers to the phenomenon that memories available in one context are not available in another context. For instance, a subject having studied the word *black* in the context of *train* cannot later remember that event when *black* is presented in the context of *white* but can remember *black* when it is presented again in the *train* context. There have been several explanations (Anderson, 1976; Anderson & Bower, 1974; Reder, Anderson, & Bjork, 1974) of the encoding specificity results in terms of semantic networks and spreading activation. The different explanations are slight variations on one another, but they all contain the same essential insight. This is that a memory laid down in the presence of two items like *train* and *black* will have associations to both of these terms. Recognition of *black* will be higher in the *train* context than in the *white* context, because there will be two retrieval entry points from which activation can converge to revive the memory.

The variation of this explanation that we have been most strongly identified with involves a notion of multiple meanings for words like *black*. The claim is that in the context of *train*, one meaning will be activated for *black*, and associations to the list-context will be attached to this meaning. When tested in the context of *white*, the subject may not be able to activate that meaning of *black* used at study. Evidence for this explanation of encoding specificity includes the fact that words with few meanings do not show much of a deficit due to a change of context (Reder, Anderson, & Bjork, 1974).

11.4   FINAL REMARKS

In summary, we see two major problems with HAM. First, the representational claims made for HAM were too strong. We did not have an adequate way to establish what HAM could represent, and it now appears that there are things HAM cannot represent. Also, the connection between data and memory representation is not as strong as we thought. However, while the HAM representation turns out not to be perfect, we are still fairly content with most aspects of it. A second problem with HAM is that the serial search of memory that we took from our computer simulation was wrong. A spreading activation model was what we needed. The data indicating this were not yet available when we wrote the original book. Indeed, the HAM theory was a stimulus for the accumulation of the necessary data to identify the limited-capacity, spreading activation model of memory retrieval.

There were other incompletenesses with HAM that account for why we have moved in our different ways from the HAM model. These are not points on which HAM was wrong; rather, it was just that HAM did not address issues that have proved to be more and more important to us. Anderson was bothered by the fact that HAM did not say much about how memories were used in thought. This led to the development of the ACT model (Anderson, 1976; Anderson, Kline, & Beasley, 1979), which has a production system model for mental procedures and which interfaced this procedural component with a memory model derived from HAM. Bower was bothered by the fact that HAM did not address the issues of how large bodies of text material are processed, how large knowledge structures are organized in memory, and how these large knowledge structures are used to interpret text. This led him to an interest in story comprehension, scripts and schemata, and reconstructive memory processes (Bower, 1976, 1978; Bower, Black, & Turner, 1979).

So, we are now much concerned with theoretical issues that HAM does not directly address. Still, HAM is very much with us and has important influences on our thinking about these new problems. In HAM, we find many concepts and analyses that we can use as foundations for our new endeavors. In this condensed book, we have tried to keep those aspects of the original book that are still cogent for us. We hope that other scientists will find these ideas useful in the 1980s.

REFERENCES

Amarel, S. On representations of problems of reasoning about action. In D. Mitchie (Ed.), *Machine intelligence III.* New York: American Elsevier, 1968.

Amsel, A. Partial reinforcement effects on vigor and persistence. In K. W. Spence & J. T. Spence (Eds.), *The psychology of learning and motivation: Advances in research and theory* (Vol. 1). New York: Academic, 1967.

Anderson, J. R. FRAN: A simulation model of free recall. In G. H. Bower (Ed.), *The psychology of learning and motivation* (Vol. 5). New York: Academic Press, 1972.

Anderson, J. R. Item-specific and relation-specific interference in sentence memory. *Journal of Experimental Psychology: Human Learning and Memory*, 1975, *104*, 249-260.

Anderson, J. R. *Language, memory and thought.* Hillsdale, N.J.: Lawrence Erlbaum Associates, 1976.

Anderson, J. R., & Bower, G. H. Recognition and retrieval processes in free recall. *Psychological Review*, 1972, *79*, 97-123.

Anderson, J. R., & Bower, G. H. A propositional theory of recognition memory. *Cognition and Memory*, 1974, *2*, 406-412.

Anderson, J. R., Kline, P. J., & Beasley, C. M. A general learning theory and its application to schema abstraction. In G. H. Bower (Ed.), *The psychology of learning and motivation* (Vol. 13). 1979, in press.

Anderson, J. R., & Ross, B. H. *Evidence against a semantic-episodic distinction.* Manuscript in preparation.

Anderson, R. C. Substance recall of sentences. *Quarterly Journal of Experimental Psychology*, 1974, *26*, 530-541.

Anderson, R. C., & Watts, G. H. Response competition in the forgetting of paired associates. *Journal of Verbal Learning and Verbal Behavior*, 1971, *10*, 29-34.

Arnold, P. G., & Bower, G. H. Perceptual conditions affecting ease of association. *Journal of Experimental Psychology*, 1972, *93*, 176-180.

Asch, S. E. The metaphor: A psychological inquiry. In M. Henley (Ed.), *Documents of Gestalt psychology.* Berkeley: University of California Press, 1961.

Asch, S. E. A reformulation of the problem of associations. *American Psychologist*, 1969, *24*, 92-102.

Asch, S. E., Ceraso, J., & Heimer, W. Perceptual conditions of association. *Psychological Monographs*, 1960, *74*(3, Whole No. 490).

Atwood, G. An experimental study of visual imagination and memory. *Cognitive Psychology*, 1971, *2*, 290-299.

Bain, A. *The senses and the intellect.* London: Edwin S. Parker, 1859.

Barlow, H. B., & Levick, W. R. The mechanism of directionally selective units in rabbit's retina. *Journal of Physiology*, 1965, *178*, 477-504.

Barnes, J. M., & Underwood, B. J. "Fate" of first-list association in transfer theory. *Journal of Experimental Psychology*, 1959, *58*, 97-105.

Bartlett, F. C. *Remembering a study in experimental and social psychology*. Cambridge: The University Press, 1932.

Battig, W. F., & Montague, W. E. Category norms for verbal items in 56 categories: A replication and extension of the Connecticut category norms. *Journal of Experimental Psychology Monograph*, June 1969.

Baylor, G. W. *A treatise on the mind's eye* (Tech. Rep.). Institute of Psychology, University of Montreal, July 1971.

Bean, J. *The effects of subject-generated strings on noun pair learning in children: Population differences*. Unpublished doctoral dissertation, University of California, Berkeley, 1971.

Beare, J. I. De Memoria et reminiscentia. In W. D. Ross (Ed.), *The works of Aristotle* (Vol. 3). Oxford: Clarendon Press, 1931.

Bergman, G. Theoretical psychology. *Annual Review of Psychology*, 1953, *4*, 435-458.

Bever, T. G. The cognitive basis for linguistic structures. In J. R. Hayes (Ed.), *Cognition and the development of language*. New York: Wiley, 1970.

Bever, T. G., Fodor, J. A., & Garrett, M. A formal limitation of associationism. In T. R. Dixon & D. L. Horton (Eds.), *Verbal behavior and general behavior theory*. Englewood Cliffs, N.J.: Prentice-Hall, 1968.

Birnbaum, I. M. Long-term retention of first-list associations in the A-B, A-C paradigm. *Journal of Verbal Learning and Verbal Behavior*, 1965, *4*, 515-520.

Birnbaum, I. M. Response-class similarity and first-list recall with mixed and unmixed transfer designs. *Journal of Experimental Psychology*, 1968, *77*, 542-546.

Birnbaum, I. M. Response selection in retroactive inhibition. *Journal of Experimental Psychology*, 1970, *85*, 406-410.

Bobrow, G., & Bower, G. H. Comprehension and recall of sentences. *Journal of Experimental Psychology*, 1969, *80*, 455-461.

Boring, E. G. *History of experimental psychology*. New York: Appleton-Century-Crofts, 1950.

Bower, G. H. A multicomponent theory of the memory trace. In K. W. Spence & J. T. Spence (Eds.), *Psychology of learning and motivation* (Vol. 1). New York: Academic Press, 1967.

Bower, G. H. Analysis of a mnemonic device. *American Scientist*, 1970, *58*, 496-510. (a)

Bower, G. H. Organizational factors in memory. *Cognitive Psychology*, 1970, *1*, 18-46. (b)

Bower, G. H. Imagery as a relational organizer in associative learning. *Journal of Verbal Learning and Verbal Behavior*, 1970, *9*, 529-533. (c)

Bower, G. H. Mental imagery and associative learning. In L. Gregg (Ed.), *Cognition in learning and memory*. New York: Wiley, 1972.

Bower, G. H. Experiments on story understanding and recall. *Quarterly Journal of Experimental Psychology*, 1976, *28*, 511-534.

Bower, G. H. Experiments on story comprehension and recall. *Discourse Processes*, 1978, *1*, 211-231.

Bower, G. H., Black, J. B., & Turner, T. J. Scripts in memory for text. *Cognitive Psychology*, 1979, *11*, 177-230.

Bower, G. H., Munoz, R., & Arnold, P. G. *On distinguishing semantic and imaginal mnemonics*. Unpublished manuscript, 1972.

Bower, G. H., & Winzenz, D. Comparison of associative learning strategies. *Psychonomic Science*, 1970, *20*, 119-120.

Briggs, G. E. Retroactive inhibition as a function of degree of original and interpolated learning. *Journal of Experimental Psychology*, 1957, *53*, 60-67.

Brooks, L. R. Spatial and verbal components of the act of recall. *Canadian Journal of Psychology*, 1968, *22*, 349-368.

Brooks, L. R. *Visual and verbal processes in internal representation*. Paper presented in a colloquium series sponsored by the Salk Institute, La Jolla, Calif., July 1970.

Brown, R., & McNeill, D. The "tip of the tongue" phenomenon. *Journal of Verbal Learning and Verbal Behavior*, 1966, *5*, 325-337.

Brown, T. *Lectures on the philosophy of the human mind*. Edinburg: Tait, Longman, 1820.

Bugelski, B. R. Words and things and images. *American Psychologist*, 1970, *25*, 1002-1012.

Buhler, K. Die "Neue Psychologie" Koffkas. *Zeitschrift fur Psychologie*, 1926, *99*, 145-159.
Ceraso, J. Specific interference in retroactive inhibition. *Journal of Psychology*, 1964, *58*, 65-77.
Ceraso, J., & Henderson, A. Unavailability and loss in RI and PI: Second try. *Journal of Experimental Psychology*, 1966, *72*, 314-316.
Chase, W. G., & Clark, H. H. Mental operations in the comparison of sentences and pictures. In L. Gregg (Ed.), *Cognition in learning and memory*. New York: Wiley, 1972.
Chomsky, N. *Language and mind*. New York: Harcourt, Brace & World, 1968.
Chomsky, N. *Aspects of the theory of syntax*. Cambridge, Mass.: M.I.T. Press, 1965.
Clark, H. H., Carpenter, P. A., & Just, M. A. On the meeting of semantics and perception. Paper presented at the Eighth Carnegie Symposium on Cognition, Carnegie-Mellon University, Pittsburgh, Pa., 1972. [W. G. Chase (Ed.), *Visual information processing*. New York: Academic Press, 1973.]
Clark, H. H., & Clark, E. V. *Psychology and language*. New York: Harcourt, Brace, Jovanovich, 1977.
Cofer, C. N., Faile, N. F., & Horton, D. L. Retroactive inhibition following reinstatement or maintenance of first-list responses by means of free recall. *Journal of Experimental Psychology*, 1971, *90*, 197-205.
Collins, A. M., & Loftus, E. F. A spreading-activation theory of semantic processing. *Psychological Review*, 1975, *82*, 407-428.
Collins, A. M., & Quillian, M. R. Retrieval time from semantic memory. *Journal of Verbal Learning and Verbal Behavior*, 1969, *8*, 240-247.
Collins, A. M., & Quillian, M. R. Experiments on semantic memory and language comprehension. In L. Gregg (Ed.), *Cognition and learning*. New York: Wiley, 1972. (a)
Collins, A. M., & Quillian, M. R. How to make a language user. In E. Tulving & W. Donaldson (Eds.), *Organization and memory*. New York: Academic Press, 1972. (b)
Conrad, C. Cognitive economy in semantic memory. *Journal of Experimental Psychology*, 1972, *92*, 149-154.
Deese, J. *The structure of associations in language and thought*. Baltimore: Johns Hopkins Press, 1965.
Delprato, D. J. Specific-pair interference on recall and associative matching tests. *American Journal of Psychology*, 1971, *84*, 185-193.
Delprato, D. J., & Garskof, B. E. Free and modified free recall measured of response recall and unlearning. *Journal of Experimental Psychology*, 1969, *81*, 408-410.
Dreyfus, H. L. *What computers can't do*. New York: Harper & Row, 1972.
Ehrenfels, C. von. On Gestalt qualities. *Psychological Review*, 1937, *44*, 521-524.
Ernst, G. W., & Newell, A. *GPS: A case study in generality and problem-solving*. New York: Academic Press, 1969.
Evans, T. G. A program for the solution of geometric-analogy intelligence test questions. In M. Minsky (Ed.), *Semantic information processing*. Cambridge, Mass.: M.I.T. Press, 1968.
Feigenbaum, E. A. Simulation of verbal learning behavior. In E. A. Feigenbaum & J. Feldman (Eds.), *Computers and thought*. New York: McGraw-Hill, 1963.
Feigenbaum, E. A. Information processing and memory. In D. A. Norman (Ed.), *Models of human memory*. New York: Academic Press, 1970.
Fillenbaum, S. Psycholinguistics. *Annual Review of Psychology*, 1971, *22*, 251-308.
Fodor, J. A. Could meaning be an r_m? *Journal of Verbal Learning and Verbal Behavior*, 1965, 1965, *4*, 73-81.
Foss, D. J., & Harwood, D. A. Memory for sentences: Implications for Human Associative Memory. *Journal of Verbal Learning and Verbal Behavior*, 1975, *14*, 1-16.
Freedman, J. L., & Loftus, E. F. Retrieval of words from long-term memory. *Journal of Verbal Learning and Verbal Behavior*, 1971, *10*, 107-115.
Freud, S. *New introductory lectures on psychoanalysis* (trans. by J. H. Sprott). New York: Norton, 1933.
Friedman, M. J., & Reynolds, J. H. Retroactive inhibition as a function of response-class similarity. *Journal of Experimental Psychology*, 1967, *74*, 351-355.

Garner, W. R. *Uncertainty and structure as psychological concepts.* New York: Wiley, 1962.

Garskof, B. E. Unlearning as a function of degree of interpolated learning and method of testing in the A-B, A-C and A-B, C-D paradigms. *Journal of Experimental Psychology,* 1968, *76*, 579-583.

Garskof, B. E., & Sandak, J. M. Unlearning in recognition memory. *Psychonomic Science,* 1964, *1*, 197-198.

Gazzaniga, M. A. The split brain in man. *Scientific American,* 1967, *217*, 24-29.

Gazzaniga, M. A., & Sperry, R. W. Language after section of cerebral commisures. *Brain,* 1967, *90*, 131-148.

Greenberg, G., & Wickens, D. D. Is matching performance an adequate test of "extinction" effects on individual association? *Psychonomic Science,* 1972, *27*, 227-229.

Greeno, J. G. A cognitive interpretation of negative transfer and forgetting in paired-associates (Human Performance Center Memorandum Rep. No. 9). Ann Arbor: University of Michigan, 1969.

Gregory, R. L. *The intelligent eye.* New York: McGraw-Hill, 1970.

Gibson, E. J. A systematic application of the concepts of generalization and differentiation to verbal learning. *Psychological Review,* 1940, *47*, 196-229.

Goetz, E. T., Anderson, R. C., & Schallert, D. L. *Models of sentence representation.* Paper presented at the meetings of the Psychonomic Society, San Antonio, Tex., November 9-11, 1978.

Graesser, A. C. Tests of a holistic chunking model of sentence memory through analyses of noun intrusions. *Memory and Cognition,* 1978, *6*, 527-536.

Guzman, A. *Computer recognition of three-dimensional objects in a visual scene.* M.I.T. Artificial Intelligence Laboratory Project MAC-TR-59, 1968.

Hartley, D. *Observations on man, his frame, his duty and his expectations.* London: 1749.

Hendrix, G. G. *Expanding the utility of semantic networks through partitioning* (Stanford Research Institute Tech. Note 105), 1975.

Head, H. *Studies in neurology.* Oxford: Oxford University Press, 1920.

Hintzman, D. L. Explorations with a discrimination net model for paired-associate learning. *Journal of Mathematical Psychology,* 1968, *5*, 123-162.

Hintzman, D. L. On testing the independence of associations. *Psychological Review,* 1972, *79*, 261-264.

Hobbes, T. Human nature. In W. Molesworth (Ed.), *The English works of Thomas Hobbes* (Vol. 4). London: Bohn, 1840. (Originally published, 1650.)

Hoffding, H. *Outlines of psychology.* London: Macmillan, 1891.

Hook, S. *Dimensions of mind: A symposium.* New York: Collier Books, 1961.

Hopcroft, J. E., & Ullman, J. D. *Formal languages and their relation to automata.* Reading, Mass.: Addison-Wesley, 1969.

Houston, J. P. Proactive inhibition and undetected retention interval rehearsal. *Journal of Experimental Psychology,* 1969, *82*, 511-514.

Houston, J. P. Proactive inhibition and undetected rehearsal: A replication. *Journal of Experimental Psychology,* 1971, *90*, 156-157.

Johnson, N. F. Sequential verbal behavior. In T. R. Dixon & D. L. Horton (Eds.), *Verbal behavior and general behavior theory.* Englewood Cliffs, N.J.: Prentice-Hall, 1968.

Johnson-Laird, P. N. On understanding logically complex sentences. *Quarterly Journal of Experimental Psychology,* 1969, *21*, 1-13.

Jones, G. V. A fragmentation hypothesis of memory: Cued recall of pictures and sequential position. *Journal of Experimental Psychology: General,* 1976, *1*, 277-293.

Jones, G. V. Texts of a structural theory of the memory trace. *British Journal of Psychology,* 1978, *69*, 351-367.

Jones, G. V. Interaction of intrinsic and extrinsic knowledge in sentence recall. In R. S. Nickerson (Ed.), *Attention and performance* (Vol. 8.). Hillsdale, N.J.: Lawrence Erlbaum Associates, in press.

Katona, G. *Organizing and memorizing.* New York: Columbia University Press, 1940.

Katz, J. J. *The philosophy of language.* New York: Harper & Row, 1966.

Keppel, G.   Retroactive and proactive inhibition. In T. R. Dixon & D. L. Horton (Eds.), *Verbal behavior and general behavior theory*. Englewood Cliffs, N.J.: Prentice-Hall, 1968.

Keppel, G., Henschel, D. M., & Zavortink, F.   Influence of nonspecific interference on response recall. *Journal of Experimental Psychology*, 1969, *81*, 246-255.

Keppel, G., & Rauch, D. S.   Unlearning as a function of second-list error instructions. *Journal of Verbal Learning and Verbal Behavior*, 1966, *5*, 50-58.

Kimura, D.   Right temporal damage. *Archives of neurology*, 1963, *8*, 264-271.

King, D. R. W., & Anderson, J. R.   Long-term memory search: An intersecting activation process. *Journal of Verbal Learning and Verbal Behavior*, 1976, *15*, 587-605.

Kintsch, W.   Abstract nouns: Imagery vs. lexical complexity. *Journal of Verbal Learning and Verbal Behavior*, 1972, *11*, 59-65.

Koch, S.   Clark L. Hull. In W. Estes, S. Koch, K. MacCorquodule, P. Meehl, C. Mueller, W. Schoenfield, & W. Verplanck (Eds.), *Modern learning theory*. New York: Appleton-Century-Crofts, 1954.

Koffka, K.   *Principles of Gestalt psychology*. New York: Harcourt, Brace & World, 1935.

Kohler, W.   *The place of value in a world of facts*. New York: Liveright, 1938.

Kohler, W.   *Gestalt psychology: An introduction to new concepts in modern psychology*. New York: Liveright, 1947.

Kolers, P. A.   A pattern analyzing basis of recognition. In L. S. Cermak & F. I. M. Craik (Eds.), *Levels of processing in human memory*. Hillsdale, N.J.: Lawrence Erlbaum Associates, 1978.

Koppenaal, R. J.   Time changes in the strengths of A-B, A-C lists: Spontaneous recovery? *Journal of Verbal Learning and Verbal Behavior*, 1963, *2*, 310-319.

Koppenaal, R. J., Krull, A., & Katz, H.   Age, interference, and forgetting. *Journal of Experimental Child Psychology*, 1965, *1*, 360-375.

Landauer, T. K., & Freedman, J. L.   Information retrieval from long-term memory: Category size and recognition time. *Journal of Verbal Learning and Verbal Behavior*, 1968, *7*, 291-295.

Landauer, T. K., & Meyer, D. E.   Category size and semantic-memory retrieval. *Journal of Verbal Learning and Verbal Behavior*, 1972, *11*, 539-549.

Lashley, K. S., Chow, K. L., & Semmes, J.   An examination of the electrical field theory of cerebral integration. *Psychological Review*, 1951, *58*, 123-136.

Lehr, D. J., Frank, R. C., & Mattison, D. W.   Retroactive inhibition, spontaneous recovery, and type of interpolated learning. *Journal of Experimental Psychology*, 1972, *92*, 232-236.

Loftus, E. F.   Category dominance, instance dominance, and categorization time. *Journal of Experimental Psychology*, 1973, *97*, 70-74.

Loftus, E. F., & Scheff, R. W.   Categorization norms for fifty representative instances. *Journal of Experimental Psychology Monograph*, 1971, *91*, 355-364.

Logan, F. A.   *Incentive*. New Haven: Yale University Press, 1960.

Loux, M. J.   The problem of universals. In M. J. Loux (Ed.), *Universals and particulars*. New York: Doubleday, 1970.

Mandler, G.   Organization and memory. In K. W. Spence & J. A. Spence (Eds.), *The psychology of learning and motivation* (Vol. 1). New York: Academic Press, 1967.

Mandler, J., & Mandler, G.   *Thinking from association to Gestalt*. New York: Wiley, 1964.

Martin, E.   Verbal learning theory and independent retrieval phenomena. *Psychological Review*, 1971, *78*, 314-332.

Martin, E., & Greeno, J. G.   Independence of associations tested: A reply to D. L. Hintzman. *Psychological Review*, 1972, *79*, 265-267.

Martin, E. A.   *Hamming it up*. Unpublished manuscript, Department of Philosophy, Indiana University, 1975.

McCarthy, J., & Hayes, P.   Some philosophical problems from the standpoint of artificial intelligence. In B. Meltzer & D. Mitchie (Eds.), *Machine Intelligence 4*. Edenburgh: Edenburgh University Press, 1969.

McGeoch, J. A.   Forgetting and the law of disuse. *Psychological Review*, 1932, *39*, 352-370.

McGeoch, J. A.   Studies in retroactive inhibition: VII. Retroactive inhibition as a function of the length and frequency of presentation of the interpolated lists. *Journal of Experimental Psychology*, 1936, *19*, 674-693.

McGill, W. J. Stochastic latency mechanisms. In R. D. Luce, R. R. Bush, & E. Galanter (Eds.), *Handbook of mathematical psychology* (Vol. 1). New York: Wiley, 1963.

McGovern, J. B. Extinction of associations in four transfer paradigms. *Psychological Monographs*, 1964, *78*(Whole No. 593).

McGuire, W. J. A multi-process model for paired-associate learning. *Journal of Experimental Psychology*, 1961, *62*, 335-347.

Melton, A. W. Comments on Professor Postman's Paper. In C. N. Cofer (Ed.), *Verbal learning and verbal behavior*. New York: McGraw-Hill, 1961.

Melton, A. W., & Irwin, J. M. The influence of degree of interpolated learning on retroactive inhibition and the overt transfer of specific responses. *American Journal of Psychology*, 1940, *53*, 173-203.

Merryman, C. T. Retroactive inhibition in the A-B, A-D paradigm as measured by a multiple-choice test. *Journal of Experimental Psychology*, 1971, *91*, 212-214.

Merryman, C. T., & Merryman, S. S. Improvement during nonreinforced trials: Confounded with backward associations? Paper presented at the meeting of the Psychonomic Society, St. Louis, November, 1972.

Meyer, D. E. On the representation and retrieval of stored semantic information. *Cognitive Psychology*, 1970, *1*, 242-300.

Meyer, D. E., & Ellis, G. B. *Parallel processes in word recognition.* Paper presented at the meeting of the Psychonomic Society, San Antonio, November 1970.

Mill, J. *Analysis of the phenomena of the human mind.* London: Longmans, Green, Reader & Dyer, 1869.

Mill, J. S. *A system of logic, ratiocinative and inductive.* London: Longmans, Green, 1889.

Miller, G. A. The magical number seven, plus or minus two: Some limits on our capacity for processing information. *Psychological Review*, 1956, *63*, 81-97.

Miller, N. E. Liberalization of basic S-R concepts: Extensions to conflict behavior, motivation and social learning. In S. Koch (Ed.), *Psychology: A study of a science* (Vol. 2). New York: McGraw-Hill, 1959.

Milner, B. Visual recognition and recall after right temporal-lobe excision in man. *Neuropsychogia*, 1968, *6*, 191-209.

Moeser, S. D., & Bregman, A. S. *Imagery and language acquisition.* Preprinted paper. Simon Fraser University, Burnaby, B. C., 1972.

Moeser, S. D., & Bregman, A. S. Imagery and language acquisition. *Journal of Verbal Learning and Verbal Behavior*, 1973, *12*, 91-98.

Morton, J. The interaction of information in word recognition. *Psychological Review*, 1969, *76*, 165-178.

Mowrer, O. H. *Learning theory and the symbolic processes.* New York: Wiley, 1960.

Müller, G. E., & Pilzecker, A. Experimentelle Beiträge zur Lehre vom Gedächtnis. *Zeitschrift Psychologig Ergänzungaband*, 1900, No. 1.

Neisser, U. *Cognitive psychology.* New York: Appleton-Century-Crofts, 1967.

Newell, A., & Simon, H. A. GPS, a program that simulates human thought. In H. Billing (Ed.), *Lernende Automaten*. Munich: R. Oldenbourg KG, 1961.

Newton, J. M., & Wickens, D. D. Retroactive inhibition as a function of the temporal position of the interpolated learning. *Journal of Experimental Psychology*, 1956, *51*, 149-154.

Nilsson, N. J. *Problem-solving methods in artificial intelligence.* New York: McGraw-Hill, 1971.

Norman, D. A. *Memory and attention: An introduction to human information processing.* New York: Wiley, 1969.

Osgood, C. E. An investigation into the causes of retroactive interference. *Journal of Experimental Psychology*, 1948, *38*, 132-154.

Osgood, C. E. Towards a wedding of insufficiencies. In T. R. Dixon & D. L. Horton (Eds.), *Verbal behavior and general behavior theory*. Englewood Cliffs, N.J.: Prentice-Hall, 1968.

Paivio, A. Mental imagery in associative learning and memory. *Psychological Review* 1969, *76*, 241-263.

Paivio, A. *Imagery and verbal processes.* New York: Holt, Rinehart & Winston, 1971.

Posner, M. J. Abstraction and the process of recognition. In G. H. Bower (Ed.), *The psy-*

chology of learning and motivation (Vol. 3). New York: Academic Press, 1969.

Postman, L. The present status of interference theory. In C. N. Cofer (Ed.), *Verbal learning and verbal behavior*. New York: McGraw-Hill, 1961.

Postman, L. The effects of language habits on the acquisition and retention of verbal associations. *Journal of Experimental Psychology*, 1962, *64*, 7-19.

Postman, L. Unlearning under conditions of successive interpolation. *Journal of Experimental Psychology*, 1965, *70*, 237-245.

Postman, L., Burns, G., & Hasher, L. Response availability and associative recall. *Journal of Experimental Psychology*, 1970, *84*, 404-411.

Postman, L., Fraser, J., & Burns, G. Unit-sequence facilitation in recall. *Journal of Verbal Learning and Verbal Behavior*, 1968, *7*, 217-224.

Postman, L., & Kaplan, H. L. Reaction time as a measure of retroactive inhibition. *Journal of Experimental Psychology*, 1947, *37*, 136-145.

Postman, L., Keppel, G., & Stark, K. Unlearning as a function of the relationship between successive response classes. *Journal of Experimental Psychology*, 1965, *69*, 111-118.

Postman, L., & Parker, J. F. Maintenance of first-list associations during transfer. *American Journal of Psychology*, 1970, *83*, 171-188.

Postman, L., & Stark, K. The role of response set in tests of unlearning. *Journal of Verbal Learning and Verbal Behavior*, 1965, *4*, 315-322.

Postman, L., & Stark, K. The role of response availability in transfer and interference. *Journal of Experimental Psychology*, 1969, *79*, 168-177.

Postman, L., & Stark, K. On the measurement of retroactive inhibition in the A-B, A-D paradigm by the multiple-choice method: Reply to Merryman. *Journal of Verbal Learning and Verbal Behavior*, 1972, *11*, 465-473.

Postman, L., Stark, K., & Fraser, J. Temporal changes in interference. *Journal of Verbal Learning and Verbal Behavior*, 1968, *7*, 672-694.

Postman, L., Stark, K., & Henschel, D. M. Conditions of recovery after unlearning. *Journal of Experimental Psychology*, 1969, *82*, 1-24.

Postman, L., & Warren, L. Temporal changes in interference under different paradigms of transfer. *Journal of Verbal Learning and Verbal Behavior*, 1972, *11*, 120-128.

Prentice, W. C. H., & Asch, S. E. Paired-associations with related and unrelated pairs of nonsense figures. *American Journal of Psychology*, 1958, *71*, 247-254.

Prytulak, L. S. Natural language mediation. *Cognitive Psychology*, 1971, *2*, 1-56.

Pylyshyn, A. W. What the mind's eye tells the mind's brain: A critique of mental imagery. *Psychological Bulletin*, 1973, *80*, 1-24.

Quillian, M. R. Semantic memory. In M. Minsky (Ed.), *Semantic information processing*. Cambridge, Mass.: M.I.T. Press, 1968.

Quillian, M. R. The teachable language comprehender. *Communications of the Association for Computing Machinery*, 1969, *12*, 459-476.

Ramsey, F. P. Universals. *The foundations of mathematics*. New York: Harcourt Brace, 1931.

Raphael, B. The frame problem in problem-solving systems. In N. V. Findler & B. Meltzer (Eds.), *Artificial intelligence and heuristic programming*. New York: American Elsevier, Inc., 1971.

Reder, L. M., Anderson, J. R., & Bjork, R. A. A semantic interpretation of encoding specificity. *Journal of Experimental Psychology*, 1974, *102*, 648-656.

Reitman, W. *Cognition and thought*. New York: Wiley, 1965.

Reitman, W. What does it take to remember? In D. A. Norman (Ed.), *Models of human memory*. New York: Academic Press, 1970.

Reitman, J., & Bower, G. H. Structure and later recognition of exemplars of concepts. *Cognitive Psychology*, 1973, *4*, 194-206.

Riley, D. A. Memory for form. In L. Postman (Ed.), *Psychology in the making*. New York: Knopf, 1962.

Rips, L. J., Shoben, E. J., & Smith, E. E. Semantic distance and the verification of semantic relations. *Journal of Verbal Learning and Verbal Behavior*, 1973, *12*, 1-20.

Robbin, J. W. *Mathematical logic: A first course*. New York: Benjamin, 1969.

Robinson, E. G. *Association theory today*. New York: Century, 1932.

Rohwer, W. D., Jr. Constraint, syntax and meaning in paired associate learning. *Journal of Verbal Learning and Verbal Behavior*, 1966, *5*, 541-547.

Rosenberg, S. Associative facilitation in the recall and recognition of nouns embedded in connected discourse. *Journal of Experimental Psychology*, 1968, *78*, 254-260. (a)

Rosenberg, S. Association and phrase structure in sentence recall. *Journal of Verbal Learning and Verbal Behavior*, 1968, *7*, 1077-1081. (b)

Rosenberg, S. The recall of verbal material accompanying semantically poorly-integrated sentences. *Journal of Verbal Learning and Verbal Behavior*, 1969, *8*, 732-736.

Rosenberg, S. Source of facilitation in recall of context material from high-association discourse. *Journal of Experimental Psychology*, 1970, *83*, 504-505.

Rumelhart, D. E., Lindsay, P. H., & Norman, D. A. A process model for long-term memory. In E. Tulving & W. Donaldson (Eds.), *Organization and memory*. New York: Academic Press, 1972.

Russell, B. On the relations of universals and particulars. *Proceedings of the Aristotelian Society*, 1911-12, 1-24.

Russell, B. *Philosophy*. New York: Norton, 1927.

Schaeffer, B., & Wallace, R. The comparison of word meanings. *Journal of Experimental Psychology*, 1970, *86*, 144-152.

Schank, R. C. Conceptual dependency: A theory of natural-language understanding. *Cognitive Psychology*, 1972, *3*, 552-631.

Schnorr, J. A., & Atkinson, R. C. Study position and item differences in the short- and long-run retention of paired associates learned by imagery. *Journal of Verbal Learning and Verbal Behavior*, 1970, *9*, 614-622.

Schubert, L. K. *Extending the expressive power of semantic networks* (Tech. Rep. TR74-18). Department of Computer Science, University of Alberta, 1974.

Schwarcz, R. M., Burger, J. F., & Simmons, R. F. A deductive question-answerer for natural language inference. *Communications of the Association for Computing Machinery*, 1970, *13*, 167-183.

Selz, O. Zur Psychologie der Gegenwart: Eine Ammerkung zu Koffkas Darstellung. *Zeitschrift für Psychologie*, 1926, *99*, 169-196.

Shannon, C. E. A mathematical theory of communication. *Bell System Technical Journal*, 1948, *27*, 379-423; 623-656.

Shepard, R. N., & Metzler, J. Mental rotation of three-dimensional objects. *Science*, 1971, *171*, 701-703.

Shiffrin, R. Memory search. In D. A. Norman (Ed.), *Models of human memory*. New York: Academic Press, 1970.

Shulman, H. C., & Martin, E. Effects of response-set similarity on unlearning and spontaneous recovery. *Journal of Experimental Psychology*, 1970, *86*, 230-235.

Simon, H. A., & Feigenbaum, E. A. An information processing theory of some effects of similarity, familiarity, and meaningfulness in verbal learning. *Journal of Verbal Learning and Verbal Behavior*, 1964, *3*, 385-396.

Skinner, B. F. *Science and human behavior*. New York: Macmillan, 1953.

Slamecka, N. J. A temporal interpretation of some recall phenomena. *Psychological Review*, 1969, *76*, 492-503.

Slamecka, N. J., & Ceraso, J. Retroactive and proactive inhibition of verbal learning. *Psychological Bulletin*, 1960, *57*, 449-475.

Spence, K. W. *Behavior theory and learning: Selected papers*. Englewood Cliffs, N.J.: Prentice-Hall, 1960.

Spencer, H. *The principles of psychology*. New York: Appleton, 1890.

Sperry, R. W., & Milner, N. Pattern perception following insertion of mica plates into visual cortex. *Journal of Comparative and Physiological Psychology*, 1955, *48*, 463-469.

Staats, A. W. *Learning, language and cognition*. New York: Holt, Rinehart & Winston, 1969.

Sternberg, S. Memory-scanning: Mental processes revealed by reaction-time experiments. *Acta Psychologica*, 1969, *30*, 276-315.

Stromeyer, C. F. Eidetikers. *Psychology Today*, 1970, 4, (November) 76–81.

Suppes, P. Stimulus-response theory of finite automata. *Journal of Mathematical Psychology*, 1969, 6, 327-355.

Thune, L. E., & Underwood, B. J. Retroactive inhibition as a function of degree of interpolated learning. *Journal of Experimental Psychology*, 1943, 32, 185-200.

Tieman, D. G. *Recognition memory for comparative sentences*. Unpublished doctoral dissertation, Stanford University, 1971.

Townsend, J. T. A note on the identifiability of parallel and serial processes. *Perception and Psychophysics*, 1971, 10, 161-163.

Townsend, J. T. Issues and models concerning the processing of a finite number of inputs. In B. H. Kantowitz (Ed.), *Human information processing: Tutorials in performance and cognition*. Hillsdale, N.J.: Lawrence Erlbaum Associates, 1974.

Tulving, E., & Madigan, S. A. Memory and verbal learning. *Annual Review of Psychology*, 1970, 21, 437-484.

Tulving, E., & Thompson, P. M. Encoding specificity and retrieval processes in episodic memory. *Psychological Review*, 1973, 80, 352-373.

Underwood, B. J. The effect of successive interpolations on retroactive and proactive inhibition. *Psychological Monographs*, 1945, 59(Whole No. 273).

Underwood, B. J. Retroactive and proactive inhibition after 5 and 48 hours. *Journal of Experimental Psychology*, 1948, 38, 29-38. (a)

Underwood, B. J. "Spontaneous recovery" of verbal associations. *Journal of Experimental Psychology*, 1948, 38, 429-439. (b)

Underwood, B. J. Attributes of memory. *Psychological Review*, 1969, 76, 559-573.

Underwood, B. J., & Schultz, R. W. *Meaningfulness and verbal learning*. Philadelphia: Lippincott, 1960.

Von Neuman, J. *The computer and the brain*. New Haven, Conn.: Yale University Press, 1958.

Wanner, H. E. *On remembering, forgetting, and understanding sentences: A study of the deep structure hypothesis*. Unpublished doctoral dissertation, Harvard University, 1968.

Warren, H. C. *A history of the association psychology*. New York: Scribner's, 1921.

Watkins, M. J., & Tulving, E. Episodic memory: When recognition fails. *Journal of Experimental Psychology: General*, 1976, 104, 5-29.

Watson, J. B. *Behaviorism*. New York: Norton, 1930.

Weaver, G. E., Duncan, E. M., & Bird, C. P. Cue specific retroactive inhibition. *Journal of Verbal Learning and Verbal Behavior*, 1972, 11, 362-366.

Wender, K. F., & Glowalla, U. Models for within-proposition-representation tested by cued recall. *Memory and Cognition*, 1979, 7, 401-409.

Wertheimer, W. Gestalt theory. *Social Research*, 1944, 11, 78-99.

Whorf, B. L. *Language, thought, and reality*. Cambridge, Mass.: M.I.T. Press, 1956.

Wichawut, C., & Martin, E. Independence of A-B and A-C associations in retroaction. *Journal of Verbal Learning and Verbal Behavior*, 1971, 10, 316-321.

Wickelgren, W. A., & Norman, D. A. Strength models and serial position in short-term recognition memory. *Journal of Mathematical Psychology*, 1966, 3, 316-347.

Wickens, D. D. Encoding categories of words: An empirical approach to meaning. *Psychological Review*, 1970, 77, 1-15.

Wilkins, A. T. Conjoint frequency, category size, and categorization time. *Journal of Verbal Learning and Verbal Behavior*, 1971, 10, 382-385.

Winograd, T. Procedures as a representation for data in a computer program for understanding natural language. *M.I.T. Artificial Intelligence Laboratory Project* MAC TR-84, 1971.

Winograd, T. Understanding natural language. *Cognitive Psychology*, 1972, 3, 1-191.

Winston, P. H. Learning structural descriptions from examples. *M.I.T. Artificial Intelligence Laboratory Project* AI-TR-231, 1970.

Wiseman, G., & Neisser, U. *Perceptual organization as a determinant of visual recognition memory*. Paper presented at meeting of the Eastern Psychological Association, Spring 1971.

Wolford, G. Function of distinct associations for paired-associate performance. *Psychological Review*, 1971, *78*, 303-313.

Woods, W. A. What's in a link: Foundations for semantic networks. In D. G. Bobrow & A. Collins (Eds.), *Representation and understanding: Studies in cognitive science*. New York: Academic Press, 1975.

Author Index

A

Amarel, S., 79, *243*
Amsel, A., 218, *243*
Anderson, J. R., 25, 68, 113, 221, 227, 231, 232, 234, 236, 239, 240, 241, *243, 247, 249*
Anderson, R. C., 225, 235, *243, 246*
Arnold, P. G., 51, 201, 204, *243, 244*
Asch, S. E., 50, 51, 83, *243, 249*
Atkinson, R. C., 203, *250*
Atwood, G., 204, *243*

B

Bain, A., 18, *243*
Barlow, H. B., 46, *243*
Barnes, J. M., 217, *244*
Bartlett, F. C., 56, 57, *244*
Battig, W. F., 177, *244*
Baylor, G. W., 195, *244*
Bean, J., 194, *244*
Beare, J. I., 17, *244*
Beasley, C. M., 241, *243*
Bergman, G., 31, *244*
Bever, T. G., 12, 13, 82, *244*
Bird, C. P., 226, *251*

Birnbaum, I. M., 221, 224, 226, *244*
Bjork, R. A., 240, *249*
Black, J. B., 241, *244*
Bobrow, G., 201, *244*
Boring, E. G., 18, 26, 56, *244*
Bower, G. H., 43, 50, 51, 52, 55, 158, 197, 201, 202, 204, 221, 240, 241, *243, 244, 249*
Bregman, A. S., 82, *248*
Briggs, G. E., 216, *244*
Brooks, L. R., 204, *244*
Brown, R., 43, *244*
Brown, T., 25, *244*
Bugelski, B. R., 197, *244*
Buhler, K., 44, *245*
Burger, J. F., 25, *250*
Burns, G., 189, 223, *249*

C

Carpenter, P. A., 195, 206, *245*
Ceraso, J., 50, 214, 223, 226, *243, 245, 250*
Chase, W. G., 201, *245*
Chow, K. L., 54, *247*
Clark, E. V., 234, *245*
Clark, H. H., 195, 201, 206, 234, *245*
Chomsky, N., 5, 40, 85, *245*

Cofer, C. N., 223, 227, 229, *245*
Collins, A. M., 4, 172, 174, 179, 239, *245*
Conrad, C., 174, 175, *245*

D

Deese, J., 23, *245*
Delprato, D. J., 225, 227, *245*
Dreyfus, H. L., 11, 44, *245*
Duncan, E. M., 226, *251*

E

Ehrenfels, C. von, 44, 45, *245*
Ellis, G. B., 176, *248*
Ernst, G. W., 44, 73, *245*
Evans, T. G., 201, *245*

F

Faile, N. F., 223, 227, 229, *245*
Feigenbaum, E. A., 4, 19, 207, *245, 250*
Fillenbaum, S., 129, *245*
Fodor, J. A., 12, 13, 30, *244, 245*
Foss, D. J., 240, *245*
Frank, R. C., 223, *247*
Fraser, J., 189, 218, 222, 224, *249*
Freedman, J. L., 176, 177, *245, 247*
Freud, S., 49, *245*
Friedman, M. J., 224, *245*

G

Garner, W. R., 64, *246*
Garrett, M., 12, 13, *244*
Garskof, B. E., 225, 227, *245, 246*
Gazzaniga, M. A., 66, *246*
Glowalla, U., 236, *251*
Gibson, E. J., 187, *246*
Goetz, E. T., 235, *246*
Graesser, A. C., 235, 236, *246*
Greenberg, G., 225, *246*
Greeno, J. G., 225, 226, *246, 247*
Gregory, R. L., 60, *246*
Guzman, A., 127, *246*

H

Hartley, D., 25, *246*
Harwood, D. A., 240, *245*
Hasher, L., 223, *249*
Hayes, P., 89, *247*
Head, H., 57, *246*
Heimer, W., 50, *243*
Henderson, A., 223, *245*
Hendrix, G. G., 231, *246*
Henschel, D. M., 218, 222, 227, *247, 249*
Hintzman, D. L., 207, 226, *246*
Hobbes, T., 18, *246*
Höffding, H., 53, *246*
Hook, S., 44, *246*
Hopcroft, J. E., 12, *246*
Horton, D. L., 223, 227, 229, *245*
Houston, J. P., 221, *246*

I

Irwin, J. M., 217, 218, *248*

J

Johnson, N. F., 122, *246*
Johnson-Laird, P. N., 96, *246*
Jones, G. V., 236, *246*
Just, M. A., 195, 206, *245*

K

Kaplan, H. L., 216, *249*
Katona, G., 55, *246*
Katz, H., 219, *247*
Katz, J. J., 40, 41, *246*
Keppel, G., 218, 219, 224, 227, *247, 249*
Kimura, D., 66, *247*
King, D. R. W., 239, *247*
Kintsch, W., 203, *247*
Kline, P. J., 241, *243*
Koch, S., 32, *247*
Koffka, K., 23, 47, 52, 53, *247*
Köhler, W., 23, 47, 48, 49, 53, *247*
Kolers, P. A., 234, *247*
Koppenaal, R. J., 219, *247*
Krull, A., 219, *247*

L

Landauer, T. K., 172, 176, *247*
Lashley, K. S., 54, *247*
Lehr, D. J., 223, *247*
Levick, W. R., 46, *243*
Lindsay, P. H., 4, 87, *250*
Loftus, E. F., 173, 177, 239, *245, 247*
Logan, F. A., 218, *247*
Loux, M. J., 85, *247*

M

Madigan, S. A., 2, 62, *251*
Mandler, G., 26, 52, *247*
Mandler, J., 26, *247*
Martin, E., 224, 225, 226, *247, 250, 251*
Martin, E. A., 231, *247*
Mattison, D. W., 223, *247*
McCarthy, J., 89, *247*
McGeoch, J. A., 37, 217, *247*
McGill, W. J., 132, *248*
McGovern, J. B., 227, *248*
McGuire, W. J., 187, *248*
McNeill, D., 43, *244*
Melton, A. W., 38, 217, 218, 219, *248*
Merryman, C. T., 220, 225, 226, *248*
Merryman, S. S., 220, *248*
Metzler, J., 206, *250*
Meyer, D. E., 172, 176, 179, 180, *247, 248*
Mill, J., 19, 21, 23, *248*
Mill, J. S., 23, 24, *248*
Miller, G. A., 52, *248*
Miller, N. E., 31, 32, *248*
Milner, B., 66, *248*
Milner, N., 54, *250*
Moeser, S. D., 82, *248*
Montague, W. E., 177, *244*
Morton, J., 57, *248*
Mowrer, O. H., 85, *248*
Müller, G. E., 37, *248*
Munoz, R., 201, 204, *244*

N

Neisser, U., 56, 58, 60, 61, 199, *248*
Newell, A., 44, 71 73, *245, 248*
Newton, J. M., 223, *248*

Nilsson, N. J., 154, *248*
Norman, D. A., 4, 55, 87, 159, *248, 250*

O

Osgood, C. E., 30, 216, *248*

P

Paivio, A., 194, 197, 198, 237, *248*
Parker, J. F., 219, *249*
Pilzecker, A., 37, *248*
Posner, M. J., 206, *248*
Postman, L., 38, 189, 215, 216, 218, 219, 222, 223, 224, 225, *249*
Prentice, W. C. H., 50, *249*
Prytulak, L. S., 68, 182, 184, *249*
Pylyshyn, A. W., 195, *249*

Q

Quillian, M. R., 4, 25, 85, 169, 172, 174, 179, 239, *245, 249*

R

Ramsey, F. P., 85, *249*
Raphael, B., 89, *249*
Rauch, D. S., 219, *247*
Reder, L. M., 240, *249*
Reitman, W., 43, 68, 207, *249*
Reynolds, J. H., 224, *245*
Riley, D. A., 52, *249*
Rips, L. J., 173, *249*
Robbin, J. W., 95, *249*
Robinson, E. G., 27, *250*
Rohwer, W. D., Jr., 193, *250*
Rosenberg, S., 121, 122, *250*
Ross, B. H., 240, *243*
Rumelhart, D. E., 4, 87, *250*
Russell, B., 34, 35, 85, *250*

S

Sandak, J. M., 225, *246*
Schaeffer, B., 178, 179, 180, *250*

Schallert, D. L., 235, *246*
Schank, R. C., 87, *250*
Scheff, R. W., 173, *247*
Schnorr, J. A., 203, *250*
Schubert, L. K., 231, *250*
Schultz, 184, *251*
Schwarcz, R. M., 25, *250*
Selz, O., 44, *250*
Semmes, J., 54, *247*
Shannon, C. E., 64, *250*
Shepard, R. N., 206, *250*
Shiffrin, R., 211, *250*
Shoben, E. J., 173, *249*
Shulman, H. C., 224, *250*
Simmons, R. F., 25, *250*
Simon, H. A., 4, 19, 71, 207, *248, 250*
Skinner, B. F., 31, 63, *250*
Slamecka, N. J., 214, 227, *250*
Smith, E. E., 173, *249*
Spence, K. W., 218, *250*
Spencer, H., 25, *250*
Sperry, R. W., 54, 66, *246, 250*
Staats, A. W., 30, 85, *250*
Stark, K., 218, 222, 224, 225, *249*
Sternberg, S., 163, *250*
Stromeyer, 198, *251*
Suppes, P., 12, *251*

T

Thompson, P. M., 240, *251*
Thune, L. E., 215, 217, *251*
Tieman, D. G., 68, 113, *251*
Townsend, J. T., 169, 239, *251*
Tulving, E., 2, 62, 182, 240, *251*
Turner, T. J., 241, *244*

U

Ullman, J. D., 12, *246*
Underwood, B. J., 184, 199, 207, 215, 216, 217, 218, 221, *244, 251*

V

Von Neuman, J., 6, *251*

W

Wallace, R., 178, 179, 180, *250*
Wanner, H. E., 129, *251*
Warren, H. C., 18, 24, *251*
Warren, L., 223, *249*
Watkins, M. J., 240, *251*
Watson, J. B., 34, *251*
Watts, G. H., 225, *243*
Weaver, G. E., 226, *251*
Wender, K. F., 236, *251*
Wertheimer, W., 45, *251*
Whorf, B. L., 83, *251*
Wichawut, C., 226, *251*
Wickelgren, W. A., 159, *251*
Wickens, D. D., 207, 223, 225, *246, 248, 251*
Wilkins, A. T., 173, 176, *251*
Winograd, T., 59, 60, 76, *251*
Winston, P. H., 127, 194, 195, 201, *251*
Winzenz, D., 201, *244*
Wiseman, G., 199, *251*
Wolford, G., 220, 225, 228, *252*
Woods, W. A., 231, *252*

Z

Zavortink, F., 227, *247*

Subject Index

A

ACT, 239, 241
Aristotle's theory of memory, 9, 12, 16–18
Associationism, 3, 9–39
  American, 16, 26–38
  British, 12, 16, 17–26
  German, 26
  See also Aristotle's theory of memory,
    Associations, Behaviorism,
    Functionalism, Ideas,
    Methodological empiricism
Associations, 22, 28
  free association, 189
  successive vs. synchronous, 22
  See also Contiguity, Similarity

B

Behaviorism, 28–27, 64
  habit memory, 33–37
  intervening variables, 31–33
Binary branching, 110–111, 234–235
  See also Ideas (duplex)

C

Complex ideas (*See* Ideas)
Connectionism, 10, 12
Contiguity, 17, 22–23, 115–121

D

Decoding process, 64–70, 153–180
  See also MATCH process, Retrieval
Duplex ideas (*See* Ideas)

E

Elementarism (*See* Reductionism)
Emergent properties (*See* Gestalt theory)
Empiricism, 4, 6
  See also Methodological empiricism
Encoding process, 68, 69–70, 129–151,
    235–238
  encoding on partial matches, 106–111
Encoding specificity, 240

F

Fact retrieval, 72, 153–180
  model for verification times, 159–171
  semantic memory, 171–180
  vs. question-answering, 153–154
  See also MATCH process
Forgetting (*See* Interference)
Form qualities [*See* Gestalt theory
    (Gestaltqualitat)]
Functionalism, 27–28, 64
  vs. structuralism, 26–27

G

General ideas [*See* Ideas (universal)]
Gestalt theory, 11, 23, 49–55
  emergent properties, 46–49, 54–55
  forgetting, 52
  Gestaltqualitat, 44–45
  Law of Pragnanz, 47
  perception, 46–48
  phi phenomena, 46
  retrieval, 53
Gestaltqualitat (*See* Gestalt theory)
Get process, 102–106, 157, 159–161
  search for GET-lists, 163–170, 208–213,
    238–239
  See also MATCH process

H

Holism, 42, 61, 66

I

Ideas
  complex, 18–19, 47–48
  duplex, 19, 84–89
  simple, 18–19
  universal, 20–22
IDENTIFY process, 101–102, 107–111
Imagery, 194–206
  conceptual-proposition interpretation
    (HAM), 197–198, 204–206
  mental picture metaphor, 194–198
  verbal learning, 201–204
Input trees, 66–67, 69–70, 80–99
  intersection of trees, 94–95
Interface, 7, 71–73
Interference, 37–38, 52, 103, 207–230
  associative matching, 220, 224–227
  differentiation hypothesis, 221–222
  generalized response availability, 223,
    227–229
  HAM's theory of, 209–217, 239
  negative transfer, 229–230
  number of trials, 214–216
  proactive interference, 211–214, 224–227
  relation to fact-retrieval, 209–211,
    216–217
  response competition, 217–218
  retroactive interference, 207–230

Interference (*cont.*)
  spontaneous recovery, 219–220, 223
  stimulus-specific interference, 211–214,
    214–217
  STOP rule in HAM, 209–211
  unlearning, 218–219
Intervening variables, 31–33
Introspection, 63–64
Intuitionism, 41–42, 61

L

Labelled associations, 24–25, 67, 79–99
Learning (*See* Encoding process)
Lexical memory, 129–131, 136–141,
    187–189, 211–212
List discrimination, 190–191, 215, 221–223
  role in response set suppression, 222–223

M

MATCH process, 101–128, 156–159
  encoding upon partial matches, 106–111
  experimental tests, 112–125
  model for verification times, 153–171
  parallel vs. single access, 170–171
  See also Decoding process, Fact retrieval,
    GET-process, Interference,
    Recognition
Mechanism, 10–11, 12
Memory structure of HAM, 69–70, 83–99
  See also Propositional representation
Metafeatures
  of methodological empiricism, 10–12
  of methodological rationalism, 40–44, 61
Methodological empiricism, 3, 9–12, 61–62
  See also Terminal Meta-Postulate
Methodological rationalism, 3, 39–44, 61
Mnemonics, 192–194, 194–198, 201–203

N

Nativism, 40–42, 61
Natural Language Mediators (NLMs),
    184–185
Neo-associationism, 4–5, 62, 63
Nonsense syllables, 182–185, 187
  See also Natural Language Mediators

O

Output trees, 68–70

P

Paired-associate learning, 185–194
  backward associations, 191–192
  double function lists, 192
  imagery, 194–198, 201–204
  response learning, 187–189
  rote vs. meaningful learning, 192–194
  stimulus learning, 187–189
  stimulus-response association learning,
    189–191
  See also Interference
Probe trees, 68, 69–70, 97–98, 155–159
Propositional representation (HAM), 3, 7,
    66–68, 79–99
  concept vs. individual nodes, 91
  conjunction, 93–94
  context-fact distinction, 87–90
  deep grammar, 92–94
  predication, 85–87, 95
  problems, 231–235
  relation-object distinction, 85–87,
    233–235
  sensationalistic features, 82–83
  subject-predicate distinction, 84–85
  terminal quantification, 90–91, 231–233

Q

Question-answering, 2, 72, 153–154

R

Rationalism, 4
  See also Methodological rationalism
Rationalist methodology (See
    Methodological rationalism)
Recognition, 101–128
  word recognition, 190–191, 215, 240
  See also MATCH process
Reconstruction hypothesis, 56–61
  evidence, 60–61
  schema, 57–58
Reductionism, 10–11, 16–17

Relations (See Labelled associations,
    Propositional representation)
Repetition efects
  sentences, 115–125
  See also Interference
Representation, 231–235
  See also Propositional representation
Representation problem, 79–83
Retrieval, 238–240
  See also Decoding process

S

Semantic memory
  cognitive economy, 175–178
  effects of associative strength, 175–178
  effects of category size, 178–181
  negative judgments, 181–182, 240
  Quillian model, 173–175
Sensationalism, 10–11, 12, 16, 46–62, 82–83
Sentence memory, 234, 235–238, 240
  MATCH process, 112–125
  partial recall, 148
  stochastic model for, 129–151
  See also Fact retrieval
Similarity, 17, 23, 52, 55
Simple ideas (See Ideas)
S-R Psychology (See Behaviorism)
Strategy-free component of memory, 68–70
Structuralism, 26–27
Subset relation, 90–91
  See also Semantic memory
Sufficiency conditions, 2
Superset relation (See Subset relation)

T

Terminal Meta-Postulate, 3, 12–15, 18–22,
    33
  mirror-image language, 12–15
Transfer (See Interference)
Type-token distinction, 18–20

U

Universal ideas (See Ideas)

V

Verbal learning, 181–206
  propositional analysis, 181–185
  See also Interference, Paired associate
    learning, Recognition (word)
Vitalism, 43–44, 61

W

Well-formedness conditions, 3, 25
Word-idea distinction (*See* Lexical
  memory)

M